HOW
TO AVOID
YOUR PARENTS'
MISTAKES
WHEN
YOU RAISE
YOUR CHILDREN

HOW TO AVOID YOUR PARENTS' MISTAKES WHEN YOU RAISE YOUR CHILDREN

Claudette Wassil-Grimm

Illustrations by Jonathan Grimm

POCKET BOOKS

New York   London   Toronto   Sydney   Tokyo   Singapore

We have endeavored, where necessary, to trace the ownership of copyrighted material and to secure permission from copyright holders. In the event of any question arising as to the use of any material, we will be pleased to make the necessary corrections in future printings.

POCKET BOOKS, a division of Simon & Schuster Inc.
1230 Avenue of the Americas, New York, NY 10020

Text copyright © 1990 by Claudette Wassil-Grimm
Illustrations copyright © 1990 by Jonathan Grimm

Library of Congress Catalog Card Number: 90-61214

ISBN: 0-671-72742-7

First Pocket Books hardcover printing September 1990

10 9 8 7 6 5 4 3 2 1

POCKET and colophon are registered trademarks of
Simon & Schuster Inc.

Printed in the U.S.A.

For Jerzy

ACKNOWLEDGMENTS

I want to express my appreciation for the support, encourage-ment, and professional advice I received during the preparation of this book.

Thank you to Denise Cross, Mary Martin, Doreen Moldovany, Jean Mosteller, Cinda Thompson, and especially Diane Andersen for serving as readers while the work was "in progress." Their responses helped make the manuscript clear enough to reach the many kinds of parents I address. Thanks also to Claire Zion, my editor at Pocket Books, who helped me enormously with last-minute touches that make the manuscript stronger and clearer.

For their professional advice and continuing encouragement I would like to thank pediatrician Glenn Austin, M.D., psychiatrist Merle Hausladen, M.D., psychologists Anthony Benjamin, Ph.D., Linda Benjamin, Ph.D., and Anita Lampel, Ph.D., and parenting specialists Jan Hackleman, RN/MFCC and Cynthia Walker, MA/ Social Work.

Finally, I want to thank my interviewees for being so open with me, and my husband, Andy, for his steadfast faith in my writing ability.

AUTHOR'S NOTE:

All the stories presented in this book are drawn from real individuals' lives but the names and identifying characteristics have been changed in order to protect their privacy.

Life is a series of challenges. My interviewees' problems are not necessarily over. I have caught many on an upswing and taken a "freeze" shot. They will continue to have problems but they will pass through the denial period more quickly each time. What is impor-tant is that they have learned from their mistakes and so will gradually climb higher and higher toward greater confidence and health.

CONTENTS

◆ 4 ◆

STRESS AND THE FAMILY   61

Normal Life Cycle Transitions • Individual and Family Life Cycle Transitions (chart) •
Parenting as Stressor • Grace's Memories • ABCX Family Crisis Model (chart) •
Jealousy of the Child • Parenting Superstressors • Judy and Carl Under Stress •
Family Reactions to Stress (chart) • Time Pressures • Family Support • Supportive
Behaviors (chart) • Child Abuse • Maryanne—Living Out Her Legacy

PART II

PARENTING HANDICAPS

Introduction: Parenting Pitfalls of Adult Children
from Dysfunctional Families (chart)

◆ 5 ◆

FEELING DIFFERENT   83

Realistic Expectations • Matching Expectations to Child's Developmental Level •
Alienation and Defensiveness • Blending In • Rosalyn as New Mother • Studying
Healthy Behavior • Grace's Mentor • Gail's Method • Avoiding Reactionary Rigidity •
Building Support Systems • Breaking Out of Isolation • Gail •
Differentness as a Virtue

◆ 6 ◆

FEAR OF INTIMACY   104

Enmeshment, Walls, and Boundaries • Personal Boundaries (illustrations) • Invasion
vs. Evasion • Triangles • Childhood Survival Habits • Susan as Co-Parent •
Parentified Child • Judy—Drowning in Intimacy • Too Close • Too Distant •
Carl—Running from Intimacy • The Child Within • Dependency Needs •
Moving Closer One Step at a Time

◆ 7 ◆

CRISIS LIFE-STYLE   125

Judy's Family Ghosts • Unrealistic Plans and Expectations • Judy and Carl in Crisis •
Lowering Expectations for Everyone • Setting Priorities • Bob and Anna—Strong
Roots • Are Your Children Stressed Out? (chart) • Teaching Stress-Management to
Children • Time Management • Bob and Anna—The Two-Career Family • Money
Management • Bob and Anna's Sensible Approach • Time to Reflect on Parenting

◆ 8 ◆
DEFENSIVENESS AND DENIAL   146

Denial • Natalie's Denial • The Family Pretense • Betsy's Family Secret •
Reestablishing Trust • Excessive Loyalty • Judy and Carl—Denial and Loyalty •
Tolerance for Abuse • Emotionally Abusive Behaviors (chart) • Challenging Misplaced
Loyalty • Grace—Fear and Lying • Lying in Children

◆ 9 ◆
EVERY DAY IS JUDGMENT DAY   165

Perfectionism • Susan—A Non-person • Learned Hypercritical Attitudes •
Underparenting • Maryanne's New Husband • Making It Manageable • Negative
Parental Expectations • Unconditional Love • Self-Forgiveness
and Acceptance • Nurture Yourself

◆ 10 ◆
CONTROLLING   183

Overparenting • Merissa—Rescuing • Letting Go • Judy and Carl—Superresponsible •
Sharing Power • Children Are Unpredictable • Power Struggles • Ginger—Food! •
Hypervigilance • The Wards—Hypervigilance • Communication Skills (chart) •
Communicating with Teens • Trusting Your Teen • Gary as Teen

◆ 11 ◆
NURTURING RESPONSIBILITY   204

Being Reactionary • The Overcommitted Child • The Irresponsible Parent • Parenting
Alone • Who Is the Grown-Up Here? • Conscious Parenting • Grace—Gaining Control
• Anticipation • Giving Positive Attention • Rules, Routines, and Rituals •
Establishing Rules • *Character* (poem) • Family Meetings

◆ 12 ◆
CONSISTENCY AND SUPPORT   229

Consistency • Being Assertive • Rosalyn's Tough Love • Facing the Child's Anger •
Approving of Yourself • Regrets and Remedies • Teaching Respect • Praising
Effectively • Uses and Misuses of Healthy Parenting Skills (chart) • The Wards—
Relaxing Their Grip • Consistency vs. Rigidity • Being a Role Model

Amazing Grace

Amazing grace—how sweet the sound,
  That saved a wretch like me!
I once was lost, but now am found,
  Was blind, but now I see.

Through many dangers, toils, and snares,
  I have already come;
'Tis grace has brought me safe thus far,
  And grace will lead me home.

                              —John Newton, 1779

PROLOGUE

I grew up in a dysfunctional family. The details are not important. As I interview people I find that the patterns are very similar whether you are the daughter of an alcoholic, the son of a schizophrenic, or the child of parents who staved off intimacy by throwing themselves into work and volunteerism. Preoccupied parents do not have time to nurture self-esteem, and their children grow up with a hole in their hearts, a yearning to be valued that is hard to fill.

In my life, I have had to work through the effects of the damage twice: once to be a functional adult who could hold a job, take care of herself, and fit in with a more stable social crowd. Just when it looked as if I had it all together (and was indeed much more stable and peaceful than I had been for the first thirty years of my life), I had a child and the rug slipped out from under me. Suddenly I couldn't remember to brush my own teeth, let alone remind my child to brush his. The stress level was just too high.

I won't state any specifics from my childhood. I believe my parents did the best they could and, in fact, were far better parents than their own had been. But they had a long way to go, and I love them too much to wave their faults around in public. They deserve the same privacy that I grant to my interviewees.

However, my own feelings and struggles are mine to share. I will interject my own experience where it is appropriate. I want you to know that I have been there, and I have come through it. I never thought I'd say this, but my formerly very difficult son has been the greatest blessing in my life. I thought I was stable, even healthy, before I had him, but what I had was a very precarious health in a carefully controlled life. His birth pitched me into the open sea of life, and before I drowned, I learned to swim like a champion. I now have a peace of mind that I had never believed was possible for me. I had given up being "happy" long before. I was content just to be out of pain. I didn't think I could do better.

But then, for my son, I had to. Like a typical Adult Child of a Dysfunctional Family, I would never have done it for myself!

1

1

FAMILIES: AN INTRODUCTION

*We marry so we can love and be loved, not feed
and be fed. We join together in a search for
intimacy, not protection. We have children so
that we can give and be given to, care and be
cared about, and share the joys of connecting
with posterity, not for old-age bread and bed.*
—Delores Curran, *Traits of a Healthy Family*[1]

How do you judge successful parenting? Why are some parents thought to be "better" than others? Were you raised in a healthy family or did you find much lacking in your home environment?

If you have gone through (or are still going through) a painful period of searching to discover who you are and what you need in order to feel happy, you are not alone. Like many others in their generation, your parents may have been ill-prepared or incapable of nurturing your self-esteem and making space within the family for your unique personality and needs. Thinking back on your childhood, you may have some clear ideas about what *not* to do as a parent, but little idea of what parents *can* do to raise healthier, happier children. If your parents were very poor role models, you may feel as if you are parenting from scratch.

What could we reasonably expect from our parents and what can our children reasonably expect from us? Up until thirty years ago there were no studies to show what parenting skills produce the most well-adjusted children. No one realized the importance of self-esteem, nor did they realize how much the parent's relationship with the young child would go on affecting that child's behavior and attitudes his or her whole life. As we know, Sigmund Freud, the

3

founder of psychoanalysis, was the first to focus attention on early childhood experiences as a source of mental illness or health, but it took many years for these theories to begin to affect early childhood educators. The full importance of parent/child relationships in those crucial early years is just now becoming common knowledge to the general population.

In essence, the average parent a generation ago had no guidance or education for this important role. They naturally relied heavily on what their own parents had done, so poor parents begat more poor parents. Yet there have always been some successful, harmonious families (who have also passed their parenting skills on to the next generation). Psychologists and sociologists have studied these families and discovered what makes them work.

We are the first generation who can use this knowledge to choose our parenting practices and techiques with some confidence. Now that we know the importance of high self-esteem, and can define it, analyze it, and understand how to nurture it in our children, we have a responsibility to use that knowledge to make our children's lives better. At the same time, our vision of a richer life for our children casts a shadow on our own past. As we struggle to raise our self-esteem as adults, we naturally wish our parents had been more capable. Now, as we set new parenting goals for our own generation, we are forced to evaluate the guidance we got from our own parents. We each must ask ourselves: How destructive or healthy was my family of origin? How much should I change my parenting methods to raise healthy, happy children?

GETTING A SENSE OF SCALE

Our need to make sense of our painful experiences causes us to look for some formula, some order to help us understand just how our experiences compare to other people's. We might ask which is worse: being the child of a workaholic and being ignored, or having a mentally unstable parent whose treatment of us was very inconsistent? Having to take care of an alcoholic parent, or being belittled and insulted constantly? Being beaten or being sexually abused? To aid in my research for this book I tried to develop some scale that would show which parental behaviors were most harmful and which were less harmful by comparison. Psychologists I interviewed acknowledged that some parental dysfunctions were more traumatic than others, but these estimations were always complicated by the individual child's responsiveness. Although we might think it obvious that physical abuse is worse than verbal abuse, this "simple truth" is muddled by the fact that some children have a high threshold for physical pain but are extremely sensitive emotionally. For them verbal abuse may be worse than physical abuse.

Of course, here too, the degree of abuse makes a difference. Even when a child is relatively impervious to pain, if the parent breaks the child's arm the incident is bound to be more traumatic for the child than being called names. On the other hand, if the parent is shocked by his or her loss of control in the arm-breaking situation and, as a result, apologizes and never resorts to physical punishment again, the damage to the child in the context of the child's entire childhood may be small. Indeed, that child may be better off than another child whose parents were never physically violent, but told him he was stupid every day of his life.

It is no simple matter to determine just how destructive a certain family situation is. Like beauty, it is in the eye of the beholder.

There are further complications to developing a simple formula to measure family dysfunction. For example, because alcohol and a lack of good judgment go together, adult children of alcoholics may also have been beaten or sexually abused as children. It can be hard for adult children of dysfunctional families (hereafter abbreviated ACODF) to put their fingers on what was most disturbing in their childhoods so that they can work through the trauma. Frightening memories will often be distorted. If the smell of liquor on the parent's breath always accompanied sexual abuse, later any whiff of liquor might trigger shameful sexual feelings in the ACODF. In another case, the adult child might clearly remember what was most traumatic and all else may seem incidental by comparison. A girl who was raped repeatedly by her father might consider drunkenness to be a very minor thing. Indeed, she may have felt so relieved when her father stayed out drinking instead of coming home for the night, that she acutally has positive feelings about heavy drinking. Therefore, as an adult and a parent, she might be overly cautious about touching her children's bodies (and, unfortunately, may also be harmfully unaffectionate), but she would think nothing of getting sloshed and leaving the children alone until 3 A.M. Will her children be better off?

Psychologist Rollo May discovered that, surprisingly, children who were rejected outright by their mothers were better off than those whose mothers professed love for them but acted in a rejecting way. As a matter of fact, the radically rejected children had greater peace of mind. They knew their mothers didn't love them. It was a simple fact of life. They could give up on their parents and move on with their lives, investing their trust elsewhere. But children whose parents professed love while acting in an unloving way were left feeling guilty and unappreciative, wondering not about what was wrong with their parents, but rather about what was wrong with themselves.[2] So it can be very difficult to sort out what parental behaviors are most damaging.

Child psychologist Anita Lampel shed more light on the subject by pointing out that one has to consider the quantitative aspect of the problem. Dysfunctional behaviors most often come in clusters. As we alluded to above, studies show that more than 60% of adult children from alcoholic homes have also been sexually abused or been victims of violence.[3] Common sense tells us, and psychologists have observed, that parents who are physically abusive are usually also verbally abusive. So we need a system that can take all these variables into account to some degree.

In the Scale of Family Functioning, I present a graph which uses a subjective rather than objective accounting of behaviors in various families. Though not scientifically scaled, it represents the observations of psychologists and the spirit of the problem.

Our scale takes into consideration both positive and negative parenting behaviors. Esteem building (+4), where parents consciously look for behaviors to praise, show children they are important by spending time with them, and frequently express their joy at being with their children, represents the highest positive parenting behavior. By contrast, fatally violent abuse (−9) is in itself so devastating that this one trait alone is equal to a cluster of many negative traits. The scale also shows us that good parenting practices come in clusters just like poor parenting practices do.

INTERPRETING THE SCALE

In our Scale of Family Functioning, Kim represents the average child's experience since, when we look across all social classes, most American families still use mild corporal punishment (spanking and slapping), verbally abuse their children ("Why can't you ever do

A SCALE OF FAMILY FUNCTIONING

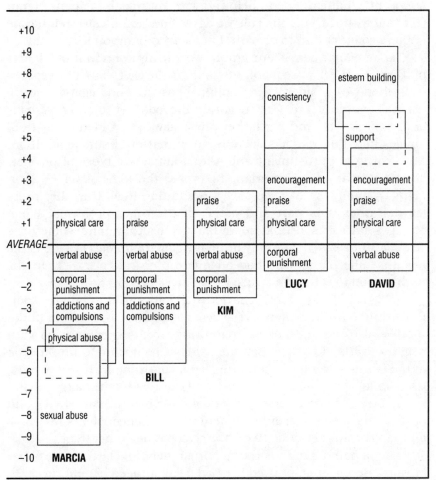

CHARACTERISTICS	POINTS	CHARACTERISTICS	POINTS
ESTEEM BUILDING	+4	CORPORAL PUNISHMENT (MILD)	−1
SUPPORT	+3	VERBAL ABUSE	−1
CONSISTENCY	+3	ADDICTIONS AND COMPULSIONS	−2
ENCOURAGEMENT	+2	PHYSICAL ABUSE	−3
PRAISE	+1	SEXUAL ABUSE	−5
PHYSICAL CARE	+1	FATALLY VIOLENT ABUSE	−9

anything right?"), yet provide adequate physical care and praise on occasion. At the same time, the average parent in the last generation neglected to foster self-esteem by encouragement ("You can do it!"), support ("What can I do to help you with your goals?"), consistency ("I'm sorry, but that's the rule we agreed on"), and esteem-building ("You're so much fun to be with. I'm lucky to have you for my kid.")

As we glance across our graph, we quickly see how much better off David ($+9 - 1$ = score of $+8$) is than Marcia ($-9 + 1$ = score of -8) when we consider their combined positive and negative scores. Marcia's parents are very negative indeed. Her mother verbally abuses her (-1), and her father physically (-3) and sexually (-5) abuses her. But Marcia's score is not a matter of simple addition. Both corporal punishment and sexual abuse are types of physical abuse, so the values overlap. Likewise, the alcoholism (-2) in Marcia's family is not necessarily in addition to all the other problems. Rather it is part and parcel of the other problems. When Marcia's father is drunk he verbally, physically, and sometimes sexually abuses her. The only mitigating factor in Marcia's life is the fact that she has always had adequate physical care ($+1$) in the form of food to eat and a house to live in.

In David's family good behaviors don't appear in isolation either. Praise and encouragement are aspects of support and esteem building. We also see that positive parenting traits, when coupled with negative traits, do help lessen the damage, so it is important to look at the family's average functioning level. For example, Kim's parents used mild corporal punishment (-1) and were verbally abusive (-1), but they also provided adequate physical care ($+1$) and praised her for her accomplishments ($+1$). Hence, she is no worse off than the average child (0 on our scale) in her generation.

Lucy's parents used corporal punishment (-1), took care of her physical needs ($+1$), praised her ($+1$), encouraged her efforts ($+2$), and were consistent ($+3$), yielding a rating of $+6$ above average ($+7 - 1$ = score of $+6$). As we can see, although Lucy's parents swatted or slapped her when she "got out of line," their positive traits gave her enough good feelings to make her more confident and competent than the average person.

It becomes a case of simple addition again when we look at the behavior of Bill's family. Although Bill's parents remembered to praise him on occasion ($+1$), their harsh authoritarian methods and beliefs rendered this praise almost totally ineffective. They were strong believers in punishment and chastised (-1) and hit (-1)

him frequently when they felt he had disobeyed or let them down. Indeed, they often treated strangers better then they treated their own son. They were active in many civic and church organizations that benefitted the poor and underprivileged, but they were gone so often to committee meetings (Addiction and Compulsion for −2) that Bill grew up feeling unloved and abandoned. His parents were never around to offer support or encouragement and rarely had time to sit down to a meal with the family. Bill, with a score of −3 (+1 −4), came away from his childhood with predominantly negative feelings about himself and life in general.

The category of Addiction and Compulsion on the chart represents many "driven" behaviors. Some are considered positive (such as working long hours or volunteering for many worthy causes), but still block intimacy as surely as alcoholism or drug addiction because they pull an inordinate amount of the parent's time and attention away from caring for the children. Other compulsive behaviors include sexual addiction, overeating, overspending, and gambling. When these "addictions" absorb most of the parent's attention (searching for sexual partners) or the family's financial resources (compulsive buying), the family is under too much stress to be able to relax and feel close.

This scale, for the sake of simplicity, is based on specific observable behaviors, but does not really show the effect of diagnosable mental illnesses. In the chart above, sexual abuse and severe physical punishment combine with alcoholism to create dangerously dysfunctional behavior in Marcia's father. But this parent might behave this way because of a mood disorder. Similarly, a family's functioning may be seriously impaired by chronic physical illness (a dying or severely handicapped family member) or mental illness such as schizophrenia, mood disorders, or alcoholism alone. Along with the symptoms discussed above, at −5 we would probably see families with very poor communication, where family members have low self-esteem and hence become violent or defensive. The bottom line is that all of these symptoms both result from and contribute to problems with intimacy, for intimacy can only flourish in a relaxed open atmosphere. Similarly, a family with a physically handicapped or fatally ill member might function in the −3 range because they are under too much stress to be able to meet the children's basic needs for security, love, and guidance. We will be taking a closer look at the effect of stress on family functioning in the chapters which follow.

As we said, the zero range would represent the average American family, but we need to keep in mind that the normal or average level of functioning is not necessarily a **healthy** level of functioning. According to Dr. Charles Whitfield, Medical Director of The Resource Group Counseling Center in Baltimore, only 5 to 20% of today's adults received enough love, guidance, and nurturing to be able "to form consistently healthy relationships, and to feel good about themselves and about what they do."[4]

To raise truly competent children parents need to nurture high self-esteem, encourage independence, and accept each child in the family for who they are. In the healthiest families adults and children alike should have a strong sense of personal identity and be confidently moving toward fulfilling their life goals. They would all support and encourage one another in a spirit of cooperation that even extends beyond the family boundaries to include healthy, limited involvement with church, school, or community groups. In the imaginary +10 range, the perfect family would anticipate every conflict and resolve it before it occurs! But, of course, nobody's perfect.

But where exactly should you aim? How should you rate your family of origin and where should you set your sights as parents? Let's use a scale we are all familiar with—the public school grading system. Looking back at our Scale of Family Functioning chart, I would give Marcia's family an "F" in parenting. They did far more harm than good. Marcia is going to have to come a long way to raise her functioning as a parent up to the average level. If you grew up in an "F" family, try not to be too hard on yourself if all your efforts never raise you above a "C." That is as much as many with the best intentions will accomplish in a lifetime.

Bill's parents would get a "D" in parenting from me because they have not put in enough effort at building their child's good feelings about himself. Kim's parents, who are average, would naturally get a "C." A "C" is not a bad grade but I would hope Kim expects more from herself when she becomes a parent. She has started out with enough stability to be able to become a "B" parent (like Lucy's parents) with a little concentrated effort. Lucy, by the same token, should be able to rise to an "A" parent (like David's parents) if she studies healthy parenting practices and spends lots of relaxed time with her family.

David is the one person on our scale who can probably get an "A" in parenting by just "doing what comes natural" (which is really doing what his parents did). The only good excuse for David slipping down to a "B" parent would be if his wife or one of his children becomes seriously ill or handicapped. If he must cope with a very severe problem (such as a deceased spouse or child with spina bifida), I would still applaud David if he only managed to function on a "C" level.

FAMILIES OF THE '90s

In America and other developed countries, most people no longer have to worry about basic survival. People can now turn their attention to what enriches life. Loving, and being loved in return, is a high priority for all human beings. Naturally, adult children from dysfunctional families are very concerned about their ability to form and maintain healthy relationships. They struggle with trying to relate in healthy ways because their parents and families often provided no role models. They might be successful at achieving the level of intimacy needed at work because they can observe many others in similar relationships. But when it comes to marriage or family life they may have few ideas about appropriate behavior. Their ideas about good parenting would have to come from observing neighbors or watching TV families. Unfortunately, these are often poor sources for seeing what actually goes on inside a home when a parent is at the end of his or her rope. The nuclear family is now often the only source for our learning about relationship. Without access to extended family and a wider variety of relationships, an awful lot rides on the health and functioning of the parents. Yet at the same time, parents juggling two careers and adjusting to the disruptive social changes that follow from this are hardly at their best. If we consider these pressures on the family, we readily believe 80 to 95% of today's families fall short of truly healthy functioning.

This book then, is not only for adult children of clinically dysfunctional families with diagnosed problems such as alcoholism, eating disorders, mood disorders, or more severe mental illnesses such as schizophrenia. It is also for the millions of today's parents whose own parents did not have the time or the inclination to consider the importance of human connectedness, and so did not cultivate quality relationships in their families. Many of us with higher expectations and no role models fall into this category, and nothing is to blame save the progress of humanity's healthy growth toward deeper intimacy in important relationships.

NORMAL FAMILY PROBLEMS

As we can see, our level of functioning is influenced by many factors, but two aspects that provide the "glue" for good family health are communication and the ability to be close and caring. Healthy family intimacy and caring relationships take time to develop. As all families experience the usual ups and downs, they are more or less open to family closeness. During the high-stress years between the ages of twenty-five and forty, when most adults are working on career, family, and personal relationships simultaneously, all adults show an increase in stress-related dysfunctional behaviors, but adults from dysfunctional families have more problems to a more severe degree. The stressful effects of childhood in a dysfunctional family leave adults weaker and less able to cope with normal adult stresses.

Periods of transition are especially difficult times. Starting college, graduating, getting married, changing jobs, moving, becoming a parent, experiencing the death of a loved one, getting divorced, or entering middle age are extremely stressful times for everyone. Naturally, they will be even more stressful for adults who have grown up in dysfunctional families.

ADULT CHILDREN OF DYSFUNCTIONAL
FAMILIES (ACODF) AS PARENTS

Because I grew up in a dysfunctional family I have long been interested in the development of children in these families. For my master's degree in special education I chose to concentrate on socially and emotionally maladjusted children, now known more commonly as "high risk" children. In the early '70s, while working for the Mahwah, New Jersey, school system, I designed one of the first programs for high risk children in the United States. As a member of the Child Study Team, as both a classroom teacher and later the Learning Disabilities Specialist, I worked with a select group of children, their teachers, and their parents. Our goal was to lower truancy, and decrease the drop-out rate. Although we had some success working with children at the junior high and high school levels, we were well aware of the pivotal role of parents and the importance of the early childhood years.

As I became more and more interested in the whole picture, I turned my attention toward alcohol studies and in 1976 began graduate work in alcoholism through the Graduate Theological Union in Berkeley, California, then one of the most up-to-date programs in the country on alcoholism, the alcoholic, and his or her spouse. I served an internship in the Ward Annex In-Patient Alcohol Program of San Francisco's Presbyterian Hospital and have recently updated my education by attending seminars for adult children of alcoholics. Across these twenty years I have seen the focus of alcohol studies shift outward in concentric circles to include the spouse, then the children, and now the adult children. Similarly, the insights gained through the study of the alcoholic and his or her family have shed light on the way families have responded to many other dysfunctional behaviors. When I became a parent, I had to take a very personal and soul-searching look at how my own "family system" contributed to my child's unmanageable behavior and the unbearable stress we felt as a family.

If, like me, you have grown up in a dysfunctional family, you are probably concerned about your own parenting abilities. Can adult children of dysfunctional families (ACODF)—whether the problem was "extreme" or "normal"—overcome their childhood handicaps enough to become better parents, even *good* parents, whose children are happy and successful? Through my research I have learned that, yes, they can.

Part I of this book will provide the background you will need to understand the concepts presented in Parts II and III. Both healthy and dysfunctional families are defined and discussed. Some of the case stories we will follow throughout the book begin here, so even if you have a strong background in adult children issues, you will want to read these more personal accounts before going on to Part II.

To pinpoint what is most essential for today's parents to know, I began by interviewing psychiatrists, psychologists, social workers, and other counselors about the way ACODF typically parent. Naturally those in the counseling professions see mainly those ACODF parents who are seeking help. So we began by defining the *weaknesses* common to many ACODF parents. The results of the information gathered in these interviews are shown in the chart that opens Part II entitled *Parenting Pitfalls of Adult Children from Dysfunctional Families*. Part II will examine each of these fifteen handicaps and show how they interfere with one's best parenting.

There, and in other sections of the book, I recount family stories that illustrate these parental behaviors. I gathered these stories by interviewing parents who identified themselves as adult children of dysfunctional families. To find subjects I attended parenting meetings, parenting classes, and self-help group meetings and announced the subject of my research. Parents came forward to share their stories with me and I did follow-up interviews which sometimes involved all members of the families. In researching this book, I have followed these families for over two years. In addition, I interviewed parents who felt they had grown up in healthy supportive families to see how their experiences differed from the ACODF. Then for the answers to the parenting problems posed in my Parenting Pitfalls list, I turned not only to the "healthy" parents, but also to those admirable ACODF parents who had created healthy families out of their often chaotic beginnings.

How can you avoid your parents' mistakes when you raise your children? First you must change yourself. This book shows you how to change the subtle negative ways of thinking about your children that you probably inherited from your parents and that will stand in the way of your becoming the best parent you can be. As each problem is discussed in Part II, new ways of thinking and acting are presented along with the problem. Then Part III opens with a list of strengths that define how you can change each of those parenting pitfalls into plusses. All you need at this point is an open mind and a willing heart.

BECOMING A HEALTHY FAMILY

After all is said and done, probably the most important trait of the healthy family is its ability to turn problems into opportunities. Any family can find itself in a crisis. In even the healthiest families children get seriously ill, spouses die, and teenagers sometimes get involved in drugs. No one is immune from life's difficulties. But when facing a crisis as severe as chemical dependency, healthy parents do not waste time whipping themselves for their failure or blaming each other. Instead, they take action to begin solving the problem. Healthy parents can recognize when a problem is severe enough to require professional help; and when problems are less severe they will already have a network of friends to use as sounding boards. The greatest gift they give their children is a model for straightforwardly facing problems and initiating quick action toward a solution.

Although healthy families soon take the steps they need to solve their problems, they still have moments when they suffer deeply and painfully, just as members of dysfunctional families do when they encounter serious problems. But healthy families make the most of the suffering, by looking for meaning in their problems. They try to learn from them. And when the problems have been worked through, the family is stronger and more able to face future difficulties. They have each learned something that will later help him or her advise, comfort, or understand another family member or friend in crisis.

Throughout this book, as I present the stories of adult children who have grown up in dysfunctional families, you will see that many of these people have been all the way down at the bottom and have suffered terrible abuse and neglect. Yet most of them have turned their problems into opportunities. I call these people *Super Survivors*. In each story you may find the sad details painful to read. However, when I bring these stories to a close in the last chapter, you will undoubtedly agree that these people could now be considered among the strongest and healthiest of parents.

May these families be an inspiration and symbol of hope for you.

NOTES

1. Delores Curran, *Traits of a Healthy Family*. San Francisco: Harper & Row, 1983, p. 10.

2. Rollo May, *The Courage to Create*. New York: Bantam Books, 1975, pp. 58–61.

3. Robert J. Ackerman, Ph.D., *Let Go and Grow*. Pompano Beach, FL: Health Communications, Inc., 1987.

4. Charles L. Whitfield, M.D., *Healing the Child Within*. Pompano Beach, FL: Health Communications, Inc., 1987.

Parenting Legacies

Adult Personality Characteristics[1]

1. I guess at what is normal.

2. I have difficulty following a project through to completion.

3. I lie when it would be just as easy to tell the truth.

4. I judge myself without mercy.

5. I have difficulty having fun.

6. I take myself very seriously.

7. I have difficulty with intimate relationships.

8. I overreact to changes over which I have no control.

9. I feel different from other people.

10. I constantly seek approval and affirmation.

11. I am either super responsible or super irresponsible.

12. I am extremely loyal even in the face of evidence that the loyalty is undeserved.

13. I look for immediate as opposed to deferred gratification.

14. I lock myself into a course of action without serious considerations to alternate choices or consequences.

15. I seek tension and crisis and then complain.

16. I avoid conflict or aggravate it but rarely deal with it.

17. I fear rejection and abandonment yet I reject others.

18. I fear failure but have difficulty handling success.

19. I fear criticism and judgment yet I criticize others.

20. I manage my time poorly and do not set my priorities in a way that works well for me.

Reprinted with the permission of the publishers, Health Communications, Inc., Deerfield Beach, FL, from Let Go and Grow, by Robert J. Ackerman, Ph.D., copyright 1987.

The most widely used description of the adaptive behaviors of Adult Children of Alcoholics (ACOA) are the Adult Personality Characteristics presented above. This list of characteristics, originally formulated by Janet Woititz, also serves to describe adult children from all types of dysfunctional families.

These characteristic fears and feelings of inadequacy produce predictable parenting problems when these "adult children" begin having children of their own. Through consultations with psychologists and interviews with parents who have overcome these problems, I have been able to define and describe the characteristics of parents who have grown up in poorly functioning homes. This book will explore how to recognize which of these "parenting pitfalls" you are most likely to fall into and will show how you can overcome them.

NOTES

1. The most widely honored analysis of the adaptive behaviors of Adult Children of Alcoholics (ACOA) are those described by Janet G. Woititz in her pioneering book *Adult Children of Alcoholics* (Pompano Beach, FL: Health Communications, Inc., 1983). Woititz, Robert Ackerman, and Tom Perrin later reframed, restated, and expanded this list for Ackerman's book, *Let Go and Grow*. This is that expanded list.

· **2** ·

THE DYSFUNCTIONAL FAMILY

*When one person in a family (the patient) has
pain which shows up in symptoms, all family
members are feeling this pain in some way.*
        —Virginia Satir, *Conjoint Family Therapy*[1]

Do you feel good about yourself? Are you generally confident, secure, and optimistic? If so, you probably grew up in a supportive, healthy family. But if you have had to struggle to raise your self-esteem as an adult, and you recall being excessively shy or unsure of yourself since childhood, you probably come from a family that was, to a greater or lesser extent, dysfunctional. It is important to keep in mind that a family can be dysfunctional whether or not they all live in the same house together. Parents who have separated through a bitter divorce are often still too preoccupied with the parental relationship to pay proper attention to the children.

Dysfunctional families are families that do not provide children with security, warmth, nurturance, and guidance. They do not build self-esteem nor do they prepare children to either enjoy life's bounty or cope with life's misfortunes. In such poorly managed families, children do not gain an internal sense of confidence and trust. When they leave their family of origin, they often lack the personal judgment they need to function effectively. Perpetually off-center, they grope for a life preserver: Someone or something outside of themselves that will relieve their pain, protect them, make decisions for them, and give them a sense of personal worth. In this way, dysfunctional behaviors such as alcoholism, addictions, and co-dependency are carried forth from one generation to the next.

The family is a sensitive system. Like the ecological system that governs life on this planet, each part interacts with the other parts

21

to create a balanced, functional whole. This means that if one person cannot function well, the whole system will have to struggle to regain balance. Once this struggle begins to take place, cause and effect can be difficult to determine. For example, if the marriage relationship is strained, the children in the family will inevitably be drawn into the conflict. Mother might be lonely because Father has lost interest in her or is excessively preoccupied with work or drink. In order to get her needs met she looks to her children for companionship and affirmation of her worth. But every child needs a mother who can comfort him, not a mother who needs comfort from him. Even though he would rather play with friends than go shopping with Mom, he will sense her loneliness and feel guilty saying no. The child who tries to meet Mother's needs will probably become disturbed and might start losing sleep, acting aggressively, or having difficulty paying attention in school. The child may be referred for therapy but, of course, he is only the *Identified Patient*; both the sickness and the cure actually lie in the parental relationship.[2]

GENERAL CHARACTERISTICS OF THE DYSFUNCTIONAL FAMILY

There are many causes and sources of dysfunctionality in the family, most of which are passed on from generation to generation, although sometimes the source of dysfunction is no longer clear— just the effects. For example, the family with an alcoholic develops predictable patterns of relating. There is usually a "problem" person, and others in the family react to that problem person by trying to rescue him or her, or by withdrawing. It is very difficult to act natural and healthy when there is a great disturbance in the family. Because we learn how to relate to others in our family of origin, these patterns of relating are repeated in the next generation whether there is an active drinker in the family or not. In other words, if you have been rescuing your mother by taking on her responsibilities, you are likely to take on too much responsibility in your own marriage. Neither situation allows a healthy balanced sharing of responsibility. Alcoholism in a family member is one of the most common causes of poor family functioning in our society, and adult children from many different kinds of dysfunctional families have related strongly to the recently much-publicized problems of adult children of alcoholics. For this reason, let us momentarily take a close look at the typical alcoholic family system to see what we can learn about how dysfunctional family systems operate.

Let's assume that the problem drinker is Mother. Perhaps Father was originally a sound, sensible, highly functional person, or perhaps he was a little insecure. Father will naturally be embarrassed by Mother's behavior and will want to protect the children from the pain and uncertainty of having an alcoholic mother. He may believe that if he simply tells the children that Mother is "sick," they will be less fearful or ashamed. Perhaps he assumes that Mother's state is only temporary anyway because he intends to help her get a better grip on her life. So it seems sensible to deny the true nature of the problem.

As Father gets into the habit of lying about Mother's "illness" he gradually realizes that Mother is *not* going to get better, but he has a great deal to cope with by then. He has had to take over a lot of Mother's chores and assign others to the children. Left unsupervised because Mother is "out of it" and Father is preoccupied with Mother, the children start to get into trouble. They don't hand in their homework, they get in fights at school, and they stop caring what happens to them because no one else seems to care. They no longer bring their friends home because they are embarrassed that Mother is still in her bathrobe at 4 P.M. and laughs too loudly at nothing. They hide in their rooms or they roam the streets. If they are older, they may drink to blot out the pain.

In such a troubled system it is easy to see how the whole family is affected. The children stand helplessly by as the relationship between their parents becomes increasingly hostile. Father is bound to resent all the extra responsibility, and a great deal of that responsibility has to do with caretaking. Hence he may ultimately resent the presence of the children, even their very existence.

When children are devalued by their parents, they have difficulty valuing themselves, and these feelings of low self-worth don't automatically disappear when the child is old enough to leave home. Their lowered self-esteem may cause them to be the drinkers in the families they create, or it may cause them to indulgently suffer the behavior of an alcoholic spouse because they don't believe they deserve better. It is easy to see how these environmental factors cause the cycle of alcoholism to be passed on from generation to generation; but there is also much evidence to support a hereditary cause for not only alcoholism but also mood disorders and other psychological disorders. When children were adopted away from their biological families, 18% born to alcoholic parents later became alcoholic, whereas only 5% of children adopted from non-alcoholic families became alcoholic. Studies of the general population show that children who grow up in alcoholic families are four times more likely to develop alcoholism as adults, than the average child is.[3] Similarly, the child of one mood-disordered parent has three times the chance of having a mood disorder than the average child, and 40% of children with two mood-disordered parents inherit the disease. Twin studies show that identical twins will both inherit a mood disorder 40–70% of the time (depending on the study) whereas only 0–13% of fraternal twins share a mood disorder.[4]

In addition to hereditary factors, the outward physical neglect and lack of emotional support in many dysfunctional families create lifelong adjustment problems for the child of poorly functioning parents. As these parents distort reality to protect themselves through denial, they undermine the child's own better judgment. Family therapists and researchers have observed four important rules that govern alcoholic or other dysfunctional homes: The Rule of Rigidity, The Rule of Silence, The Rule of Denial, and The Rule of Isolation.[5]

THE RULE OF RIGIDITY

One of the most predictable characteristics of an active alcoholic or emotionally disturbed parent is his or her unpredictability. As the behavior of the parent becomes more irrational, the resultant chaos is very uncomfortable for the family. They struggle to bring some order into their lives. They begin to adopt rules and adhere to them rigidly so that at least some aspects of their existence are predictable. This reactionary behavior quickly creates an inflexible lifestyle. Change is discouraged.

However, there is no growth without change. Children naturally go through stages—it is well-known that children can be stubborn and obstinate one year (when independence is a high priority to them) and then "outgrow" this stage only to be delightfully coopera-tive the next. But children in a rigidly dysfunctional home can be frozen at any developmental stage, depending on when the trauma occurs. If the child is going through a reckless stage when the difficulty with the dysfunctional parent escalates, then the child becomes viewed as a reckless child. Once the child has been pigeon-holed, the family finds it easier to continue to regard that child as the reckless one. For, if they permitted or acknowledged his or her transformation into a more self-disciplined child, the family members, and indeed the entire family system, would have to readjust. They would have to learn new ways of thinking about and interacting with the child. Any change produces stress and the family is already heavily stressed. It is just simpler and less challenging to keep everyone the same by reminding them about their limitations. ("Well, look at Billy! He's clean for a change. That won't last long.")

In a healthy family these stages are worked through more fluidly. The parents, who can effectively manage the normal stresses of daily life, are often the first to notice a change in the child's behavior. When the child stops at the curb and looks carefully up and down the street instead of dashing heedlessly out, the parents praise this new behavior and thereby reinforce the positive change that is germinating. Likewise, they are able to notice negative attitudes early and offer extra support at these times. Thus the children work through their various stages with the help, support, and encouragement of their families.

Without the opportunity to progress through these developmental stages, the child in a dysfunctional family may go on into adulthood with unconscious childlike behaviors or fears that get in his or her way. Psychologists have observed that certain types of learning are blocked when the child is preoccupied with survival or has no one to reflect and encourage new behaviors. The body grows, but the emotional understanding does not. These children reach "adulthood" with an underdeveloped sense of independence, often feeling like helpless children trapped in adult bodies that prompt everyone else to expect adult behavior from them. They may have moved away from the disturbed parent and hence no longer need to hide this shame, but they must now hide their own insecurity. They try to control everyone and everything around them in order to hide this new secret. Thus they go forth taking their rigidity with them.

When we are not careful to attend to individual preferences, we believe "What's best for me is best for you."

◆ PENNY'S RIGIDITY

"My mother's favorite cake was German Chocolate cake," Penny recalls, "so every time it was someone's birthday she would make a German Chocolate cake. I loved white cake. The week before my birthday I would start working on her, saying how much I liked white cake, and couldn't I have a white cake for my birthday. She'd say, 'We'll see.' And then on my birthday she'd serve German Chocolate cake. She'd dig in and say, 'Isn't this delicious?' She had made it so many times that everyone was sick of German Chocolate cake. I think my father was afraid to say anything because she was also very proud of her German Chocolate cake. If you liked German Chocolate cake, she probably made the best German Chocolate cake around." In her new family, Penny now makes each person's favorite cake for his or her birthday.

But Penny couldn't expand on this "correction" of old family ways and apply it effectively to new situations. For example, her childhood family had always used Russian dressing on their salad, but Penny had tasted Italian dressing at her friend's home and liked it. On shopping day she had asked her mother to buy some Italian dressing. Her mother's reply? "You think we're all going to eat a dressing we don't like just so you can be happy?" It never occurred to Penny's mother that they could buy two different bottles of dressing. Likewise, when I interviewed Penny she was still eating Russian dressing because, "That's the only kind the kids will eat." (And Penny doesn't want to make the mistake of forcing her children to eat a dressing they don't like.) When I suggested she buy two bottles of dressing, she balked. It seemed so extravagant and she prided herself on keeping up her mother's frugal ways. She was astonished and relieved when I explained how long the Italian dressing would last if only she were using it, and how much longer the Russian dressing would last if she no longer used it. In other words, it cost no more to have a choice.

Penny is a bright young woman perfectly capable of figuring out the mathematics of this situation on her own, but she has grown up in a system of rigid thinking and unless she puts forth an extra effort, she cannot find more creative solutions to even simple problems.

THE RULE OF SILENCE

Overtly or covertly the dysfunctional family agrees to keep silent about the pain and confusion everyone is feeling. The parents may directly instruct (or threaten) the children never to tell outsiders what goes on at home. For example, children are often told not to tell friends, neighbors, teachers, or social workers about their parents' drunkenness or abuse. Sometimes the parents model this secrecy. When a neighbor drops by for a visit, the children hear Mother tell the visitor that Dad is sick and mustn't be disturbed. If the children point out that Dad is drunk, they will probably be slapped for their impertinence. The children become afraid to discuss it even among themselves. In this way, they come to believe that there are many things one simply should not talk about.

However, "talking it out" has long been accepted as a good method for discovering solutions to problems and relieving the stress of strong feelings. Not only does talking help the talker analyze the situation, but talking to someone who is part of the problem is the first step in solving the problem. Adult children who have been "shut up" as children carry a threefold burden. First, they come to adulthood with pent-up emotions from childhood; second, they do not know how to constructively vent tension they now feel as adults; and third, they cannot even begin to discuss interpersonal problems with their adversaries. As parents, not only will they fail to model the power of talking over problems, they have been programmed to silence their own children's complaints.

THE RULE OF DENIAL

If the dysfunctional family could clearly identify their problems through talking or reflection, they would then have to do something about the problems. Dysfunctional families use this silence of mind and mouth to avoid taking action. Rarely do we hear family members say, "Yes, we see there is a great problem here which will become worse and worse with time, but we choose to do nothing about it." Instead, they minimize, rationalize, or deny. They might admit that the parent's destructive behavior is "a bit of a problem sometimes," but it's nothing they can't handle themselves. They deny the seriousness and hope the problem will go away of its own accord in time.

For example, when Daddy comes home drunk and irritable, the children are asked to be quiet so that Daddy can rest from his tiring workday; or when Mother is too depressed to fix dinner, the party line is that Mother was too busy and they are lucky that they get to eat fast-food. The children probably feel frightened that Mother isn't responding to them, but they are expected to act glad and excited about the opportunity to eat out. In Carolyn's family her older sister Glenna was bulimic and could be heard retching in the bathroom during dinner, yet family conversations would continue without pause. When Carolyn pointed out Glenna's vomiting and weight loss, she was chided for being jealous of her sister's attractive figure. As long as Carolyn persisted in believing her sister was in trouble, the strong denial of the other family members made her feel crazy, wrong, and not really "part of the family."

In the alcoholic home "blackouts" add to the confusion. Problem drinkers forget what they have done, heard, and said for anywhere from a few seconds to a few weeks. Dad might hand his son a twenty-dollar bill and tell him to buy tickets to the circus or insist his daughter buy "something nice to wear." When he snaps out of his blackout he is likely to accuse his child of taking money from him while he was asleep. Dad will vehemently deny that he made promises or certain statements because he truly has no recollection of the incidents. What he did was simply not recorded in his memory. While drunk, the parent might terrorize the child with threats—behavior that he might regret and apologize for if he recalled it. Instead, when the parent is sober, there is no mention or acknowledgment of the encounter. The child is left confused, wondering why her parent would lie about something they both know is true, or aching because the terrible argument that took place a few hours earlier is still horribly painful for her while the parent seems totally unaffected. To survive the agony of such nonsensical behavior, the child may have to suppress the memories, telling herself that she must have been mistaken.

ACODF who have grown up in families that constantly practiced denial are likely to doubt their perceptions and sanity. They may have come to believe that they are "too negative" and so now discount their negative or apprehensive feelings. If an ACODF's son is behaving aggressively at school, she might brush it off with a comment like, "Boys will be boys." Her common sense might tell her that repeated fights on the playground indicate a serious problem, but then her old "parent tape" will tell her to stop being so negative. Her self-doubts will delay acceptance of the problem and consequently prolong her son's bad behavior until it becomes a habit. By the time she can recognize the problem and take action, the molehill will have become a mountain.

THE RULE OF ISOLATION

The dysfunctional family does not want to know the truth. They do not want the clearer perspectives of others. They fear interference. Outsiders who try to offer help are seen as meddlesome busybodies out to make trouble for the family. With an "us against them" attitude, the dysfunctional family makes every effort to shield itself from other influences. In most cases the members of a dysfunctional family physically withdraw from society. They form no bonds with neighbors, join no churches or organizations, and seek no help for their problems. On the other hand, those more skilled at keeping up appearances may become active (or hyperactive) in sports or church in order to appear normal enough to discourage snoopers or even convince themselves that everything is fine. However, they are never open to the ideas of these acquaintances and will likely belittle others to the children, implying that their own family is better.

Obviously, any truly open interaction would chip away at the rigid beliefs that hold the family together. They are united in their denial, their own distorted reality. For a dysfunctional family, this unified belief in their superiority may be the only thing they feel they can depend on. The fantasy of happiness must be protected at all costs. They cannot accept help from others because they would first have to acknowledge a need for help, and a perfectly happy family wouldn't need help—or would they?

By contrast, one of the things that characterizes the healthy family is its ability to seek help during difficulties. The healthy family expects life to contain some rough spots. Confident parents realize they cannot know all the answers. Because they have a strong sense of self-worth, they do not fear the judgments of others. They assume that everyone realizes problems are a normal part of life, so they don't expect to be harshly judged for having difficulties. The parents who least need it are often the participants at parenting workshops. They realize the complexities of parenting and want to be prepared, whereas the dysfunctional parents have the mistaken idea that good parents will automatically know what to do.

Rigidity, silence, denial, and isolation create a system of relating that becomes the model for children of dysfunctional parents. Absorbed unconsciously, these ways of relating will feel "right" or comfortable to these children when they grow up and look for a mate. If the adult child's parents were sarcastic and verbally abusive, she will admire a potential spouse's "sense of humor" expressed through sarcasm. That special person who attracts them "at first sight" is likely to be someone from another dysfunctional family— someone who has the "right" attitudes—someone who knows the rules.

OTHER COMPULSIONS

It is important to realize that there are many other destructive compulsions besides alcoholism that create a dysfunctional family system. Workaholism, volunteerism, overscheduling, overeating (or bingeing and purging), gambling, compulsive shopping, compulsive jogging, relationship addiction, and compulsive sex are just a few addictive behaviors that create and perpetuate dysfunctional families. These behaviors often become compulsive habits for the children of such families because as adults they seek relief from their feelings of low self-worth or sadness. Initially these activities might bring enjoyment, a sense of worth, or just simple diversion, but since they do nothing to solve the ACODF's basic problems, these compulsions will soon lose their newness and their effect. Just as the addict needs higher and higher doses to get the same effect, the compulsive ACODF needs to eat, drink, jog, or shop more and more to get that same sense of satisfaction.

In *Breaking the Cycle of Addiction*, therapists Patricia O'Gorman and Philip Oliver-Diaz neatly define the dysfunctional family as one which organizes around a *substance* or *act*, as opposed to the healthy family which organizes around *people* and *feelings*.[6] That "happy" family which skis together every weekend may be quite dysfunctional if they are not also allowing time to talk and interact on a deeper level. If they are always too busy skiing, watching TV, or attending church meetings and functions ever to have time to discuss their problems, they cannot achieve good family health. We sometimes hear the term "positive addiction" applied to habits such as running that improve some part of us. However, the bottom line is, compulsions or addictions that are so absorbing that they cause parents to neglect their children, or children to stay away from home too much to form intimate bonds with their parents and siblings, are not positive; they are dysfunctional. To illustrate this we will next look at an addiction that has been revered by past generations and is only beginning to be questioned by today's mental health specialists.

WORKAHOLISM

Workaholism serves as a wonderful example of a good habit gone amuck. Not only is workaholism epidemic in America, it is revered and reinforced at all levels.[7] A self-questionnaire from Workaholics Anonymous[8] clarifies the destructive relationship that can develop between work and family. Some pertinent questions it asks are:

—Do you get more excited about your work than about family or anything else?
—Do you take work with you to bed? on weekends? on vacation?
—Have your family or friends given up expecting you on time?
—Do you get impatient with people who have other priorities besides work?
—Do you get irritated when people ask you to stop doing work to do something else?
—Have your long work hours hurt your family or other relationships?

Workaholism follows the same pattern as active alcoholism. Children of alcoholics complain that their parents were rarely there. When the alcoholic parent was at home, he or she was too preoccupied or cross to approach. The children had to tiptoe about because Daddy was "sick." As they were departing for family outings Daddy was often too drunk to come along (or would weasel out at the last minute to go down to the bar with the boys). If they insisted he come, he would ruin the outing. Everything from dinners to vacations had to be planned around Daddy's drinking.

Likewise, grandchildren of alcoholics talk about Daddy's workaholism, the most common second-generation compulsion.[9] Daddy was never around because he worked long hours each day and went into the office on weekends. When he did come home, he was too stressed-out to be with children. They had to be quiet because Daddy had a headache, and if they weren't quiet he might explode with tension. There were no family outings if they depended on Daddy going along since he was always working; and if mother insisted he come along, he either grumbled all day or ran the outing as if it were a race or competition. They gave up having dinner with Dad and the family rarely took vacations because Daddy was always in the middle of an important project that no one else could handle. Of course, he couldn't ever be expected to leave work to see them in a school play, or even high school graduation for that matter. The workaholic may not drink, but his neglectful behavior will have an equally destructive effect on his children.

ARE YOU FROM A DYSFUNCTIONAL FAMILY?

You may be confused about whether or not you come from a dysfunctional family. Perhaps you have a vague sense that your parents didn't do the best job, but you aren't sure whether your expectations are simply too high. If you have identified with much

Healthy vs. Dysfunctional Families

HEALTHY FAMILY	DYSFUNCTIONAL FAMILY
Open system	Closed system
Accepts each child as a separate person with his or her own unique personality. Each child is encouraged to pursue his or her own special interests.	Children expected to mold themselves to family identity such as sports family, musical family, extroverted family. Parents choose the child's activities rather than child.
Children are gently pushed toward self-reliance and independence as is appropriate for his or her age.	Either child is kept dependent by parents doing everything for him or her or child is given adult responsibilities at too early an age.
Family roles are clear: Parents function as nurturers and children are only expected to concern themselves with their own personal problems.	Parentified child syndrome: One child is given the role of "little mother" and is expected to care for siblings and sometimes even parents.
Although they are not expected to solve their parents' problems, children are often willingly responsive to parent when extra help is needed.	If kept overdependent by placating parent, children resent being asked for help. Mother becomes an abused slave and parental burn-out occurs.
Family interacts with a wide network of people through scouts, church, school, etc.	Family does not socialize or seek help from others. Unhealthy isolation occurs.
Children willing to reveal their mistakes or admit to shortcomings because they know they will be loved "no matter what."	Children fear loss of love and may lie or hide their mistakes. When something is broken no one admits blame and each points a finger elsewhere.
Balanced relationships within the family: Child is comfortable with both father and mother.	Unhealthy alliances form. Two family members "gang up" on another. Child forms a triangle with favored parent.
Each child feels important. No one is the favorite.	One child's problems or achievements on center stage.

of the material presented but cannot imagine why, there may be a secret in your family history. Often, such as in the case of grandchildren of alcoholics, the connection between the origin of the dysfunction and the present generation has been lost. The dysfunction becomes so unconscious that it is very difficult to identify but it continues to be felt. Many reach adulthood believing they have come from a healthy family because they were no worse off than other families they knew as children. Keep in mind, that birds of a feather flock together and what is common is not necessarily healthy. Follow your instincts for the time being and see if you can discover what has left you feeling so unsure of yourself.

The degree of damage you might have suffered could be minor and poses little threat to your present family, or it might be severe and debilitating. As we mentioned in Chapter 1, some families are more dysfunctional than others. In the worst families there are either many dysfunctions clustered together or the children are subjected to the most abusive behaviors. There are matters of degree. The girl whose father pays little attention to her because he is constantly out running or at work has not been damaged as much as the girl whose father has raped and beaten her. We will be discussing these more serious abuses in chapters to come but it is important to mention them here for the sake of perspective. What we suffer as children forms our attitudes about life and our expectations for ourselves and others. To get an idea of your level of health or dysfunctionality try using the checklist below.

The Dysfunctional Attitude Checklist[10]

_____ **1.** I feel very upset when I am criticized.

_____ **2.** I need other people's approval in order to be happy.

_____ **3.** My value as a person depends greatly on what others think of me.

_____ **4.** I cannot find happiness without being loved by another person.

_____ **5.** When people I care about reject me, I feel there is something wrong with me.

_____ **6.** In order to be able to consider myself a worthwhile person, I must be truly outstanding in at least one major aspect.

_____ **7.** If I am not a useful, productive, creative person, my life has no meaning.

_____ **8.** When I fail at my work, I feel like a failure as a person.

_____ **9.** I believe in the old adage: "If you can't do something right, don't bother doing it at all."

_____ **10.** I can't help getting upset when I make a mistake.

_____ **11.** When I deserve something, it is only fair that I should get it.

_____ **12.** If I have put other people's needs before my own, they should help me later when I need something from them.

_____ **13.** When I do nice things for someone, I expect them to respect me and treat me just as well as I treated them.

_____ **14.** I am responsible for the way people close to me feel and behave.

_____ **15.** To be a good, worthwhile, moral person, I must try to help everyone who needs it.

_____ **16.** If a child is having emotional or behavioral difficulties, I believe the child's parents are to blame.

_____ **17.** I try to please and be liked by everybody.

_____ **18.** I cannot control how I feel when something bad happens.

_____ **19.** My moods are created by factors beyond my control, such as my past, my body chemistry, hormones, biorhythms, or bad luck.

_____ **20.** I would be happier if I were better looking, more popular, wealthier, or more famous.

Any attitudes you checked off above show your emotional weaknesses. 1, 2, 3, 4, & 5 show your need for love and approval; 6, 7, 8, 9, & 10 indicate you need to excel; 11, 12, & 13 show your high expectations of others; 14, 15, 16, & 17 indicate a belief that you have a godlike control over others; and 18, 19, & 20 show how much you feel in charge of your own emotions. Those not checked indicate relative emotional strengths. If you checked 10 or more items, you have probably grown up in a dysfunctional family.

The above attitudes are the norm in dysfunctional families. They are a set-up for failure and disappointment. They reflect excessively high expectations. Life is often not fair. People can disappoint you even when they love you and want to come through for you. No matter how well-organized or pure-intentioned people are, there are just too many unexpected things that can go wrong. The happiest people are those who learn to appreciate who they are and what they have. They can see how green the grass is on their own side of the fence.

Part of self-acceptance is understanding and accepting our genetic strengths and weaknesses. Psychologists now understand that behavior is not all learned. Studies of the brain and mind reveal a chemical basis for personality variables such as gregariousness, aggressiveness, positive vs. negative attitudes, activity level, attention span, and many other characteristics once thought to be controllable or learned behaviors. In Part III we will take a closer look at how our inherited family brain chemistry has contributed to generations of dysfunctional behaviors, but let's preview what disorders are likely to reappear in families despite changes made by one generation.

HEREDITARY FACTORS

Handicaps may be physical or psychological and many difficulties which affect children are now understood to be disturbances in both mind and body. Through taking case histories on several generations, psychological researchers have discovered a number of behavioral and psychological disorders that show up repeatedly in some families. Probably the most common of these are alcoholism, mood disorders (depression or manic-depression), schizophrenia, and childhood syndromes such as hyperactivity.

These disorders are so hard to live with—not just for the afflicted person but also for other family members—that they are bound to cause a disturbance in the way family members relate to each other. It is not surprising that children of depressed or schizophrenic parents are often depressed or disturbed because they have probably had very chaotic or painful childhoods. Moreover, studies with twins and adopted children have shown that there is also an important genetic component in these disorders.[11] So if your parents had any of the above disorders there is a higher probability than normal that you too could develop these disorders and your children may very well have inherited a genetic tendency toward them.

However, self-aware, well-trained parents can reduce the risks for their children and teach them the skills they need to live normal, happy lives. Although these disorders are not caused primarily by environment, they are usually triggered by environmental factors such as traumatic childhood experiences, stress, illness, financial difficulties, poor nutrition, or poorly developed coping patterns. By the same token, these disorders can often be prevented or mitigated by correcting the child's dysfunctional habits or teaching good life habits from the start. For example, children who develop good self-esteem and learn to avoid overextending themselves may never experience the intense stress that would trigger a depressive episode.[12] Specific steps parents can take to reduce the risk of their child being handicapped by these disorders will be presented in Parts II and III.

HISTORY REPEATS ITSELF

If you have come from a dysfunctional family there is no escaping the fact that it has had an effect on you. Leaving that family does not automatically give you the psychological understanding or emotional strength to be a confident person or a mature parent. Unfortunately, much of the damage is buried in the unconscious and has been processed through childish perceptions and knowledge about the world. If you grew up in a family that survived from crisis to crisis, whatever the source, you have become used to the excitement of "living on the line," of using adrenalin for fuel. Perhaps you will avoid the specific mistakes that made your childhood uncomfortable, but you will follow a crisis life-style in other areas. For example, if the crises in your childhood were caused by mismanagement of money, you may budget expenses in advance and be extra cautious about buying on credit. However, your childhood crisis life-style training might come out in an inability to manage your time. You might neglect all your household chores until your in-laws are about to arrive, never realizing that you are repeating a behavior pattern from your family of origin. Nonetheless, as your children rush around trying to clean up the house before Grandma arrives, while you and your spouse scream at each other, your children will feel the same terrible anxiety you felt when your parents fought over money matters.

On the other hand, many do the polar opposite of what their parents did and think this will guarantee their success as parents. But such thinking is hardly objective and danger lies in any extreme. If your parents were 100% rotten and you did the opposite, it might work—that is if you had any idea what the opposite was. But how could you? Parenting, even for healthy parents from healthy families, requires a lot of self-examination and sorting. What works for one set of parents may not work for another, and neither will its opposite. Each child within the same family may require different parenting techniques. Parents must keep an open mind and remain responsive to their particular children. Parenting exactly as your parents did, or the exact opposite, are both ways of following that Rule of Rigidity. To break free you must really take the time to think through your parenting style.

In this book we will analyze the most common dysfunctional behaviors and beliefs of children from poorly functioning families so we can pin down what probably needs to be changed. And by studying what healthy families do and believe instead, we can get ideas about what to do that is better than what our families have been doing for generations. It won't be easy, but if you can determine where it is best to put your time, money, and energy and can avoid wasting your resources, the task is manageable. However much you can raise your child's self-esteem, confidence, and functioning, it is well worth the effort. For your child's level of functioning can be passed on to your grandchildren and influence many generations to come.

◆ ═══════════ **SUMMARY** ═══════════ ◆

Unless there is some kind of intervention or education, a family's dysfunctional ways of relating will be passed on to the next generation whether or not the problems were originally hereditary. Although dysfunctions come in many forms, they all really represent an avoidance of intimacy.

◆ ═══════════ **POINTS** ═══════════ ◆

1. The family is a system of interdependent parts. If one member is disturbed, the balance of the entire family is disturbed.

2. Unless there is intervention, family dysfunction is passed on to subsequent generations.

3. Because any change (good or bad) creates stress, dysfunctional families often defend themselves by becoming rigidly opposed to change.

4. Dysfunctional families frequently deny their problems and withdraw from social contact. Unfortunately, this shuts them off from avenues of help.

5. The healthy family organizes around people and feelings, but the dysfunctional family organizes around a substance or act.

6. Parents who are chronically overoccupied with work, volunteering, or sports leave their unattended children feeling just

as neglected as children who have been emotionally abandoned by alcoholic parents.

7. Many disorders are hereditary but even these dysfunctions may be controlled by learning a less stressful life-style and teaching it to our children.

N O T E S

1. Virginia Satir, *Conjoint Family Therapy*. Palo Alto, CA: Science and Behavior Books, Inc., 1967.

2. In her book *Conjoint Family Therapy*, Virginia Satir popularized the concept of the family as a system—a concept that is now widely accepted by therapists.

3. David C. Lewis, M.D., and Carol N. Williams, Ph.D., *Providing Care for Children of Alcoholics*. Pompano Beach, FL: Health Communications, Inc., 1986.

4. Mark S. Gold, M.D., with Lois B. Morris, *The Good News About Depression*. New York: Bantam Books, 1986.

5. Using the alcoholic family as a representative dysfunctional family, Wayne Kritzberg *(The Adult Children of Alcoholics Syndrome*. Pompano Beach, FL: Health Communications, Inc., 1985) presents the general characteristics of the dysfunctional family. These rules are a response to and a way of coping with an alcoholic in the family.

6. Patricia O'Gorman and Philip Oliver-Diaz, *Breaking the Cycle of Addiction:* Pompano Beach, FL: Health Communications, Inc., 1987, p. 33.

7. Anne Wilson Schaef and Diane Fassel, "Hooked on Work," *New Age Magazine,* Jan/Feb 1988.

8. Workaholics Anonymous, % Westchester Community College, 75 AAB Grasslands Road, Valhalla, NY 10595.

9. Ann W. Smith, *Grandchildren of Alcoholics*. Pompano Beach, FL: Health Communications, Inc., 1988.

10. This checklist was adapted from a shortened version of Dr. Arlene Weissman's *Dysfunctional Attitude Scale (DAS)*, copyright 1978, as it appears in *Feeling Good: New Mood Therapy* by David D. Burns, M.D. (New York: Signet, 1980).

11. Studies which look for higher incidence of similar disorders in identical twins versus fraternal twins, and which examine children adopted away from their natural parents who have psychological disorders (including alcoholism), help distinguish which disorders are hereditary and which are simply dysfunctional behaviors that have been learned in a poor family environment. For further information see Donald W. Goodwin, *Is Alcoholism Hereditary?* New York: Ballantine Books, 1988.

12. Mark S. Gold, M.D., with Lois B. Morris, *The Good News About Depression*. New York: Bantam Books, 1986.

· 3 ·

ADULT CHILDREN FROM DYSFUNCTIONAL FAMILIES

*The co-dependent person is one who gives up
his or her own sense of healthy independence
and power to another. It is a one-directional
relationship in which the co-dependent person is
always a reactor to someone else's acting.*
—Robert J. Ackerman, *Let Go and Grow*[1]

In Chapter 2 we took a look at the family as a system and realized that one family member's problem will affect everyone as they react to it in healthy and useful ways, or in destructive ways. Children in dysfunctional families are really in a rather helpless position. They are also very vulnerable. Yet they must learn to survive in whatever situation or family they find themselves. Consequently, the child who is severely beaten for any transgression is bound to become a liar and a "sneak" instead of imitating George Washington's exemplary honesty. **Survival does not always mean doing what is right or good. It means doing what is necessary.**

In this chapter we will be taking a closer look at the adaptive behaviors of the children in dysfunctional homes and how these adaptations have affected these children as adults. Frequently, adult children have learned no constructive ways to deal with conflict. They may be pleasers, fixers, or caretakers because past experience has taught them that if they don't give in, violence will erupt. Without intervention, the ways of relating to others learned in childhood will pattern the way people relate to others as adults. Let's take a look at some of these unhealthy patterns.

VICTIMIZATION

Children are dependent on their parents for food, guidance, and a place to live. The impact of being a small, truly helpless person dependent upon irresponsible and often abusive adults is different from the impact on an adult-sized person legally able to obtain a job or other outside assistance.[2] In order to survive, children must adapt to their dysfunctional parents and do whatever is necessary to please them. Even if they can see that their parents are wrong and that what their parents demand of them is unreasonable, they do not have the option of divorcing their parents and getting a new set who appreciate them more.

Unfortunately, these dependent children often have difficulty attracting others to help them; for the behavior modeled in their homes most frequently is dysfunctional behavior—behavior that doesn't work to bring social acceptance, intimacy, or positive reinforcement. For example, as the family, and especially the spouse, puts all its energy into an alcoholic, depressed, or otherwise dysfunctional parent, the child sees that the very attention he longs for is lavished on his self-centered, uncooperative, destructive, or helpless parent. It is no wonder that children from dysfunctional families often use destructive behaviors to try to capture attention; the attention they get, however, will rarely be positive.

In addition, children do not have the objectivity to realize they are being mistreated. Until the child is old enough to go to school or play in other children's homes for extended periods of time, he has no model of what is normal, reasonable, or acceptable. The abusive parent and the observing spouse are capable of knowing that the abuse is wrong, but the child has no reason to believe that the abusive treatment is not what goes on in every home. Therefore, he is not outraged by his abuse; he believes he deserves it. If the family has made it clear that we don't talk about these things to outsiders, it may be a long time before the child hears a contradictory view. Instead, the child can grow up thinking that love and violence go together, never realizing that tenderness might be part of love too.

To change this pattern, ACODF need to clearly identify how they were mistreated as children. For if an adult child continues to rationalize her parents' behavior ("Mom was tired . . . I must have deserved it . . . Everyone's parents treated them that way"), she is likely to make similar excuses for abusing her own children ("I was tired . . . He deserved it . . . All parents beat their children on occasion"). It is painful to acknowledge how much it hurt to be sworn at, hit, and belittled, or neglected and discounted. Remembering oneself as a small, helpless child being chastised, threatened, or ignored can often bring on a flood of agonizing tears, but being truly open to the memory will bring a sense of relief. Only when we can get in touch with our own childhood feelings, can we realize the intense sensitivity of all children, our own included, even if they are standing before us in arrogant defiance—"looking for a beating," as Mother might have said.

◆ MARYANNE—ABUSED AND NEGLECTED

"I always wanted someone to hang my pictures on the refrigerator," Maryanne confessed as we stood in front of her refrigerator pleasantly cluttered with her son's drawings. Keith dashed by and she grabbed him and pulled him to her for a hug. "And I always wanted someone to hug me. I guess you could say I rely mainly on my memories of what I didn't have as a child."

What Maryanne remembers most clearly is the loneliness. She was the youngest of two children in an alcoholic home. Her mother had been drinking heavily since shortly after she was born and her father was seldom there. Her parents hated each other but were afraid to separate. They had done the next best thing—her mother took an evening waitressing job so she would be gone before her husband returned from work, and Maryanne's father went out drinking on weeknights and was gone as much as possible on the weekends. Maryanne, age seven, had only her eleven-year-old brother, Jim, for company.

Maryanne would get herself up for school in the morning and make herself a bowl of cereal. She was forbidden to wake her mother, who "worked late." (Although the restaurant closed for dinner at 9 P.M. her mother generally stayed on "relaxing" until the bar closed.) Maryanne would scrounge around in the laundry looking for something to wear. Sometimes her clothes were clean, sometimes ironed, sometimes neither. The school was a long walk but she always managed to get herself there on time although Jim was often still sleeping at home and rarely made it to school.

When Maryanne arrived home, artwork and school papers in hand, her mother would nod a greeting as she rushed around getting ready for work. If Maryanne set her papers out hoping to catch a compliment, her mother would yell at her to get that mess off the table. There were no questions about her day, about her schoolwork, about her feelings. The only communication was instructions about dinner. There was generally a stew or other easily heated meal for when her father got home. It was Jim's job to fix the dinner but sometimes he was not there and Maryanne had to fix it if she didn't want to be beaten by her father. When her father was very angry he would strip her and beat her bare flesh with a belt to make sure she felt it and learned her lesson.

Maryanne was an early maturer and had the body of a woman by the time she was ten. Her brother, Jim, was fourteen years old then and he and his friends were growing curious about girls. One of them got the idea of using Maryanne for kissing practice. They told her they were playing "married." For Maryanne, who still played with dolls, this was just a more advanced game of playing "house." It felt strange to have these boys kiss her, but it also felt good to have some affection. Maryanne's mother only hugged her when she was drunk and stank of booze, and her father never touched her except to beat her.

One evening when Jim was not at home, three friends came in to wait for him. They were drunk and began kissing Maryanne, but the "game" got out of hand and turned to rape. Afterward the boys were so ashamed they fled the house: all but the oldest boy, Skip, who stood dazed in the doorway, stunned by what he had done. Moved by Maryanne's tears, he decided to stay with her.

Skip was eighteen, a high school dropout who lived with his wretched, demeaning mother. He had never known his father. He was looking for love and attention himself and Maryanne, a very confused child at this point, forgave him the rape. As Skip filled her lonely evenings, Maryanne felt loved and cherished for the first time in her life. Skip had a job and money and bought her presents such as little plastic horses. Skip hunted up all Jim's friends to issue a warning that they had better keep their hands off. Maryanne felt flattered and warmed by his jealousy and possessiveness. She had never been so prized.

The next few years were intense with pain and confusion. Maryanne's father was diagnosed as having cancer and lay at home dying. He had lost his two outlets—work and alcohol—and was like a penned-up raging beast. He didn't have the physical strength to overpower her anymore but his verbal insults were constant.

With her father home constantly, Maryanne was no longer available as a sexual outlet for Skip and he stopped coming around. Maryanne found her years of hatred toward her father coming out in shocking meanness. She would hurl insults back and run beyond his grasp. By the time he died she felt like the worst monster on earth. Maryanne had wished him dead so many times that she believed it was her ill will that had killed him. She had begun eating and eating to soothe herself and weighed nearly 200 pounds.

(Continued in Chapter 4)

Although Maryanne lived in a suburban home, her experience resembles that of a child of the streets. There was little direct parental supervision and Maryanne felt so disconnected from her parents that she didn't feel safe telling them about the rape. She feared they would, at best, do nothing about the incident, and at worst, get angry at her. Besides, in her childish understanding she felt grateful to her victimizer since he was now offering her warmth and security. These are the acts of a desperate child.

Being a true victim in such circumstances results in certain behaviors and beliefs that are carried into adulthood. Victims characteristically have identity problems: They are uncertain about what they want, like, believe, or feel. Thus it is difficult for them to set limits on other's demands and dictates.[3] They have no sense of personal rights. For example, an adult abused as a child might not realize that she (*not* her spouse) has a right to decide how to dress or wear her hair. Consequently, as a parent she may have difficulty letting her children make such decisions. Another result of letting others run her life might be that she becomes overcommitted to activities and obligations that don't interest her, and saves too little time for activities that stimulate, relax, and renew her.

The victim's underdeveloped maturity provides few tools for dealing with the usual parenting difficulties. Because she has learned to repress pain, the victim-as-parent may underreact to what is a crisis, but explode over a minor incident. When panic sets in she may resort to extreme thinking. For example, if her pre-schooler is bitten at school (a rather common occurrence at that age) she might withdraw the child immediately even though she had selected the facility with great care, endured a long waiting list, and had been pleased with the staff and program. Some victims make many impulsive decisions they later regret, while others find it impossible to make any decision even after long deliberation. Rather they "get stuck," endure the crisis, and eventually wallow in self-blame. This inability to cope with crisis and stress can also lead to physical illness, or a sense of hopelessness.

If you were a childhood victim of physical, sexual, or psychological abuse in your own home or neighborhood, your perceptions and beliefs about personal rights are probably very distorted. Not only will you probably allow others to trample over your feelings and take advantage of you in many ways, you will have little understanding of the respect your child needs to grow up into a capable, healthy adult. Children are very demanding and your background gives you two disadvantages that work against your being kind, calm, and firm. You are likely to be chronically exhausted from meeting the demands of others so that you bring little patience to parenting, and you will probably be outraged by what your children feel they deserve. Your expectations and ability to respond are bound to be far from normal. You may need to seek counseling with a therapist to help you establish a sense of your personal rights and be able to accept your children having rights too.

CO-DEPENDENCE

Co-dependence has become a much talked about issue and everyone has his or her own definition. The notion of co-dependence grew out of the study of family dynamics of alcoholism. Al-Anon was originally established to be a support group for spouses of alcoholics. Together, these spouses began to discover what actions on their part seemed to prolong the problem, and what actions they could take to protect themselves and avoid playing into the "game of alcoholism." They dubbed themselves co-alcoholics.

Now we understand that many people play a "helping" role also to drug addicts, workaholics, and others addicted to love, sex, or failure, to name a few. The notion of being addicted to destructive love relationships was popularized by Robin Norwood in her book *Women Who Love Too Much*,[4] and Melody Beattie has raised awareness about how this self-sacrificing "servant" role can be carried over into all relationships in her book *Co-Dependent No More*.[5] Another popular term used to describe this syndrome is *enabling*. In looking at co-dependence most current books focus on the over-controlling martyred partner in the dance, but I prefer to look at the reciprocity of the relationship, so I will define co-dependency with that aspect foremost in mind.

Co-dependency is an unhealthy relationship between two people who depend on each other too much. This two-way dependency may not always be obvious. For example, in marriage many couples seem to have a strong partner and a weak partner. At first glance we might say, "It's obvious she depends on him too much, but he doesn't seem to need anybody!" Yet there are no supermen without the people who believe in them. She depends on him to protect her. He depends on her to need his protection so he can go on feeling strong (and superior). For generations women have been programmed to marry someone who would "take care of them." In the ultimate "being cared for" scenario, the spouse would not only feed and clothe you, but also make decisions for you and intervene in social situations, offering your excuses, and saving you from any confrontations. Of course, only a Prince Charming could meet all these needs. But both men and women can wish for such a savior— female saviors can end up supporting helpless men who can neither keep a job nor make a sandwich. Although this male/female relationship style has been the norm in past generations, it is not the ideal.

Co-dependency is also the natural result of growing up in a dysfunctional family. The parents in a dysfunctional family are not "fully functioning" human beings. Someone must compensate for what the parents lack. If an ACODF has played the parent in her family of origin, she will probably try to parent her spouse. Likewise, she may not be able to share parenting without resentment, because being totally in charge of the family is the only way that feels right to her. Thus, she takes on a disproportionate amount of responsibility and thereby trains everyone else to depend on her to an unhealthy degree.

Commonly, ACODF have learned the importance of keeping up appearances and so they may appear to be strong, competent, and emotionally healthy. However, the adult child inwardly feels confused, lost, lonely, and dependent. Co-dependent people avoid recognizing these painful feelings by focusing on outside stimulus. The resulting symptoms are:

Symptoms of Co-Dependence

1. Depression

2. High tolerance for inappropriate behavior

3. Self-defeating coping strategies that cause neglect or abuse of self

4. Strong need to be in control

5. Physical stress symptoms[6]

If you are experiencing any of the above symptoms, you have probably learned co-dependent habits and behaviors in your family of origin. You may be wearing yourself out fixing others instead of taking the time you need to nurture yourself. Or you may have come to believe that you cannot change and you simply must put up with abusive behavior from others because you are no prize yourself. You will need to go "back in time" and take a more rational look at the child you once were. It is never too late to learn to take good care of ourselves. We'll explore this in detail in Parts II and III.

You might be silently asking, "Why would anyone stay in a relationship with a dysfunctional or abusive spouse if they didn't have to? Doesn't she understand that I would take care of myself if I wasn't married to this lug-head?" This is when we have to really challenge ourselves to take a look at our part in the dance. For example, when a woman stays in a co-dependent relationship with an alcoholic spouse there are certain hidden benefits. The alcoholic husband can become her excuse for never fully developing her own capabilities. She would go back to school if it weren't for him; she would quit her depressing job and look for a better one if he were working; she would be calm enough to treat the children better if she weren't so exhausted from caring for her alcoholic husband; the children would be better behaved if they had a father who would discipline them. Whatever is wrong with her or her life can be blamed on him, so she does nothing as she waits for him to change (and become Prince Charming). Meanwhile, no one can blame her for being a failure. It's important to remember that co-dependence serves both the helpless one and the helper.

In the same way, many ACODF waste a lifetime blaming their parents for all that's wrong with them, instead of taking responsibility for changing themselves now that they are adults. But waiting for "the other" to change is a learned response. Adult children have grown up in an atmosphere of blaming. The adult child must first be able to recognize how nonproductive blaming is before he or she can learn a new behavior.

Our co-dependent tendencies can best be sorted out in relationships because it is when we interact with others that our overcontrolling behaviors become obvious. At work co-dependents are generally workaholics who unconsciously grab responsibilities from others or overvolunteer until they are stressed-out by the expectations others then have of them. In churches, co-dependents are often the heads of several committies and, for a time, flourish under the admiration of others for their superhuman capabilities. In love, co-dependents play superparent or rescuer to the loved one. In parenting, co-dependents are overprotective and stifle the growth of independence in their children by doing for them what they should be learning to do for themselves. Marriage is a perfect "natural laboratory" for observing co-dependence in action. Due to poor parental role models, few of us have any idea what a healthy relationship looks like, and yet the way we relate to our co-parent is likely to have the greatest impact on our children's notions of how to be in relationship. Let's take a look at how a healthy interdependent couple function in a marital crisis.

THE HEALTHY MARRIAGE

Family systems counselors believe that a healthy family begins with a healthy marriage between two "whole" self-actualizing people. Each member of the partnership realizes he or she is responsible for his or her own actions and happiness. John Bradshaw uses the analogy of two people making music together: Each may play a different instrument and his or her own part of the harmony, but the combined result is a well-orchestrated complete piece of music. Each parent satisfies his or her own individual needs and the partnership satisfies their need for mature companionship.[7]

◆ GARY AND RACHAEL—A HEALTHY COUPLE

By their mid to late twenties Gary and Rachael were well on their way to realizing a dream that many only approach at mid-life. Gary, accomplished in the art of carpentry, had built up enough of a professional reputation to be successfully running and living off his own cabinet business. With Rachael's steady income as a classroom teacher they were able to purchase some land on the side of a mountain and begin building the dream house that Gary had designed. It was a goal they shared with enthusiasm.

Still, it was their first big project as a couple, even as adults, and despite their careful planning, there were unexpected challenges to meet. They were working toward their vision of a shared nest; they not only wanted the house they would build together, they also planned to start a family. When it looked as though the house would easily be finished in six months, Rachael became pregnant. She would be finishing up the school year just as the house was ready to move into and then she would have three months to get settled before the baby arrived. At least that was the plan.

Gary managed to keep to his time schedule for the house, but there were delays with the electrician and the plumber. To top it off, some new building codes caused some unexpected expenses and the price of lumber had risen sharply. Gary decided to put on the roof himself to save money but time was lost in the bargain. By Rachael's ninth month of pregnancy the house was still not ready to be moved into and the expenses had exceeded their savings. As interests rates climbed, the cost of their future mortgage loomed as a threatening unknown.

Rachael had a baby girl and returned to her teaching job in the fall to earn the money they needed to cover the unexpected expenses. She cried each day as she drove away from the caretaker's, yearning instead to be at home in her new house with her new baby. Gary felt bad that he was not earning enough money to make it possible for Rachael to stay home, but Rachael did not blame him. She knew he had worked as hard and as fast as humanly possible. They were in this together. They had made all the decisions together and they faced the consequences of the unexpected delays and expenses together. Together they had learned that one should always expect the unexpected and they were both able to recognize that they could only have had this wisdom in hindsight.

By the end of the school year they were one year's salary richer but were stressed to their limits. They were into the house, caught up on their big cash outlays, and able to make future mortgage payments. They each had had to draw on their reserves of emotional strength, and both sets of their parents had pitched in with child care and moral support. They were grateful for the help but realized they could not keep up this pace much longer. More time had to be devoted to home and family. As Gary saw it, his panic had driven him toward putting in far too much time at the business and he needed to start cutting back. Rachael felt her full-time work had drawn too much energy away from their relationship and their child. Each saw things he or she could do to reestablish their harmony and equilibrium.

This pattern of taking personal responsibility and not blaming each other for difficulties has characterized their marriage and brought them through the birth of a second child. Rachael has had a healthy sense of personal progress in career advancement as she worked toward her master's degree while being at home to nurture her children. Gary has been able to support her efforts while still making steady progress with his cabinet business. They are two strong, stable people moving compatibly toward realizing both personal and shared goals.

By contrast, a dysfunctional family is likely to be headed by two incomplete adults. People with low self-esteem tend to be attracted to one another, although each party is seldom aware of his or the other's inadequacies during courtship. The attraction is unconscious. They are each half-realized people looking for a partner to complete them. If a man lacks social skills, rather than increasing his own social functioning, he may look for a woman who will bring him in comfortable contact with people. Likewise, a woman who fears competing in the business world may look for a man who can support her rather than developing the skills and contacts she needs to succeed in a career. Initially this can solve each person's problems by seemingly filling in their deficits, but the system falls apart under stress. The stress produced by adding a child to the relationship is often enough to undermine this delicate balance.

The pressure of having another mouth to feed (while going to work without adequate sleep) can lower Father's job performance, and Mother may be much too tired and distracted to make social plans. If either spouse can no longer compensate for the other's shortcomings, the disappointed spouse is likely to panic and become hypercritical. The partners become alienated and a dysfunctional triangle is bound to form: Mother or Father, disappointed by their spouse's human failings or hurt by their spouse's criticism, often turn from the other spouse and look toward the child for comfort and proof of their worth. Soon it is Mommy and Baby against the "cruel" daddy, or Father and Son against the "overly emotional" mother. The child who learns to read her parents well can often play on both teams, siding with whatever parent is most useful for getting what she wants at a given time. In these scenarios family members use each other to gratify their own needs without regard for what this does to the member used.

RIGID ROLES

As we discussed in the last chapter, one central characteristic of dysfunctional parents is their inability to let each child's personality unfold. Rigid systems such as the dysfunctional family require each person to take a fixed role. If the system is to work, the people must fit in around each other like pieces in a puzzle. Often the children in the family must play their roles so that their parents are able to think of themselves as good parents. But when the parents' functioning is actually very inadequate, this means two things: Someone in the family will have to pick up the parenting responsibilities; and someone in the family will have to be blamed for the things that go wrong. For the dysfunctional family to remain in balance, the system must provide compensations for the deficits.

Here we will primarily concern ourselves with the adaptations of the children. Once again we will look at the research on adult children of alcoholics, since psychologists and adult children of all types of dysfunctional families find similar adaptations have to be made no matter what is the exact source of the poor functioning in the family.[8] Many authors have tried to describe the roles and characteristics that result from adapting to an alcoholic family, and there is general agreement in the counseling community about certain personality types that are formed in response to living with dysfunctional parents.[9] If you have grown up in a dysfunctional family, if your parents were not effective as parents and did not provide you with the love, security, and nurturance that every child needs, then you will probably identify with one or several of these roles. Actually, most people find they identify with more than one of these character types, having taken on different functions as they grew older, or as siblings abandoned certain roles.

Sources on the alcoholic family describe a variety of rigid roles children are forced to play in order to keep the family system in balance, but we will focus on the five most commonly reported: The *Black Sheep*, who takes all the blame; the *Mascot*, who uses humor to draw attention away from family problems; the *Lost Child*, who just tries to stay out of everybody's way; the *Placater*, who plays the role of family arbitrator; and the esteemed *Family Hero* (or heroine), who brings the family glory while training for an adult career in co-dependence. We will take a brief look at the first four roles and how they affect our parenting as adults, and then focus in on the popular role of "Hero."

THE BLACK SHEEP

The Black Sheep (sometimes called the scapegoat) is the one who draws attention to himself or herself with antisocial behaviors such as lying, cheating, stealing, taking drugs, indiscriminate sexuality, and any and all other forms of acting out. If anything else is amiss in the family it can be blamed on him or her. After all, how could a family function in the midst of the chaos caused by all this misbehavior? This is the most tragic role because, as the Black Sheep tries to strike back for the pain of his neglect, he strikes himself. The Black Sheep, not the neglectful or rejecting parents, is the one to end up in jail or dead. The Black Sheep is likely to become a parent "by accident" at a young age. If he or she does not simply flee the responsibility, the Black Sheep is not likely to make a good parent. Tragically, the low self-esteem and repressed anger that have built up during childhood is likely to erupt as abusive behavior toward any children the Black Sheep parents.

THE MASCOT

The Mascot is responsible for providing more pleasant distractions than his counterpart the Black Sheep. The family clown, he acts out his tension and anxiety by joking around. However, he does not grab attention to fulfill his own needs, for unconsciously he knows that it is his job to divert attention away from the family problems. The Mascot avoids conflict and stress by manipulating the situation with humor. Unfortunately, when he avoids working through normal developmental crises this way, he never really has the opportunity to grow up. He or she will remain overly dependent into adulthood.

Because they are accustomed to making light of any situation, Mascots-as-parents are not likely to treat children's problems and concerns with respect. Nor can Mascots provide a stable supportive harbor for their children since they themselves have not worked through the stages of development that lead to maturity.

THE LOST CHILD (OR QUIET ONE)

This child attempts to be invisible. She doesn't want to cause any trouble so she blends into the background of chaos. She will rarely assert herself to get any of her own needs met; in fact, she may come to believe that she has no needs, or that her needs are too unimportant to consider. Shy and retiring, she will sacrifice for others without show. If there isn't enough food to go around, she will say she is not hungry. These quiet children are valued for never being a problem and can be ignored so completely they may come to doubt their own existence, or at least their right to exist. The lost child will make any adaptation to avoid conflict. Often thought to be the dreamy one, she will spend a great deal of time alone, failing to establish bonds with either peers or family members. As parents, lost children are likely to be too permissive since they have had too little experience with being assertive or resolving conflicts. They are also likely to be distant and emotionally inaccessible.

THE PLACATER[10]

One child often feels responsible for and shows a talent for smoothing out all the rough spots in the family. Very sensitive to the feelings of others, this child listens to and comforts Mom or Dad, doing what she can to alleviate the pressures on her poor parents. This child is the one who arrives with the pipe and slippers before they are requested. The Placater seems to be a mind-reader. Some psychologists believe that the Placater's insecure mother often unconsciously transmits her all-consuming need for nurturance during infancy. Before language can make the child consciously aware of what exactly is expected, the child begins to form the desired personality characteristics.[11] Because the infant is so dependent on the mother (or other primary caretaker), the baby's survival instincts click in. The infant senses what will most endear him to his mother and abandons his own natural preferences, sometimes even ignoring his own needs for independence or any other development of his own unique personality.

The Placater is also available to soothe Brother or Sister, or even the neighbors if it becomes necessary. As they grow older they become counselors or mediators for family and friends, never saying no to anyone's needs but their own. As a parent the Placater may continue this pattern of avoiding his own problems by losing himself in others' conflicts. The Placater often intervenes overprotectively in his children's lives. This intrusive behavior robs the child of the opportunity to learn from her mistakes or gain the sense of power or accomplishment that comes from successfully working through a difficulty on her own.

THE FAMILY HERO (HEROINE)

As a child, the Family Hero is the high-achiever, the family showpiece. It is his responsibility to get good grades and be an exemplary citizen so that he casts a good light on the family. He wins awards for scholastic achievement, stars on the basketball team, is admired by his peers, and is pointed out as an example by everyone's parents. The Family Heroine often takes on the additional role of the "little mother," filling in the gaps for her neglectful mother.

Whether boy or girl, as an adult this heroic child goes on achieving—capturing prestigious jobs, early promotions, and the admiration of all. In fact, the hero thrives on this admiration for he has always experienced love as conditional and his self-worth is tied up in accomplishments. If he is not *Numero Uno*, then the hero believes he is not even on the list. The hero has come to believe that nothing about him is lovable except his accomplishments, and when he fails to meet his own excessively high standards he feels like a total failure. This is likely to happen when the hero or heroine comes up against the stress of a normal adult developmental crisis, such as mid-life, and simply hasn't the reserve energy to go on being a top achiever. The female version is probably Super Mom—the full-time career woman who makes her own bread, does volunteer work, and still has time to chauffer her children to piano and soccer. This workaholic pace can only be escaped through debilitating burn-out or the numbing effects of something like TV or alcohol. As a parent, the family hero has little time for intimacy. He may set for his children the same excessively high standards of achievement that he had set for himself. Since his self-esteem is based on achievement, he will naturally expect his children to reflect his great parenting skills.

◆ JUDY AS FAMILY HEROINE

Judy was the daughter of two mood-disordered parents who medicated themselves with alcohol. Judy's mother would cry a lot and seemed incapable of taking care of her children. By the time Judy was twelve she was the main caretaker for three younger brothers and a sister. Her mother had taken a job working evenings so that she left as soon as Judy arrived home from school. Judy would do the laundry, make the dinner, bathe and put the children to bed, and then wash the dishes. Her father was hypercritical of her dinners, finding something wrong every day. He muttered his complaints into the air because he never directly addressed the children. Most nights he went out drinking, but when he was at home everyone had to be silent as he lay on the living room couch resting. If one of the children giggled or coughed her father would leap off the couch and start beating them all.

Judy vowed her life would not be like that when she grew up. Despite her heavy load at home, Judy was bright enough to get good grades, and she saw college as the ultimate salvation. She earned a scholarship for tuition and her parents begrudgingly allowed her to continue living at home "for free," although they thought she ought to be working and contributing money to the family. Judy continued to care for her brothers and sister and took a part-time job so she could pay for her on-campus expenses. By this time her mother's drinking had escalated and the situation at home had grown so bad that Judy had begun drinking herself. She wanted to leave but felt guilty about deserting her younger brothers and sister. She began seeing the campus psychologist and he convinced her that her siblings would benefit from her example in getting out more than they would from her hopeless presence. She took an apartment with friends and her outlook improved a great deal although she still struggled with her own drinking. She scraped through college by "going on the wagon" periodically.

Although her grade point average was low, Judy scored high on the state Social Worker test. She got a job working with the public schools, creating a program that would reduce truancy and dropouts. Advice from her brothers made her a smashing success with the hard-core delinquents and she was encouraged to go to graduate school so she could move up into an administrative position.

With a straight A graduate degree behind her, Judy gave up drinking and took up working as a new escape. Within a few years she was "high" on her success, serving as the learning disabilities specialist on the prestigious child-study team. Although Judy had "arrived" professionally, she had become isolated socially. She frequently felt lonely, depressed, and defective because she had no marriage prospects.

Judy dedicated the next few years to finding a husband and joined every club and social group she could find, attacking the dating game as vigorously as she had graduate school. She dated a lot and started up many relationships, but either she couldn't make herself love the men or they dropped her when she came on too strong. These failed attempts were grinding her down and she frequently thought of suicide. At the bottom of one of her all-time lows she forced herself to go to a party. It was here that she finally met her "soul mate." Recently divorced, Carl was rather down-and-out at the time, but Judy saw him as having all the right qualifications and saw herself as lucky for finding him while he was in the "bargain basement" of life. He was good-looking and had a high-paying job with an established corporation. However, he had committed most of his salary to child support and alimony payments in his desperate rush to get out of his marriage and he was drinking heavily.

Two weeks after they met Judy moved in with Carl and started straightening out his life. He was impressed by her sobriety and willingly gave up drinking. With someone to take care of him, Carl pulled his life back together, and began climbing his own career ladder again.

Judy and Carl actually began to grow up together, subtly rotating roles as child and nurturer. Judy knew Carl's first marriage had failed partly because of his tremendous need for attention. Despite the fact that Carl's first wife had had three children in rapid succession, he expected her to "be there" for him when he got home. Even though no one else competed for her attention, Judy found it difficult to give Carl the response he seemed to need. She knew that if they had children too soon, their marriage would be doomed too. And there really was not enough money. His company had begun moving them around and Judy found herself taking lower and lower paying jobs at each new location.

Besides, Judy instinctively knew that she had to have her childhood first. Sometimes using Carl's visiting children as an excuse, sometimes not, Judy and Carl went to amusement parks, zoos, museums, hiking, boating, camping—all the things Judy had not done with her family of origin. After six years (and despite some very difficult times with her stepchildren) Judy felt ready to have a child and their finances had improved enough to make it possible. Judy felt like she had it all together now, and this child would have everything—all the attention, love, and advantages that she had been denied. This baby was bound to be the ultimate satisfaction of her life.

(Continued in Chapter 4)

Judy will soon learn that parenting introduces a whole new set of factors that must be coped with. Even adults who have grown up in healthy families are surprised at the amount of time and attention children need. Those who have grown up in dysfunctional families are further handicapped, not only by having no reliable basis of comparison, but also by the quotient of stress they still carry from childhood. Unfortunately, as much as we may disapprove of our parents' methods and attitudes, we are likely to backslide during parental stress.

All parents, whether from a good family or bad, will mimic the parenting in their family of origin unless they have worked hard to establish different patterns. We each carry an "inner parent" that may act with or without our conscious approval. The more we know about this "inner parent" the more we can hope to control it. One good way to start bringing these unconscious parenting messages up where you can see them is to make a list of your parents' strengths and weaknesses. With paper and pen sit down and list all the traits of your parents that you wish to change in yourself, and in a second column list all their positive traits (no one is *all* bad). If you find yourself blocked into thinking your parents had no redeeming qualities, you may be able to let go of some of this negative feeling by thinking about each of your parents' childhoods. What kind of family did they grow up in? Can you picture them as small, helpless children and imagine what they felt? What do you think they vowed to change? Was your childhood any better than theirs as a result?

CONFRONTING, FORGIVING, AND HEALING YOURSELF

Can you acknowledge the effect your past has had on your present functioning? Are you able to admit that the lack of good role models leaves you confused about what to do as a parent? Realizing you do not have all the answers is a prerequisite for healthy parenting, whether you came from a dysfunctional family or a healthy one. Only someone from a very dysfunctional family would believe he or she is already a perfect parent and has no need to read books or take courses on parenting.

Admitting you have been affected by growing up in a dysfunctional family is vital to being able to change. Unraveling the negative parental practices that have affected you is a murky and often difficult process. One of the most crippling traits of a dysfunctional family is *denial*. You may have felt devastated when your mother didn't show up at your recital. This is normal. But you may have been told that you were being overly sensitive when you voiced your disappointment. You may still have difficulty being with small children because you remember feeling overwhelmed by your screaming two-year-old brother whom you were expected to care for when you were only ten years old yourself. But you remember your mother saying casually, "Just ignore him." You may remember trying to talk to your sister about how miserable and nervous you felt at home only to have her scoff at you and insist that you had the happiest family on the block. You may have come away from your family believing that there was something wrong with you, so that you now badger your own children about being overly sensitive.

Denial, rationalizations, and selective memory all befuddle the process of coming to terms with your childhood traumas and learning from them. In addition, the low self-esteem that is the inevitable result of living in a dysfunctional family can make it difficult to accept that you have problems with parenting. Your resentment of your parents and your determination to do it differently may make it hard to admit that you resort to the same tactics under stress. Before you can change, you have to be totally honest about where you are now. This done, skip the guilt. It drains energy you need for constructive change. If you are reading this book you already have the most important characteristic of a good parent—the willingness to explore and examine your own techniques as well as new techniques.

If you have children you may wonder how much they have already been affected by your unconscious messages or your low self-esteem. Has your hesitation, ambivalence, unnecessary harshness, or conflict with your spouse created damaging stress for your children? Children under stress often appear moody, irritable, easily angered, complaining, or shy. When stress increases, children may regress or become withdrawn, physically ill, secretive, belligerent, or hostile. You may remember using these coping mechanisms yourself, and if you recognize them in your own children, despite your efforts to be a kinder or gentler parent than you had, you may find yourself angry at your children or embarrassed by them. You might ask: "How can they feel bad when they have it so much better than I did?"

Indeed, it can be very difficult to understand our parental shortcomings when we compare well to our very dysfunctional parents. We may do many things a whole lot better, but fail to improve in the most important areas. Ann Smith, in her book *Grandchildren of Alcoholics*,[12] describes the stressful conditions that often occur in second-generation dysfunctional families—families headed by adults who put a great deal of energy into not repeating their own parents' mistakes. Despite their good intentions, the parents, who are adult children of alcoholics, are already stressed-out by the time they have children. And they haven't had much training for the job.

The ACOA-as-parent often has low self-esteem, a vision of herself as a victim of circumstance who cannot change, and an inability to ask for help. Left to her own devices, she can frequently change the outward appearance of her new family, so it appears to be more healthy than her family of origin. For example, if her own mother never attended to the kids' physical needs, the ACOA-as-parent can see this as a problem. She can solve it by scrubbing and feeding and dressing her children. She might take the kids on frequent family outings because this is what healthy families do (whether anyone enjoys these outings or not). Her home may be decorated like *House Beautiful* and she may be the Brownie leader, soccer coach, and classroom mother. But if she is only mimicking externals she may fail to do these things in a healthy spirit. Her children might rather have a messy house, skip Brownies, and sit around talking over their day with a relaxed Mom and Dad.

For this reason grandchildren of alcoholics (GCOA) often grow up confused. It looks as though they have come from a "good" family where the parents were active and concerned about them, but for some mysterious reason they don't *feel* loved. The GCOA will generally conclude there must be something lacking in him—a despicable inability to appreciate or be grateful for the sacrifices his parents have made. Because the ACOA parent erroneously believes that healthy families don't fight, get confused, or have problems, she puts the lid on all conflict. Then her child, the GCOA, senses his parent's need to have the perfect family. He doesn't want to "break his Mom's bubble" by admitting he has any personal problems. He accepts that anyone who has grown up in such a "good" family should be happy all the time and feels that he is to blame if he is unhappy. If you are having trouble identifying why you grew up feeling so insecure when you came from such a "good family," try taking a close look at your grandparents. Were they hypercritical, extremely negative, or "party animals"? Your parents may have failed to meet your needs because they were too preoccupied with their agenda of doing the opposite of their own dysfunctional parents without examining if the opposite was the *healthy* thing to do.

There is an old saying: If you take the alcohol away from a foul-mouthed, abusive, resentful alcoholic, what you get is a foul-mouthed, abusive, resentful, non-alcoholic. The liquor may have caused the original problems but merely taking the liquor away does not cure them. Behavior patterns must be changed. And so it is for the family of an alcoholic or for any other dysfunctional family. The nonproductive patterns of relating must be corrected. The families must learn to talk about feelings, to admit to failures or shortcomings, to apologize, make amends, forgive and forget. Your parents may not have been able to move beyond surface corrections to building positive intimacy.

If you have come from a dysfunctional family you have a lot of unlearning to do before you tackle the stacks of helpful parenting books available. At this point, you may feel as if you are at − 10. But what's important is that you are willing to move away from there.

SPECIAL STRENGTHS OF ADULT CHILDREN
OF DYSFUNCTIONAL FAMILIES

At this point you may feel like you will never be able to be a good parent because you've been programmed by poor role models, weakened by childhood trauma, and patterned to be co-dependent. But all of these experiences can be put to constructive use. For example, the almost clairvoyant sensitivity that the Placater has developed can help the ACODF-as-parent be exceptionally perceptive about his child's feelings. He may see that although his child is *acting angry,* he is *feeling hurt.* This helps the ACODF parent respond more effectively.

Neither will the ACODF suffer from blind overconfidence. As stated earlier, since parenting is stressful and ACODF are very vulnerable to stress, they are likely to realize early on that they must give more thought to their parenting methods. While many parents are caught off guard when their children hit the teen years, ACODF will probably encounter difficulty when children are younger. To survive they will have to learn *Conscious Parenting* or parenting governed by daily self-examination. (We'll be taking a closer look at Conscious Parenting in Chapter 11.) By questioning their parenting practices early, ACODF can catch their mistakes before their kids are alienated teenagers with problems much harder to tackle.

Indeed, all of today's parents should examine their parenting methods—even if they have grown up in healthy families. For the parenting practices that worked fine for their own parents in the 1950s and '60s are not necessarily appropriate in today's more democratized society. Parenting research shows that neither the traditional authoritarian model of the '50s nor the permissiveness of the '60s prepare children to deal with the many complex decisions they will have to make in today's fast-changing world. (Nor does it prepare them to say "no" to adults who would take advantage of them, as in the case of sexual abuse.) Obedience is no longer the most desirable trait in children, and yet we have learned that children do need some structure. The delicate balance between responsibility and freedom that our children must achieve cannot be taught without much thought and self-examination on every parent's part.

It is easy to see why today's best parents must be open to new ideas. Since many children of dysfunctional families have no old models they wish to cling to, they will be more receptive to new models. Hence, a difficult childhood plus self-awareness may be the best preparation anyone can have for parenting.

◆ ══════════ SUMMARY ══════════ ◆

As children we had to learn to cope with the people in our immediate environment and we had no choice about who those people would be. Now that we are grown we can decide who we want to become close to, what kind of relationship we want to have with each person in our lives, and insist on our right to be respected. Regardless of what our parents did in the past, we are in charge of our lives now.

◆ ══════════ POINTS ══════════ ◆

1. Children in dysfunctional families may have adapted to their environment in unhealthy ways to ensure their temporary survival.

2. As parents, we need to allow ourselves to feel our old childhood vulnerabilities so that we can be appropriately sensitive to our children's problems.

3. ACODF often have unhealthy dependency patterns. They either depend on their spouses and children excessively or take over all responsibility making it difficult for others to help them.

4. In healthy marriages, husband and wife share responsibilities smoothly. If something goes wrong, they look for a way to right it instead of wasting time blaming each other.

5. Dysfunctional marriages are often formed by two half-realized people. Rather than working to overcome our weaknesses, we may each seek someone to complete us—to do for us what we lack the courage to do for ourselves.

6. Recognizing that we don't "have it all together" as parents is the first step to becoming healthy parents.

7. A difficult childhood, and resulting doubts about parenting abilities, often makes us more open to new ideas and methods.

NOTES

1. Robert J. Ackerman, *Let Go and Grow*. Pompano Beach, FL: Health Communications, Inc., 1987.

2. Jael Greenleaf, "Co-Alcoholic, Para-Alcoholic:" Presented at the National Council on Alcoholism 1981 Annual Alcoholism Forum, New Orleans, LA, April 12, 1981.

3. Smith, in *Grandchildren of Alcoholics* (Pompano Beach, FL: Health Communications, Inc., 1988), describes the victim life-style.

4. Robin Norwood, *Women Who Love Too Much*. New York: Pocket Books, 1985.

5. Melody Beattie, *Co-Dependent No More*. New York: Harper/Hazelden, 1987.

6. John C. Friel and Linda Friel (*Adult Children: The Secrets of Dysfunctional Families*. Pompano Beach, FL: Health Communications, 1988) offer further clarification of co-dependency as a dysfunctional pattern of living. They point toward the significant difference between the *outside* and *inside* of the co-dependent person. Friel and Friel see our society as one that fosters co-dependence through the encouragement of conformity in the schools, the American dependence on technological cures and fixes, and authoritarian leadership models. Their book provides an excellent self-quiz for co-dependent tendencies.

7. John Bradshaw, *Bradshaw On: The Family*. Pompano Beach, FL: Health Communications, Inc., 1988.

8. Herbert L. Gravitz and Julie D. Bowden report in their book *Recovery: A Guide for Adult Children of Alcoholics* (New York: Simon & Schuster, Inc., 1985) that during speaking engagements many audience members from non-alcoholic families resonate with the problems faced by adult children of alcoholics. Indeed, the characteristics of adult children of alcoholics seem to apply to anyone from a dysfunctional home.

9. The roles presented in the next few pages are based on Sharon Wegscheider-Cruse's classic roles published in her book *Another Chance—Hope and Health for the Alcoholic Family* (Palo Alto, CA: Science and Behavior Books, 1981) and expanded upon by other experts in the field of alcoholism such as Claudia Black and Robert Ackerman.

10. Claudia Black, in her book *It Will Never Happen to Me* (New York: Ballantine Books, 1981), was the first to identify the role of Placater in the alcoholic family.

11. Both Jael Greenleaf ("Co-Alcoholic, Para-Alcoholic:" speech delivered at the National Council on Alcoholism, 1981) and Alice Miller (*The Drama of the Gifted Child*, New York: Basic Books, Inc., 1981) comment on the "clairvoyant" qualities of children from dysfunctional family systems.

12. Ann W. Smith, *Grandchildren of Alcoholics*. Pompano Beach, FL: Health Communications, 1988.

4

STRESS AND THE FAMILY

*Some learn to control family stress; others allow
stress to control their family lives.*
—Delores Curran, *Stress and the Healthy Family*[1]

Perhaps one of the greatest dividers between the healthy family and the dysfunctional family is the way they each deal with stress. Unfortunately, the dysfunctional family, which often encounters more stress than the average family, has developed many behaviors that produce stress but has the fewest tools for overcoming stress. Thus, the dysfunctional family is often chronically stressed. In fact, some therapists have observed that the trauma of living in an abusive family, alcoholic family, or a family which has been torn apart by a bitter divorce is comparable to the stress felt by soldiers during a war. (Others compare the powerlessness and cruel treatment of some children to the helplessness and fear experienced by concentration camp victims.) Just as combat veterans often feel the effects of their terrible experience long after they come home from the war, children who have grown up in such families begin their adult lives already depleted. They have little emotional energy in reserve to deal with stress and little knowledge of behaviors or techniques they can use to reduce stress.

NORMAL LIFE CYCLE TRANSITIONS

Stress is caused by each of our normal life cycle transitions and these times are therefore periods of extra vulnerability. Three aspects contribute to a family's tension level during each transition: each person's individual developmental stage, each person's sexual

61

identity development stage, and the family developmental stage. Obviously, if one's individual developmental crisis coincides with a family developmental crisis (such as a critical time in one's career coming at the same time as the birth of the first child) the stress for both the individual and the family will be greater. Unfortunately, they will also have less energy to cope with each of these normal life-crises. The chart below shows the stages of life and what tasks we need to accomplish at each stage to move on from that developmental level to the next one.

The stress is always greatest at the time of transition or change. For example, as an adolescent moves from high school to college

---◆---

Individual and Family Life Cycle Transitions[2]

(F = Female), (M = Male)

STAGE	TASKS
Infancy	Establishing trust
Early Childhood	Establishing autonomy
Play Age	Taking initiative
School Age	Becoming industrious
Adolescence	Establishing Identity
Young Adulthood (18–25)	Individual: college/first job Family: marriage, intimacy
Stage 2 Adulthood (25–30)	Indiv.: M-promotion, F-quit job Fam: first child
Stage 3 Adulthood (30–35)	Indiv: M-career, F-parenting Fam: second child, school age
Stage 4 Adulthood (35–50)	Indiv: M-career, F-menopause, return to work Fam: adolescent children
Stage 5 Adulthood (50–65)	Indiv: M-career decline, retire F-second career Fam: launching children, grandparenting

there are many challenges to face. Within the first important year of college he may be expected to make all new friends, find his way around a new place, and decide what he would like to do with the rest of his life. Then things calm down for a few years until he faces college graduation and his first career position. If he marries straight out of college he will have to adjust to a new level of intimacy with a significant other at the same time he is trying to look like a go-getter in his new job. By looking at the chart we can see how and when these various stress periods are likely to overlap. Each individual can have personal transitions that overlap with each other as well as personal stress periods that fall just when a spouse or child is facing one of his or her own important transitions.

PARENTING AS STRESSOR

Adjusting to the birth of the first child is perhaps the most difficult task a couple has to accomplish. It marks the onset of parenthood for each adult and the end of the couple's easy opportunity for intimacy. Many psychologists consider this stressful event to be of crisis intensity. The first child is often born just as the man is establishing his career. Ironically, the baby frequently causes the woman to abandon her career plans and lose the social support of her career-oriented co-workers, just as she is losing easy access to her husband as a companion. The transition for the child's primary caretaker (usually Mom) is very intense and can be aggravated by the husband's lack of first-hand experience with stay-at-home parenting. Meanwhile sleepless nights affect the husband's job functioning and increase his stress too. The couple is suddenly faced with the problem of trying to find time for uninterrupted sex or even conversation.

The scenario for the two-career family is even harsher. In her landmark study of contemporary marriage entitled *The Second Shift*, sociologist Arlie Hochschild points out that although men often verbally commit to part of the housework, few actually do it.[3] The more liberal men who agree to wash dishes when the wife cooks often relegate all the child care to the woman as if it is just one chore on the list. "You take care of the kid, and I'll take out the trash." Since most women cannot anticipate how much time caring for a child really takes, we can understand how a man could fail to appreciate the magnitude of the extra burden that has fallen on his wife with the birth of a child. At the same time, the woman who has chosen to plunge on with her career full-speed despite the birth of a child is often surprised to find how difficult it is to tear herself away from her infant each morning. Many two-career couples who now look back on their children's early years have regrets about the time they missed with their children.

In addition to the career-vs-family-vs-intimacy stresses that each new parent faces, the onset of parenthood naturally restimulates each parent's memories of childhood and the way he or she was parented. If the parent's childhood was difficult and his or her parents were neglectful or cruel, the memories will be painful and the new parent's knowledge and emotional reserves for parenting may be inadequate.

◆ GRACE'S MEMORIES

When Grace was pregnant with her first child, her daughter Candace, she became extremely depressed during the sixth month. She had been an aggressive, outgoing person before the pregnancy and suddenly she was withdrawn and suicidal. "I was scared of everything, and anything my husband, John, said to me would make me cry."

Following the birth Grace fell into a deep postpartum depression that left her nervous and irritable. "The baby wouldn't quit crying and I kept screaming at her, 'Shut up! Shut up!' I kept telling John, 'I need sleep. I need somebody to help me.' "

But Grace's husband, locked into some kind of macho-male role, would stay in bed and refuse to help her. Grace began to get more depressed as the hours without sleep piled up. "Then one day I was totally exhausted. I remember jerking the phone cord out of the wall because my husband threatened to call the authorities and have my baby taken away from me. I knew in my mind that I wasn't going to hurt nobody. I just wanted somebody to help me. I remember I took the baby's swing and I hit it and hit it and made it like a pretzel and I knocked stuff off shelves and then John tackled me and held me down."

Grace became so anxious that she called her brother long distance in the middle of the night. Candace was three months old by then, and Grace's brother, who had been warm and reassuring on the phone, made her promise to call her mother for help the next morning.

"When my Mom came over I was just sitting there moaning and crying. All I could think about was my dad molesting me. I could see my dad in my mind. He was trying to make me have oral sex with him. He had a dish of candy in his hand that he planned to give me afterwards. I didn't want the candy but I would look at it so I wouldn't have to look at him. I could remember how the candy looked in the dish, what the dish looked like. I could see me as a little girl just standing there and looking up and crying and begging him, 'Please don't make me do this.' And what would bother me so bad was to think that this was my dad."

Grace felt as if she had been thrust back in time, to when she was a helpless child. Sensing the helplessness of her baby, being wrung out with the terrible stress of exhaustion, had driven Grace into this emotional state. "I couldn't even talk. I didn't know what was going on. My mind was running too fast and I couldn't control it."

Grace's mother persuaded her to sign herself into the hospital. During the two to three weeks Grace was in the hospital her husband came to see her every night, but she dreaded the visits. Although her husband was kind, she couldn't bear to be with him. This frightened her and she asked her staff psychiatrist why she didn't feel love for her husband anymore. The doctor replied, "You're going to have to answer that question yourself." Grace thought, "God help me. Somebody help me. I can't answer it myself." But no one helped her answer this terrifying question.

She eventually calmed down enough to be able to return home but soon her anxiety focused on her relationship with her husband again and they split up. "I was very insecure and afraid I wouldn't be able to provide for the baby. I think that from not having the proper love myself, I didn't really know how to love Candy. I didn't want the responsibility for her because I felt like I couldn't even take care of myself mentally, and then I didn't know how to love her right."

(Continued in Chapter 5)

Children do remind us of our childhoods. For some this is one of the greatest joys of parenting—to be able to relive those carefree moments. For others, it is a return to terror. It is easy to see why parenting would be especially stressful for one who has grown up in a dysfunctional family. But restimulated memories are not the only stressful aspect of parenting. The challenge of parenting goes on and on. The poorly prepared adult has to learn how to parent from scratch, not once but again and again, each time the child reaches a new developmental level and his or her behavior and needs change accordingly.

Any family's reaction to a stressful event or developmental crisis will be based on a complex combination of three factors as illustrated in the chart below:

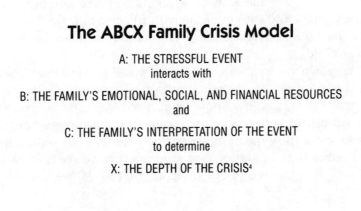

The ABCX Family Crisis Model

A: THE STRESSFUL EVENT
interacts with

B: THE FAMILY'S EMOTIONAL, SOCIAL, AND FINANCIAL RESOURCES
and

C: THE FAMILY'S INTERPRETATION OF THE EVENT
to determine

X: THE DEPTH OF THE CRISIS[4]

For example, an event that would be only slightly stressful for a family headed by stable parents with high self-esteem, strong social support systems, and adequate financial resources, could be crippling to an isolated family where the breadwinner has just lost his job and consequently his main source of self-esteem. Similarly, the family's attitude toward the event—whether they see it as one of life's challenges and an opportunity for growth, or as the final blow from a cruel, arbitrary world—will strongly influence their ability to cope with the stress.

JEALOUSY OF THE CHILD

With the birth of a baby jealousy crops up everywhere and this jealousy increases tension and stress in the family. Every new father has probably seen his newborn baby as a rival for his wife's attention. It is a natural reaction and is harmless if not taken too far. The emotionally mature parent soon comes to appreciate how much the infant needs his mother's care and can wait (patiently or impatiently) for Mom to have time for Dad again. New mothers can feel "left out in the cold" too. They are usually unprepared for how much work an infant is, and they inevitably feel jealous of the husband's greater freedom. Even healthy parents have these feelings. It's just a simple fact that everyone must do a lot more work once there is a child in the family system. Until the couple has a chance to absorb this harsh new reality, each partner often feels they are being taken advantage of, that the other is not doing their fair share. Dysfunctional partners, who each suffer from low self-esteem, are bound to get caught in a blaming pattern at this point. They blame the partner for not doing enough, and they blame the baby for needing too much. As the child grows, the poorly prepared parent inevitably compares his child's functioning with his own at a similar age and lacks the objectivity to judge what should be expected from the average child.

"Why, when I was your age . . ." is a well-used sit-com line. The parent goes on to describe scenes of yesteryear where he had to walk four miles to school in a snowstorm. For generations parents have been exhorting children to appreciate the advantages they have. This takes on new meaning when the parent is the adult child of very dysfunctional parents. Sometimes when we see how easy our kids have it compared to our difficult childhoods, we feel resentful that our children are not more grateful. We are really jealous of their good luck in having us for parents. We feel as if we would have been absolute angels if a parent had attended us the way we care for our children. But, in truth, we probably would have been less well-behaved than we actually were because, had our parents really been attentive and nurturing, we would have felt *safe enough to misbehave.*

We have often had such distorted childhoods that we find it very difficult to judge how much children really need materially or emotionally. Poor judgment about children's needs at each age and stage can be at the root of child-neglect. A working parent may leave her seven-year-old at home to care for herself during summer break because the child seems so responsible. Even if the child may be trusted not to hurt herself on the stove, or do other dangerous things, this does not address the child's emotional need to feel cared for. She may be intensely lonely and frightened by every noise in the house. If parents do not understand children's normal fears and feelings, they may overstress their children emotionally.

In a similar way, we may neglect our children materially when we use ourselves as a scale for how much children should get. If a mother who grew up in a dysfunctional family only had two dresses to get her through the school week, she may find herself furious when her daughter cannot seem to keep a dress clean for more than one day. But normal children, allowed a healthy amount of movement and freedom to explore, are bound to dirty their clothes in the day's activities. It is not appropriate to expect them to stay spotless all day; nor is it fair to become angry when they can't.

Privileges are another touchy area. If we "survived all right" without dancing lessons or designer jeans, we may feel our children are being greedy when they want what other kids have. I am not suggesting that children should be given everything they want or that it is even good to have what other children have, but we must calmly and objectively consider their wishes. If designer jeans are that important to your child, set a limit on her clothes budget and let her decide if she would rather have one pair of designer jeans or three pairs of Brand X. Letting your child set her own priorities like this may prove to be a real eye-opener into the depth and intensity of her preferences.

The best way to cure your feelings of jealousy toward your child is to begin by giving yourself some of the love and care you never received. By faithfully parenting yourself you will also discover how wonderfully secure a child can feel when she is well cared for. You will come to understand that this is a true human need.

PARENTING SUPERSTRESSORS

Some stressors go beyond the normal transitional stresses that everyone experiences.[5] The stress of a "different" child (socially, emotionally, or physically handicapped) is often chronic because the duration of the problem is usually longer than those problems caused by normative transitions. For example, a hyperactive child is likely to need special attention and thoughtful training throughout his childhood. Family schedules and habits may have to be changed, special diets, medication, or professional help may have to be sought, and school and friends often react adversely to the behavior of the child, increasing the strain. Common dysfunctional methods of coping include overprotection by a parent (sometimes resulting in a coalition between the parent and child which excludes the other parent), withdrawal from friends due to embarrassment, anger and resentment that is unleashed in hostility toward the child or the other parent, and using the child or situation as a scapegoat and source of blame for all family problems.

If the parents do not take the necessary time to help the hyperactive child cope with his transitions and challenges, the whole family is likely to be disrupted by his behavior and the other children will begin to show symptoms of stress that, in turn, will have to be dealt with. Likewise, the entire family system will be adversely affected if Father or Mother choose to escape these pressures by working longer hours or numbing themselves with drugs or alcohol, instead of devoting their energy to working on the solution. Flexibility, courage, and social support are essential when coping with these "super-stressors" or with a pile-up of normative stressors. Unfortunately dysfunctional families (who have a statistically higher incidence of hyperactivity, mood disorders, or inability to handle alcohol that is believed by many to be hereditary) are characterized by rigidity, fear and isolation.

◆ JUDY AND CARL UNDER STRESS

   Casey, Judy's first child, was born into an already highly charged, stressful atmosphere. When Judy was seven months pregnant, Carl's former wife had sued them for a substantial increase in child support. Judy had already quit her job so that she could stay home with her newborn baby. Anxious about the mounting lawyer costs, Judy was unable to sleep. She developed toxemia and had to have an emergency Caesarean.

Determined to be a perfect mother, Judy stood stubbornly by her decision to breast-feed even though the baby's constant need to nurse interrupted her rest and delayed her recovery from the operation. To save the family money she signed on to a breast-feeding study which provided free infant care to babies whose mothers were willing to breast-feed exclusively for the first six months. Since Judy was also trying to lose weight, her dieting plus the baby's growing demands for milk left her physically depleted.

Despite Judy's many stresses, Casey appeared to be happy and healthy. He slept through the night early and was cooperative when she took him along to La Leche meetings and visits with friends.

All this changed when Judy was offered a good salary to be a Learning Disabilities Specialist for the public schools; two weeks into the job everything began to fall apart. Casey's caretaker quit unexpectedly and Judy hurriedly placed Casey with a caretaker she found through an ad in the paper.

Recently divorced, the new caretaker had a two-year-old girl who was having adjustment problems. Casey, unable to get away from this disturbed, aggressive child, frequently came home with bitemarks and bruises. Judy was upset by the situation but felt helpless because she would lose her job without care for Casey. She put him on a waiting list at a day-care center but when the center finally took him she found they were so understaffed that Casey was confined to a playpen most of the day. He would scream and cling each morning when she dropped him off, and when she picked him up in the afternoon he would punch her face and have a violent tantrum all the way home in the car. She was guilt-ridden and searched newspapers and child-care agencies for an alternative, but it was several months before she could find a replacement. Meanwhile Casey had become chronically aggressive. He attacked children at the new babysitter's, and when they visited friends he would bite and hit his playmates. Judy tried to tell herself this was the "terrible twos" setting in, but regardless, she found herself refusing more and more invitations to get together with other mothers because Casey's behavior was so embarrassing and she had no idea how to control it.

About this time Carl was offered a promotion that would require relocation. He would receive a raise and Judy had been able to save part of her salary against hard times. She thought that perhaps Casey would recover his old cheerfulness if she could spend more time with him.

Shortly after they moved, Carl was sent out of state for a month-long training program and Judy began her long-awaited life as a stay-at-home mother. Judy had not been with Casey much for the last year and was used to the stimulating companionship of adults in a prestigious job. She was bored by routine household and child-care tasks and became irritable and depressed. At the same time, Casey's disposition had not improved. He was cranky, demanding, uncooperative, and exhausting. He would run through the house pulling things out of cupboards and off shelves and would punch and bite his mother when she tried to get him to stop. He would exhaust himself so much that he took two long naps each day, but Judy would just spend this time crying or staring at the wall, feeling somewhat healed by the silence and the relief from Casey's frantic activity. She tried to read, to keep up with her professional journals, but she was too exhausted to concentrate and lapsed into watching mindless TV.

Judy tried to get out to church and mothers' groups but Casey continued to be aggressive and she found that the other mothers shunned her. One said Casey needed a good beating; another said that perhaps he wouldn't hit others if Judy didn't hit him. Judy didn't know what to say to either of them. She had never hit Casey and was strongly opposed to spanking, but she was beginning to wonder if that was what he needed.

During the third week of Carl's long absence Casey became so wound up and anxious that he stopped sleeping. And every time Judy fell asleep, Casey would shake her awake as if he was afraid that she would disappear like his dad. After forty-eight hours she felt herself becoming dangerously irritable. She kept imagining herself smacking Casey down, as she had been smacked down so many times as a child, but everything in her struggled against it. Suddenly, she felt herself reach the breaking point and she ran for her bedroom, locking Casey out so that she couldn't harm him. He screamed and pounded on the door for more than half an hour and then finally fell asleep from exhaustion. The two slept for more than twelve hours.

Judy dragged Casey along to look at day-care centers the next day and placed him in one by the end of the week. Still upset by his father's abrupt and total absence, Casey apparently believed his mother was abandoning him too, and he screamed in terror each day when Judy left him at the day-care center. It took so much energy just to get Casey ready and then tear himself away from him at day-care each day, that Judy usually spent the whole four hours in an exhausted heap on the couch, resting up to be able to survive the rest of the day with Casey. The next week when Carl returned energized and stimulated from his training, he found the house a shambles and Judy despondent. Casey refused to go near him and would not look at him. This was not the reception he'd expected. He almost wished he hadn't come home.

Casey continued to resist being left at the day-care center, but he began to calm down a little at home when he realized Carl was back to stay. Judy decided that she needed to go back to work, telling herself that Casey would adjust to the day-care center as soon as things settled down from the move. Besides, it was just too crazy-making to stay home with Casey, and the month had made her aware of how lonely and isolated she was. Within a few months she found a part-time job doing educational testing for a school system in the next county. Although it was a long commute, she only had to go in to test or report results two days out of every other week and could write up her evaluations at home.

(Continued in Chapter 6)

Regardless of Judy's background she is now in a stressful situation that is common to many American parents. Relocation is unavoidable in many careers and moving is considered to be a major stressor. To make matters more difficult, Judy and Carl had not yet learned to handle the stresses of new parenthood. The move has pushed them both beyond their limit. Gary and Rachael (Chapter 3) were also under considerable stress when the birth of their first child coincided with an unexpected increase in debt-load and a move to a new home. Yet that stress ultimately strenghtened their relationship. Why do some families cope with stress better than others? Here is a chart showing the basic differences between stress-effective families and those who are overrun by stresses:[6]

---◆---

Family Reactions to Stress

STRESS-EFFECTIVE FAMILY	STRESSED-OUT FAMILY
1. Sees stress as temporary, perhaps growth-producing.	1. Feels guilty that the stress exists.
2. Works together on solutions to minimize stress.	2. Seeks scapegoat to blame rather than seeking solutions.
3. Prioritizes time and shares responsibilities.	3. Gives up rather than trying to master the stress.
4. Accepts stress as a normal part of family life.	4. Focuses on family problems rather than strengths.
5. Feels proud and strong for overcoming stresses.	5. Feels weaker from stress.
	6. Dislikes family life as a result of stress.

On the other hand, if one or both of the parents have grown up in a dysfunctional family and have "worked through" their experiences until they have mastered their feelings and made sense of their childhoods, they may be well prepared to cope with the special needs of family members in a crisis. By contrast, those who grew up in functional families would have to change their expectations and learn new coping skills.

TIME PRESSURES

Families without time are common in our culture. The lack of time, itself stressful, creates impatience, frustration, and ill-thought-out responses. These behaviors increase tension, perpetuating a vicious cycle. Such destructive habits in the stressed-out family produce a continual sense of urgency, no relaxation time, tension which increases quarreling (and no opportunity to resolve conflicts), a need to get away by oneself, and a constant frustration about things left undone. These overscheduled families often fail to schedule in time for error—the common mishaps of daily life—such as an unexpectedly unavailable caretaker, a car repair, or even a long line at the supermarket fast-check lane. If a child becomes ill, the parent with an important meeting at work is likely to be furious and resentful—just when that child needs a calm and nurturing parent.

The families caught in this stress-trap are often responding to cultural directives that tell them Mom *should* work outside the home (*and* take a cooking class at night), boys *should* play soccer, girls *should* have dancing lessons, Dad *should* head up the scout troop, and the family *should* be active in a church. This is what we have been told will create the healthy family, and ironically, the dysfunctional family is the one most vulnerable to trying to live up to all these expectations. They don't realize that no one could juggle all these commitments. All families may experience this level of stress-reaction at some time or another, but stress-effective families learn to recognize these symptoms earlier and earlier with each successive "stress-test" and work toward a solution before things get out of hand. The dysfunctional family, by contrast, becomes paralyzed, allowing the effect of each successive stressor to pile up until everyone is overwhelmed and the system falls apart.

The low-stress family works as a team. For example, if Mother decides to take a job outside the home, Father takes over a greater portion of the household chores. Children also contribute to the family's maintenance by doing their share of cooking and cleaning. Families of today with destructively high stress levels are generally those who have not been able to make a smooth transition to this new family life-style. Often Mom is still expected to meet everyone's emotional and physical needs while pursuing a career. In the healthy home, family members realize that if Mom is overworked and unhappy the whole family's quality of life will suffer. By contrast, the dysfunctional family remains entrenched in the old roles, putting all their energy into trying to make Mom do the impossible, and resenting her if she doesn't. The stressed-out family does not understand that it would actually take less energy to just share the housework. Until dysfunctional families realize this, they will continue to be exhausted by their unresolved conflicts while stress-effective families use their energy to move ahead and find solutions that consider everyone's needs.

The truly healthy family isn't controlled by its involvements, but rather controls and limits its activities, signing up for only those which fit *after family time is scheduled*. If they miscalculate and become overcommitted, they are not afraid to cancel activities or drop memberships. The family as a whole has the strength to say "no," despite peer pressure.

FAMILY SUPPORT

Family systems researchers have studied the way families act under extreme stress and have sorted out the family behaviors that are most helpful when one member is facing a crisis:[7]

Supportive Behaviors

1. Emotional support in the form of love and affection, accompanied by a feeling that the family is on their side.

2. Encouragement.

3. Advice or useful information about resources that can provide help.

4. Companionship to take their mind off their problems.

5. Tangible help such as lending money, providing transportation, or helping with chores.

Unfortunately, those who have grown up in dysfunctional families often have too little emotional energy in reserve to be able to help others in a crisis. In addition, the parent who has grown up in a dysfunctional home may come up blank when her teen needs advice. The parent's naturally controlling behavior may make her a poor listener, and she may become so anxious about the child's problem that the child feels worse after confiding in her. As the child finds no relief from his crisis, his problem may escalate until the whole family is stressed-out from the repercussions. Common symptoms of stress that characterize the stressed-out family are increased tension and arguments or fights, sleeplessness, headaches, and lowered resistance to illness.

Adults who have grown up in a dysfunctional family are generally very vulnerable to stress because they do not have emotional stores in reserve. For this reason, it becomes very important for them to learn to recognize the signs of stress early. For example, all parents need a break from their children sometimes, and the ACODF parent may need longer and more frequent breaks. She must learn to seek help and schedule relief instead of trying to tough it out and be a "superparent." But asking for help can be extremely difficult for someone who has grown up in a dysfunctional family. Because her own parents frequently failed to respond to even simple requests (such as for food or a ride), the ACODF has come to believe that any need she has is unreasonable. As a child, she was probably rewarded for being totally self-reliant because her "not having any needs" relieved her parents' guilt. Now, instead of asking for help when she is depleted, she may even offer help to others. She might hope to get support in return, or might simply be seeking a feeling of competence, thinking, "If I can help others, surely I can manage my own problems!"

When she abruptly comes to the end of her rope, the ACODF parent is likely to blame the child rather than taking responsibility for the fact that she has let herself get stressed out and may be overreacting as a result. We all know that on some days we don't even notice a child rocking in a chair or playing his radio. In fact, if we are very relaxed these behaviors might make us smile wistfully. Is it the child's fault then if this same behavior gives us a pounding headache on another occasion?

There is nothing wrong with asking children for special treatment when we are headache-prone by requesting they not play music this particular day (or asking them to turn it down.) Children will usually be glad to help a stressed-out parent in this way. But it is wrong to yell at the child accusingly, as if they have played the music for the sole purpose of giving us a headache. When we have let ourselves get too tired and overwhelmed we cannot think clearly and quickly enough about what is the right thing to do. Responsible parents take care of themselves so that their children do not have to suffer the consequences of their self-neglect. In some cases too little attention to a parent's own need for space and quiet can even push her over the edge to child abuse.

CHILD ABUSE

Children are most frequently abused—physically, emotionally, or sexually—by their own parent or guardian rather than outsiders.

The parent loses control of himself or herself because of a complex combination of factors. Experts commonly agree that there are four primary variables that contribute to child abuse:[8]

1. **The childhood experience of the abusing parent.** Over 90% of abusing parents were abused and neglected as children.[9] With no model for warmth and affection, they have difficulty being appropriately responsive to their own children. In addition, they have low self-esteem and easily become frustrated or lose their tempers.

2. **The temperament of the child.** A child who cries a lot, is hyperactive, or has special physical or emotional needs can try the patience of any parent. Many conditions such as hyperactivity, mood disorders, or alcoholism occur more frequently in dysfunctional families, so the child of an ACODF is more likely to be difficult. A parent who has a short fuse or has learned only spanking or hitting as a way to discipline, is likely to become stressed out by the child's excessive needs and "go over the line" to physical abuse. Small children, who naturally need a lot of time and attention, are even more likely to be abused.

3. **Isolation.** A parent without a network of family or friends to provide relief or support during stressful periods is more likely to lash out at the child.

4. **A crisis situation.** When the parent or family is in crisis, child abuse is more likely to occur. The loss of a job, money problems, health problems, drug use, or alcohol abuse can all precipitate a crisis. Depending on the stability of the parent, even a burnt dinner or broken TV can trigger an episode of abuse.

Those who were physically abused as children might vow not to hit their own children, but will tear away at the children's self-esteem through veiled insults, believing all the while that this is normal parent/child communication. One parent may know this is destructive but will permit the other parent to verbally abuse the children, because he fears losing the love of his mate by criticizing her. If the young couple's parents were physically abusive, the new parents may take great pride in abusing their children only verbally, failing to see the very destructive effect of this "lesser" abuse.

◆ MARYANNE—LIVING OUT HER LEGACY

For Maryanne, whom we met in Chapter 3, the only warmth in her life had come from Skip. Maryanne's father died when she was thirteen. Jim had gradually moved out of the house at some indistinct point and drifted off into the drug crowd. Now it was Maryanne alone with her mother. Her mother alternately clung to Maryanne out of loneliness and abandoned her to drunken bouts.

Maryanne had more freedom again and liked the sexual attention she could get from boys at her new high school. Because she was so overweight she felt she couldn't hope for a real relationship with a boy, but one nice-looking overweight boy kept coming back for more and she gradually settled into dating Gilly exclusively. His parents were alcoholic and he seemed to understand her pain. When she became pregnant she ran off to get married.

Marriage and a baby were going to solve all her problems, she thought. She would never be lonely again. Gilly made enough money to support them and Maryanne devoted herself to home arts. She cooked and ate, cleaned and ate, and cared for her baby and ate. She had grown so fat that she began to worry people would make fun of her if she went out and so stayed in more and more. She had no friends. Gilly began to criticize her constantly; then he began to beat her. One night, when an argument had turned into a fist-fight, little Keith rushed into the fray, wrapped himself around his father's leg, and begged, "Please don't hit my Mommy. It makes her cry." The terror in Keith's eyes made Maryanne realize that these scenes had to stop, and she needed outside help.

She began to see a counselor covered by Gilly's insurance. The counselor helped her see that she did whatever Gilly wanted because she was afraid to be on her own. In her mind she was still a helpless child and he was a daddy who had pledged to take care of her. Sometimes daddies beat you, but what can you do? Go live in the street?

Through counseling, Maryanne realized she was grown up enough to get a job and that she could not give Keith a better life than she had had unless she began to show him that people can solve their problems. Gilly was unable or unwilling to change and Maryanne left him.

By the time she was twenty-five she had lived through several lifetime's worth of painful experience and was able to learn from the pain. She was not a perfect mother by any means. She recalled Keith's early years and knew that she had hit him too severely. But her measuring stick had been naked beatings with a belt. A talk show on child abuse made her realize that she was hitting Keith in anger, not as a method of discipline. Now she sends him to his room or takes away TV privileges.

"It really wasn't doing any good to hit him anyway," she says. "It would make him more stubborn or something, and then I would realize that I was hitting him harder and harder—that there might be no end point, no amount that was enough. I suddenly saw that I was like my father, that things could go that far if I kept it up."

"The next thing I'm working on is my mouth," she adds. "I still say terrible things to him sometimes. It's just what comes out of my mouth naturally. My parents were always swearing at me and calling me stupid. I know he'll feel awful about himself if I don't learn to control my mouth."

Maryanne has awareness and Keith has time to be healed. Meanwhile, when Maryanne slips up and says hurtful things, she always remembers to apologize later and tell Keith that she is the one to blame. She believes he is a loving, capable boy and she tells him so often.

(Continued in Chapter 9)

The adult who has grown up in a dysfunctional family is at high risk for child abuse. It is likely that he himself was neglected if not abused during childhood. As a result he probably has low self-esteem and little experience with positive parenting methods. If he has come from a typical isolated dysfunctional family he may lack the social skills he needs to "get connected" to healthier influences. On top of this, chances are he is frequently "in crisis" because he has not learned to budget time or money. To cope with their own stresses, his parents probably escaped through alcohol, drugs, or TV. Since these methods avoid problems rather than solving them, the ACODF parent, who knows no other methods, is likely to let problems build up until the family is in crisis.

Parents who function best are those who establish support systems, learn to balance the demands of the parenting role with their other needs and identities, and seek knowledge through media or professional resources. Interaction with friends, neighbors, church or social groups, or extended family not only relieve pressure through social opportunities, but also bring the parent in casual contact with other parents who can offer advice or support.

With so many demands on our time, time with spouse, time with children, and time alone must be planned into the weekly schedule or it will be squeezed out. The stress-effective family prioritizes their activities, and Family Time is right at the top of the list.

◆ ═══════════════ **SUMMARY** ═══════════════ ◆

Stress ruins our health, turns our lives into chaos, and brings out our worst dispositions. When we learn to control the stress in our lives, we can achieve our greatest goals and still fulfill our deepest needs.

◆ ═══════════════ **POINTS** ═══════════════ ◆

1. ACODF often inherit stress-producing disorders but have not learned any useful methods for coping with stress.

2. The birth of one's first child is one of the most stressful events each person encounters in life. And because children's habits and needs change constantly as they grow, the stress of parenting is unrelenting.

3. If our own childhoods have been very difficult, we will have a hard time judging how much nurturing and attention the average child needs. As a result, we may neglect or resent our children.

4. Due to low self-esteem, the ACODF parent feels inadequate when he or she experiences parenting as stressful. Therefore, the parent's first reaction is to deny or hide the stress and attempt to "do it all."

5. Stressed-out parents need to accept their limitations, lower their demands, and learn to ask for help from others.

6. Healthy parents build support systems among friends or relatives so that they will have someone to turn to in times of crisis.

N O T E S

1. Dolores Curran, *Stress and the Healthy Family.* Minneapolis: Winston Press, Inc. 1985, p. 6.

2. Charles R. Figley and Hamilton I. McCubbins borrow from Erik Erikson, R. Havinghurst, and K. Riegel to form charts for individual and family developmental transitions, and I have combined these to form the chart. For more information see Charles R. Figley and Hamilton I. McCubbin, eds., *Stress and the Family, Volume I:* New York: Brunner/Mazel Publishers, 1983.

3. Arlie Hochschild, Ph.D. with Anne Machung, *The Second Shift:* New York: Penguin USA, 1989.

4. McCubbins and Figley analyze the impact of stress on the family by using the Hill ABCX family crisis model. For more information see Charles R. Figley, and Hamilton I. McCubbins, eds, *Stress and the Family, Volume I:* New York: Brunner/ Mazel, 1983, p. 6–15.

5. Adapted from McCubbins's and Figley's second volume on stress and the family. For more information see *Stress and the Family, Volume II:* New York: Brunner/Mazel, 1983.

6. Information from Dolores Curran, *Stress and the Healthy Family.* Minneapolis, Winston Press, Inc., 1985, p. 12.

7. McCubbins and Figley (Vol II.) cite studies that clarify the essential elements of family support in dealing with an extreme crisis in the family. For more information see *Stress and the Family, Volume II:* New York: Brunner/Mazel, 1983.

8. *The World Book Medical Encyclopedia:* Chicago: World Book, Inc., 1980.

9. However, this does not mean that 90% of abused children become abusing parents. As an article in the magazine *Parenting* points out, some abused children actually become excellent parents because they are aware of how much pain certain parental behaviors can inflict on a child. For more information see Anthony Brandt, "The Sins of the Children," *Parenting,* May 1988, pp. 84–90.

PARENTING HANDICAPS

Parenting Pitfalls of Adult Children from Dysfunctional Families

1. ACODF overidealize normal family life and have inflated expectations for themselves as parents and for their children.

2. ACODF lack confidence in their judgment as parents and consequently may avoid important social networking.

3. ACODF may become so overwhelmed by the needs of their young children or so fearful of their children's rejection that they withdraw into work or neglectful behavior.

4. ACODF may become so close to their children that they cannot allow the child to have a separate identity.

5. ACODF have little experience anticipating problems and are often too impulsive to make careful, considered judgments.

6. ACODF have difficulty determining how much time child-rearing takes and consequently become stressed out.

7. ACODF often fail to recognize a child's difficulties or other family problems, thus postponing any movement toward a solution.

8. ACODF are often so critical of others that they alienate all potential sources of support.

9. ACODF fear harsh judgments of their parenting ability and consequently become hypercritical of their children's behavior.

10. ACODF are often excessively rigid and fail to consider children's individual differences or better solutions to a problem.

11. ACODF engage in frequent power struggles with their children and may feel dangerously angry when they cannot control them.

12. ACODF either model irresponsible behavior and create irresponsible children or are so superresponsible that they become burned out and dysfunctional.

13. ACODF have difficulty following through on promises and agreements about such things as trips, outings, transportation, or allowances.

14. ACODF often seek approval from their children and consequently fail to be consistent with discipline or act responsively to the child's own need for approval.

15. ACODF have few skills for dealing with conflict effectively.

On a bad day, even the most healthy parents can identify with the "pitfalls" described in the table above. The behaviors are just more chronic in adult children who have grown up in dysfunctional families—and usually, the more dysfunctional the family, the more severe problems the children will have when they grow up. Some of the characteristics on the list are neutral behaviors that should simply be controlled. For example, being superresponsible is just a few steps away from being very responsible.

A strong sense of responsibility is usually a wonderful trait in a parent. It can be very reassuring to have a Mom who fixes you breakfast every morning, and always picks you up from school when it rains. On the other hand, if you are twelve years old and you're dying to learn how to use the stove, but Mom thinks it's too dangerous; or all your friends walk to school together, but your Mom insists on driving you every day; you may feel incompetent, untrusted, and humiliated.

In Part II we will be looking at each trait in detail and analyzing how much is too much—describing the good and bad applications of each trait, especially as it pertains to parenting. The characteristics are grouped in the order that they will be addressed in Part II.

Perhaps the most important strength that comes from surviving childhood in a dysfunctional family is the heightened awareness about poor parenting, and the resultant desire to be better parents. If we have been burned we will have a greater respect for fire than one who has not been burned. We are likely to read about fire safety and have fire extinguishers available. Our new knowledge will make us more safety-conscious around fire than those who have not been burned.

So it is in parenting.

• 5 •

FEELING DIFFERENT

*1. ACODF overidealize normal family life and
have inflated expectations for themselves as
parents and for their children.*

*2. ACODF lack confidence in their judgment as
parents and consequently may avoid important
social networking.*

Many parents who have grown up in dysfunctional homes have inflated expectations for themselves as parents as well as impossibly high standards for their children. They believe they should all be like the "Father Knows Best" family. They idealize "normal family life" and imagine that other people come from near-perfect families. It is hard for an ACODF to get a sense of scale, and errors can happen in both directions—they may expect too little from their children or too much. They may give too little to their children or they may give too much.

How do ACODF get a sense of scale? How can they tell when they are giving their children enough nurturance without being overprotective? Where will they find role models? Even "average" is not a meaningful goal for ACODF now trying to create a better family atmosphere, because the average American family in the last generation knew far too little about developing self-esteem, and the average American family in this generation (often with two working parents) has too little time even to spend with the children, let alone to consider what is best for them. Knowledge about how the average family functions can downscale our expectations a little and relieve some guilt we may have, but what ACODF really need to ask is: What is *healthy* behavior? What parenting practices will produce competent, happy children who will become productive adults? One of the key aspects of the healthy family is that the parents' expectations match the children's capabilities. We can get a sense of what to expect from our children from child development books, parenting classes, and talking to our children's playmates' parents.

Because ACODF often believe that most other parents are having an easy time of it while ACODF struggle blindly with their parenting problems, they are reluctant to get out and discuss problems with these other "perfect" families. ACODF think they are "different" and are ashamed that they have problems with their children. The truth of the matter is that most parents struggle with parenting, and we would all be better off being more open about it. Probably that neighbor who looks so perfect to you has never dared admit to you that she has parenting problems because you have never mentioned problems to her and she fears *your* criticism.

REALISTIC EXPECTATIONS

If you grew up in an unhealthy home, you may have been expected to take on adult tasks too early. If your mother was alcoholic, depressed, or severely ill, you may have been called upon to care for her and your younger siblings. Perhaps when you were twelve you had to make dinner and care for the younger children while your mother worked nights. If so, you should have felt over-whelmed or used. In order to keep her own guilt at bay, your mother may have told you you were being selfish and spoiled for expressing such feelings. She had to convince herself that you were being unreasonable. Where does that leave you? When you ask your daughter to make a simple salad for dinner and she leaves an important ingredient out of the dressing, do you think she is being stupid, sloppy, lazy, or resistant? The pained look on her face when you are criticizing her should tell you your expectations are too high. But if your heart has been hardened, you may interpret her reaction as a manipulative play for sympathy.

In dysfunctional families a child as young as six years old may be expected to get himself up and dressed for school because Mom has given strict orders not to wake her. Sometimes a six-year-old is capable of getting his own breakfast and feeding his two-year-old brother, who is up and hungry, but that does not mean this is a reasonable expectation. Six-year-olds typically have a poor sense of time and still want the warmth and care of their mothers. Tiptoeing around the house and keeping a constant eye on the clock are stressful for a child that age. Having to think about the welfare of younger siblings adds still more stress. In short, although some six-year-olds may be capable of these tasks, that does not mean they are developmentally ready. They are likely to feel lonely, anxious, and emotionally abandoned when they leave for school each morning.

Parents in a healthy home have realistic expectations for their children. They may have read developmental books that describe what children are capable of at each age. They may spend time with other children the same age as their child, so they get a sense of the norm for that age. They may base their expectations on their actual experiences with their own child, becoming sensitive to the child's frustration level and respecting the child's individual growth rate. They allow the child time to master each level of behavior before presenting him or her with a new challenge. If a parent has come from a healthy home, she may be able to do this without much thought. But if your parents had unrealistic expectations for you, you will have to slow down and try to understand what is appropriate at each age and stage.

MATCHING EXPECTATIONS TO CHILD'S DEVELOPMENTAL LEVEL

As you design your family rules, keep in mind that ACODF often have very distorted ideas about developmental stages and what it is appropriate to expect of children at various ages. That's a major reason they get frustrated with their kids. They can't understand why their two-year-old can't sit still for a half hour (when they haven't brought anything for the child to play with). Sometimes it's hard to remember just how difficult it is to tie a shoe before you've had years of practice. If you can't understand how your child could be so slow at reading, take a piano class that requires you to read notes in both clefs, or try learning a foreign language. One way to get in touch with your child's frustration at using a fork is for you to try eating with chopsticks. You will soon realize that your child is not "just being stubborn" when he eats with his fingers.

There are many resources for learning about children's developmental stages. Child development courses are offered at most community colleges; there are many books on the market that describe the skill level of each age child (my favorite is the *Your Two Year Old* series);[1] and *Parents Magazine* has articles every month on what you can expect from children at certain stages. Here is a quick list of what chores children of various ages can be expected to do:

AGE 2–3: Put away toys, make food choices, use toilet, brush teeth and hair, put dirty clothes in hamper, dress with help.

AGE 4–5: Set table, fetch things at grocery store, feed pet, dust, get mail, help fix simple dessert, sandwich, or bowl of cereal, share toys, clean room, make bed, choose clothes and dress, answer phone, put away clothes.

AGE 6–7: Make toast, fix sack lunch, rake leaves, walk dog, tie shoes, carry money and notes to school, take phone messages (if reading and writing), run errands near home, sweep patio, water lawn, wash and wipe dishes.

AGE 8–9: Peel or cut vegetables with supervision, mop floors, select clothes when shopping, sew on buttons, cook simple family meals (hamburgers), paint fence, vacuum rugs, babysit with adult supervision nearby.

AGE 10–11: Change sheets, operate washing machine and dryer, plan own parties, schedule own homework and practice times, earn money by doing chores for neighbors, manage money, transport self by bike, babysit, pack own suitcase.

AGE 12–13: Mow lawn, deliver papers, check oil in car, check tire inflation, cook more elaborate meals (spaghetti), clean oven and stove.

TEENS: Earn money at job, use own checking account, use credit cards, care for self when parents on trip, help decide curfew, drive self to activities.[2]

After reading the above lists do you feel you have expected too much from your child? Too little? Just the right amount? There are also other considerations that influence your child's readiness for a task. If your child has been under a lot of stress because he has a new sibling, your family has moved to a new town, or you have recently divorced, lower your expectations until his adjustment period is over. Don't be too critical of your child's performance at any time. For example, when she is ready to select her clothes and dress herself, really let her do it. Keep in mind that this does not mean she will choose clothes that you feel go well together. Avoid criticizing her choices. If you must guide her in some way, compliment her profusely when she happens to make a combination that pleases you. If she asks your opinion you could offer an alternative selection, but don't expect her to follow your advice. Try to separate your self-esteem from your child's appearance. Anyone else who lets her child dress herself will know immediately why your daughter is wearing a purple dotted blouse with red-striped shorts. Those kids who are always color-coordinated are probably not dressing themselves!

Participating in Sunday school, scouts, or sports is another good way to see how other kids your child's age function. You might realize you have been expecting too much or you might discover you have been expecting too little of your child. If your child seems to lag behind his peers, try to raise your expectations a little and watch carefully for his response. If your child repeatedly and consistently cannot function as well as others his age, don't assume he is defying you. Lower your standards until you have reached down to his level of success. Your child might be fully capable of achieving and behaving like others his age, but if he *believes* he can't, he won't be able to. You may need to build his confidence first. **Remember, criticism does not build confidence; success does.**

When a child frequently misbehaves in public the parents may be tempted to withdraw from social contact. If you have been on the go too much, streamlining your social plans may be all your child needs to help him stop his tantrums. But you can't stay hidden away all the time. The only way a child can learn how to behave in public is by being out with other people and succeeding or failing. Although children often should be taken home immediately when they are misbehaving in public, it is not healthy for any of you to cut yourselves off completely from social contact because your child's behavior is imperfect. You will have to fight against your need to look like the perfect family and get out there and make a fool of yourself with the rest of us!

On the other hand, some ACODF parents keep such a tight reign on their children through threats and punishments that the children never misbehave in public. When these parents see other children misbehaving they imagine that the other parents simply do not know how to "control" their children. The healthiest children will not be perfect angels in public. Because they realize children must be allowed some freedom to express themselves and make their own mistakes, the best parents have not instilled a "controlling" amount of fear in their children. When we threaten our children into perfect behavior and buoy our spirits by judging other parents inferior, we are just acting out our own fears of inadequacy in another way. Let's take a look at where these exaggerated feelings of inferiority come from and what we can do about them that is more constructive.

ALIENATION AND DEFENSIVENESS

Ever since childhood adult children of dysfunctional families have felt "different," and because they typically have low self-esteem **they rarely regard that difference as a positive virtue.** Instead they feel defective or inferior. A very common defense for this feeling is an "I'm OK, you're not OK" stance. Because ACODF often must grow up too fast and lose childhood illusions early, they may cynically and defensively see themselves as better than their "naive" peers. This can lead to an isolating "chip-on-the-shoulder" family attitude.

It is well known that people who feel inferior often try to bolster their self-esteem by finding fault with others. The more people they can denigrate, the higher up on the heap they see themselves. In a dysfunctional family, conversation may be dominated by stories of triumph over imagined adversaries. A basically negative life-view can color everything. An encounter with a store clerk who is distractedly thinking of her boyfriend becomes a story about the clerk who purposely ignored you and had to be put in her place, while a store clerk who was especially nice becomes a naive fool to mock for your more "savvy" family. Almost any human interaction can be interpreted as hostile if the viewer is defensive or insecure. In a dysfunctional family, life—or the whole world and everyone in it— may be seen as an enemy or colored by disdain. Mr. Rogers is a wimp, "Sesame Street" is a bunch of stupid puppets, churches are filled with hypocrites, scouts are nauseating do-gooders, and teachers and cops are out to get you. These litanies teach children to be suspicious of everyone no matter how warm the overture.

The children in these families will often grow up to be defensive ACODF parents who think everyone means harm to them and their children. They feel that it is only safe to stay within the family, socializing exclusively with their parents and adult siblings. In these families the ACODF parents resist any dubious "help" from outsiders. And so the cycle will continue with each generation because these families are too isolated from sources of help. With such training, the children of ACODF parents are often too guarded to form meaningful relationships with peers or teachers. Their only conversation topics may be put-downs of themselves or others. They may be strongly attracted to subcultures whose main common ground is a shared rejection of mainstream values. It's easy to see the trouble this can lead to when the child approaches the teen years. Teens see drug use as a quick, efficient way to escape the pain of loneliness, gain an instant sense of belonging in a subculture, and thumb their noses at culturally acceptable morals.

At the same time, the child who can see straight while growing up in a twisted family will have to overcome a great deal of resistance. Perhaps some of you experienced this. If you were bright as a child and did well in school, the praise you received from your teachers probably felt much better than the criticism you received at home. Even in a chaotic home you may have managed to do enough schoolwork to keep your place of esteem in the teacher's eyes. You may have been accepted by classmates from more stable homes and wanted to join wholesome activities such as Girl Scouts. But if your home values were in direct opposition with society's values, you eventually had to choose sides. Most dysfunctional homes have a "with us or against us" rule. The very adept child may manage to arrange her own transportation to activities, but every time she comes home she will feel her mother's sense of being betrayed. **For, in the family's eyes, the child is becoming one of "them."**

In these circumstances, a dysfunctional Mom or Dad typically worry about what the child is telling the teacher or troop leader. They may refuse to give the child money for dues. They may use being grounded from the activity as punishment for every small infraction. They may even feel the child needs to be protected from the inevitable rejection she will suffer at the hands of her "snobby" new friends. If the parents have never been able to fit into the mainstream, it is hard for them to imagine that their daughter can succeed socially. At this point of resistance you probably made your choice. You either became a rebel marching off to college as if you were joining a crime ring, dropped your family altogether and took up with a surrogate family that had positive values, or gave in to the pressure and decided your parents were right after all. If you've done the latter, reexamine your values and look at what you are communicating to your children about their healthy pursuits.

For the dysfunctional parent's defensive stance generally forces him to see healthy activities as frivolous self-indulgence at best, and at worst, as deceitful setups for bitter disappointment when the child finally has to face reality. He may come across as a "holier than thou" parent, believing that he has some secret wisdom about parenting because of what he has suffered. Perhaps long ago you dreamed you would go to college but your parents were unable or unwilling to give you any money for that purpose and your grades were not good enough to win a scholarship. It may have been hard for you to make the sacrifices necessary to work and put yourself through college while your family jeered at you from the sidelines just waiting for you to fail. If your family was successful at defeating your ambitions probably all you remember now is the humiliating sting of trying and failing. In your mind it may be a noble and protective gesture to spare your daughter that disappointment. In your distorted protectiveness you might make sure your daughter gets the unrealistic notion of going to college out of her head as early as possible.

Try to overcome the negative life-view your parents gave you. By virtue of the fact that you are reading a parenting book and looking for better ways to parent, your children have a much better chance of succeeding where you failed. Try not to let your pessimism color their lives. They live in a new time, perhaps with opportunities you never had. You can improve their likely success rate tremendously by just being supportive. They don't have to face the "reality" you had to face. There are many "realities," and with our attitudes we actually choose which one will rule our lives.

BLENDING IN

The softer-style dysfunctional parent is one who may have learned enough social skills to be able to blend in with healthier families despite her feeling of inferiority. This parent would under-standably live in constant fear of "being found out." She strains to imitate "normal" topics of conversation and tries to discover what normal families do for recreation, carefully studying and mimicking the surface appearance of health. Naturally, it will be hard for her to learn better parenting skills from other parents because she will be afraid to be open about everyday family problems. Instead, she will have to rely on accidently overhearing the advice she so desperately needs. For she fears that talking about any of her own family problems will immediately tip her hand. The "normal" parents will discover she is "different" and she will be ostracized.

The insecure parent who has grown up in a dysfunctional home thus cuts herself off from opportunities to sort out what feelings of hers are destructively different and which feelings or actions are within safe bounds. How angry or helpless do other parents feel when confronted with a crying baby or a temper tantrum? How have her own childhood experiences affected the way she is reacting? Can she say how she feels without shocking others?

◆ ROSALYN AS NEW MOTHER

Rosalyn is a career counselor in a New Jersey college and has had some success as a professional artist. Like many blacks who have learned to be careful with people outside their tight family network, Rosalyn has been cautious about what she shares with others. No one at her workplace knows about the history of mental illness in Rosalyn's family, nor does anyone know the horribly difficult postpartum depression Rosalyn lived through, terrified all the while that she had inherited her father's schizophrenia. For the world, Rosalyn is just an outgoing successful career woman, but Rosalyn's brother, like his father, is in a mental hospital for schizophrenia.

Rosalyn often paints sad melancholic pictures of family life. The paintings inspired by her early life have a hollow lonely quality, but she also has lighter portraits inspired by her son and the warm family life she has had with her husband. Many of her paintings have a strong social message.

Rosalyn's son is her "love child" conceived out of wedlock when she was in her early twenties. Rosalyn had an AA degree and had been working toward her BA when she became pregnant. Her schooling was halted and Rosalyn, wanting to be a "good mother," had quit her nursing job and gone on welfare so she could stay home with her newborn son. Like all babies, her son Richard cried a lot and required much boring physical care. This was a sharp contrast to Rosalyn's life in her early twenties. She had been working her way through school, holding down two jobs, and studying, full of ambition, enjoying the social contact vital to her. Now she was alone, depressed, and overwhelmed. She began to think violent thoughts about her baby. While she was cutting open a melon her baby woke again, screaming and demanding her attention when she herself was hungry and in desperate need of an island of quiet. She looked at the knife and thought of stabbing the baby. She sometimes thought about smashing him against the wall or putting a pillow over his face. This violence never went beyond thought into action. She would close herself up in her bedroom or go for a walk around the block, but her thoughts frightened her. Rosalyn naturally thought about her father's schizophrenia and feared she was losing her mind. She began to worry that she would snap and harm her child. She finally worked up the courage to tell her older sister about it and the sister took her to a therapist.

Going into therapy determined to tell the truth, Rosalyn worried that her baby would be taken away from her. If that was what was best, she was ready to accept it for her child's sake. But after hearing her story the therapist, a warm older man, assured her that she was experiencing prolonged postpartum depression and showed no signs of schizophrenia. He advised her to get back to work or school, explaining that she was simply not the "stay-at-home-mom" type. He told her that there was no reason for her to give up her baby, pointing out that thinking and doing are two different things. He reminded her that even at the "end of her rope" she had restrained herself.

(Continued in Chapter 12)

Many mothers, from all kinds of families of origin, are unprepared for the demands of a newborn infant. The supermellow mother with a full-term baby who has delivered without complications may have an easy time of it, but such scenarios are rare for a first-time mother. Most new mothers are nervous and babies sense this. Some babies are born with underdeveloped digestive systems and will have colic for the first three months, screaming and crying unconsolably around the clock. More and more mothers are delivering by Caesarean and don't realize that this is a major operation that would take six weeks of recovery for anyone who is not caring for a baby at the same time. Postpartum depression is common even in mothers who have grown up in the most supportive homes; although usually short-lived, it is a body-chemistry problem that a loving childhood does not cure.

But for the mother who has grown up in a dysfunctional family, her first thought when problems with the new baby arise is that it is all her fault because she'll never be a good mother. It is easy for a postpartum depression to take hold and add to the naturally low mood she has brought with her from childhood insecurities. When a woman has been happy most of her life and finds herself very irritable, depressed, or feeling violent following the birth of her child, she is likely to go off to her doctor and talk about it. Then the doctor can take steps to help relieve the depression and recommend ways the new mother can lower her stress and get more relaxing rest. But the mother who fears the depression and exhaustion are the result of her "bad genes" or her great inadequacy, may be reluctant to tell anyone the depth of her feelings.

Often mothers raised in dysfunctional homes (who see that parents like their own are now having their children taken away from them by Child Protective Services) fear losing their children. Rosalyn had a healthy streak in her that superseded her pride and desire to be a parent. She reached the point that she was ready to give up her baby if that were best for the child. Because of this healthy willingness to face her problem, Rosalyn was able to get help before she did any harm. Another ACODF mother, equally savable, might have stayed in the situation until she harmed the baby—all because she feared what would happen if she "told on herself." Like Rosalyn, when we fear our thoughts or behavior are going "out of bounds," we need to have the courage to seek professional help. For our smaller fears, it is good to look around us for healthy parenting models.

STUDYING HEALTHY BEHAVIOR

When a new parent has no healthy role model, each challenge of parenting is a vast mystery she is expected to solve without clues. For example, Grace's father used harsh beatings as discipline. Grace had vowed never to hit her child, so she screamed and hit things. Though this terrified everyone around her she kept it up because she had no other alternatives in her mind. Her husband offered no solutions to the problem. He felt mothers should automatically know how to take care of their babies.

But many mothers raised in dysfunctional homes come up blank when confronted with a child-care crisis. **Just as one would study a foreign culture, parents from unhealthy homes must observe and read about parenting practices in healthy families.**

◆ GRACE'S MENTOR

Fortunately, Grace's Aunt Serena, a warm, loving person, was able to take in Grace and Candace. Serena had been Grace's babysitter when she was little. "Out of my whole life," recalls Grace, "she was always the person who was really warm and affectionate to me. She never judged anybody."

Grace had to work late hours at a nightclub, often running the whole place herself. "I would be so exhausted when I got home about two or three in the morning. Candy would come in and wake me up early in the morning and I would beg her to please go away and let me sleep. I would start off being real sweet to her and asking her nicely to let me sleep, and to just go out and watch TV until I got up. But she would just come in persistently and keep waking me up, so I would get more and more irritated. Then I'd start screaming at her. I would get so mad I can remember hitting the door with my hand because I didn't want to hit her. But I was terrifying her." Fortunately Aunt Serena would come in and take Candy away so that Grace could get some sleep.

Serena had always been good with children and she watched Grace's baby while Grace took classes and worked. She welcomed Grace home each night with big dinners and gave Grace the love and support she so desperately needed at the time. "The thing that really helped me learn to be a better mother was this time I spent with my aunt, because she really helped me out and she was so loving."

Once she recovered from her long period of exhaustion Grace could be the mother she wanted to be. With the support of her aunt, Grace finally was able to be on her own with her child after about a year.

"It's only been in this last year that I feel like I am the way I want to be with my daughter. And that's sad because she's ten years old."

(Continued in Chapter 8)

In addition to role models other than parents, there are many ways to learn parenting skills in both school and private settings. Support groups, study groups, family therapy, or trips to the park can all be vehicles for learning healthy parenting.

Many school districts now offer free parenting classes for parents of school age children and many preschools can refer you to parenting groups. Parenting classes such as STEP (Systematic Training for Effective Parenting), P.E.T. (Parent Effectiveness Training), Confident Parenting, or the new P.R.I.C.E. (Positive, Responsibility, Influence, Consequences, Encouragement)[3] curriculum generally offer a broad approach that focuses on communicating effectively with your child and approaching your child with an attitude of respect. They generally provide opportunities to discuss specific disturbing behaviors of your child and the instructor or fellow classmates can offer suggestions on how to change that behavior. Healthy parents as well as confused parents take these classes. Parenting classes are a good place to make friends with someone who may have more answers at the tip of her tongue than you do.

Parenting books are a good source of information, and parenting courses may also be found through the Y.W.C.A., adult education, or community colleges. Parents have been sharing tips at play groups, swim lessons, gymnastics, or scouts for generations. These discussions can help you sort out whether or not your child's behavior is typical for her age. In a large group setting others may ask the questions that have been haunting you or describe situations you haven't even encountered yet so that all questions become part of your personal education as a parent. If your problems are more serious, there are many family-oriented counseling centers that offer both group and one-on-one parenting instruction.

Organizations such as La Leche League, the Childbirth Education Association, PTA's, and churches often have educational and support groups for new moms. The groups are out there but news of them is usually spread by word of mouth. Once you find one parenting group, you will hear of many others from the leaders and parents you meet. On the other hand, if your child begins to make enough trouble to get the notice of society, you may be referred to a parenting program and required to attend. If this happens to you, try to take the attitude that such "punishments" are often really *blessings* that come when you "hit bottom" with your child.

Remember, many parents from dysfunctional homes who cannot find new methods to deal with their children will fall back on the hitting and screaming tactics of their own parents even though they had vowed not to. Learning to parent your child more effectively often has many side advantages that you could never have imagined. In order to be an effective parent, you must reduce your own stress and learn to organize your own life better. On the road to discovering better parenting methods, you will find much that will improve the quality of your own life. Remember, an essential part of being a good parent is being a happier person. Time you spend on self-improvement, even if it does not apply to parenting per se, will benefit your child. Just try to keep the best balance you can between meeting your needs and your children's needs.

Generally, anything that brings you into contact with other parents can be an opportunity to learn from others. Watch how other parents interact with their children. When you see a child who looks happy and confident, watch how the mother or father communicates with her and treats her. If you like what you see, ask for advice. Most parents are glad to give suggestions to those who ask and will be flattered. But ignore any advice forced on you by someone who has a sour or timid child. Instead, as Gail did, cultivate the friendship of parents you admire and be open and willing to learn.

◆ GAIL'S METHOD

Gail was twenty-eight when her daughter Ariel was born. It was very stressful because the pregnancy was unplanned and, although Gail had always meant to be a stay-at-home mother, she had to go back to work. Her husband was still in college and she couldn't help feeling resentful that he wasn't ready to support her and the child. Gail worked during the day and her husband went to school at night. She was always alone when the baby would cry in the evening and she felt overwhelmed. As a high school teacher she had lessons to prepare and papers to mark. There was stress on the marriage, and stress on her relationship with the baby. Gail felt she had very little emotional energy at the end of her workday. She simply took care of the baby's physical needs.

"When I was still working, I felt like I was a lousy mom. Most of the mothers I knew were stay-at-home moms and not only did I have a terrible upbringing, I worked full-time."

As soon as her husband finished school and got a job, Gail quit so she could stay home. "I feel much better now that I'm not working and I can just concentrate on being a mom. The feeling of belonging is a key thing for me. Before I was a stay-at-home mom I felt like I didn't belong in my group of friends. I don't like to be too different. But then one of the hardest things I faced was being at home with Ariel. I didn't know how to relax at home and just get down on the floor and play. I would find it boring. I really didn't know how to enjoy just being with Ariel. Instead, I'd take her out to a coffee shop." Gail is beginning to learn how to be with her daughter, but she is still most comfortable when they are doing something productive (like baking a cake together) instead of just playing.

"I've always had trouble having a close relationship with someone I'm living with. I was never good at my roommate relationships. I probably had an instinctive desire to get out of the house because when I was little I got out of the house as much as I could and I just went on 'getting out of the house.'"

Gail's father was a violent alcoholic who would blow up over every small thing. "When I was a child, I used to think about killing myself. I remember lying in bed at age five or six and putting the pillow over my head to try and suffocate myself. Every night my father would beat one of us to a pulp and I just felt so frightened and depressed. The schools never noticed. I was always a straight A student; in high school I was a cheerleader and student body president. I liked anything that gave me a reason to get out of my house."

Despite Gail's success at school, she had no confidence in herself. Her father was very controlling and had convinced her she wasn't competent at anything. "In high school he was still choosing my clothes for me. I think my mother was depressed because years of his controlling behavior had made her helpless. She couldn't even drive on a highway. She was always afraid of something and was easily overwhelmed. Four kids were too much for her. She had a very passive personality. You couldn't have any other personality if you lived with my dad. I remember her always being confused. I think my parents knew they should have stopped at two children, but they were Catholic and they couldn't practice birth control."

In high school Gail had a boyfriend from a strong and stable family. "Paul's mom was loving and warm. We'd come home from school in the wintertime and she would have a fresh-baked apple pie for us. We'd sit down with her and talk over pie and tea. I did everything with his family, even summer camping trips."

After three and a half years of being part of this boy's family, Gail found herself on the outside when Paul broke up with her. "Six months later my dad committed suicide, so that was a very hard year for me. I went through the whole gamut of things to deal with the anxiety. I did drugs and I got into drinking, but I could see that I didn't feel any better. Then I met this girl who was very religious and she seemed to have it all together. I really admired her and she befriended me and took me to all her church meetings. Her friends, who weren't doing drugs like my friends, just seemed so much more sincere and dependable. They'd go bowling on Friday nights instead of hitting the bars. I looked at her life and I said, 'This is what I want.'"

Gail started seeing a counselor through the church and the therapist teamed her up with an older woman in the church who became like a mother to Gail. "The therapist believed that God uses people in the church to heal you. If I hadn't been so bad off to begin with, the church may have been all I needed, but I could see I needed both the intellectual knowledge of the counselor and the love and acceptance of the church. The church is there to give you better role models and give you new, more positive experiences that will heal you and make up for some of your bad experiences. This approach has really helped me."

Gail stopped being self-destructive and eventually met her husband, Steve, a stable, supportive man. "I was fine until Ariel was born. But then I started freaking out; I was depressed; I would get angry at Steve all the time, so I went back into counseling."

Gail feels that she will always be more prone to depression than most people, but now she has a lot more coping skills. "I have so much more to feel grateful for now. When I get depressed I say to myself, 'What are you so depressed for? You've got a wonderful husband, a wonderful child, and a wonderful house. Everything's going your way.' And I can get through it better."

(Continued this chapter)

Since high school Gail has understood the need to surround herself with healthy role models. Each time she neared "bottom" she looked around herself for people who looked happier. She was open to their influence on her life. Later we will see how Gail applied this method to her parenting.

AVOIDING REACTIONARY RIGIDITY

If your childhood was painful you may have vowed to do things differently from your parents. If they were strict and unyielding, you might hold flexibility as your highest goal. By contrast, if your life was chaotic and unpredictable, your first priority might be establishing some clear rules. Identifying what your parents did that made you uncomfortable is a good place to start. However, keep in mind that any extreme is not healthy. Many dysfunctional families see everything in terms of black and white, so **if you do not examine your motives and opinions carefully, you might make the mistake of going overboard in the opposite direction.** Healthy families have clear rules but remain flexible so they can respond to personality differences in the children. They also work for a midrange in closeness. The family should have some activities they do together, but if each person cannot also enjoy some solitary activity it may be a sign that the family is too close and encourages unhealthy dependency.

Without conscious correction the rigid thinking patterns you grew up with may cloud your judgment. You need to be out interacting with other families to get a sense of what the norm is. However, in your rush to end the uncertainty with a decision, don't just adopt someone else's values. They might not know any more than you do. Discovering what is best for your particular child is often an agonizing process of trial and error, and sometimes there are no shortcuts. Consult more than one source. Like Gail, cultivate friendships with competent parents but also consult books or professionals and be open to opposing views. That is the only way to sort out exactly what degrees of freedom, closeness, and flexibility are best suited to the unique personalities of you and your child.

BUILDING SUPPORT SYSTEMS

If both you and your spouse grew up in dysfunctional homes where your emotional needs were neglected, your current nuclear family unit may simply not have enough emotional energy in storage to meet your children's needs. You will have to get some emotional energy from someone or something outside your family unit. While healthy families often have grandparents and other relatives to lessen their burden, your dysfunctional parents will probably be no more supportive as grandparents than they were as parents. You will want to have better options anyway. Your parents may not have the skills needed to step in and help care for children in a way that makes those children feel good about themselves. Having realistic expectations about your own parents will not only lessen your disappointment, it may also protect your children from unnecessary negative treatment.

Parents need to build a wide safety net of child-care support that they can fall back on as they strive to become increasingly comfortable with their child's level of dependency. If the family can afford it, the best solution is often paid child care at either a day-care center or in the home. This is a complete transaction. You get what you need (time away from the children to renew yourself or keep your relationship with your spouse healthy), and your obligation to the caretaker is completely satisfied with cash. If the caretaker is well chosen and affordable, the transaction is a total plus for conserving emotional energy. If you simply don't have the money (and look at your budget carefully before you decide this—paid child care is worth more to your family system than anything beyond rent and the simplest food), there are other options. Many families who cannot afford to pay sitters use exchanges with neighbors, mothers of classmates, or through formalized baby-sitting co-ops. However, exchanges mean that you will be caring for other people's children as often as you have a free space off. If you are still feeling very uncertain of your parenting skills or are still having difficulty learning to assert yourself with your children, taking on other children may use up more emotional energy than you have gained during

your free time. In order to benefit from a child-care exchange arrangement, you must actually come out ahead. Your neighbor's
children must be easier to care for than your own, and they must be
compatible enough with your children that even your own children
are easier to care for when the neighbor's children are there for
company.

Seek the healthiest families to exchange with and keep the
terms of the arrangement modest. Don't start with an overnight.
Ask only for as much time as you can comfortably handle when your
turn comes around. If you have taken two hours to go shopping and
your neighbor asks if you will watch her children for an eight-hour
stretch, you need not feel guilty saying you just can't help her out
this time. Explain that your kids don't do well with other children
for more than two hours, or that at the end of your workweek you
can't handle that many children for that length of time. Then
reinforce that you would be glad to sit for two hours at some other
time. Pushing yourself beyond your limit will not benefit you in the
long run. If you agree to watch the neighbor's child for longer than
you can manage to be warm and calm, the child and neighbor are
bound to want to end the arrangement. Few parents will appreciate
you doing a poor job for eight hours, more than your doing a good
job for two. Build trust in your exchange sitter and confidence in
yourself by keeping it manageable.

BREAKING OUT OF ISOLATION

That feeling of being different or defective, of not belonging
anywhere, can be one of your great stumbling blocks, or the feeling
can make you uncomfortable enough to seek help. Your poorly
functioning family probably kept itself isolated from the influence
or possible criticism of others. You, too, may want to shy away from
other parents. If you were criticized mercilessly by your dysfunctional family and friends, you may be hypersensitive to criticism. Or
perhaps, as a child you had very little contact socializing with other
families (except relatives who shared the same peculiar values), so
you have no role models for achieving comfortable closeness with
other families. At first, reaching out may be awkward and perhaps
even frightening. No one likes to feel the pain of rejection, and your
poorly developed social skills may not be polished enough to bring

you instant success in making new friends. Perhaps a good starting point is other people in the same boat as you. There are now organizations for Adult Children of Alcoholics all over the country, and they attract the participation of people from many different kinds of dysfunctional families. It may be a smaller risk to begin opening up in one of these groups. To feel a sense of connectedness one needs to look for similarities, and you may find you have a lot of common ground with other ACOA. From there you can move on to groups of more general interest such as churches, youth league groups, or any other groups which are based on a shared interest such as Sierra Club. As you strive to develop your social skills you will be models for your children.

Children will benefit from simply seeing their parents "fitting in." This at least challenges that isolating feeling of differentness. Once you have gained some social skill from putting yourself out there in social situations, you will have first-hand experience with making friends that you can share with your children. Children often need help making friends. Your son may talk about a classmate that he likes but have no idea how to approach his school friend about coming to your house for an after-school visit. If you still have a lot of trouble socializing, it may be because your parents did not have the tools to help you at that state of your childhood social development.

In order to break the cycle, you will have to take some initiative. Commonly, children's first after-school visits are arranged by the children's mothers. You will have to pluck up the courage to make conversation with the mother of your son's friend. Both children may only be ready to socialize in the presence of their mothers, so you may have to spend a few hours at the park with this other mother.

If you are shy or fear rejection, this might seem insurmountable. But taken one step at a time you can get through it for your child's sake. Make the initial contact with just a simple introduction and work up to taking the conversation further each time you see the other mother. Then suggest an activity that provides some distraction, such as a visit to a hamburger stand with a playground or a trip to a movie. Think of topics for conversation before you go. The place where your children have met will be an easy topic. You can talk about the teacher or troop leader and the activities your children have shared. You might want to brave sharing a child-rearing concern. Perhaps you are worried about your son's fear of the dark. You can ask the other mother if her child has the same fears and, if so, what she has done about it. Most parents like to give advice, and admitting you don't know everything about parenting yourself will make it easier for the other mother to open up.

◆ GAIL

"If I like the way someone's kids behave and I like the feeling of the family unit, then I ask a lot of questions about how they do things. My pastor's wife is a wonderful mother and I often ask her for advice. But I don't automatically follow the advice if it doesn't feel right to me." Gail has also read many parenting and child development books. "I think there is a general standard of what is realistic to expect, but every child is different. You need to be flexible."

(Continued in Chapter 14)

If your child has had trouble making friends in a large group such as his school class, create opportunities for your child to get together with kids his age in smaller group settings such as scouts, team sports, lessons, or Sunday school classes. Keep working at it until you find a step that you and your child feel comfortable taking. You'll find you are developing your social skills along with your child. Then you will see how the child has begun to change your life for the better in broader ways than simply giving you love and affection.

DIFFERENTNESS AS A VIRTUE

Remember, what is average is not necessarily what is healthy. Materialism and excessive TV-watching are still problems in most families, but many of these same families are not even aware they have a problem. If you recognize that your family of origin was dysfunctional and that you therefore cannot rely on your parents as role models, you will have the heightened awareness that all parents need in this fast-changing age. Parenting courses all emphasize that the methods that were effective a generation ago are not adequate to prepare children to thrive in today's world. Many parents may not realize this until their children are in their teens. But you will not be lulled by a false confidence. Your strength begins with the ability to see the complexity of parenting and is backed by the wisdom that comes from having struggled. The depth that comes from having to humbly admit your parenting inadequacies will help you become a far more compassionate parent. It is easier to create something new when you have bravely swept away the old structure. Your family has the potential to be more stable than those families who are still patching up old parenting models.

◆ ═══════════════ SUMMARY ═══════════════ ◆

We humans are social animals and we need the company of other humans in order to feel truly good about ourselves. When we feel self-conscious and different, we do not attract friends. We need to let ourselves feel our "human bonds" and reach out to others.

◆ ═══════════════ POINTS ═══════════════ ◆

1. Adults who have grown up in dysfunctional families will need to study child development so they have realistic expectations for their children.

2. An overly defensive family attitude can distort our perceptions of other's actions. Parents with low self-esteem may be teaching their children to be unrealistically suspicious of other's motives.

3. Insecure parents may become overly protective and inadvertently discourage their children's participation in healthy activities.

4. Parents from dysfunctional families need to look for healthy role models and seek out opportunities to be with other parents so they can see healthier parenting in practice.

5. Parenting classes are an excellent place for us to learn healthy parenting behaviors so we can prepare our children to function well in our fast-paced stressful society.

6. There is great value in analyzing what our parents did wrong. However, doing the polar opposite of our parents is seldom a good route to better parenting.

7. We need to build support systems that give to us at least as much as we give to them. Options such as paid baby-sitting provide rest spaces from our children that carry no obligation to return the favor.

8. We each need to reach out and establish healthy friendships with other parents at a pace that is comfortable for us.

NOTES

1. Louise Bates Ames, and Frances L. Ilg, *Your Two Year Old*. Gessell Institute of Child Development. New York: Dell Publishing, Inc., 1979.

2. Adapted from lists prepared by Community Parent-Teacher Education Center, Cooperative Counselor Education Project, Phase II: Counseling and Guidance Department, College of Education, University of Arizona, and Pupil Personnel Service, Tucson Public Schools, Tucson, Arizona, 1971.

3. **STEP**

The Parent's Handbook (Systematic Training for Effective Parenting) by Don Dinkmeyer and Gary D. McKay, American Guidance Service, Circle Pines, MN, 1982.

P.E.T.

Parent Effectiveness Training by Thomas Gordon, New American Library, New York, 1975.

Confident Parenting

Confident Parenting Workshop Leader's Guide, by Robert Aitchison, Center for the Improvement of Child Caring, Studio City, CA, 1976.

P.R.I.C.E.

P.R.I.C.E. Parent's Manual by Lou Denti and Kevin Feldman, Riverside County Office of Education, Riverside, CA, 1988.

· 6 ·

FEAR OF INTIMACY

3. ACODF may become so overwhelmed by the needs of their young children or so fearful of their children's rejection that they withdraw into work or neglectful behavior.

4. ACODF may become so close to their children that they cannot allow the child to have a separate identity.

How close is close enough? How close is too close? If you watch people talking at a stand-up party, you will see that each person has a different "comfort zone." Some people want to stand up very close, so that they are practically touching the person they are addressing. Others like a four-foot invisible zone around them and will step back each time the speaker steps closer. Some nationalities customarily stand closer than others. Americans in general like to be near each other when they talk, but a wide range of comfort zones can still be observed in a group with a common nationality. That's where the influence of personal experience comes in. If physical closeness was a positive aspect of your family, then nearness will be appealing to you. If your parents were psychologically or physically distant, so that your needs for closeness were never met, you may still be seeking closeness from others, and you may sometimes make others uncomfortable with your level of need. On the other hand, if you were often beaten as a child, if stepping up close to your parent meant coming into a range of striking arm, you will probably like to keep a wide safety zone around you.

How close do children need a parent to be? What personal experience do they bring to bear? They come from inside their mothers—that's pretty close! When they are born, that is their norm. If a child is allowed to experience and meet his or her intimacy needs, his or her physical distance from the mother's body will gradually expand as the child grows older. Newborn infants like to be molded to the mother's body, while teenagers dodge kisses (from their parents anyway). What if you need a wide zone around you but your child likes to be right up next to your body? What if you want to hold your child close to you, even when she struggles? In both cases, you two have got a problem with intimacy.

ENMESHMENT, WALLS, AND BOUNDARIES

Psychologists call this comfort zone a boundary. A boundary is like a fence around us. It is the line that divides the *me* from the *not me*. We all need boundaries to protect us and help define us. But boundaries can range from rigid to flexible to diffuse. People who are fearful of intimacy often have rigid boundaries or *walls*. They are so afraid of being hurt or taken advantage of that they close themselves off from close relationships. Others, who totally lack the ability to assert themselves, seem to have no fence around them, nothing that defines the beginning or end of their psychological property. People trample through their feelings. In dysfunctional families, parents and children alike often swing from rigidity to unlimited giving. They might do everyone's bidding for a while and then find that the only way they can say no is to scream, "No!" and retreat into a rigid, cold withdrawal. Then as they become more and more isolated and lonely they go overboard trying to win back love, again giving until they are overextended and stressed. Healthy boundaries are flexible boundaries that never reach either of the above extremes. A healthy person will give what they have to give; they will give what is comfortable and stop short of giving so much that they resent the "loved one" they are giving to. This describes one aspect of boundaries: personal boundaries.

If you have a clear idea of your own boundaries, you will know when someone tries to violate them and can protect yourself. However, children are not born with boundaries. It is part of the normal infant/mother relationship to be "bonded." As the infant was, in fact, once part of mother, for a time afterward he still perceives himself as part of mother. In a healthy family, during the first year the infant will begin to perceive he is different, and at about age two (the "NO!" stage) boundary-setting takes place.

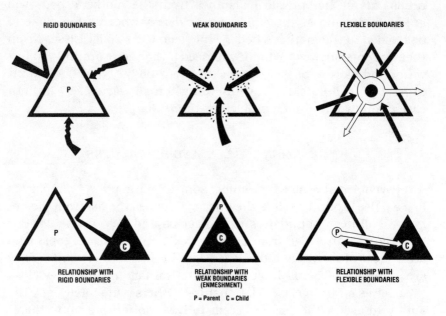

The family is where we begin to learn to set our boundaries, and boundaries between individuals in a family are very important. As children, we learn about boundaries from interacting with our parents and from observing how they set their own boundaries. Many dysfunctional families have *walls* that block out all interaction and intimacy, while other families are *enmeshed*—without boundaries between the varying members. They all try to think alike and feel alike. Parents in such families think, "If I am hungry, you must be hungry, and if you refuse food, you are being defiant."

In addition to personal boundaries, families have a boundary between the family unit and the outside world. Again the boundary may be a rigid excluding wall, too open to allow for a "family identity," or appropriately flexible and healthy. Our feelings of loyalty often show something about our boundaries. At the point of marriage our parents should have left their families of origin psychologically as well as physically. The partners in a healthy couple will each be closer to each other than they are to their own parents. If the husband is closer to his mother than he is to his wife, there will be trouble in the marriage. One of the couple's first jobs is to set up the boundaries that separate their new family from their families of origin. Family boundaries can function well whether they are large (including grandparents, aunts, uncles, stepchildren, former spouses, etc.) or small (nuclear family only) as long as the two parents agree about the family boundaries. But if the husband sees extended family as outsiders who have no business poking their noses in, and the wife wouldn't dream of making important plans without consulting everyone, there will be problems.

There can even be disagreement about boundaries within a nuclear family. Here territorial feelings influence boundaries. If the couple have a rigid sense of what is "man's work" and what is "woman's work," Dad will feel personally violated if Mom mows the lawn. A destructive outcome of such rigidity is the common case where a father does not see why he should attend family therapy since the children are his wife's responsibility. At the same time, a mother may be so emotionally involved with her children that she has no emotional energy left for her husband, thus drawing a circle around the family which leaves Dad on the outside.

Boundaries can be kept flexible and healthy if the marriage partners communicate clearly and regularly about their emotional and physical ups and downs. Be open with your spouse and let him or her know when you are emotionally or physically available and when it is too stressful to "be there" in any sense of the word. Couples can take steps to clarify and strengthen necessary boundaries. The husband and wife must each spend time by themselves discovering their personal interests and rhythms, and developing their capabilities so that they can function independently. Likewise, children should learn to spend time by themselves finding their own entertainments and developing their personal interests, rhythms, and capabilities so that they can function independently when they reach adulthood.

Probably the most damaging boundary problem that can take place in a family is confusion about boundaries between parent and child. Role confusion (when daughter is asked to play "little mother") would be the mildest form of family boundary problem, while the most serious boundary violation is incest between a parent and child. Although we hear more and more reports about how common physical incest really is, there is too little recognition of emotional incest. When a divorced mother makes a son into her "little spouse" or a father favors his daughter over his wife, the parent is committing emotional incest. The children are drawn into the role and lose their opportunity to complete the tasks of childhood development. Being excessively needed or favored by a parent can be very tempting, but children need to be developing friendships among their peers and need to feel the protection and discipline of a parent, not the adoration of a "pretend spouse."

INVASION VS. EVASION

Dysfunctional families frequently function at one extreme or another. If they are not excessively distant they are pryingly close. As we grow up in a dysfunctional home we learn either to evade closeness or invade others' private space. When we follow a parent's modeling, we may read at the breakfast table because we have come to believe this is the appropriate way to act when we share a meal with our children. Or we might *react* to the parent's example by going to the other extreme. Instead of reading, we might ask our children so many questions about what they are planning to do that day, how they *feel* about what they're planning to do, who they are planning to do it with, and what they will be thinking every minute they are away from us, that they don't even have a chance to eat!

Both behaviors will erode our children's self-esteem. The very evasive parent sends the message that the kids are not important (hardly even noticeable), while the invasive parent gives her child the feeling that he cannot be trusted to make even simple decisions about his own life. Both of these extremes spark intense emotions. The child who is starved for attention and warmth will perceive intimacy as salvation and will seek intimacy with those outside the family at all costs. We all remember children who were cruelly nicknamed "leeches." This clingy child was always available to play and would do anything you ordered her to do, just to be allowed to hang around you. But she was boring and suffocating. She never dared to have ideas of her own, and when you were ready for a break she had no place else to go. She usually wore out a new friend in a day or two and then was banished again to her lonely island.

By contrast, the extreme evader is generally terrified of intimacy. If the child has been made Mother's confidant, he has probably experienced intimacy as an overwhelming burden. When adults share adult emotions with children, it robs them of their childhood. They struggle to understand things beyond their experience, all the while feeling inadequate to meet Mommy's or Daddy's needs. It is not unusual for a mother in a dysfunctional family to complain about the father's extramarital affairs to her six-year-old son. How can a child understand this? All he can understand is that Daddy has done something to hurt Mommy very much and now he must be faithful to Mommy so she won't be hurt even more. He can feel the mother's loneliness and will consequently feel guilty when he goes off to play with his friends. As the child grows up and is able to pull away from this obligation, he will have formed an idea of closeness that is riddled with guilt and suffocation. He may then be an intimacy evader as an adult.

TRIANGLES

One of the symptoms of unhealthy intimacy patterns in a family is the emotional triangle. In the above example, since Dad is having affairs, Mom is more or less without a spouse. She looks toward her son to meet those emotional needs. In the same way, a father who does not feel "respected" by his wife will turn to his daughter and make her Daddy's little girl. Mom and Dad do not have a relationship that meets their mutual needs without pulling in a third party, in this case, the child.

However, triangles can form between any family members, or might even include outsiders. Mom can form a triangle by pulling her mother into the relationship on some level. What happens in triangles is that the person with a complaint does not voice that complaint to the one who has caused the pain. Instead, Mom might complain to her mother about Dad's ill treatment of her. This is a way people diffuse the emotional energy that surrounds a conflict, but it is rarely healthy or productive. Rather it is always best to resolve conflicts with the person who is causing you the discomfort. Meek or manipulative people love to try to find someone else to come to their aid, or simply to take the flack. Dad sends his son in to Mother with the message that he would like his dinner served soon because he is starving. Son goes to tell Mom and she shouts, "Well, you tell him that if he were out here helping me we could all eat a lot sooner!" The "messenger" has received the angry feelings of both parents while the parents have avoided addressing their own conflict.

CHILDHOOD SURVIVAL HABITS

Triangles leave the child walking a tightrope. Have you ever said too much as you sympathized with a friend who was dropped by a lover, only to be accused of maliciousness when your friend later patches up the relationship? Children sense the potential danger in taking sides. And yet sometimes these situations are an "opportunity" too tempting to pass up. The child who has been emotionally neglected or ignored is suddenly presented with a chance to gain his or her parent's affection. If they take the bait, they are bound to lose the love of one parent and might ultimately lose the love of both. In any case, parents who are willing to use the child as an emotional crutch for their own personal problems are not considering the child's emotional needs.

◆ SUSAN AS CO-PARENT

During her early childhood, a tremendous weight came to rest on Susan's shoulders. "I can remember my mother taking me aside when I was only eight and explaining that my father was an alcoholic and since she had to do his chores, I would have to take over many of her responsibilities. I was made the family nurturer." Susan was also her mother's main confidant, so she carried the emotional burden of her father's alcoholism.

When Susan was twelve, she was expected to start earning money to help put her older siblings through college. She worked in a nursery and later did bookkeeping for a local veterinarian, giving about half of her earnings to her mother. "It was implied that I, in turn, would get money from the family when I went to college." But her sisters were married with families by then and the father's alcoholism had progressed and put greater demands on the family, so the subject was dropped when Susan reached college age.

"I think the fact that there was never anyone being supportive of me, but I was expected to be supportive of everyone else had an impact. It made me see myself as a less valuable person. I was only valued for what I could do for everybody else, not for me. I needed the assurance that I was OK, that I was important. If they had at least expressed appreciation instead of just asking for more, it would have helped."

(Continued in Chapter 9)

If your parents used you for emotional support and did not return support when you needed it, you have probably grown up with a lot of unmet emotional needs. In a healthy parent/child relationship the child naturally looks to the adult for affirmation and approval. ACODF did not get this kind of reinforcement from their parents. In some cases the parents were simply too wrapped up in themselves to notice their child's positive traits; in other cases the parents were hypercritical; and, probably in all cases, the parents received little positive reinforcement from their own parents so they had no idea how to express approval of their children. The result is the same for the ACODF. Without affirmation their self-esteem is very low. As the healthy child matures he or she becomes increasingly able to look inward for approval and to perform well for a personal sense of satisfaction rather than praise from others. Praise is always nice, but for the maturing child it is no longer a critical need. The child from a dysfunctional home, on the other hand, is like a hungry child that has not been offered food. They are starving for attention and desperate for approval. Some learn to hide it as they grow older but the emptiness is ready to overwhelm them as soon as their guard is down. Their terrifying needs cause them either to run from intimacy or smother anyone who comes near enough.

If you can clearly identify how your parents used you, you might draw back from your own child in a genuine gesture of protectiveness, vowing not to take advantage of them emotionally. On the other hand, you might also draw back from your own child because you learned that to become close is to become vulnerable and you have little tolerance for emotional pain, since you were "used up" during childhood. On the deepest level there is the fear of abandonment—of being hurt—a vestige of childhood when those closest to you (parents) could not "meet" you emotionally. Most children who have been emotionally neglected feel despair, anger, and fear. They sometimes feel invisible, since their needs don't seem to be visible to anyone.

If you don't have it, you can't give it to your children. Parents from dysfunctional homes often have not yet learned how to take care of themselves or give to themselves. Consciously or unconsciously they hope that the child is going to give to them and meet their long-ignored needs. They still have a tremendous need to be taken care of. If they don't recognize and try to outgrow this need the roles will be reversed for another generation.

PARENTIFIED CHILD

One of the greatest dangers in seeking the approval from your child that you did not receive from your parents, is that the roles of parent and child can become reversed. For it is not just simple approval or compliments that the adult seeks; there is also a longing for care left over from childhood. Gloria's mother used her as a servant. Gloria was a naturally accomodating child anyway and liked to do things to please her mother. But before long it became Mother parked in her chair sending Gloria off to get her a soda, an ash tray, her cigarettes, her magazine. When Glorida wanted to sit and be pampered, her mother was too tired. Now Gloria is an adult with children of her own. Having played her mother's mother, Gloria cannot help but feel that it is her turn to be waited on now. It may be a bitter pill to swallow, but Gloria missed her turn. If she turns her daughter into a servant, her daughter will miss her turn too. Does that mean that Gloria cannot ever have these needs to be cared for met? Not necessarily, but it is better for Gloria's children if they are not called on to be the caretakers. Glorida found an appropriate remedy by asking her husband if they could "take turns waiting on each other." If Gloria had sat back in her chair and demanded her turn without being willing to give back some nurturing, she would not only have been disappointed, she may also have been abandoned as she alienated those around her. Yes, Gloria's mother recieved more than her fair share, but that does not mean that Gloria, for having paid the price, will now be able to get a full share. Still, coming from nothing, Gloria has consoled herself by focusing on the 50% improvement in her circumstances.

A naturally nurturing child with a very needy parent is bound to take over parenting the parent. These children commonly had to be caretakers both for their parents and other siblings at a very young age. It goes without saying that they also had too much responsibility for themselves. Children will rise to the occasion; they really have no choice. It is a question of survival. They were stressed and exhausted, but they kept putting one foot in front of the other and got through it. Many looked forward to the time they could get out of the house and leave all that responsibility behind.

The superresponsible ones often postpone children for a while, feeling as if they have already raised one family. But even when they wait, they may find themselves not "up to the task." It is hard for any new parent to anticipate the utter dependence and demandingness of small children. Once the child is born, the only escape is emotional or physical withdrawal. The ACODF parent may feel like he will drown if he doesn't get away.

◆ JUDY—DROWNING IN INTIMACY

There was no doubt that Casey was difficult, but then everyone had warned Judy that boys are difficult and her brothers hadn't been easy either. It was impossible to write up her evaluations when Casey was at home, and she had to extend his day-care hours. At first she faithfully went to get him when her written work was done for the day, taking him along on her errands. But at every parking lot he would get away from her and run out in front of cars; in the shops he would pull things off the shelves; or if she put him in a cart he would stand up and try to jump out. When she tried to do any business that required talking to anyone he would either yank on her arm and scream at her the whole time, or quietly disappear, sometimes exiting the store and wandering into the street. She felt as if she wanted to chain him to her, and whenever they were at home she would either lock him into the house or lock up the fence so he couldn't leave the yard.

One day as she headed for the day-care center she realized that she could get her afternoon chores done in half the time if she didn't pick Casey up until afterward. Then she discovered that the less time Casey spent at home, the fewer things he could pull out and throw around the house. Carl had been complaining about what a mess the house was all the time and it had been getting her down. She decided to let Casey stay at day-care eight hours a day, vowing she would start picking him up earlier again when she got caught up.

Casey started going through another "bad stage." He would cling and scream when she left him and hit her when she came to get him, saying he didn't want to go home with her. Judy would often find the teacher scolding Casey when she arrived, and the teacher seldom had anything positive to say about him.

There was trouble at church school too. Judy hadn't wanted to be Casey's teacher, but she couldn't get anyone else to take his class. She tried to persuade Carl to come help with the Sunday school class but he often felt he had to work weekends to keep up with his job and said he just couldn't do any more. Casey couldn't bear to have Judy pay attention to the other kids in the class and would do whatever he could to keep her attention on him. This included hitting her or the other kids, refusing to do the scheduled activity and creating a mess instead, or running out of the classroom building so that Judy had to abandon the other kids to go after him. It was maddening.

One day the minister came and told Judy that a woman had quit the church because she didn't want her daughter to be in a class with Casey. Judy was hurt, exhausted, and bewildered. She became genuinely worried that there was something wrong with Casey. Yet, when she tried to discuss this with Carl, he insisted that Casey was just "all boy" and he would grow out of it. Judy pointed out that Carl hadn't been around much lately and maybe he was mistaken about Casey's behavior. Maybe he was "more boy" than most. Carl shrugged.

But Carl didn't act so calm about Casey's behavior when they were at home. Carl would play with him for about a half hour each night, then lose patience with him, and either blow up or retreat to the garage. He turned more and more of Casey's care over to Judy. After being with Casey in the late afternoon, Judy felt all used up and wanted Carl to put Casey to bed. But Carl always had something more important to do.

(Continued this chapter)

Judy is feeling overwhelmed by Casey's needs. She wants to get her errands done without a major struggle, but she has taken an all-or-nothing stand. It felt so good to be independent that she is escaping her problem with Casey's demandingness. She needs to learn to set reasonable limits so that she doesn't have to resort to rejecting Casey outright. Casey senses her need to get away from him and it frightens him. He shows her what he thinks of her new policy by getting angry at her—by hitting her and saying rejecting things when she comes to pick him up. Of course, this only makes Judy wish she hadn't come for him at all. They are caught in a self-reinforcing downward spiral that interferes seriously with their ability to become close.

How does the healthy, secure parent cope with the needs of small children? For one thing, she probably learned about setting reasonable limits from her own parents, and can keep demands at a more manageable level. For another, her initial emotional response to her child is more relaxed. When the child cries, it is perceived as a communication rather than a demand. The mother seeks to find out the cause of discomfort. The ACODF parent, who inevitably has a much more nervous disposition, may not be able to control the initial feeling of panic when the child cries. Then her own fear, anxiety, and uncertainty is communicated to the baby through her tense muscles, and the baby's discomfort becomes anxiety in response to the mother. Hence, a cycle of anxiety and tension between Mother and Baby is set into motion.

But some ACODF parents have the opposite problem with intimacy. Their childhood unmet need for closeness causes them to be so intimacy-starved that they try to hold their children too close. Some children are not cuddly from birth and almost all children reach a time in their second or third year when they want less physical contact with Mom or Dad. Parents who try to hug and kiss a child who wants to be on the go will also experience rejection. If they override the child's need to be more separate and insist on physical closeness, the child may cooperate temporarily but will experience his parents as suffocating. When he is older and has a choice he is likely to flee his parents' presence.

TOO CLOSE

Healthy intimacy involves being able to merge with others at moments and then return easily to ourselves. However, many ACODF were forced to be excessively close to their parents and were not allowed the time or emotional space to form their own identities. They merged with the parent in a half-developed way, with parent and child creating one whole (as overly close married couples sometimes do). The ACODF grows up as a half person with the need to seek another half to merge with. Even when she is married, she may form an unhealthy symbiotic relationship with her child because closeness with her child may seem less threatening than closeness with her spouse would be. Symbiosis is appropriate between mother and infant, but when the child starts becoming independent at age two and the parent blocks that independence, symbiotic closeness is unhealthy. The parent unconsciously (or sometimes blatantly) gives the child the message, "You need me. Without me you won't be safe." If the child has a dependent-type personality, he or she will be very vulnerable to an invasive mother. By contrast, if that same child were raised by healthier, more secure parents, they would gently push the child toward being more independent, all the while being supportive and saying through words and actions, "You can handle it."

Some ACODF parents become so close to their children that they cannot allow the child to have a separate identity. They simply project all their preferences and fears onto the children. "I was always afraid of thunder, too," the parent announces proudly. He screws up his face as he feeds the baby spinach and then feels some secret satisfaction when the child spits it out. "What do you mean you don't like strawberry ice cream?" he asks, sounding as if he has been insulted. The child soon learns that Daddy's approval hinges on her close imitation of all of Daddy's likes and dislikes.

Uncertain parents are also drawn to the lure of being needed.

Making themselves slaves to their childrens' every need is so absorbing that they can forget their aching loneliness. Many mothers become compulsively preoccupied with what is best for their children and use this as a way to postpone their own growth. The mother plans to improve her appearance, finish her degree, or look for a job when the children are older, but the thought of taking these steps toward her own independence is so threatening that she will keep moving the deadline farther and farther away. "When they're all out of diapers," she'll say. "When the last child goes to school . . . then, oops! I'm pregnant again . . . maybe five years from now."

TOO DISTANT

Because ACODF had no adequate role models they have difficulty determining how much time child-rearing takes. Even the healthy parent will underestimate this. It takes many years of parenting to fully appreciate how personally strong you have to be to raise children. When the ACODF parent finally realizes how much the child needs from him or her, there can be an overwhelming desire to escape. A respectable retreat is career or volunteer work. Work serves many purposes in the struggle to avoid intimacy. A child cannot reject, on a personal level, a dad who is never at home. Dad does not have to deal with the feelings of jumpiness that emerge when the child is cranky and in need of calming attention. He has a societally sanctioned reason for not being with his children. Dad can justify that he is being a better parent by providing more material goods, or Mom can overvolunteer as she "makes the community a better place for the child to grow up in."

◆ CARL—RUNNING FROM INTIMACY

To hear Carl tell it, he came from a "Father Knows Best" family. His mother, a former home economics major who had dropped out of college to marry his father, had "been there" for Carl throughout his childhood. She cooked wholesome meals, kept a clean house, and occasionally scolded him gently. His father, a college graduate with a good job working for a secure corporation, had taken him hiking, camping, and hunting. Other weekends he would let Carl help out on home repairs, learning the homecrafts a man would need.

But, in contrast to this idyllic description, there had been problems in Carl's father's family; his father's brother was alcoholic and Carl recalled that everyone said Grandpa drank too much too. His father's sister had been crippled by an accident as a child and required a lot of her parents' time. Later, she was dependent on her brothers (but the drinking brother was never around so the responsibility for her had fallen on Carl's father.) Carl's family led a very orderly existence. Their daily schedule was predictable and he could even remember what they had had for dinner every Monday night, because it was always the same. They took their family vacation to the same place at the same time every year.

But Carl wasn't close to his father. He never seemed to quite measure up to his father's expectations. Other family members told Carl how stubborn and independent he was as a child, but all he could remember was that he never seemed to win any confrontation with his father. His happy childhood memories centered around time spent with his friends. When he tried to remember his experiences at home, his mind would come up blank. He only had the vaguest impressions; one couldn't even call them feelings. He believed his mother loved him and possibly even favored him over his two sisters, but he didn't think his father liked him much.

Carl's college education was interrupted when he became a father at age twenty, and further delayed when he had another child at age twenty-two and a third at age twenty-four. He had thought his girlfriend, Trina, was taking care of birth control; she had thought he was. He was overwhelmed with college, fatherhood, and a job. Every night he came home tired, needing some support, but his wife was always busy with the baby, and there was always a baby. He coped by drinking a six-pack of beer or getting stoned, but after six years finally decided to leave before there was a fourth baby to make him feel even more guilty.

Unlike Trina, Judy (his second wife) was a planner. When Carl was too paralyzed with guilt to arrange a visit with his kids, she took care of it. She convinced him to finish his graduate degree and she typed his papers. She was dependable and solid. He had never expected her to fall apart from having just one child. Suddenly she was whiny and dependent, asking him to make decisions about Casey when he didn't have any idea what to do about him. She was the one with the psychology background.

In Carl's mind, Casey just didn't seem much different from his other boys. True, he was aggressive and stubborn. That kid could make him furious sometimes—no one had ever made him so angry. He certainly didn't want to spend more time with him until Judy had him behaving better.

All Carl knew was that he certainly didn't have the time or energy to help. He needed help himself. He worked sixty- and seventy-hour weeks, suffered jet lag from traveling every week, and then Judy wanted him to teach Sunday school or take care of Casey. It wasn't fair for her to expect him to do half her work.

He was back in the same rut again. He was working like a dog for his family and no one appreciated it. When he returned from a trip she would jump on him right away about how she was exhausted and needed a break from Casey. If she wasn't after him to take care of Casey, she was trying to talk him into blowing a whole Sunday at the beach. As if he had time for such things.

His only salvation was the company trips he took. He looked forward to the long plane rides, even though the time changes wore him out, because he could at least be alone for awhile. Judy complained of loneliness. He'd like to try loneliness for awhile. Or frittering away afternoons in the park while the dishes stood unwashed. She didn't know how lucky she was.

(Continued in Chapter 7)

Carl obviously deals with his fear of intimacy by getting as far away as possible. Even when he is at home, his fears seriously impair his ability to relax or play with Casey. Like other ACODF parents, Carl probably feels the pull of his child's attempt to bond, and fears "losing himself" in the moment. To play is to let go, but any loss of emotional control can be extremely threatening to an ACODF. To begin with, they have usually had far too few actual play experiences when they were small. Because play was discouraged in their childhood homes, they now feel guilty if they "waste time" playing. The only play that feels at all comfortable is very structured play. They "teach the baby to read" as a form of recreation or sign the boys up for soccer so that they will learn team skills. An open afternoon playing in the yard would feel somewhat frightening. Father might ask himself, "But what will we *do* for all that time?" Soon he will be out in the yard exhorting his son to rake the leaves. Still, structured fun such as sports and games may be the easiest to approach initially. Games can be a stepping stone to spontaneous fun, if the ACODF can let go of competitive feelings. Don't worry about winning, play for the fun of it! Then move on to more casual activities that provide opportunities for conversation. Paint with your child, walk the dog together, play house and let your child be the parent while you play baby.

However, be careful not to structure out intimacy. Often entire families keep up a frantic schedule that provides a socially acceptable excuse for never having a meal together. Either every family member goes his or her separate way, running into each other infrequently like "ships passing in the night," or the whole family becomes compulsively involved in some activity. For example, some families deeply involved in their church may be together constantly but there is always an audience of other congregants present. Gung-ho skiiers or "party families," who perpetually have extra people around, also manage to schedule out intimacy while looking all-American healthy. Children who have grown up in such families are often very confused. They feel this horrible sense of loneliness, but Mom and Dad were always there (and so was Aunt and Uncle, the cousins, the neighbors, and sometimes passers-by). How could they be lonely? What is wrong with them? Each child feels crazy and doesn't express the need for time alone with the parents because he or she is certain he or she is the one to blame. Everyone else looks like they're having such a good time. Scheduling the kids for a million activities also relieves the parent of the guilt they feel for not being there for the kids emotionally, for they too feel the loneliness in quiet moments.

Parents need to be able to "just be" with their children. Children wait for such spaces to ask important questions or tell fears and joys. To feel safe enough to reveal intimate thoughts, we each need to sense that there will be time to finish the talk. No one wants to open up their vulnerable places if they have reason to believe the talk will end abruptly with their tender insides exposed. Children function mainly on an intuitive level. They may not know what is bothering them on a rational, explainable level. When one relaxes totally, unconscious messages can be heard. Parents who can relax with their children are privileged to hear the child's innermost thoughts.

THE CHILD WITHIN

At first it may be very difficult to relax with your child. True play seems to draw from the unconscious, and for many ACODF, awareness of unconscious messages is very frightening. Having grown up in an environment that made denial and repression essential defenses, all those hurt, lonely, and scary feelings have been locked away in the unconscious. Really giving yourself to the experience of play is bound to start releasing those feelings and images. The longer these feelings have been bottled up inside of you, the more wrenching it will be when they are released. Just being fully in the presence of your young child will remind you of that time in your life and bring up contrasting images. You may even find yourself feeling jealous and impatient with your child. You think of how little attention or play time you had and maybe you feel as if your child is not appreciative enough. Right in the midst of giving attention to your child, you may remember the attention you never received and feel weepy. You may see yourself as a young, vulnerable, neglected or abused child and find that you feel compassionate for yourself for the first time. You might have hated that child within you before because that child carried the emotional component of your being and without him you would never have had to hurt. In the past, you might have denounced that child within you as a self-pitying cry-baby that should straighten up and not be so sentimental. In fact, you may have done such a good job scaring him into silence that you must now actively coax him out of hiding. Be as gentle with your child-within as you are with your real child in your best moments. As you learn to nurture yourself and permit the relaxing joy of play, you will also become gentler and more responsive to your real child. The ACODF who have the hardest time playing, have the greatest need to play.

Not only do we need to allow ourselves to play, we need to allow ourselves to *need.* If our parents were distant and preoccupied with their own problems, they discouraged us from expressing our needs or making demands. We probably learned, at a very young age, that our parents were not willing to meet our needs and it hurt less just to deny that we had them. We did our best to meet our own needs for physical care and reprimanded ourselves for having emotional needs. Now, we are far from being able to recognize that we have emotional needs even as adults. Interacting with our vulnerable, needy children reminds us of our needy child-self and our unmet adult needs, and that is threatening.

DEPENDENCY NEEDS

Family inevitably creates conflict over dependency needs and this is an even greater source of anxiety for ACODF. Everyone in the family has needs. Whose needs should have priority? Many ACODF parents put their needs last, believing that is what is best for the child. But it is a paradox. If you have unmet needs from childhood, you really have to meet those needs before you can fully meet the needs of your child. Naturally, you can't just forget about taking care of your children for a while. Your children have needs of their own from the day they are born, and will go on having them day-in and day-out. But lower your expectations for yourself as caretaker until you are feeling stronger. Just meet your children's most basic needs and let the rest go while you save some of your nurturing energy for yourself.

"I'm over the starved-child stage," states Raylea. "I've eaten enough meals." Raylea, who has been giving herself permission to get more involved in career, feels she has been meeting her needs for power and effectiveness, but still neglects her need to be nurtured. She doesn't take enough time off just to relax. When she first experimented with trying to combine relaxing with "being there for the children," it did not work for her. But Raylea persisted and eventually discovered that doing art projects with her children helped them all relax and feel nurtured. Now she can genuinely enjoy these moments with her children.

Before an ACODF learns to really let go and play, play is just something else they are trying hard to achieve. "Sometimes I don't feel the children's needs are being met and I do feel guilty about that," said Raylea. Raylea and her husband, Ken, reached a critical point in their marriage and, on top of Raylea's increased career demands, she and Ken had to take a lot of time out to work on their relationship. "The kids are sort of left on the sidelines waiting for Mom and Dad to get it together and be able to pay attention to them again. I'm afraid of repercussions in years to come as they recall when Mom and Dad were all wrapped in their own conflict." However, if Raylea and her husband stopped working on their relationship and put the kids' needs first, the kids would not learn how to resolve conflict in an adult relationship.

MOVING CLOSER ONE STEP AT A TIME

As you gain emotional strength, you will gradually be able to spend more and more time with your child. If you have avoided closeness with your child for a prolonged period, it can take a long time to reestablish an atmosphere of trust. Take your time. Try to move so slowly that you will not have a need to draw back. At the same time, keep in mind that your readiness and willingness is not the whole answer. If you and your child have not spent time alone together talking about sensitive subjects, you cannot expect an immediate warm response from your child. He or she will probably be cautious and suspicious. The child will be afraid to trust, afraid to believe in your apparent change of attitude.

Imagine that you are taming a gentle wild animal. In the well-known children's book *The Little Prince*,[1] the prince decides to befriend a fox. He comes to the same spot, at the same time each day, so that the fox can learn to trust and look forward to the little prince's coming. On each consecutive day the prince sits a few feet closer to where the fox stands than he had the day before. In time he tames the fox and then the fox reminds him: "You are responsible forever for what you have tamed."

Keep these principles in mind when you try to build your child's confidence in you so that intimacy feels safe. Take it in small steps. First try doing something structured with your child—something that does not demand you be in intimate conversation. Play catch, board games, or simply read to your child. By relaxing together you and your child will become more and more comfortable with each other. Let your attention drift away from the game, or discuss the characters in the book you are reading. After small talk, you might try sharing a childhood memory where you felt very vulnerable or very happy. Without probing aggressively, ask your child how he or she feels about what happened in the story, or about his or her own friends at school. Whatever your child says, don't lecture, criticize, debate, or advise. Just listen and accept. Repeat to your child what you think he or she meant or felt and then ask the child if you have understood him or her correctly. In this way you will slowly build the atmosphere and relationship needed for true intimacy.

You may need to approach touching in the same way. If you have not been affectionate with your child in the past, the normal parent/child touching may be uncomfortable for both of you at first. You might have an aversion to touching that comes from being physically abused, or you may lack the ability to cuddle with your child because your parents did not cuddle with you. Try sitting near each other as you read to the child. Some children are very abrupt in their movements and need to be taught how to touch gently. Model warm, safe touching by moving slowly from sitting or standing near the child to slipping an arm around the child. If the child is preadolescent, tousling his or her hair is a nice way to show affection without being overbearing. As you grow closer in your relationship, touching will begin to feel more natural and less threatening for both of you.

Most ACODF have a strong set of defenses that can be as impenetrable as a brick wall. You must be able to let down your defenses before you can be intimate. The heavily defended person is often critical and hostile in order to keep others at a safe distance. Before you can move beyond your child's protective shield, you must first allow your child beyond the buttressed gate to your most vulnerable self, by reigning in the guard dogs that would frighten him or her. You may need to keep reminding yourself to be warm, open, and vulnerable. Contact with other parents and children in a supportive atmosphere such as church, scouts, Sierra Club, or other caring low-key environments will reinforce your newly developed intimacy skills. Seek out places where you feel safe and accepted so that you can enlarge your capacity to be unguarded. Select people who treat you respectfully and warmly and avoid those who are harsh or critical.

If you have the opposite problem—that you want far more closeness than your children or mate are able to give—you may need to supplement your family relationships by cultivating a strong network of close friends. Remember that no one person can meet all your needs for intimacy. If you are a single parent you probably have many intimacy needs that are going unmet. It will be difficult to resist expecting too much from your children, but this is when you need to be most cautious. Join support groups such as Parents Without Partners, Adult Children of Alcoholics, Bible study groups, or even exercise classes that make after-class socializing easy. Begin by establishing many casual friendships so that you don't overwhelm a new friend with your needs. Then gradually test out these relationships until you feel like you have gathered enough supportive people around you not to feel so needy anymore.

Whether you fear intimacy or hunger for it, surround yourself with as much love and positive energy as you can so that you will not need to be stingy with your love. Bank as much support as you can so that you can give to your child out of abundance.

◆ ═══════════════ S U M M A R Y ═══════════════ ◆

In order to establish the most healthy level of intimacy with our children we need to become objective about our own needs for closeness. We should always have friends our own age that we can rely on so that we are not tempted to lean too heavily on our children.

◆ ═══════════════ P O I N T S ═══════════════ ◆

1. It is important to have flexible boundaries within our families that respect individual rights and differences while allowing healthy interdependency and closeness.

2. The parent/child relationships within the family become the central models for intimacy. If parents are too distant or too close the child will imitate this model (or its polar opposite) in his or her later adult relationships.

3. To grow up healthy, children must be free to love both parents. When there are problems in the parental relationship parents must be very careful not to push the child to take sides.

4. Instead of passing our "intimacy hunger" on to our children by seeking their approval and demanding inappropriate closeness with them, we must find adult friends to meet our emotional needs.

5. If we find we are "burnt-out" on intimacy before our children are born, we must struggle against our excessive need for distance so that our children do not feel unwanted.

6. As parents we must consider our own needs as well as our children's. None of us can give from an empty well.

7. If we have already avoided intimacy with our children for a long time, we will need to be patient. Children cannot learn to trust overnight, but our gentle steady efforts will eventually win back their hearts.

NOTES

1. Antoine de Saint-Exupéry, *The Little Prince.* New York: Harcourt, Brace & World, 1943. Even though this is a "children's book," it is a beautiful book about relationships which has a lot to say to adults.

7

CRISIS LIFE-STYLE

5. ACODF have little experience anticipating problems and are often too impulsive to make careful, considered judgments.

6. ACODF have difficulty determining how much time child-rearing takes and consequently become stressed-out.

In troubled homes, periods of unemployment, frequent moves, and abandoned plans routinely create stress and an unsettling and unstable atmosphere for children. The adrenaline rush of crisis and stress feel normal to these children, and as adults they will have difficulty recognizing tension as a possible cause of problems. As children they were not taught to plan ahead and as parents they have trouble managing their own lives, let alone the lives of their children. If they feel tense, instead of suspecting that they have tried to take on too much, they will assume they are weak and deficient. If they go into therapy, they initially seek ways to cope with the chronically stressful life they have created **rather than trying to prioritize their commitments and let some go.** They are sure that all the normal people are capable of what they can't handle and in some ways they are right. Anyone who has grown up in a dysfunctional family is often already "used up" by the time they become adults. They have not learned how to replenish their energy along the way, and until they do, they will never be able to function as efficiently as those who had solid, dependable parenting.

As we mentioned in Chapter 2, many dysfunctional families also have hereditary problems such as hyperactivity or mood disorders. The depressed mother with few learned coping skills, who must care for a hyperactive child, will be far more stressed than the healthy mother caring for a child with a normal activity level.

◆ JUDY'S FAMILY GHOSTS

Mrs. Bronson, the director of Casey's day-care center, asked Judy and Carl to come in for a conference. Carl was out of town so Judy went alone. The director said that several of the parents had threatened to take their children out of the school unless they were transferred out of Casey's class. She wondered if Judy knew why Casey was so disturbed.

Judy talked about the move and Carl's increasing absence. Mrs. Bronson interrupted to say she had noticed bruises on Casey—did he fall frequently? Judy explained that he was always in motion, bumped into things, and fell down often, but he wasn't a crier and would just bounce back up again. (It was one of the things Judy especially liked about him.) Mrs. Bronson asked Judy if she had considered trying gentler means of discipline.

Judy suddenly realized what the director was getting at. She felt furious and trapped. The woman was being very cautious with her. Judy remembered being on the other side of these conferences when she was on the Child Study Team in Denver.

Judy carefully replied that she thought she disciplined him appropriately—that she would confine him to his room. (She also knew that she had often had to drag him kicking and screaming to the room and they had had to install an outside lock to keep him in it. He would hurl himself against the door and throw himself around the room. She knew she might have bruised him getting him to his room, or he might have bruised himself thrashing around, but she didn't dare point this out to the director. She had never struck, never even spanked him, although he had kicked and bruised her many times.)

Mrs. Bronson began asking Judy about the family background. Judy truthfully replied that her parents had been alcoholics, proudly adding that she herself didn't drink. The director asked if anyone had had school problems and Judy admitted that all her brothers had had trouble with school but only one was a fighter. When the director suggested that perhaps Judy shouldn't let Casey watch so many violent shows, Judy hotly informed her that Judy and her husband were educated people and did not watch much television. They certainly didn't let their son watch violent shows.

Mrs. Bronson took Judy down the hall to watch Casey's class through a two-way mirror. Casey flew around the room bopping the other children on the head with a toy car. The teacher was busy with a small group of children up to their elbows in clay. The director motioned toward Casey and explained that they didn't have enough staff to assign an aid to Casey and he seemed to need constant monitoring. She suggested Judy have him evaluated and consider shortening his day.

Judy felt sick to her stomach. It was like ghosts coming to haunt her. She didn't get drunk. She didn't neglect him. She didn't hit him. She fed him nutritious food and refused him junk food. She got him to bed on time. What more could she do? The day-care center didn't look like a good place for Casey, but she was afraid she would crack under the strain if she spent more time with him at home. She had been marshaling all her energy every day to treat him calmly and kindly, even when he was kicking her and screaming at her. But she just couldn't do it for more hours a day.

Judy decided to try changing schools. There were certain things she had always known about keeping Casey calmer. He liked predictability. She looked for a school that was highly structured and was pleased with the routine at the Montessori School. Judy was frank about Casey's previous problems and she questioned the Montessori director closely to make sure they wouldn't give up on Casey if he had trouble adjusting to the new system. The Montessori director said that they had worked with children like Casey before and they understood it could take a while. Besides, they gave all children a sixty-day trial period. Judy was sure that Casey could adjust to anything given sixty days to do it, so she gave notice at his day-care center and moved him the next Monday. Ten days later the Montessori director called her early one afternoon and told her to come get Casey. They simply couldn't handle him.

(Continued this chapter)

In a sense Judy has created this crisis by pulling away from Casey as we saw in Chapter 6. Casey is a difficult child by nature, more active than the average child and probably more sensitive. He would require more attention than the average child needs under the best of circumstances. Judy's life has been so full of struggles and changes that she does not even recognize that she and her family are under great stress. They have moved to a new location where they do not have established friends. In Denver, networking with other mothers, Judy would have had access to information that could help her pick the best preschool for Casey. But friends are not available to Judy now—either as advisors or as temporary child-care sources. Judy and Carl are both adjusting to new jobs, and Casey, too young to understand what "moving" means, has just lost all the familiar people in his life, save his parents. Dad has been increasingly absent and Mom is pulling away too. Casey has actually done what he needed to do to insure his survival. He has gotten himself thrown out of preschool back into his mother's arms.

Another mother might have seen this coming, but Judy feels Casey's need for her is an inexplicable and unfair low blow of fate. Her expectations for Casey's level of independence are based on her own distorted childhood memories. By age six she was helping care for her younger brother and getting herself ready for school. Why would Casey, almost four years old, need so much attention from her? Why can't Judy work, adjust to a new town, volunteer at the church, and care for one child? Instead of using this crisis as *useful information* about her particular child's needs at this critical time,

Judy blames herself for being so "weak" and her child for being so "dependent."

UNREALISTIC PLANS AND EXPECTATIONS

Because they did not grow up in child-centered homes, parents from dysfunctional families of origin cannot judge how much time child-rearing actually takes. They typically try to go on with all their former activities despite their new, tremendously time-consuming job of raising a child. Their own parents probably failed to set aside adequate time to carry out their parenting tasks. Perhaps the parents cut corners by never signing their children up for enriching activities or attending school functions. The next generation, now trying to parent, must determine how much is reasonable and healthy to give to their children.

At the same time, ACODF may not be capable of doing as much as parents raised in a healthy family can do. Unresolved emotional struggles drain their energy every day, and the constant stress of evaluating choices wears them down in ways that don't affect the child who has been raised in a healthy family. When the adult child from a healthy home is too tired to think, she can fall back on what her parents did and be reasonably sure that it won't do too much harm. But the adult child raised in a disruptive home can never relax into "whatever solution comes to mind first" without worrying about the potentially destructive effect. Parenting from scratch, they often must think through hundreds of decisions daily, especially with the first child. If the parent cannot rely on a spouse or supportive structure such as school or day-care to relieve the burden, the tension can become paralyzing.

◆ JUDY AND CARL IN CRISIS

As she drove Casey home from the Montessori School, Judy worried about the thirty evaluations that were due Monday. The Denver house had still not sold and they would have to borrow money if she lost her job. She was irritable and wanted to cry. Casey was looking tremendously pleased that she had come early for him. As she reached over to undo his seat belt Casey grabbed her around the neck and pulled her toward him to give her a big hug. An intense pain shot up Judy's back and she broke out in a cold sweat. Still bent over, she pushed herself out of the car. When she tried to straighten she was paralyzed with pain. Even walking doubled-up sent a shooting pain up her back as she took each step. She slowly made her way to the door and into the house. Casey followed quietly behind her, frightened by his mother's behavior. As she flopped onto the bed he hovered near her and asked if she was going to be all right. She could see how afraid he was and wanted to reassure him, so she whispered that she would be OK now. He ran toward her and before he could even touch her, a pain shot up her back in anticipation. She screamed, "Don't touch me!" and he ran from the room.

Judy couldn't move out of the bed. When Carl came home she asked if he could stay home a few days until she could get back on her feet. He said that was impossible but he would see if he could find another school for Casey. The next day Carl couldn't get away from work for even a half hour. His desk was piled high with work that had accumulated while he was out of town. And so it went for the rest of the week.

Judy's reports were late, but she had taken no sick days before so she managed to keep everything on hold for a couple of weeks. Judy frantically telephoned schools from her bed and found that everyone had long waiting lists. Casey would sit by her crying and whining saying he hated school and he just wanted to stay home with his mommy. Everytime he tried to climb on her lap she'd get another shooting pain. The more she needed him to stay away from her, the more he needed to be close to her. He was content just to be allowed to lie in her bed with her and she got through half the day that way. But the time came when she had to face giving notice at work.

After that her mood dropped drastically each day until she could not even convince herself to get out of bed to eat. Casey made himself peanut butter and jelly sandwiches and poured himself drinks. She knew the kitchen must be an incredible mess. She'd had Carl bring the TV into the bedroom and she and Casey just sat and watched cartoons. She would cry and sleep. Carl was disgusted with her and complained bitterly about how all this chaos was affecting his job performance. He told her she better go to a doctor and see what was wrong with her. She knew what was wrong with her. She was depressed, just as her mother had been, and she doubted anyone could help her. She thought about killing herself, but there would be no one to take care of Casey. Carl had worked a full day, every day, throughout this crisis. She thought about killing Casey too, because he probably had the same mood disorder and there was no one who seemed willing to put up with him.

As a last-ditch effort she opened the phone book and called a counseling center. She had nothing to lose. She could live one more day and see if there was anyone to help them. She could always kill herself tomorrow.

(Continued in Chapter 7)

The parent who has grown up in a dysfunctional home has a lot of difficulty judging just how much activity she can handle, and equal difficulty deciding how much stress her child can handle. The process of discovering her limits is often prolonged and painful, because every time she feels overwhelmed she doesn't think about lowering her work load. Instead she puts her problem-solving strategy into trying to find a way to "do it all." At this point, Judy should realize she needs more help from her husband and question his overcommitment to work. But Carl has similar behavior patterns. He has too little self-esteem to feel safe if he is not the number one producer at the office each and every day. And Judy has too little self-esteem to realize that she deserves some physical care. She has run her body down to the point where she can no longer function, and without hope of help from other sources, suicide is almost logical.

LOWERING EXPECTATIONS FOR EVERYONE

Obviously, **adult children of dysfunctional families need to learn time management, setting priorities, allowing for relaxation, and other coping techniques.** In the beginning, a good rule of thumb is to take on far less than you think you are capable of doing. You can always add on more volunteer projects, a part-time job, or an extra child later if you find you really have too much leisure time. However, that is not usually the case. An ACODF who cuts her commitments in half has probably just begun to approach a manageable level.

If you're having trouble getting down to a stress-free level, take a month's sabbatical leave from all plans. Pretend you are leaving town but stay home and think. If you work full-time, make a committment to work only forty hours a week for that month. If you work part-time, curb your impulses to stay after hours to get ahead on a few things. If your job requires setting up and cleaning up, consider that part of your work time. Just work (if you already have a job) and take care of the physical needs of yourself and your children. Refuse all plans unless they are open invitations to recreational activities where you are only expected to show up and play. (Even those should be kept down to about one a week.) And make no firm commitments. If the day arrives and it feels like a chore to go off on that church picnic, don't feel obligated to go.

Imagine that it is your birthright to receive instead of give for a while and assume that the only people you should give to are yourself, your spouse, and your children. (Even your mother and siblings can take care of themselves for one month.) Work the system around so that you have lowered not only what you expect of yourself, but also what others have come to expect from you. Train them to *expect nothing* of you and then if you have extra time and energy you can make an unexpected gift of your time and effort. But first get all the way back to start. Add on pressures one by one until you feel mild discomfort: then stop!

A tricky area where many determined ACODF fail to set limits is in demands made by friends. If you are used to spending time in a "problem exchange" with a friend, avoid this activity for the month. You might believe that you get rejuvenating energy from venting your dissatisfied feelings to a close friend, but this can be deceiving. **Discussing problems can sometimes become a negative addiction.** Try to avoid troubled friends for the month; their problems may be just too draining for you. Tell everyone you are taking time out to think about some changes you need to make. Rehearse what you will say if they call. Begin the conversation by saying you really don't have time to talk now, and after five minutes terminate the conversation with a promise that you will call when you have time next month. Remind yourself that you are not personally responsible to sustain or save them. You are only responsible to sustain *yourself*, and that is where all your energy should go during your "month off." Toward the end of the month spend some time reflecting on how much you actually get out of each relationship, compared to how much you give to it.

SETTING PRIORITIES

Healthy parents consider the effect each of their choices will have on their family. If they are thinking about going back to school for a higher education, they pace their course work so that it is not detrimental to the family's stability. If their children are small and need lots of support and attention, they resign themselves to getting their degree at a snail's pace. If they must get through school more quickly because the family desperately needs the added income they can bring in, they give up all volunteer activities to devote themselves to school. In short, they don't try to do it all. They decide what is most important right now and let the rest go until some future time when it is more feasible.

◆ BOB AND ANNA—STRONG ROOTS

Anna and Bob, who both work full-time while raising two children, are competent, confident adults. Yet, Bob is the child of divorce and Anna's father died when she was five years old. What brought them through these crises without serious damage?

Anna feels that family was a high priority for both sets of parents and she and Bob have inherited that value. Despite their personal difficulties, their parents were always there guiding them. The kids couldn't go out until the homework was done. They attended church regularly and the whole family participated in church activities. Although Bob and Anna do not attend church as adults, they feel confident about their ability to instill good values in their children. They are politically active and put their energy into social action, trying to make this a better world. Their two daughters, age eight and eleven, are developing a strong, clear sense of right and wrong. They believe that there are rules and one should follow the rules. Anna has taught them the golden rule as part of their socialization.

Anna sees herself as being very positive. She was recently listening to a friend's troubles and went home thinking how grateful she was that she had had such a carefree pleasant life. But then she stopped and thought, "Wait a minute! My dad died when I was five, I lived in a very troubled blended family for a while, my sister committed suicide . . . I've had my share of troubles!" Anna had also had a child unexpectedly while her husband was still in college and they had very little money, but she never seemed to skip a beat. She does have a special endurance. The message came across very strongly from her Mom: "You can be anything you want to be. Just go ahead and do it."

Anna's parents had married late in life and started their family when they were in their forties. Her father died in a car accident when she was five and her brothers were two and one. Anna's mother had been one in a family of eighteen children and her own father had died when she was in her twenties. She had raised her two younger brothers and was a strong, independent woman by the time she married and was later widowed.

Anna remembers her family as calm, stable, and supportive before her mother remarried when she was twelve. Although she didn't feel mistreated in her new family, she felt all the tension in her home caused by two families with very different styles coming together, as well as the crush of two extra people sharing their small house. Anna's mother and her stepfather worked through their differences and have a strong, stable marriage that has lasted twenty-three years. Recently, the family has been rocked by the tragic suicide of her stepsister. Apparently very depressed after her divorce, the stepsister disappeared from sight and took an overdose of barbiturates.

Although Anna's daughter Francie was only eight at the time of the stepsister's suicide, Bob and Anna did not hide the details. Naturally, Francie wanted to know why Aunt Laura had killed herself, and Anna was concerned that Francie would see this as a way to solve one's problems. She explained that her sister had been very very sad and had not gotten the help she needed to get over it. This explanation satisfied Francie, who commented, "It's like people who smoke even though everyone knows it's bad for your health."

What was Bob's childhood like before his parents divorced when he was fourteen? He remembers both his mother and father as being warm and loving to him. His family went fishing, camping, and boating together. His mother was happy with the role of wife and mother and even participated in the PTA. Like other fathers in the 1950s Bob's father worked long hours, but Bob felt his father was very responsive to him when he was at home. In Bob's mind, all the time his father spent with him was quality time. His childhood was balanced and stable.

When Bob's parents married, his father was seventeen and his mother was nineteen. Anna and Bob also see themselves as having married "young." Anna was nineteen and Bob was twenty. Anna had held off marrying Bob straight out of high school because she was going to college and wanted to see "what the wide world out there" offered. After one year she decided that there was no one she would love more than Bob and has been satisfied with her decision. Both sets of parents approved of the marriage because they trusted these two young people to go on developing themselves and saw the relationship as a very positive one.

Francie was conceived unexpectedly when Bob was in his sophomore year of college on the GI Bill. They had meant to wait until Bob had finished school, but they just took the pregnancy in their stride. "There really is no perfect time to have kids," Anna comments philosophically. "There is always some good reason to wait." She doesn't feel as though she or Bob have suffered for it. Bob had wanted to be a dentist but decided it required perfect grades and he wasn't the "perfect" type anyway. He finished his BA, got a good job, and is now getting top grades in graduate school, despite the delays and responsibilities of having two children. He is more satisfied with his well-rounded life that includes a family along the way. Anna had finished her BA before she got pregnant and was able to go on with her career. She doesn't feel as if she has missed any promotions because of her children.

But then, Bob has always been supportive. When they were first married, whoever got home first would make the dinner. When the baby came along Bob pitched in with parenting. Anna had six weeks' leave from her job and then Bob's summer break began. He took a few courses and was Francie's main caretaker for three months. Bob simply took Francie along in a back carrier. That time is a happy memory for Bob, who feels glad he had the chance to bond with his child, which so many other men have missed.

Anna has cultivated her mother's life attitude, which she describes as: "You've got to make the best of what life gives you. Don't fell sorry for yourself, just get on with it."

(Continued in this chapter)

Healthy families listen to their bodies and cut back when they feel stress mounting up. They can resist pressure from others to take on more, as well as internal pressure motivated by a false sense of guilt.

Last year Janice found herself directing the Sunday school, and running her daughter's Girl Scout troop, while her husband (who commuted two hours to work each way) took a major role on the church board and ran his son's soccer team. They were caught in a common trap facing parents today. With so many two-career families there is only a small pool of volunteer parents available to run these childrens' activities. But Janice's family is suffering from burn-out and she is beginning to look ahead and realize that her children may soon need her to work and earn money for their college tuitions. She has done more than her fair share and it's time to cut back. These are tough choices, but Janice is finally getting tough.

She has run both the Sunday school and the scout troop for three years now. It is time for someone else to take a turn. She has given notice to both and begun to consider how to better meet her own needs and the long-range needs of her family.

After streamlining their own schedules, each parent must take a critical look at activities available to the children. Children need to learn to set limits too, and being pushed to meet the demands of so many activities becomes training for leading an overstressed life. There is also a societal push toward quantity instead of quality. Can your child really do her best at piano, scouts, *and* soccer? Is she able to *enjoy* any of these activities or does she feel like she's been entered in the "stress olympics?"

How much of their stress can you handle? Seven-year-old Jessica was interested and talented in violin, dramatics, and gymnastics, and decided to join Brownies to be with her classmates. She seemed to be handling it all fine but her mother Nancy was becoming burnt-out and snappish driving her daughter to all these activities while trying to keep up in law school. With a guilty heart Nancy told Jessica that she was going to have to drop two of these activities. After a lot of agonized complaints Jessica dropped dramatics and gymnastics. Jessica found herself fiddling away the extra time prolonging her violin practice each day. She quickly began to climb from being a good violinist to being an exceptional one. With her overcrowded schedule no one had suspected that she had this much talent. The simple act of having to make a choice had alerted Jessica to how important violin was to her, and the empty space allowed her to act on this attraction. Before their "trimming back" exercise, Nancy had actually been considering pulling Jessica out of violin because she would argue about practicing. Apparently, even Jessica had been a little burnt-out and could have lost sight of an important part of herself in the shuffle.

Try to help everyone in your family set priorities by training them to question the effect of each proposed activity. They should consider whether they are truly interested in the activity or just responding to peer pressure. (This goes for Moms and Dads too!) What have they been doing with the time that would now be taken up by the new activity? Even if they had a "free" Saturday afternoon, one must examine carefully how the loss of unscheduled time will affect their quality of life right now. Was the time spent spontaneously with friends or family members, or in recreational reading and relaxing games, or perhaps simple housework that lessened distracting disorder? What will happen when that time is no longer available? How will the loss of time affect the individual and how will it affect the tension level and closeness of the whole family? Do the benefits outweigh these losses? In order for a family to become or remain healthy they must spend time together developing trust and intimacy. When activities interfere with these two vital functions, they are never worth the sacrifice.

ARE YOUR CHILDREN STRESSED OUT?

Here are ten symptoms of stress in children.[1] How many of these behaviors do you see in your child?

---◆---

Signs of Stress in Children

1. Is your child extremely shy or sensitive?
2. Is your child frequently moody or irritable?
3. Does your child have difficulty making friends?
4. Does your child have a "short fuse" or quick temper?
5. Does your child constantly whine and complain?
6. Is your child often withdrawn or preoccupied?
7. Does your child often complain of headaches, stomachaches, or other vague illnesses?
8. Has your child been very secretive or noncommunicative?
9. Has your child been very belligerent lately?
10. Does your child frequently have nightmares?

The greater the number of stress symptoms your child has, the more concerned you should be. If your child is showing any of these signs over a prolonged period of time (say three months), you need to begin to reduce the stress factors in his or her life. Even if these characteristics are part of your child's inborn temperament (see Chapter 14), he or she will respond well to lowered stress.

Cut back on scheduled activities and lower expectations for performance until the symptoms disappear. Then, after a several-month period of stability, try to add the activities back one at a time. Wait three to six months before you add each new activity. If you are anxious for him to try something different that you are sure he will enjoy, have him give up one of his current activities. As soon as you see signs of stress again, stop! Talk about this process with your child, and involve him in analyzing how much he can handle before he becomes stressed out.

TEACHING STRESS MANAGEMENT TO CHILDREN

Children are not "little adults." They don't reason like adults and they have a different sense of time. They function very much in the here and now. As they move toward adulthood they need to learn to plan ahead and to postpone gratification, but these concepts must be gradually and gently developed. You may already have experienced the frustration of telling your child what chores she needs to do to get her allowance and found that on allowance day nothing has been done yet. Unfortunately, however well-organized you are, giving your child a week's worth of tasks to do at her discretion is bound to end up in failure. A daily list is more useful. Tasks broken up into "before school" and "after school" chunks are better yet. And keep in mind that some children may only be able to handle *one* task at a time.

Children need to be taught step-by-step (one-bite-at-a-time) problem-solving so that life feels manageable. Without intervention children cannot "keep their room clean" on a daily basis so that it is already clean on allowance day. They will not learn that it's easier in the long run to put a few things away each day if you simply let them experience how overwhelming it is to clean up a week's mess on Saturday. Instead, they will learn how overwhelming (and depressing) it is to clean their rooms once a week. They need to *experience* a better alternative and *feel* the difference.

It's true that the close daily supervision needed to teach children one-bite-at-a-time methods is initially much more effort for the parent. Think of it as an investment. The time you take now to gently lead each child through new methods will pay off later as your more skilled children become able to take charge of their own tasks.

To solve the messy room problem, schedule routines that keep the room from getting out of hand. What can you do to make it easier for him to clean? If he has clothes all over the floor, give him a hamper in his room and tell him you won't go in to tuck him in until the clothes are in the hamper because you are afraid of tripping (this is stating an objective fact, not scolding or threatening him). If he has toys all over the floor tell him to pick out his favorite three and put all the others in a check-out box. When he wants one of the other toys, he has to put one of the three original toys in. Then he'll only have three toys to keep picked up. Then set aside a time each day to get caught up with that day's mess. Schedule this catching-up time so that it comes before a reward. For example, he must clean up his room before he watches TV, *not* "before he goes to bed."

What you say is critical to success here. "You better clean up that room or there will be no TV tonight," is an invitation to a power struggle. "Honey, hurry up and clean your room so you can watch some TV before dinner!" is a way to be on the same side as your child, with the "no TV" rule sitting out there as a "condition of life" that has to be gotten through like an occasional cold. After the child has repeatedly experienced how little effort it really is to clean up a daily mess, you can step back and let him fail to do this. Then when he has an overwhelming mess to deal with on Saturday, he already has experienced the pleasanter, more managable alternative. He can put it together himself that it was easier to do a little work every day than it was to confront all that mess at once. But he might still need your help the next week to get back on track. Move in, back off, test it out, and move in again if necessary.

Homework is another frontier for stress-management training. Long before your child gets to junior high, where he will have long-term assignments, he should have established a routine of doing his homework when his energy is high. Every child is different. Some come home from school so wrung out that they need a play break before starting homework. Others are still in "school gear" when they get home and can finish their homework in twenty minutes if they sit right down and get to it. Experiment with your child's schedule and discuss the results as you go. Point out to him that the same spelling lesson takes him fifteen minutes at 3:30, thirty minutes at 4:30, and two hours at seven o'clock. Talk about the fun things he could do with the extra hour and three-quarters if he does his homework at his best energy time.

Each person has his or her own way of getting overstressed and needs to find the best way to avoid getting stressed out. For some children, being with other kids too much is stressful, while others never seem to completely relax except when in a group. Help your child discover these things about him- or herself by observing and discussing, keeping in mind all the while that there are many right ways to do things, many paths to the same end.

TIME MANAGEMENT

Both you and your children need to organize your lives so that you have time for relaxation and rejuvenation as well as work and skill development. Have each member of your family make out a schedule for the week, and then for the month if you have meetings or outings that occur on a monthly basis. Now have each person go over his or her own schedule to check for hidden errors. For example, did you include the time it takes to get to and from work, school, or the activity named? That should be considered part of the time taken up by that activity. Have you included time spent at home on that activity—homework, practice, phone calling, papers brought home from work? Add that too. Did you schedule time to clean your room, make dinner, wash dishes, do laundry, mow the lawn, water the grass, pick up your socks or toys? Don't forget time for sleeping and eating. Did you schedule time to brush your teeth or take a bath? How about walking the dog or cleaning up after the cat's mistakes? Create an imaginary schedule time for every event or mishap that happens on a regular basis. Do you have a neighbor who stops by for "a minute" that turns into an hour at least twice a week? Did you allow time to put gas in the car or time to walk to the gas station if you regularly forget to get gas in your rush to get everything done? How about food shopping and the day-to-day errands to pick up all the items you missed when you were food shopping? Did you schedule for a cat, dog, child, or parent to need the doctor or dentist once a month? How about trips to the post office, shopping for gifts, assembling items for a science project? Think of every unexpected thing that created a crisis last month. You many find that some are really not so unpredictable.

When you've written down every obligation that comes up on a fairly predictable basis and allowed room for some unknowns, look at how much time is left for developing family intimacy, relaxing, or reflecting. How much of what you do is rejuvenating or fun? Do you allow any time to resolve conflicts between family members or ponder better ways to do things? Compare schedules. Do any of you have free time at the same time? What does this map of your present life say about your priorities? Consider the *quality* of the time you spend with various family members. For example, if you spend many hours a week driving kids to their various activities, you may feel as if you are devoting more than enough attention to the kids. However, **if none of this time you spend with them allows for intimate conversations or quiet appreciation of their accomplishments, they may *feel* neglected despite the sacrifices you are making.** Be realistic. Is the car filled with four other screaming kids? Do you generally leave so little time for the drive that you are tense the whole way, or is your child so tightly scheduled that she is doing her homework on her way to dance class? Is it even possible to turn this into time for intimacy?

If you cannot imagine when your family could sit down together to do this exercise, then you all probably need to consider the "thirty-day vacation at home" option. If no one wants to cooperate with making assessments and changes, then you will need a lot of support to get your family back on track. Seek a counselor or support group that affirms your healthy family values and goals. You will need to borrow some strength before you begin the arduous task of reeducating your family.

◆ BOB AND ANNA—THE TWO-CAREER FAMILY

So how do Bob and Anna manage to "do it all?" They lower their expectations for themselves and each other to a comfortable level, just like they spend only as much money as they have. Anna and Bob want to be financially secure, but neither one is dreaming about being "President of the Company." And the way the family has always shared the chores it is evident that no one's life or interests are considered less valuable than anyone else's in the family. When Bob was still in school and Anna provided the financial support, Bob did an extra share of the home responsibilities. Now that Bob is working and going to school, Anna and the girls have taken over most of the domestic chores. Who does what around the house was never determined by standard husband and wife roles. Instead, who does what is determined by who has time to do what. Everything is shared in a mature and truly equitable way, with the girls gradually taking on more and more responsibility as they grow older.

Anna, the family organizer *par excellence,* simply incorporated a baby into the daily routine when Francine was born. Bob remembers trying to play the "nice-guy" parent, but Anna had a "no-nonsense" approach from the start. She had friends who complained about having to play with their babies in the middle of the night, but Anna simply did not let it happen. If Francie wanted to cry after the feeding, that was her prerogative. Anna went back to bed. On the other hand, when Francie slept through to 4:30 A.M. and was too well-rested to go back to sleep, Anna adjusted her own schedule to accomodate Francie, starting her day at 4:30 too.

Anna knows her strong personality can make her a little too controlling. She is ready and willing to schedule every mintue of everyone's life in her family, but she is open to changes and suggestions. Anna sometimes feels impatient with her "dreamy" daughter Karen, but she realizes that Karen's apparent inattentiveness has its good side. Karen is introspective and able to entertain herself for hours, whereas Francie always needs company. Anna has realized that she must "relax her standards" a little for Karen.

Bob doesn't resist Anna's scheduling efforts unless she tries to take over his solitude time. He is not necessarily shy or timid; he merely prefers being alone to being in a group, although he can rouse himself to go to parties with Anna and even have a good time. Anna is extremely outgoing and has had to learn to let Bob have time alone. They have peaceably accepted these differences in one another and even value them. Anna sees herself as a little too hyperactive and appreciates the steadying tone of Bob, while Bob enjoys the social contact that Anna so easily brings into his life, content to listen to the conversation that she keeps stirred up around her. Now that Bob is thirty-five, he has learned to be more sociable and has even grappled with giving presentations in front of an audience because he knows it is necessary for him to get ahead. But given a free choice, he would keep to himself and his family without missing the world. Time to think is essential for him, and Bob is such a natural introvert that he has to watch out that solitude doesn't become withdrawal. A few years ago Bob got overinvolved with his bike riding and running and began to see too little of the kids. Anna gently pulled him back.

(Continued this chapter)

Bob and Anna manage their time so that it reflects their values. Everyone pitches in so that each person still has personal time. At the same time, saving time for intrafamily relationships is one of their highest priorities.

MONEY MANAGEMENT

Money, like time, must be managed if you want a life that is relatively crisis-free. Most dysfunctional homes fail to take a long range view of money needs. If your parent was paid monthly, you may remember running out of food by the end of the month. If pay was received weekly, you may remember Friday as "sky's the limit" day.

Many dysfunctional families live beyond their means or fall prey to impulse spending. If they take out a loan, they often fail to remember the considerable expense of interest. Buy now, pay later. They count on pay raises that have not been promised yet or surprise windfalls. Did you live in a home where the lights or phone were turned off because the utility or phone bill had not been paid?

Ruth remembers her mother's surprise every three months, when the property tax was due. Her mother was always running off to some relative to borrow enough money to "save the house," as if tax time were an unexpected crisis. Yet the taxes had been due quarterly for every one of the previous ten years. Ruth also remembers her mother's credit card routine. When they were totally out of money her mother would begin charging things. She had cards in both her maiden and married name so that she could charge up to twice her limit. Then back to the relatives she would go, begging them to lend her the money to get out from under these expensive debts.

Understandably, Ruth had an aversion to credit. She wanted to pay cash for everything and had trouble functioning in our credit society. For many years she resisted her husband's plans to buy a house, even though they could afford it and it was a sensible investment. When she finally gave in she was anxious for years. Still, she was too tight-fisted with money for her children. Although Ruth and her husband have a comfortable middle-class income, she often kept her children in clothes that were worn, stained, or too small. If the family went on an outing or trip, she compulsively insisted that they bring all their own food in a cooler because, in her mind, spending money at restaurants was courting bankruptcy. Ruth was stockpiling money for "unexpected emergencies," even though her husband was quite responsible about setting aside sums each month for recurring expenses. She was not able to begin to change her anxious money habits until she realized that her children's self-esteem was being affected by their shabby clothing and home haircuts.

◆ BOB AND ANNA'S SENSIBLE APPROACH

Money has never been a problem for Bob and Anna. *They simply keep their wants within their means.* Despite their difficult start raising children while Bob finished school, they now own a beautiful home and are very comfortable materially.

Bob can see the roots of financial stability in his early childhood. Every Friday evening his family would get in the car, drive to the bank to deposit Dad's paycheck, and go out to dinner. Everyone got their allowance after dinner. Saving money was a part of Bob's family plan. He was required to put half of his allowance into the bank each week to save up for big purchases. If Bob needed or wanted an expensive item, his parents created opportunities for him to earn money doing extra chores, or working on family projects like painting the house. He remembers the satisfaction he felt when he bought himself a ten-speed bike.

Anna's parents had both worked and established themselves before they married and started a family. Because they had been wise enough to have plenty of insurance, Anna's mother was able to stay at home and care for her children after the death of her husband. Anna does not remember being deprived either financially or emotionally.

The healthiest families live within their means and do set aside some money for emergencies or future needs such as retirement or college for the children. But they do not force an unreasonable poverty on their children. Money spent on the children's appearance or interests now may prevent high therapy bills later. On the other hand, healthy families do live by budgets and don't feel compelled to wardrobe their children in designer outfits. They budget first for fixed expenses—house payments, utilities, car payments, insurance payments, and a reasonable amount for food. Clothing, entertainments, and special foods or eating out are provided for after the necessities. Vacations aren't put on the charge card to be paid for next year, but instead the family saves what it can each month and takes the vacation they can afford on the amount they have accumulated.

Children can be involved in these money decisions. It is easier for a child to pass up an expensive toy, or seeing a popular movie for the second time, if he or she can see that these little sacrifices are contributing toward the fund that will put the family at the beach next summer.

Just as you examined your time priorities by looking at past patterns, you need to sort out your money priorities by taking a look at your checkbook. As a matter of fact, keeping little cash on hand is a good way to get a grip on where your money is going. If you pay for most things with checks you will have a thorough record of your expenses. Little notes at the bottom of checks written to variety stores will help sort out how much was spent on household necessities as opposed to clothing or frills such as music tapes. If your records from the past are too poor to give any reliable picture of your spending practices, be very conscientious over the next month about keeping track of expenditures. At the end of each errand trip, shopping day, or outing, write down what you spent on what. Your children might happily eat food brought from home if they are shown in dollars and cents what the expensive concession-stand food would cost and are told a more fun way the family can use the money. (Of course, your actual concern might be saving for a down-payment on a car, but all money spent is linked to the central problem of keeping a balanced budget. The kids can appreciate saving toward a trip or piece of sports equipment more than they can helping with the insurance payments.)

When analyzing your money habits, be scrupulous about your hidden costs and unreasoned priorities. How often do you resort to expensive fast food? Do you really need new mixing bowls because the old ones are stained? Have you budgeted for gas in the car? Vitamins and medications? Doctor bills or deductibles not covered by insurance? Lunch money for the kids? The inevitable breakdown of household appliances? As you become better and better at record keeping, you will be able to assess your money needs more and more realistically. Soon you will have no more disastrous surprises that exceed the amount you had set aside for emergencies.

Count only on actual income you have coming in on a reliable basis. If your ex-spouse fails to send the child-support payments two out of three times, this money should not be budgeted for necessities. If you can't pay the rent without it, rent a smaller place. Many people live contentedly on a meager amount while others feel strapped and victimized even though they have substantial income. It's all in the attitude and planning.

TIME TO REFLECT ON PARENTING

The way to avoid crises is to catch problems while they are small. But small problems are always subtle. A busy person will miss any warning signals. When you have grown up in crisis and have few learned skills for avoiding crises, you must spend a lot of time carefully considering alternatives and reassessing choices before you act.

So much of what you will do as a parent must be consciously decided. Others can rely on "instinct." What just "feels right" to the parent raised in a healthy family are tried and true parenting techniques that are passed down on an unconscious level. If you have grown up in a dysfunctional family, your unconscious has received a lot of destructive, unhealthy programming. You will have to think about everything you do in order to overcome that programming. That makes parenting a far more time-consuming job for you than it is for many other parents. You simply can't take anything for granted.

Not only do you need to keep demands low in terms of time, you need to guard against the stress of intensity. If you allow yourself to get all wound up in office politics or frustrating church projects, that precious time you have set aside to think about parenting each night might become polluted by the smog of relentless, stressful, circular and negative thoughts. Try to put yourself and your family first in your daily priorities so that your mind is clear and open by the day's end. Then think about what you can do to be a better parent tomorrow.

◆ ═══════════ **SUMMARY** ═══════════ ◆

One of the most important tasks we have as parents is teaching our children how to have the richest life possible given their unique talents and weaknesses. We need to help them learn how to plan ahead, anticipate problems, and keep their stresses and commitments at a manageable level so that they have a sense of being in charge of their own destinies.

◆ ═══════════ **POINTS** ═══════════ ◆

1. Child-rearing is stressful even for the healthiest of parents. ACODF come to parenting emotionally depleted and with few stress-reducing skills. They can become so exhausted that they suffer a physical or mental breakdown.

2. Frantic activity has often been a defense ACODF use to avoid feeling their pain. We may need to take a "month's sabbatical" from all activities in order to sort out how much activity we and our families can comfortably handle.

3. Because ACODF often become overcommitted, we need to learn to set priorities by deciding what tasks and commitments are most important and most fulfilling. This means we may need to drop out of some worthwhile activities.

4. By modeling low-stress living, setting limits on our children's commitments, and teaching our children to prioritize their activities, we can help our children learn low-stress life-styles for adulthood.

5. Often it is more time-consuming to teach our children self-care than it is simply to do the tasks for them, but our efforts will pay off in the feelings of mastery and confidence our children achieve for adulthood.

6. We must involve our children in planning and evaluating their own schedules. By teaching them to break tasks into manageable bite-size pieces, we help them experience the rewarding, self-fulfilling joy of success.

7. As we teach our children time-management, we must make sure they honor and schedule time for play, rest, and intimacy.

8. Learning to manage money is as important as learning to manage time. By giving our children steady allowances and involving them in family money decisions, we can teach them vital money-management skills.

NOTES

1. Adapted from Avis Brenner, *Helping Children Cope With Stress*, Lexington, MA: Lexington Books, 1984.

8

DEFENSIVENESS AND DENIAL

7. ACODF often fail to recognize a child's difficulties or other family problems, thus postponing any movement toward a solution.

8. ACODF are often so critical of others that they alienate all potential sources of support.

The new "positive thinking" philosophy of today tells us to look as if we are what we wished we were. We hire consultants to help us with our image. We "fake it" when we are shivering in our shoes. And no matter what our own attitudes are, we must compete against the false images of perfection that surround us.

Every profession and occupation has its ideal image, and parenting is no exception. We all know that the "ideal parent" has total control over his or her child. On the rare occasions when he must discipline, the "ideal parent" walks quietly over to his child and whispers some calming reminder in the child's ear. The parent is clean and tidy and so is the child. The most serious problem this perfect parent faces is convincing the child to eat her peas.

That is the public image—the showpiece parent. But for most, parenting is not really like that. As a matter of fact, the parent who quickly controls his child with a whispered message has probably just hissed, "You're going to get it when we get home." **Unfortunately, the well-behaved child has become part of the success image along with the Mercedes and the ten-room house,** and, as a result, parents are motivated to hide their child's problems from neighbors, friends, and even themselves.

The ACODF is very vulnerable to wanting a showpiece child. Many ACODF have been through incredible struggles before becoming parents. The shame they feel about their family of origin has often pushed them to be better than average in everything, because they feel they must compensate for their family's image deficits. A young single, or a married couple without children can often put on a show of perfection, but once children enter the scene that glowing image is bound to be tarnished.

The average child is a tremendous challenge for the average parent. That is a fact. All children have problems and create problems for their parents. It is part of normal maturation. But the ACODF often thinks that he or she is the only parent who finds his or her child difficult. Hiding problems from themselves and others is a defense ACODF develop in childhood. As a child, the ACODF usually did not have the power to change the family circumstances, and hiding embarrassing details from classmates may have been a useful defense. Now that they are adults ACODF need to realize that they can find the help they need to change what has gone wrong and make it go right.

The first step in solving a problem is seeing the problem. When denial delays movement toward a solution, the child's problem may become greatly aggravated by the time the parents can be convinced to take any action. In fact, many ACODF wait until a crisis has swept away almost their entire perfect-parent facade before they act.

DENIAL

Denial comes in many guises. Parents are notorious for overlooking their own children's faults. In the healthy parent, some of this rose-colored vision is the result of overflowing love. The child's strengths may be so noticeable to the healthy parent that the faults seem insignificant by comparison. But ignoring your own child's misbehavior, and blaming other children in conflicts that involve your child, can also be motivated by your need to preserve a tenuous self-image as the perfect parent. It's hard for any parent to step back and be objective about her own child, but when her ego is wrapped up in the issue, the parent can become blinded to important facts.

◆ NATALIE'S DENIAL
Natalie could never find the right situation for her son, Jerry. In preschool he was wild and distracting. A good-natured boy, his impulsiveness was neither

purposely destructive nor mean-spirited. As he ran across the playground, arms outstretched, he would unintentionally knock down playmates who couldn't move out of his way fast enough. During quiet activities he could not pay attention, and even though he tried hard not to talk to the other children while the teacher was explaining the activity, he would make just as much noise rocking in his chair or singing to himself.

Although he was large for his age, the preschool teacher recommended holding him out of kindergarten the next year. Natalie had not been able to get pregnant a second time and she was happy to "hang onto her baby" a little longer by delaying his entry into school; but she decided to pull him out of the preschool since it couldn't "provide enough stimulation" for her son. Despite the fact that Jerry was having difficulty learning to recognize letters, his mother felt that he was gifted and the school had failed to take his "right brain approach to learning" into consideration.

The following year Natalie enrolled five-year-old Jerry in enrichment activities instead of a preschool program. Unfortunately, in crafts class Jerry was grouped with two "hyperactive" boys. They seemed to stir each other up constantly. Natalie had recommended some parenting classes to the boys' mothers, but if they had taken them, she saw no positive result. The swimming class was problematic too, because all of the children were at least a year younger than Jerry and were always distracting him. As a matter of fact, finding good peer groups for Jerry was a constant problem that year. Since he was school age he was perpetually in the company of younger children, and his mother felt these preschoolers brought out the worst in him.

When Jerry entered kindergarten the next fall he was still more active than many of the other children. By midyear the teacher reported that he was having problems on reading-readiness activites. Natalie had some background in education and felt they should be using a sight-reading approach instead of phonics. She decided to use her own methods with him at home. At the same time Natalie began "shopping" for a good first-grade teacher for Jerry. She was not pleased with what she had heard about the first-grade teacher at Jerry's home school, so although she did not need child-care, Natalie signed Jerry up for before- and after-school care in a nearby district that had better schools. That fall Natalie learned that the teacher she had hoped to get for Jerry had transferred to another school, so Jerry was stuck once again with an incompetent teacher. Two weeks into the school year, the principal of Jerry's new school recommended that Jerry be tested by the school psychologist.

Natalie wanted an unbiased opinion, so she decided. to take him to a private psychologist instead. The psychologist found symptoms of a possible attention-deficit disorder and an above-average IQ. Jerry did not seem to be learning anything at the new school, so Natalie decided to enroll him in a private school. However, when Jerry couldn't pass the entry test (due to his earlier poor training), Natalie had no choice but to provide home-schooling for Jerry herself. She didn't know how long it would take for her to undo all the damage that been done to her son by poorly qualified educators, but she was willing to try.

Natalie is denying Jerry's very real learning problems. She has gradually closed both of them off from the mainstream, where there are people who could contradict her clouded perceptions, and provide the special help he needs. She may stumble on the right teaching methods working one-on-one with him at home, but he will not be learning the social skills he will need to get along with kids his own age. While criticizing and rejecting his potential play-mates, she has alienated herself from other mothers. She and Jerry now exist in a sterile vacuum in which Natalie can imagine Jerry has no problems. But she has simply taken him out of all challeng-ing situations, and Jerry will not be stimulated to grow and change. He will eventually have to rejoin society and it may be far harder after years of social isolation.

THE FAMILY PRETENSE

Some families create an elaborate system of lies or denials that protect the family honor or support an idealized family image. I recall my family, which was really very unhappy, constantly compar-ing ourselves to situation-comedy families on TV. We would joke around and frequently remark, "We should be on TV." It is often said that alcoholic families put on a show for people outside the family—the show of the happy family. My family put on a show for people outside the family even when we were alone in our house. The show never ended so that real life could begin. Everyone else in my family maintained that we were a jolly, happy family and there was some-thing wrong with me because I thought we were miserable.

Sometimes the denial is directed at the relationship between Mom and Dad. Daniel's father left the family when he was seven years old, but he remembers his mother keeping up a facade for ten years, telling the neighbors that his Dad was constantly on the road with his job. Privately his mother would admit that the father had gone for good, but she explained to Daniel that the family would get more respect from the neighbors if they thought his parents were still married. When neighbors came to visit, Daniel's mother would quote his father as if he had been there commenting on their family life all along. The children were asked to keep up this pretense, but such story-telling was not in Daniel's nature. Consequently, he became shy and withdrawn around the neighborhood adults. Al-though Daniel never admitted the truth about his father to his friends, he suspected they knew. They never asked him about his father and Daniel never had to make up an answer, but it embarrassed him when his mother would talk about "dear old Dad" when his classmates came to the house.

For Daniel, who tended to be shy, this family pretense was too difficult to bear during his teen years. He stopped inviting kids over to the house and dropped many of his childhood buddies for new classmates that didn't know anything about his family. At times he feels like a person without a past. **Thinking back on his childhood is more like remembering a movie he once saw.**

This example is somewhat extreme, but milder "little white lies" can do a lot of damage. Betsy's parents had separated and divorced when she was four and then reconciled and remarried when she was seven. In the interim Betsy had some traumatically difficult times with her mother's live-in boyfriend, who would chase Betsy out of the house whenever he wanted privacy. Betsy's father eventually got custody of her. Later, the mother tired of the boyfriend's crazy behavior, "grew up," and went back to her husband. But Betsy's mother is embarrassed by this time of separation and, after insisting that they move to a new state, has instructed Betsy never to tell anyone about her parents' separation. Not only has the mother modeled and sanctioned lying behavior, she has required her daughter to lie. Betsy, now eleven, is obligated to pretend the family has been intact throughout her childhood. What began as occasional fabrications of life with her mother and father when she was six years old (and actually living with only her father) has ended in a pattern of chronic lying. Betsy seems to actually confuse reality with fantasy at times.

◆ BETSY'S FAMILY SECRET

Betsy had leaked the family secret to Paula, a friendly and supportive neighbor whose house was a refuge and activity center for the neighborhood children. Paula's daughter brought Betsy over to play one day. After several weeks of confusingly contradictory stories from the two girls, Paula realized that Betsy was a chronic liar.

Paula, a very easygoing person, liked Betsy despite the lying. Paula had several talks alone with Betsy, showing she could accept some of Betsy's worst behaviors, and she persuaded Betsy to try trusting her with the truth from then on.

Betsy began on the most primitive level. She would run to Paula to report every time she farted or burped, apparently considering these acts to be the most intimate of confidences. Once Paula had accepted these confessions with equanimity, Betsy expanded her trust and began to talk about her early childhood, describing the beatings by her mother's former boyfriend. Betsy showed a new authenticity and sincerity and Paula was hopeful that Betsy might no longer need to lie to her.

One day Betsy called to ask if she could come swimming. Paula said that she had too much work to do and couldn't be outside with the girls so they would have to wait until some other day. Betsy told Paula that she knew life saving and the girls would be safe with her. Paula laughed and asked Betsy if she had seen someone do lifesaving on TV. Then she explained that it was more complicated than it looked and she wouldn't let the girls swim unless their attendant had had a lifesaving course. Betsy said she had had one. Paula was certain that this was not true. She reminded Betsy of their agreement about lying and asked if Betsy wanted to change her story. Betsy again insisted that she had had lifesaving. Paula asked her if it was the certified Red Cross class, and Betsy replied that it was.

Paula asked Betsy to bring down her Red Cross lifesaving card, but Betsy said they hadn't given her one. After several attempts to allow Betsy to gracefully retract her story, Paula felt angry. She knew that this lie of Betsy's could be dangerous. What if Betsy was baby-sitting and the parents had left her in charge of children in a pool whom Betsy really could not save? Paula said she would come up and talk to Betsy's mother about Betsy's lifesaving training. Betsy said that was fine. In front of the mother, Betsy continued to insist that she had had lifesaving training at the Red Cross although her mother said that was preposterous. Betsy began crying in a very wounded way, sobbing that no one ever believed her.

At this point it seems as though Betsy has lost touch with reality. What began as a fib to get into the pool has now become a lie she must defend with all her might. Perhaps she was worried about losing Paula's friendship and decided it was better to stick by her story than get caught in a lie. On the other hand, she may have actually convinced herself that she has taken a lifesaving course. Maybe she thinks she really could perform artificial respiration and her lie is just a way of allaying Paula's foolish fears. For whatever reason, she never changed her story.

Lying functions like an addiction—the more you do it, the more you need to do it. The lies in Betsy's family began harmlessly enough. Her mother had regrets and simply wanted a fresh start. She has spared the neighbors the details to enhance her image. If Betsy believes she could perform artificial respiration in an emergency, then she believes she is just altering the details by saying she has had special training. Betsy has followed her mother's example; she is trying to improve her image too.

Parental lying not only serves as a poor role model, it also undermines the child's faith and trust in her parents. After watching the parent lie to others, the child is bound to wonder if the parent is telling the truth at home. This can color the child's whole relationship with the parent.

The children may also be caught in destructive conflicts of loyalty between their parents if the "white lie" has been told by one parent to the other. The "white lie" could be something as serious as being asked not to mention Mother's male company to Daddy when he gets back in town, or something as minor as Dad letting his daughter eat ice cream instead of her dinner when Mom is not at home (as long as she promises not to tell Mommy). Any secrets kept from one parent by the child in collusion with the other parent creates an unhealthy triangle. Ultimately, the child may be forced to side with one parent against the other, because the "lying parent" generally has a "with me or against me attitude."

REESTABLISHING TRUST

Trust between parent and child is worth their combined weights in gold! If you have told what you felt were harmless lies in the past, neither your child nor your relationship with your child is ruined for life. It is sometimes difficult, but trust can be regained. Admit to past lies and clarify for your children what is true and what is not, including your more enlightened opinion about the importance of truth. Having humbly and fully admitted your error, you can pledge a new commitment to truth. Then be patient with your children's doubts until you have proven yourself worthy of trust through repeated examples of truth-telling.

Alcoholics and people in a very stressed emotional state sometimes block out painful memories or simply forget whole chunks of time. These are called blackouts. The alcoholic is often unaware of blackouts until other people complain about or mention incidents he or she cannot recall. A blackout can take place between two moments of conscious memory, selectively blocking out some act or curse that the person is very ashamed of. Many alcoholics resist believing they could have done such things and so accuse everyone around them of being liars.

You may have done things that you truly do not remember. If you have had blackouts, you may be surprised to learn that even after you have been told about an embarrassing thing you did while drinking, you will still not be able to remember the incident. It has simply not been stored in your conscious memory. Whether or not you remember the insult or beating, someone has been hurt by it and deserves your humble and sincere apology. If your child reports an embarrassing or hurtful incident you do not recall, it is generally wise to make amends. Tell her that you don't remember dancing on the table, hitting her, or whatever, and would never do that in your "right mind." Then explain that although you don't remember the incident, you are as sorry as you would have been if you had consciously done those things.

Telling "little white lies" to make the day go smoother is a great temptation, but this too undermines trust. If, to stop a temper tantrum in front of the ice-cream truck, you promise your child that you will buy him an ice cream at the store after dinner (knowing he will forget about it by then), you have planted a seed of distrust that will grow. Or if to get quick cooperation you tell your daughter you will pay her for baby-sitting her little sisters when you get ahead on your money (even though you feel she should be baby-sitting the family for free and you don't have the money to pay her), the effects can be long-reaching. Maybe you find life is smoother when you pretend to your husband that you got your clothes on sale for half the price on the tag (knowing that by the end of the month he won't be able to tell what was spent on food and what was spent on luxuries). Being honest can sometimes be more of a hassle than lying, but it is the only way to build trust. Later we will discuss when "little white lies" are justifiable, but a quick rule of thumb should be: "When in doubt, don't."

If you have been lying to yourself or others, make a vow to stick to the truth one day at a time. Then at the end of each day, if you find you have lied, try to discover what motivated your lie. Were you afraid someone would get angry at you? Did you want to be admired? Were you trying to hold onto some freedom you feel you have lost? What did your lying accomplish? How else could you accomplish the same thing? Telling the truth is often more confrontational than telling "little white lies." You need to develop the courage to stand up to other people when you state your beliefs or desires. A course in assertiveness training can change your approach to people by providing you with new tools to get your way.

EXCESSIVE LOYALTY

The most damaging type of "lie" is denial. If your spouse is alcoholic, manic, or abusive, you may find it very painful to admit that fact even to yourself. It is easier to excuse behaviors one at a time, imagining that they are isolated, unrelated incidents. However, you owe it to yourself and your children to stop and analyze your spouse's behaviors. Did he come home drunk once in two years after a big family wedding, or does he come home drunk every Friday night after he gets paid? Did he only hit the children once when he was sick with the flu and obviously not himself, or does he hit them every time they get on his nerves too much? (And is he "nervous" so often that he hits them hard once or twice a week?) If your children run for cover everytime Dad goes on a rampage, something is wrong. By minimizing these incidents to your children, you will lay the groundwork for them to put up with abuse in their later lives.

One outcome of the ridigity seen in adult children of dysfunctional families is a tendency toward excessive loyalty. Many self-help parenting books exhort parents to support each other in every decision, regardless of each parent's personal judgment. I disagree. When children are asked to suffer unfair punishments, they get the message that their feelings do not matter, that they do not matter. We must objectively evaluate our co-parent's behaviors and act on what is right. There comes a point when one parent must step back and condemn wrong actions by the other parent. Some parents fail to do this out of loyalty to the spouse or just plain fear for their own safety; some have a heightened tolerance for punative behavior cultivated during their own childhood punishments; others lack confidence in their own perceptions. One moment the ACODF parent feels appalled at the other parent's physical brutality when the father smacks the child repeatedly. The next moment she is remembering her own father beating her with a belt and her mother coldly commenting that she deserved it. If her beating with a belt for coming home ten minutes late was deserved, then surely her son deserves such a beating for coming home thirty minutes late. Or does he?

The ACODF has no sense of reasonable consequences for misbehavior and will have little confidence in her ability to judge punishments. Although it is easier and less anxiety-provoking just to let the other parent make these decisions, the ACODF must learn to stand up for what he or she thinks is right.

◆ JUDY AND CARL—DENIAL AND LOYALTY

The counselor, a man about Judy's age, was warm and reassuring. He wanted to involve the whole family in working on their mutual problems, but Carl could only get away from work for the intake interview. Throughout this initial session Carl talked about how well they were doing. Judy wondered if they lived in the same house. As Carl painted his rosy picture, Judy interrupted him, giving her contradictory viewpoint. Carl became angry and complained that Judy was always criticizing him. Judy drew back, saying that she was probably too negative, but the counselor reassured her that there were problems they needed to work on and that those problems could be worked on.

After the first few sessions, Judy felt so much better from just having someone to talk to that she was up and about again, trying to find satisfaction in being a stay-at-home mother. The one positive thing that had come from her illness was that she had quit her church position (and was freed from all the committee meetings she had had to attend because of it). She now realized how much she had needed a break from all that responsibility and was feeling lighter and less troubled.

Then Judy and Carl got a much-needed financial break. After nearly two years of double house payments, their Denver house finally sold. They decided to use a few thousand dollars cash from the sale of the house for a family vacation. She went to a travel agent and got brochures to plan a trip.

The prospect of taking a vacation perked her up so much that she was able to think more creatively about how to be with Casey. She started getting out to the park with him and planning activities for him at home. The busier she kept him, the easier he was to be with. And he was soaking up her attention, finally trying to control his behavior for one of her smiles.

Because of the exchange rate, they got a good deal on a small condo at a beach in Mexico. There were sights a reasonable drive away, but Judy thought they could spend most of their time just relaxing on the beach. She had been learning that Casey did best with space and a relaxed parent.

Carl decided to make the most of his vacation by starting a running program, so he got up at six each morning to go running on the beach. He would come back from his run all charged up and start making a big breakfast. At 7:30 A.M. he would get Judy and Casey out of bed. Following breakfast Carl would march them all down to the beach. By 10:00 he would be bored and restless, suggesting places they should go sightseeing. Within the first few days they'd exhausted the nearby sights and they started going off on drives of several hours, spending a long day looking at ruins and museums. Casey was getting cranky and was often ill-behaved in the car.

The fourth night they returned to the condo dead tired and all headed for the bathroom. Casey used the toilet first and when he was done he began struggling with the zipper in his pants. Judy knew how adamant Casey could be about doing his own pants so she stood patiently by while he worked at it. Carl was hopping nervously from foot to foot and finally reached for Casey's pants to zip them himself. Casey angrily jumped back and shouted, "No!" Carl grabbed him by the front of his shirt and slammed him against the wall. Casey screamed as his head thudded against the concrete. Judy stepped between them and told Carl he was out of control and should go to bed by himself.

Judy calmed Casey and reassured him that Daddy was just tired and already regretted what he had done. Casey did not want to leave the bathroom. She finally got him out into the hall where Judy found Carl waiting for them. Judy thought Carl wanted to make up for what he had done, so when Casey clung to her and said he didn't want to go near Daddy, she gently pushed him toward his father. Carl grabbed

Casey by the arm and roughly dragged him down to his room. Casey began screaming hysterically and Judy pushed past Carl to wrap her arms around Casey in an effort to calm him down. Carl stormed down the hall to bed.

The next morning Carl got up early as usual and went running. When he returned he fixed breakfast only for himself, letting Casey and Judy sleep in. When they got up Casey insisted on fixing himself some cereal. He missed the bowl and the cereal spilled all over the floor. Carl stood up and bellowed at him for being so sloppy, and when he stepped toward the boy, Casey screamed and ran behind his mother. Carl tried to reach around her to get Casey but Judy backed out the door, shielding the boy as she went. Casey was crying and begging Judy to keep Daddy away from him. He said he hated Daddy.

This suddenly struck a familiar chord for Judy. She remembered hiding in the closet when her father was on the rampage, and she remembered staying in bed until he went to work in the morning because it was too risky to be up while he was still there. She kept hoping he would die or just not come home someday. When she was older she would beg her mother to divorce him.

She had never expected Casey to feel this way about his father, but Carl had changed with this new job. It had been gradual and unnoticeable to her until today, even though this was not the first time he had manhandled Casey. Carl had never been as adamantly opposed to spanking as she had been and he had dragged Casey off to his room a little too roughly at times. But Judy knew it could be hard to get Casey into his room, and she believed that it was important for parents to stick together in disciplining the child. She didn't like to see Carl shoving and smacking Casey toward his room, but she didn't think she should interfere. She had reasoned that Casey was annoying and he needed to feel the consequences of his behavior.

But Carl had crossed the line. She began to realize that there was a limit to what she could allow. She remembered her mother standing silently by watching while Judy's father beat her. She could never understand why her mother wouldn't help her. Yet Judy had been standing by for months now. She couldn't see it coming because Carl was so much more human and compassionate than her father had been. At least he used to be. But she realized it had been a long time since Carl had acted compassionately. Even to her. Throughout her illness he had seemed disgusted with her, and he was still criticizing the way she kept house as if there had been no change, never acknowledging her improved mood and capability. Instead, he seemed to act increasingly annoyed.

They kept their distance from him for several hours and Judy carefully orchestrated the rest of the week to avoid a confrontation.

(Continued in Chapter 10)

As Judy learns to value herself and her own perceptions more through therapy, she is able to "see" things that escaped her before. She no longer blocks the painful childhood memories that can inform her about how her child feels. By being open to her old feelings she can see what she must do in this abusive situation and begin to take action, so that her son does not grow up in the kind of fear she endured as a child.

TOLERANCE FOR ABUSE

In Chapter 4 we learned that abuse is very common in dysfunctional families. Of the ACODF who seek therapy, 90 percent report being verbally, sexually, or physically abused as children. The other 10 percent have often been abused too but have little understanding of what abusive behavior is. Beatings and harsh scoldings are just normal parenting behavior to them.[1] If the ACODF was beaten as a child, he would think his spouse's caustic verbal insults are mild by comparison. The ACODF has lost perspective. Smith, in her book *Grandchildren of Alcoholics*, defines abuse as any parental behavior that deliberately or unintentionally damages the self-esteem of the child. There has been a lot of attention given to sexual and physical abuse in recent years, but few can define emotional abuse. The following list describes some emotionally abusive behaviors defined by Smith.[2]

---◆---

Emotionally Abusive Behaviors

1. Harsh controlling discipline that employs sarcasm, humiliation, name-calling, or severe criticism.

2. Rigid parenting or excessive rules that prevent children from expressing themselves or making decisions.

3. The "silent treatment" that nonverbally says, "I don't love you anymore."

4. Parental moodiness or inconsistency that makes children anxious as they adapt to wide mood swings.

5. Parental dependence on a child for emotional support.

6. Passivity and inaction on the part of one parent while the other parent abuses the child.

7. Neglect of the child's physical or emotional needs.

8. Threats of beatings, abandonment, or other harsh punishments.

9. The forbidding of emotional expression such as crying, laughter, or fear.

10. Expecting far too much of the child for his or her age or overprotecting to the point where the child cannot learn self-help skills or develop independence.

For some ACODF the above list may seem like a list of all the "persuasive" methods their own parents used in disciplining them as children. Hence, these may be all the choices that come to mind for an ACODF when a situation calls for discipline. What, then, is acceptable discipline? Alternative methods such as "time-out," "natural consequences," and "conflict resolution" will be discussed in upcoming chapters.

CHALLENGING MISPLACED LOYALTY

Misplaced loyalty can be perceived and challenged. Parents must first gain a sense of what is reasonable or healthy loyalty. By interacting with other families, parents can see what normal behavior is like and put family behaviors in perspective. How do the people you admire treat their children? Do your spouse's punishments or expectations seem harsh by comparison? Strive to become more objective. It's possible that you have bought your spouse's devotion with your unquestioning loyalty, so challenging him or her can be frightening. There may have been a time when that loyalty was totally appropriate, but now it's time to stop living in the past. Don't retain loyalty because he was once so good to you and the kids. Objectively examine what is happening now. You must set aside your own fears of abandonment and confront your spouse for the sake of your children and your spouse. Sometimes confronting can be the greatest act of loyalty.

Few parents intentionally hurt their children. Instead, the child is hurt as the adult reacts to the pain in his or her own life. If your spouse is mistreating your children, he is damaging his own relationship with those children. Over time they will grow to hate him. This is probably not the outcome he desires or sees himself moving toward. By intervening, you may save your spouse's relationship with his children before it is too late (and even after it seems too late). If you do not intervene, your children may ultimately hold you responsible for their pain because of your silent approval. Studies show that the adult children of alcoholics who function best as adults usually had one parent who remained in touch with reality and "played fair" with the children.[3]

◆ GRACE—FEAR AND LYING

Grace, whom we met in Chapter 4, had to deal with beatings as well as sexual abuse. "My dad would say I had lied about something and he would say he would beat me until I told the truth. He would grab boards out of the garage to beat me with. But I had told him the truth, so finally the only way to make him stop beating me was to say whatever he wanted me to say I'd done. And then he would say that for lying to him, he'd spank me again. So he spanked me again." Even as Grace remembers this twenty years later she cannot help but cry at this crazy betrayal, the horrifying impossibility of the situation. Obviously there was no way for Grace to win at this game, or even to withdraw and stay out of the race. Her father had a sadistic streak, a need to terrorize someone smaller and weaker.

"Sometimes he would come at dinnertime and he would tell me I was going to get a spanking right after dinner. I wouldn't be able to eat my dinner thinking about the spanking I was going to get. He'd twist and twist my arm. I can remember beatings when I was on my tricycle, that's how little I was. I would be so scared that I would pee all over myself and he would beat me and he just wouldn't quit.

"My mom has told me that she would come home after shopping and I would have welts all the way up my back and I would be in the bathroom crying and my dad would say it was because I wet my pants."

The terror these beatings produced in Grace compelled her to play into her father's hands again and again. "I used to have nightmares all the time. I'd dream there was witches outside my door waiting to get me, or I'd see things in my room and I'd get so scared in my room that I could feel my heart pounding in my chest. I'd get so scared that I would go into my mom's room, and sleep on the floor at the bottom of her bed. But all the time I knew if they woke up and caught me there I'd get a beating.

"I was only nine when my dad left. My sister and my brother and my stepmom all thought I was crazy when I said my father molested me. I had done a lot of things when I was growing up that made them think I made things up.

"When I was about thirteen I was sent to live with my father and I wanted to move back with my mother. But my dad wouldn't let me. So I made up a story that these kids had jumped me. I was trying to make sure they would send me back home to my mom. I slashed my arms all up to make it look good. But I ended up telling the truth because I knew the cops knew I was lying."

(Continued in Chapter 16)

For Grace, there seems to be no objective reality. Whether she lied or told the truth she would be beaten, and she was repeatedly forced to contradict herself. To her family (except for her father who knew the truth), this made Grace look like a chronic liar. By the time her father left the family, Grace had no credibility in her mother's eyes. No one would believe her about the molestations (and they were all minimizing or denying the beatings, for which there had been physical evidence). The truth had not worked to keep Grace from being sent to live with her father, so once there she "staged" an elaborate lie to get herself out of the situation. But in the end, Grace could not lie to the police. Why didn't Grace try to tell the police her real reason for making up this story: that she wanted to get away from her father's abuse? She had concluded by then that no one would believe her anyway. What really happened at any given time had little relevance for Grace. Her primary concern had to be: What can I say that will bring me the least punishment?

LYING IN CHILDREN

What motivates children to lie? There are a number of different categories of lies that children tell. Some are harmless fantasies or simply wishful thinking uttered aloud. A more troublesome category might be "brag" lies, where children lie to others about their accomplishments or belongings. Often they do this to try to "look better" to their peers. If your son's friend has just been to Chuckie Cheese, your son might start telling everyone that he too is going there this weekend (or just went last weekend) even though your family has never been there and has no plans to go. It's just his way of trying to "keep up with the Joneses." If the child is age six or under, this is probably harmless and should just be ignored. If this kind of lying persists as the child grows older it would be a sign that the child has pretty shaky self-esteem. He will need to be reassured that he has many good qualities and needn't tell stories to impress others.

If the child's lies or omissions are designed to cover up for embarrassing family incidents, a therapist may be needed to help you all straighten out when silence is more appropriate than self-disclosure. There are times when "lying," or failing to tell the whole truth, is appropriate to protect ourselves. You have a right to privacy, and if others do not respect that right you needn't feel compelled to confess your secrets. Perhaps you have just made the difficult decision to have an abortion because you feel you just can't do a good job parenting more than two children. You don't need to tell everyone you meet, and you especially don't need to debate the issue with every anti-abortionist. Some people and places can't handle dark family secrets and you don't need to serve the world as a walking shooting gallery. On the other hand, your therapist or your child's teacher should probably be told what disruptive things are happening at home so that he or she can be supportive. It is healthy to be selective about where you tell the bald truth.

If you have grown up in a dysfunctional family, it will be very difficult for you to tell what is denial and what is reasonable self-protection. Chances are you have provided a pretty fuzzy model for your child in this area. So if your child is "denying" problems at home (or her own personal problems) and seeming to whitewash her difficulties, take it slowly. It will take a lot of sorting and thinking to come to an understanding about how much openness is healthy and necessary to function well in the world.

Probably the type of lying that most often distresses, frustrates, and even infuriates parents, is lying designed to cover up for a child's transgressions. This type of lying is often most disturbing to parents because the parent has a sense of "being out of control." The child might just be trying to avoid disappointing you, but you can't help feeling he is out-and-out disobeying you.

Often children lie because their parents expect too much of them. For example, a child might falsely report he is doing well in school but come home with a report card that tells a different story. Why would a child lie about such a thing when he knows he is going to get caught? The child may hope against hope all marking period he is going to pull through in the end, or he might simply realize that he'll be grounded once he brings home the report card, and decide he doesn't want to be grounded two weeks before as well. Children often have very logical reasons for lying and the reason is rooted in fear of consequences. If this seems to fit your situation, you need to ask yourself if you are being too harsh or demanding.

For example, how would you react if your seven-year-old son came home from school and reported that he had gotten a "warning slip" for running into another boy during recess and knocking him down on the pavement? He complains that he has lost a week of recess as a punishment.

Some parents would begin scolding the child immediately, reminding him that he knows that running on the pavement is not allowed and he had no business running during recess. They might take away his TV privileges for the evening or spank him. Their final comment on the subject is often phrased, "I better not hear you've been running on the pavement ever again!"

What is this child likely to do if he forgets and runs on the pavement the next week? Let's say that this time he has not injured anyone but has gotten another "warning slip" just the same. First of all, he will not come home and volunteer the information. If his mother happens to ask him if he has been good and not run on the pavement (in either a threatening or expectant voice), the child is likely to give in to the temptation to lie. When he gets a third slip and the principal calls, that mother will be shocked, hurt, and angry that her son had not told her about slip #2. She will probably greet the child with fury, feeling let down all the while that he does not confide in her anymore. Because of the negative reaction to the first slip, the child has changed from an innocent, open child to a sneaky, withdrawn child who no longer shares his thoughts with his parents.

What is the alternative? When the child came home with the first slip, the mother might have sympathized. In an understanding tone she could have said, "It's hard to remember not to run when you are having a good time, isn't it? What would help you remember not to run during recess?" This opens further communication on the spot and keeps the control with the child, where it needs to be anyway. The school has already punished him and he needs to learn to control himself when you are not around to remind him. You really can't control whether or not he runs on the pavement at school.

In this second scenario, what is likely to happen the next time the child gets written up for running on the pavement at school? He'll probably come home and tell you because he has no reason not to. He may also be looking for you to express your continued confidence that he will eventually learn to control his impulses. He probably feels bad about messing up again.

At first glance this might seem to be an irresponsible approach. If your child did hurt somebody, he could hurt somebody again if he doesn't learn to control himself. However, threatening him probably won't solve that problem. It will just create a new set of problems. I think that, as a general rule, you should lessen the punishment for something the child had freely confessed to you. (Even the government gives felons who cooperate shorter sentences.) This doesn't mean that you can't use the situation as an opportunity to teach right from wrong. **You can disapprove of what he has done while still approving of him as a person.**

If it is something really alarming, help him atone for his error. For example, if he tells you he has been taking money from the younger kids at school, without lecturing or treating him like an enemy, explain why it was wrong to take the money. Then help him figure out how he can correct the error. Obviously, he should return the money. If he has spent it, find a way for him to earn some money and send him to school with instructions to return the money to the children, along with an apology. Do it in a supportive way, pointing out that he'll feel better afterward, and then let him know how proud you are of him that he is learning to do the right thing. At the same time, you might give some thought to why your child would have taken money from other children. What did he feel he needed that money for? Is it time he started getting an allowance? What can you do to lessen his temptation to take money in the future?

In other words, whatever the lie, you want to think through why the child is lying to you. Are your rules unrealistic for a child his age? Are all the other ten-year-olds allowed to ride their bike in the street while yours is still required to ride on the sidewalk? Does this cause him to ride in the street whenever he is out of sight of the house, being in a state of constant sneaky disobedience because he cannot live within the narrow boundaries you have set? Are your punishments too severe? Do you ground your daughter for two weeks every time she yells at her little brother, so that now instead of shouting at him she pinches him when you're not around? Do you overreact to every little thing so that your child feels he must protect you from the truth? Do you tell him he must stop playing with his best friend because the boy knocked him off his bike? Then does he sneak off to play with the boy and hide a scraped knee until it is badly infected, to avoid reporting the latest routine skirmish?

These are very important things to sort out when your child is small. If such patterns of lying, withholding information, or concealing incidents are established by the teen years, the possible consequences become far more threatening. You want to do everything you can to keep communication open between you and your children.

◆ ══════════ **SUMMARY** ══════════ ◆

Honesty between family members is essential to developing and maintaining trust. Without this honesty, we cannot become fully intimate; for we cannot open our innermost selves unless we feel totally safe.

◆ ══════════ **POINTS** ══════════ ◆

1. The first big step in solving a problem is being able to admit that something is wrong.

2. If we have had to lie as children, either to protect ourselves from parental cruelty or because we were required to keep the "family secret," we may find it difficult to break out of this lying pattern as adults.

3. If we have lied in front of or to our children in the past, it may take quite a bit of time and patience to regain their trust, but it is well worth the effort.

4. If we gloss over or deny family problems in front of or to our children, they will not only suffer from the anxiety created by the problem, but may also begin to doubt their own clear perceptions and judgment.

5. It is best not to let our feelings of loyalty toward our spouses cause us to side unfairly with them against our children. When a spouse is being abusive, we must step in and defend our children.

6. If our child has been lying, we should first determine why he or she would need to lie. It is best to address the root of the problem—his or her fear or insecurity—instead of reacting to the behavior alone.

NOTES

1. Ann W. Smith, *Grandchildren of Alcoholics*, Pompano Beach, FL: Health Communications, Inc., 1988, p. 65.

2. Ibid., p. 72–74.

3. Robert J. Ackerman, Ph.D. *Let Go and Grow*. Pompano Beach, FL: Health Communications Inc., 1987, p. 149.

9

EVERY DAY IS JUDGMENT DAY

*9. ACODF fear harsh judgments of their parent-
ing ability and consequently become hypercritical of their children's behavior.*

*10. ACODF are often excessively rigid and fail
to consider children's individual differences
or better solutions to a problem.*

Adult children from dysfunctional families are often
perfectionists with unrealistic standards for both themselves and
their children. We can immediately see the roots of this in the
fantasies ACODF have about life in the healthy (but they really mean
perfect) family. Trying to be perfect starts in early childhood. When
you were vulnerable and dependent on your parents to mirror your
positive aspects, your parents were probably focusing on your faults.
**One of the hallmarks of dysfunctionality is the inability to take
responsibility for one's own actions,** so blaming is a defense often
used in dysfunctional homes.

Children, because they are dependent and unskilled, often require a lot of care and attention. They can be tremendously distracting. If your parents' hold on stability was tenous to begin with,
having children probably pushed them over the edge. This could
have led to their blaming all of their misfortunes on you. Dad says,
"I planned to get training for a good job but then your mother got
pregnant with you." Mom remarks to a neighbor, "If it wasn't for
these kids, my husband and I would still be together," or "Every
time I get the house in order, the kids mess it up." "See what you
made me do!" is the central message.

165

Low or high levels of self-esteem run in families as surely as blue or brown eyes do. Until this generation, parental self-esteem building habits have been unconscious. In certain families parents just naturally praise their children's every accomplishment because their own parents had praised their accomplishments as children. Just as consistently, most parents whose own parents communicated through sarcasm and insults will use these methods with their children today. But there is more backing these destructive habits of communication than simple imitation. If your self-esteem was attacked constantly as a child, you probably feel very inferior as an adult. As you compare yourself unfavorably to others, you may feel as if you have to be perfect to be minimally acceptable. Your anxiety about your "image" will also cause you to worry excessively about how your children look to others. You will want them to behave perfectly so that others will admire your parenting. This creates a rigid standard for your children that does not even begin to consider their individual talents, weaknesses, and personalities.

It can be hard to sort out exactly how your self-esteem was damaged, but it is important to define and examine the process. If you do not bring the sources of your low self-esteem into your conscious awareness, you may think you are not parenting as your parents did, but you will unconsciously pattern yourself after them. Parents can damage the self-esteem of their childen in both passive and active ways. When parents do not understand what behavior is appropriate for children at each age and stage, they can become unfairly critical. In this chapter we will look at ways parents damage children's self-esteem, how this affects them later as adults, and how we can parent so that we don't pass this damage on to our children and generations to come.

Causes of low self-esteem can quickly expand exponentially. The parent has unrealistic expectations, so that even a child doing well for his age-level begins to believe he is clumsy or slow. The child then develops performance anxiety and even as he tries to be neater, he is so nervous that he messes up. The parents become angry at his incompetence and frustrated that their effort at correcting the child hasn't paid off. They blame each other for his "inherited incompetence." Now the child feels worse still because he has caused trouble between his parents. Since he may not be able to do what they ask (because no child his age would have the coordination or concentration to do it), all his efforts make him feel more and more incompetent. Parental critical messages become part of his inner voice and when he is grown he can still hear them commenting on his every mistake. Eventually he becomes a parent with a harsh self-critical attitude. This harsh self-critical attitude inevitably spills over onto the children.

PERFECTIONISM

Perfectionism is a deeply internalized unconscious drive. It is most apparent in overachievers. They often come so close to actually being perfect, that we find their self-criticism baffling. No matter how much they have achieved, in their minds, one error can negate years of success. And that error is, of course, inevitable. Perfectionists can frequently go very long periods without "slipping up" like everyone else. But when they do err, the crash is deep and devastating by contrast.

◆ SUSAN—A NON-PERSON

"My father never said, 'I love you' or 'I'm proud of you.' I never did anything well enough for him," states Susan, whom we met in Chapter 6.

Susan had to earn her own way through college, and one semester her tuition check bounced because her father had "borrowed" money from her account without telling her. Still, she struggled on through and graduated a single woman with plans to be a teacher. "However, my family was disappointed because they felt girls should come out of college with an MRS instead of a BS." So Susan did her best to meet her parents' expectations. Shortly after graduation, she met a young Naval officer and accepted his impulsive marriage proposal before she'd had time to decide if he was right for her.

Susan's husband, Bart, was very critical of her for not being a "good military wife." "If we went to a party and I dared to disagree with military policy or question our being in Vietnam, my husband would tear into me when we got home. Any thoughts that came from the 'true me' were not acceptable." He frowned on her teaching because the "good military wife" does not have a career: Her only "career" should be social networking to promote her husband's career. So, like a proper military wife, Susan gave up her teaching, had two babies, and devoted herself to supporting her husband's ambitions and raising their children.

"You would not have recognized me when I was in that marriage. I had become someone else. I had totally submerged my true personality because what he wanted in a wife was not the woman he married. So I turned myself into the woman he wanted. I was my own worst enemy."

Susan shook loose from this self-abnegation during a highly energized marital crisis. "I had extremely high morals about what was proper and what wasn't, but when my husband went to Vietnam I tried to be realistic about what a year apart would mean. I said that if something happened and he became sexually involved, we should just accept that it happened and move on. But he insisted we swear on the

Bible that neither of us would get involved with anyone." When he returned from Vietnam, he questioned Susan closely and swore to his own faithfulness. A month later Susan, who had been faithful, found out she had a sexually transmitted disease. She had to learn about her husband's infidelity from her doctor.

"It was the straw that broke the camel's back. There had been too many things in the ten years that we'd been married and, in anger and hate, I kicked him out of the house.

"I was afraid. I felt worthless. I came from a background where you did not get divorced and I had destroyed a marriage. I felt like I had an obligation to stay with my husband and I shouldn't be feeling what I was feeling—I shouldn't be wanting to leave my husband." She was emotionally exhausted and turned to her family for support, but found none. Like Susan, they thought only bad women divorced and they chastized her. After she had given so much, there was nothing there when she needed it.

She briefly fell into an affair because she needed some nurturing and she didn't know where else to look. But having sexual relations with another man, even though she and her husband were legally separated, went against her personal moral code. "In my muddled mind I felt that only crazy people got divorced and I was unfit to be a mother. I had convinced myself that I was insane and everyone around me began agreeing with me."

Susan's daughter, Jennifer, was eight and her son, Brent, was four. For years Susan had been functioning well as a single parent because Bart was either off at sea or too busy with work to be with the children. When he was home, Bart made it clear that it was Susan's job to take care of the kids while he had his "peace and quiet."

Yet, Susan let her husband and his lawyer convince her to give up the children. The lawyer told Susan that since she was emotionally unstable and had no income of her own, the children would be better off with Bart right then. "I wanted to do what was best for my children. The lawyer gave me the impression that this was just a temporary arrangement and I would be free to change my mind once I got reestablished in my career."

Within a month Susan realized that she could not bear to be separated from her children and she wanted to change the custody agreement. "I missed my children so much that I cried every night. That's when I learned that the custody arrangement was considered final."

Susan would teach all day, attend night classes, and cry all night. Then she would get up the next day and go teach again. "I was exhausted and went down to 108 pounds. I was like a zombie. I was careful not to drink alcohol because I was terrified of sinking lower. You would have to say I'd had a nervous breakdown. My counselor explained that I had had years of emotional deprivation. Suicide was never on my mind, but I knew that I had reached the bottom of the pit. There was just this extreme and total exhaustion. I dragged myself out of bed each day and forced myself to get dressed and go to work. I performed by job because I could put on the efficient face—I was a very good face-maker. As the child of an alcoholic, I'd learned how to cover up anything. But the dam had broken. There wasn't anymore left and I couldn't pretend anymore.

"It was from that misery that I was able to gain back my true identity."

(Continued in Chapter 13)

Susan, a strong and capable woman who had faultlessly taken care of her children during her husband's long absences, allowed herself to be convinced that the children would be better off with the father they had rarely seen, a father who had never even helped in their care when he was at home. We marvel that this same woman who put her siblings and then herself through college and provided emotional support even for her own mother, could doubt her ability as a nurturer. But low self-esteem is not a rational matter. Many ACODF, no matter how much they accomplish or how much praise they receive, are not able to value themselves any more than their parents did. With the encouragement of teachers and friends they can often achieve much success by outward standards, but deep inside of themselves they still feel small and inadequate. They are just waiting to be "found out." And in Susan's case, ten years of good parenting were not enough to make up for a brief socially and legally acceptable sexual affair. She could be convinced that her children were better off with their disinterested father, who had concealed his own sexual affair while he pretended to keep a vow of fidelity to Susan.

A primary source of harsh criticism, whether directed at one's self or one's children, is black and white thinking. Something is all good or all bad. The ACODF wins the race nine times, but when she comes in second on the tenth race, she will think of herself as a failure. However, in viewing or judging both ourselves and our children, we need to focus on each small step of progress as one in a series of successes. Look at the doughnut, not the hole. If your child has a temper tantrum after two weeks of cooperative behavior, don't view this as proof that "he's *still* having temper tantrums," Focus instead on the fact that he's *only* having temper tantrums once every two weeks now instead of once a day. Don't scold him, congratulate him!

LEARNED HYPERCRITICAL ATTITUDES

Being hypercritical of others generally has one or more of three basic motivations:

1. A belief that others will be grateful for our advice.
2. An unconscious need to compare well to others: (I'm OK; you're not OK)
3. A *conscious* need to feel superior to others: (I'm not OK, but you're worse.)

In the first case, we might think that, like us, others want to be perfect and will be grateful for our advice. We might believe we will spare them the embarrassment of having others see them flawed. It is a form of rescuing, but we may be killing them with our kindness.

This nitpicking and criticism is most destructive when leveled at our children, because they are so dependent on us for our support and encouragement. The hypercritical parent not only notices each child's personal shortcomings, but may also project her loathing of her own faults onto her children, exaggerating flaws of actual little consequence. It is not uncommon to see an overweight mother restricting her child's food intake to spare her the pain of a chubby adolescence. Parents do often come down hardest on the faults of their own that they see in their children.

Similarly, a sloppy parent who has left ten personal items strewn around the living room may not "see" his own shoes lying on the floor. When the child comes home, and in imitation slips off his shoes and tosses down his backpack, this second pair of shoes may function as the "straw that broke the camel's back." This new item in an already cluttered room may be just what it takes to make the room look unkempt. So the hypercritical parent blasts into his sloppy child. **We humans have a tendency to ask, "Who ate the last cookie?" rather than, "Who ate the first forty-nine cookies?"**

Our second motivation might be an unconscious need to compare well to others. In terms of transactional analysis, it's the "I'm OK, You're not OK" position. We raise our self-esteem by finding faults in others so that we seem better by comparison. In a parent/child relationship this often takes the form of competitive or overbearing instruction that displays one's knowledge more than it teaches. Many a child has been bored to tears on the tennis court as his father shows him the *right* way to do it, before he lets the child play. The child would just like to have fun hitting the ball back and forth but Dad insists that the child learn how to serve first. Under this system, the worse we feel about ourselves, the worse we will see others as being (so that they can compare unfavorably to us). So it also reinforces a very negative life-view.

A third motivation might be a *conscious* need to compare well to others—*I'm not OK, but you are worse.* When we are aware of our feelings of inferiority, we still want to improve our public image despite our personal vision of ourselves as incompetent. Hence, we point out the faults of others to keep them on an "equal basis with us. It's a "Get them before they get you" approach. A strong offense can be the best defense. Also, a parent who is consciously aware of feelings of inferiority, might hope to improve her public image or community status through a high-achieving child and so she pushes the child instead of herself.

ACODF want their children to behave well so that their parenting ability will be admired by others. Because they themselves are hypercritical, they assume others are judging them as harshly as they judge themselves (when in truth most others don't have the time or energy to be thinking about the ACODF's parenting skills because they're too busy dealing with their own problems!).

This fear of being criticized can make us hypercritical of our children. If we let the child choose her own clothes and she wears a purple dotted blouse with pea green–striped pants, we worry that others will think *we* don't know how to make a match. We may become hypervigilant about their table manners, their personal habits, their academic success, and so on, making them and ourselves nervous wrecks. This hypercritical attitude can destroy their self-esteem.

It is also destructive for our kids if they hear us criticizing others constantly. They will inherit this hypercritical attitude and it is an isolating, alienating habit. Judge others as gently as you want to be judged. Whether family or friends, those you judge gently will form your support group.

UNDERPARENTING

Not all adult children of hypercritical parents become hypercritical of their children. Often the parent with low self-esteem will "forgive" and let slide antisocial or self-destructive behaviors in her children because she feels personally to blame for all her children's problems. This reactionary permissiveness can be just as destructive as constant criticism. Studies show that permissive parenting produces even fewer competent children than harsh authoritarian parenting. When Maryanne (from Chapter 3) found a new stable husband, her problems were not miraculously over.

◆ MARYANNE'S NEW HUSBAND

Ronnie, Maryanne's second husband, was like a dream come true. He was stable, hardworking, mature, and warm. He loved her and wanted to be a "good father" to Keith.

Keith, now six years old, still had a lot of trouble with self-control, and Maryanne, not wanting to be harsh like her father, had been too permissive with him. Keith was unusually active and distractible for his age. When he was tired, his behavior would spiral out of control. Maryanne felt humiliated by Keith's misbehavior, particularly at events with the new in-laws. Ronnie, as a stepparent, was struggling with the self-imposed pressure to prove he could be a more effective parent than Keith's father had been.

Ronnie's brother's son (about the same age as Keith) made them all painfully aware of Keith's immaturity and lack of control. Ronnie began a "crash program" to catch Keith up. After school Keith was expected to clean his room, feed the dog, and do his homework, before his parents arrived home from work. Few six-year-olds are self-motivated enough to handle this much responsibility, and due to the many stresses Keith had experienced in his short life, he was functioning more like a four-year-old. He was overwhelmed by his messy bedroom, he would forget to feed the dog, and he would daydream over his homework. When his mother arrived home from work, none of these chores would be done.

On top of this, Keith had many annoying behaviors. He had trouble making friends and complained of loneliness. Whenever his parents were home he wanted them to play with him because he had not had anyone to play with all day. If they were too busy he would whine and cry, or he would try irritating, silly antics to get their attention. He also had trouble letting his mother be alone with her new husband and would actually physically squeeze between them.

Keith was a difficult child who had had a difficult life. Even under the best circumstances he would have needed more care and guidance than the average kid. Before he could work on the usual skills a six-year-old should have, he needed to heal from the stress caused by the divorce, adjusting to a new father, and moving to a new area. After thinking the situation through, Maryanne realized that although Keith was only one child, he had about "three-children's-worth" of problems.

Ronnie, too, needed to lower his standards for both himself and Keith, so that they could each start to feel good about the things they did right. He began by attending scout meetings with Keith and got a better idea of what other kids Keith's age were like. Surprisingly, Keith was neither the most active nor the most distractible boy in the den. By seeing a wider range of six-year-old behavior, Ronnie began to feel better about Keith and could relax about "correcting" him.

Although parenting and child development books give us a good idea what we can generally expect from a child at each age and stage, we need to remember that each child is different and matures at a different rate. Along with age, one must consider the child's personality and stamina, as well as his life experiences and stresses. In the first four years of his life, Maryanne's son, Keith, had been through a great deal, and his first year in school showed he had some learning disabilities. Now Keith had to adjust to a new father. The blended family introduces many complications that even those who have grown up in healthy families don't know how cope with.

Ronnie needed to realize that, unlike his brother, he was working against tremendous handicaps. Keith had gotten off to a bad start and would need a lot of patient attention to help him catch up to other kids his age. Ronnie had missed out on early experiences with Keith that would have helped them bond and be more comfortable with one another. Natural parents have the opportunity to grow into their children gradually from infancy on. It is *much harder* to be a stepparent. The natural parent has an emotional bond that can smooth out some of the rough edges on the child. That affection makes it easier to be with the child when he is being horrible (and all children are horrible sometimes, even healthy ones).

For Ronnie and Maryanne, the most critical areas were where they both shared a weakness. They both felt very vulnerable to being judged bad parents—each for a different reason. Maryanne had had bad parents and worried she would be like them. Ronnie had had good parents but he was starting out with a "damaged" kid. Fortunately, they were both genuinely concerned about being good parents and they were willing to keep reevaluating how they were doing things.

There were obviously many things about Keith's behavior that it would be desirable to change. Although Keith had learned some bad habits that he must unlearn, most of his annoying behavior was caused by anxiety. His life had been unstable, his anxiety had caused him to behave poorly in the past, and his self-esteem had been affected by people's reactions to him while he was not his "best self" under so much stress. By helping him feel less anxious and more likeable, his parents began to change his annoying behaviors. Going at it from the other end (behaviors first) would only have continued to frustrate everyone.

MAKING IT MANAGEABLE

**It is best to create small goals that your child can do well at
and gradually increase what you expect of him.** If you have a child
who has been under stress, give him lots of kind gentle attention
and opportunities to do things right so he can get praise. This does
not mean "giving in to him" or "not disciplining" him. We can object
to behaviors we don't like; it is simply very important to make the
distinction between behavior and being. Make sure you have let your
child know that even though you don't like *what he did,* you do like
him.

Pick something your child does now that drives you crazy. Let's
say your child interrupts you and your spouse when you want to
talk to each other. You've told him not to interrupt, he remembers
for a few seconds, and then he interrupts again. You feel that by his
age he should be able to exercise enough self-control to let you and
your spouse finish a conversation with each other. But if he is not
able to, there's no point in banging your heads against a wall. Try to
break it down into some small task that he can master. Maybe he
can let you talk to each other if he can sit on your lap while you're
talking.

But what if your child is simply too big to sit on your lap? Well,
physically he might be too large, and psychologically he shouldn't
need to sit on your lap at his age, but maybe he hasn't gotten over
that need yet. As an interim measure, let him stand close to you.
Put your arms around him while you are talking. He may be a nine-
year-old but if he still thinks and feels like a three-year-old you can't
"grow him up" over night. He's got to work through all the stages
along the way. Give him the amount of attention a three-year-old
would need if that's what he needs. It will pay off later.

Whatever the task, try to think of the smallest unit. Let him do
something right and then praise him enthusiastically for it. Forget
about all those people who think he should be doing better. He'll get
there. If you sense someone judging you, just look toward your child
with compassion and say to yourself, "We've had a lot of stress in
our family this last year, and that poor kid has had a lot to deal with
in his short life. But we're all gradually making progress!" You'll be
able to find friends who appreciate your constant steady efforts and
can accept you all before you're perfect.

NEGATIVE PARENTAL EXPECTATIONS

Unfortunately, when we criticize our children we often produce the very negative traits we are trying to diminish. Rebellion is sometimes a part of this but more often it is the "self-fulfilling prophecy" effect. If the parent frequently tells the child she is incompetent, she will begin to believe it. The power of suggestion is a strong tool, and when it is accompanied by the wearing away of self-esteem, children have little internal strength to resist such suggestions.

If children need correction, it must be done in an atmosphere of acceptance, emphasizing that we are all good at some things and not so good at others. Respect must be fostered between all family members, regardless of their position in the family. Children should receive as much respect as parents. They should be respected for all the great things they do. This will be easier if you take the time to think about and appreciate how difficult these developmental steps are. For many parents this is a very new idea and it will take much practice to change the way we speak to our children. A good rule to keep in mind is to talk to and treat your children the same way you treat your close friends. If a friend entered your house with muddy shoes you wouldn't scream at her. You would politely ask her to go back out and wipe her feet on the mat or take off the muddy shoes. If you don't shout at your friends, don't shout at your children.

At the end of each day ask yourself, "Have I praised my child more than I have criticized her today?" For some crazy reason we have been led to believe that the main task of parenting is "correcting" our children. Probably your parents modeled this negative nit-picking. We watch for an error and then yell, "Don't do that!" We hover over the child as she sets the table, waiting for her to make the inevitable mistake of putting the fork on the wrong side. Then we pounce on her. That is what we have been taught to think a "good parent" does. It is our duty to make sure that they don't get away with anything. How else are they going to learn?

Believe it or not, children can learn far more by example and personal experience. A better approach is to begin by having the child help you set the table. Set one place and then have her set the next. After several "lessons" let her try it on her own. Be available if she has questions, then next time leave the room.

Setting a table can be a complex task for a five-year-old. First they must remember what utensils to put out. Then there is a napkin, cup, and plate. They must figure out how many place settings there will be. If they do manage to get out all the right things and give everyone one of each, praise them! Praise them for remembering the variety of items. Praise them for not forgetting any of the people in the family. Praise them for getting it done so quickly (even if it took half an hour). After they have done this successfully several times, you might politely mention that the fork *usually* goes on the left.

No matter what the task, begin with something positive. Correction need not always be criticism. The *tone* of voice as well as the "spirit" behind the correction make a difference. **Offer direct criticism only if there is no other way to make the child aware of the mistake and it is important that the mistake be corrected.** For example, does it really matter if your child has placed the forks on the wrong side of the plate? Can you still eat with those forks? Try to focus on the big picture and don't get bogged down by unimportant details. The gentlest way to approach criticizing your child is to ask first if he would like correction. Maybe your child rushes to show you a story he has just written and it is full of spelling errors. Remember, when the teacher assigns homework to a child, she is not testing *the parent's* spelling ability. Have your child read you the story and then, *without indicating whether or not there are any errors,* ask your child if he would like you to look for spelling errors. If he says no, you know he is feeling too sensitive about it right now. If he says yes, find two or three and ask if he would like you to look for more. Children are often more sensitive to a parent's criticism than they are to the teacher's. If your child begins to look hurt or embarrassed, stop and point out some words he has spelled right and let the teacher find the rest of the errors. Some teachers don't even check spelling on certain assignments where they are focusing on content. Why should you play the heavy when the teacher might not even care?

By looking for the good in your child, you will show him how to look for the good in himself.

UNCONDITIONAL LOVE

All children need their parents' unconditional love. They need to feel secure that you will always love them, no matter how many mistakes they make, no matter how many bad days they have. The three-year-old needs to know that you still love him even if he wets his pants, the ten-year-old needs to know that you still love her when she gets an "F" on the spelling test, and the teenager needs to know that you still love him after he slams the bedroom door in your face.

Love should not have a price tag attached to it. Your child needs to feel that there are not certain "conditions" under which you will stop loving her. If we make too much of achievement, the child may feel we will stop loving her if she fails to come out first in the contest. There is a difference between encouragement and expectation. You should encourage your child to do *her* best, not *the* best.

A good time to do this is each night at bedtime. It is good to talk over the day's problems and put all the bad feelings away before sleep. People do naturally think over the day as they are falling asleep. If your child has had an "angry fit" that day, he may go to sleep worrying that he has lost your love. Bedtime should be a time when you are both feeling calm (if not, see the chapter on stress!) and so it is a good time to put away grudges and resolve conflicts. In the heat of an argument we can say many irrational things. Both parents and children can slip into the absolutes—the always and nevers—such as, "You never pay any attention to me!" or "You always leave your things all over the floor!" A good technique is to pick an "always" or "never" from the day and be rational about it. Make a joke about it if you can, particularly if it was a very heated argument. Say, "I know right before dinner I said that you always leave your clothes all over the house, but of course that's silly! A bunch of your clothes are in the hamper right now and I know you put them there. Besides, there have been no clothes on the roof ever!"

It is also a good time to talk over deeper issues and apologize for behaviors you regret. People who love and respect each other should not scream or yell at each other, but sometimes they do. Say you are sorry you screamed at your child, that you felt very angry at the time and you lost control, but it does not mean that you don't love your child. Humbly apologize even if your son started the argument. Most of the time your child will pipe up immediately with his own apologies. Children learn by example. Ask your child how he thinks the situation could be handled better next time. Often parent and child can agree on a code word or phrase that signals it's time to calm down and cooperate. If your child has agreed beforehand to slow down and really listen when you say, "I think things are getting out of control," you may both be able to avoid losing your tempers next time. Talking over the day's conflicts like this keeps problems from becoming too large to manage.

SELF-FORGIVENESS AND ACCEPTANCE

You also need to give yourself some unconditional love. If you grew up in a dysfunctional home, what love you received from your parents probably came with many strings attached. Susan felt she had to be the family caretaker in order to be loved. She still fights against overvolunteering her time, because she has retained that unconscious message that she must earn her love and even her right to be on this planet. If you were raised in an atmosphere of guilt and blame, you may still have trouble believing that you deserve good fortune, or even rewards you have clearly earned through hard work!

Picture yourself as a young child. This may be frightening at first because you were very vulnerable then—literally without protective defenses. Close your eyes and picture your hair, your clothes, your house, your mother, your father. Do you look cared for and happy? How do your parents look at you? If their faces are not pleasant and welcoming (or even responsive), then become your own loving parent in the scenario. Hold onto the thought that you are very vulnerable and imagine how your best self would treat you. That is how you deserve to be treated. Feel compassion for yourself as a child. Think of the ways you could care for you; think of what a small child needs. Think of ways you can meet those needs now. It is never too late to get a cat, take art lessons, or simply go to the beach.

Be good to yourself. Parenting, even as difficult as it is, is a wonderful opportunity for healing. If you had not become a parent you would not have been bombarded with the message that children need to feel loved, lovable, and good about themselves. You wouldn't know what "self-esteem" means or how one goes about getting it. But even birth preparation classes now push information about self-esteem. At first all this can seem overwhelming. You may feel deep sadness when you realize you missed out on that kind of parenting, only to feel panic next when you learn that your child cannot thrive without having this thing you don't know how to give. Perhaps you feel resentful that you who have so little self-love stored up should be expected to give so much love to someone else.

There is only one solution for this. You must begin to love *both* yourself and your children simultaneously. You cannot fill your children from your empty bucket. We have no choice but to give, but we must give to ourselves as well. Share and share alike. We need to be fed too.

Think of the things that make you feel cared for and don't wait for someone else to do them for you. Don't sit around wishing someone would take you to dinner. Take yourself to dinner. If you want company, invite a friend. If you have no friends, start by making some. Pinpoint the things that make you feel good and do what you need to do to make them happen. This may seem like a contradiction at first. Haven't you grown up with a deficit because your own mother or father put themselves first? It may appear that way at first. But probably your parent didn't really know what his or her needs were or how to meet them. They may have worked long hours trying to get approval from the boss when they really needed to learn how to give approval to themselves. Or they may have spent excessive amount of money on beer, clothes, or betting, trying to fill that hole in their souls. Their real needs weren't met and so they never had the emotional energy to think about meeting yours. But you will be more selective when you nurture yourself *along with your children.* A hot bath will do more for you and those around you than a martini. You want to nurture yourself, not try to forget that you were never nurtured as a child.

You will probably need to go very slowly at first, trying things out and thoughtfully determining which things really make you feel better deep inside. The most efficient activities will be those that both you and your children enjoy. Maybe a day at the beach, where they get to jump and play in the water while you read a novel on the blanket, is a good way to start. Or perhaps what you really need is to spend some time *alone.* Grant yourself that. It is a human right. Actually *schedule* into your week whatever nurtures you most. Herbert L. Gravitz and Julie D. Bowden, therapists and authors of *Recovery: A Guide for Adult Children of Alcoholics*, suggest the following bill of rights:[1]

> These rights include the right to personal needs, including time for yourself, the right to your own feelings, the right to your own opinions, the right to decide whether you will meet others' expectations or not, the right to decide what to do with your own

body, the right to say no as well as the right to say yes, the right to change your
mind, the right to succeed, and the right to make mistakes.

If you have difficulty grasping what makes you feel good or
allowing yourself to do it, you will need outside support. You may
need someone to cheer you on and challenge you on your self-care.
Some friends can serve that purpose, but sometimes a group or a
therapist can offer more constant, steady support. A therapist is a
wonderful gift to give yourself. In many ways the therapist's role is
to be a nurturing supportive parent. If you haven't had all that
healing approval and encouragement, a therapist's office can be a
wonderful place to get it. On the other hand, some people feel more
nourished in a group setting. Al-Anon has begun to meet the needs
of adult children of alcoholics, and Parents Anonymous groups are
great places to discuss your parenting frustrations and get over
feeling like "the worst mother (or father) in the world." Both these
groups are free and many other support groups are available for
whatever ails you. Ministers and rabbis often act as referral services,
keeping themselves aware of what healing opportunities are available in your community.

Remember, kids learn more from what parents do (modeling)
than they do from what parents preach. If you want your children
to be happier than you are, you will have to become happier yourself.

NURTURE YOURSELF

Whatever nurturing your parents failed to give you, you can now
give to yourself. Make a self-nurturing tape. Pull out your recorder
and talk gently into the microphone, saying loving, reassuring,
appreciating things that you would want to say to your own small
child at bedtime. Tuck yourself in at night and play this loving tape
to yourself.

You cannot really give your children your love until you can give
it to yourself. Before then, there will be a barrier of jealousy, caution,
or fear. When you think of all you missed as a child, you may
begrudgingly parcel out love to your own children as if you are
resentful of their better fortune. For even when you treat your child
ten times better than you were treated, the child may show little
appreciation. What seems like miracles of generosity on your part,
your children may nonchalantly receive as if it is their due. And it

probably is! Many ACODF parents strive to give their children a better life and then feel jealous as they watch their children enjoy it!

Or perhaps your barrier is caution. You may fear that you cannot keep up such nurturing care for your child for an extended period of time. It *is* hard to give when you haven't received. So you hold back to avoid disappointing them on your down days. Raising their expectations for love can be frightening. Perhaps you don't want your children to expect more from you than you were given because you have not yet learned *how* to give love. Nurturing can be a frightening and overwhelming obligation at first. Take it in small steps. Give half of your daily love-quotient to yourself each day so that your capacity to love grows larger along with your child's responsive trust. Overcome your fear of being hurt. To love your child is to open yourself to being wounded or rejected. Move beyond your fear by loving yourself a little each day. It is like a tonic and will strengthen you so that you can safely take love risks.

You must begin by accepting yourself, faults and all. No one is perfect. Like Keith, you have had a difficult life and you need to be healed before you can take on the full responsibility of being a good parent. With loving patience you will grow into the role. But first you have to be a loved child, and it's time to stop waiting for your parents to be loving. Take your fate into your own hands and appreciate your good qualities. For until you can appreciate yourself despite your faults (despite the flaws that have grown out of never being loved enough) you cannot appreciate your child despite her faults (her flaws that have grown out of never being loved enough.)

◆ ══════════════ **SUMMARY** ══════════════ ◆

Praise, more than criticism, will help our children feel capable enough to do their best. If we learn what it is reasonable to expect from each of our children, we can better appreciate their accomplishments and reflect a positive image back to them.

◆ ══════════════ **POINTS** ══════════════ ◆

1. If we were criticized severely as children, we will have to guard against being hypercritical of our children.

2. We may become hypercritical because we believe others need our advice, we want to feel superior, or we need to cut everyone down to our size.

3. We often criticize our children because we fear others are judging *us* by our children's appearance or behavior.

4. Some reactionary ACODF who have been harshly criticized as children embrace the polar opposite attitude and become destructively tolerant of their children's unacceptable behavior.

5. Children's accomplishments and abilities must be judged on an individual basis. We must remember that temperament, intelligence, and life-experience all contribute to each child's level of achievement.

6. If our child has had a stressful early life due to his parents' divorce or other difficult circumstances, he may be developmentally behind others his age. We will need to lower our expectations for a while.

7. We can build the child's self-esteem by matching our expectations to the child's ability, arranging small successes, treating the child with the same respect we give our friends, and praising more than we criticize.

8. We need to tell our children that even when we do not like some of their behaviors, we still love them as people. There is no price tag on our love. It is guaranteed.

9. When we make a mistake it is best to humbly admit our error, and apologize to the child. Then we must forgive *ourselves.*

10. Although we may never get it from our parents, it is never too late to give ourselves the love, care, and acceptance we missed as children.

NOTES

1. Herbert L. Gravitz and Julie D. Bowden, *Recovery: A Guide for Adult Children of Alcoholics.* New York: Simon & Schuster, 1987.

· 10 ·

CONTROLLING

*11. ACODF engage in frequent power struggles
with their children and may feel dangerously
angry when they cannot control them.*

Adult children from dysfunctional families often grew up in chaos. There were no clear rules, and what rules there were were inconsistently enforced. They could seldom count on their parents to follow through on promises or commitments. Anything could change at a moment's notice. Some of those ACODF simply could not find clear enough role models for a more orderly existence and so have grown up to be irresponsible and unpredictable themselves. But most struggled to bring order to their lives by making up their own rules and rituals. Cinda's parents didn't care what time she came home from dates, but Cinda herself was concerned about not getting too sexually involved and becoming pregnant. So Cinda made up her own curfew and told her dates that "her parents would kill her" if she got home after midnight. Many ACODF taught themselves to brush their teeth and iron their clothes. They did everything they could to build some routine into their lives so that they would have less anxiety to live with. Sometimes their efforts to control their environment paid off; sometimes they were still sabotaged. But whatever predictability they could build into their lives at least added some comfort and security.

Children who have had to learn how to manipulate their parents, and who have taken on more responsibility than the adults around them, often have an exaggerated sense of their own power. They may come to believe that through enough effort they can control anything. At the same time, they are often left feeling that if

183

they don't control everything, the world will fall apart. As adults they compulsively overcontrol and believe organizing everyone's lives is a moral duty that is part of their destiny.

OVERPARENTING

We have all seen the mother who still ties her seven-year-old's shoes and races off to school with his lunch when he forgets it (even if this is a daily occurrence). **Some parents do everything for their children with such steady devotion there is never an opportunity to find out what the child can do for himself.** If he could not make a sandwich at four years old, they assume he cannot make one when he is ten.

◆ MERISSA—RESCUING

David had been very insecure as a preschooler and his mother was still feeling guilty about going back to work so soon. She was able to work shorter hours now and she was making an effort to "make up" for nurturing he might have missed at earlier stages.

David was seven years old and his mother Merissa knew that he needed to be pushed to overcome some of his fears. He still begged her to go to the bathroom with him because the shower stall scared him. Likewise, at bedtime he wanted his mother to lie down with him until he fell asleep. He had other dependent behaviors. He was perfectly capable of tying his shoes but he would have "frustration fits" or delay until he would miss the bus, manipulating his mother into tying his shoes for him. He also wanted Mother to cut his food.

David's mother was reluctant to push him too fast, feeling she might have unrealistic expectations. Merissa acted the part of the nurturing mother but in reality she resented all these demands. She was constantly behind on her housework because she lost much precious time each day accompanying David to the bathroom, tying his shoes, lying down with him. Still, Merissa was so worried about being a "good mother" that she could not follow her family therapist's urging to ignore David's protests and just assure David that he could handle these things himself. At the same time, she felt the therapist was right.

Merissa needed to come up with consequences that she could be comfortable with, or else she knew she would fail under pressure and decide she had been too harsh. She came up with some fairly good compromises that let her push David toward independence without feeling too guilty. First, she got him a dog to sleep with and take to the bathroom. Then she hinged the whole morning routine to the TV. David could not watch TV until he was fully dressed and had cut his breakfast pancakes into bite-size pieces. Merissa posted a family rule that stated if David missed the school bus, she would drive him to school (it would have been a four-mile walk in a rough neighborhood), but he would miss TV privileges for two days. Then she let it happen.

David only missed his TV privileges twice before he decided he really could tie his shoes and cut up his pancakes.

Merissa's guilt and overconscientious nature caused her to give in too easily to David's pleadings. A simple warning from the therapist was not enough to convince her to change—she needed to be certain it would do David no harm. Two experiences of the ACODF make them especially vulnerable to overparenting their children. As we mentioned earlier, ACODF often have an overdeveloped sense of responsibility gained by caring for themselves at a very young age. Also, they can remember just how lonely and abandoned they felt with no one to take care of their needs for them. They want to do better by their children but they often have no idea what is reasonable. They judge the needs of their children against the tremendous neediness they feel. While they are focused on making sure they do not neglect their children, it never occurs to them that **they may be robbing their children of the opportunity to become responsible for themselves.**

LETTING GO

The child's entry into school is often a very difficult time for the ACODF parent. The safety and well-being of her child is now in the hands of others for seven hours a day. She worries that no one can understand her child as well as she can, that the teacher will damage his or her self-esteem, that other children will pick on her child and no one will intervene. Indeed some parents become so frightened by the possibilities that they choose home-schooling so that they can go on controlling the child's total environment. However, this is rarely a healthy alternative. Children need to spend time with their peers and even occasionally get picked on. Someday they will have to interact with others. To be successful, they will need to know how to win an argument and how to brush off insults.

Putting your child in the hands of strangers is scary, but there are ways to bridge the connection between home and school so it is less traumatic for the parent and child. Most children can simply be sent off to school on the school bus after the first day, and most parents can let them go. But if you need more reassurance, you are entitled to get it. You might take your child down to the school a few days before each school year and meet the teacher. If you keep in mind that teachers work hard and are seldom appreciated, you can set the groundwork for your child to have a good relationship. Approach the teacher with a supportive attitude and focus on how you can become "partners" with the teacher in educating your child. Then step aside and allow the teacher to do her job. Every now and then the teacher may "pick on" your child for something he didn't do. Don't interfere unless there is a great injustice (like a five-day suspension for a window he didn't break). Life isn't always fair. Mistakes happen. You need to let your child cope with the consequences. If your child forgot that there was a rule about not bringing toys to school, and he takes along his new set of micro-machines only to have them confiscated by the teacher for the rest of the school year, so be it. He will not forget the rule again, and next year he will listen very carefully to the class rules when they are first presented. Resist the temptation to "rescue" your child from life's lessons.

◆ JUDY AND CARL—SUPERRESPONSIBLE

When Judy returned from the diastrous family trip to Mexico (see Chapter 8), she told her counselor about Carl's frightening behavior. The counselor suggested that Casey might be just too much for Carl and everyone would be better off if Casey took medication. A psychiatrist had confirmed that Casey was hyperactive and the counselor explained that taking care of Casey was like taking care of three children: There were few parents who could withstand the stress his impulsive behavior created. But Judy was adamantly opposed to drugs and decided to work around Carl by planning breaks between him and Casey. They would take no more trips until Casey had outgrown this behavior.

"And if Casey does not outgrow this behavior?" the counselor asked. Judy replied that she would then have to consider divorce.

When Judy realized that Casey would have to go to kindergarten next year, and she might have to get a job, she began to orchestrate Casey's reentry into the outside world. He cried and stormed when they went to look at preschools, then finally agreed to go to a parent-participation school where Judy could be with him every day. At this school Casey's teacher was opposed to medication for small children and so was willing to work with Judy.

At first, Casey needed constant surveillance, but when Judy tried the Feingold diet, he became a bit more manageable. It was a hassle. She had to prepare all his food from scratch and she couldn't allow him to eat the school snack or any food she had not prepared. Birthday parties were especially hard on him.

Judy followed Casey around the classroom watching carefully so that she could intervene before he could start a fight. If he was well rested he had more self-control, and she could get him to go to sleep earlier if she lay down with him. She chopped all her errands down into short trips, and if she couldn't get done quickly, they would just do without the item. She had written down all of his routines so they wouldn't forget and get off schedule. For the time being she was successfully controlling his environment.

On the other hand, there were a lot of elements that weren't under Judy's control yet. Casey was still disturbed by Carl's absences, and although Casey was doing progressively better at preschool, he was still the only child who had to sit in the time-out chair at least once a day.

About this time an old friend from Denver moved to the area and contacted Judy. When Judy thought of Donna, she could not help but think of Donna's boy Andy, six years old when she last saw him. He was the terror of the neighborhood, constantly in motion. He couldn't go into anyone's house without breaking something. Judy was now embarrassed to think about how many times she had pretended to be too busy to see Donna because she couldn't stand to be around Andy. But even Donna had once confessed that she would often shut herself in the closet because she couldn't bear to be with Andy, and since she knew he just couldn't help himself, she didn't want to punish *him*. Now Judy understood what Donna had meant, and she was anxious to have her over to see how Andy was doing now that he was older.

It turned out that Andy was taking medication and doing very well. Donna talked about how she had realized she was neglecting her other children before, because Andy's needs were so overwhelming. She had let it go on and on, even when Andy was having trouble in school and suffering from nervous ticks, because she was opposed to drugging kids. She'd tried the no-sugar diet, the no-wheat diet, the no-milk diet, and the Feingold diet. Each diet mysteriously helped for a little while, but then the novelty would wear off and they'd be back to square one again. Finally, when Andy threatened to kill himself with a kitchen knife after a disastrous day at school, Donna decided she had to accept professional help. Andy had been on medication for a year and had gone up three levels in reading and one in math. Everyone in Donna's family was feeling better.

Donna was certainly more relaxed and happy than Judy had ever seen her. If Donna needed to give her child medication, Judy didn't want to make her feel bad about it. However, Judy was sure that if she just continued to control Casey's environment, she wouldn't have to resort to medication. Still, Judy envied Donna's freedom to come talk with a friend while her kids played peacefully in the yard.

Judy would have liked to spend longer with Donna, but one hour was the absolute *maximum* Casey could stand to have her visit with someone, so she had had to ask Donna to leave when the hour was up.

(Continued in Chapter 15)

In her effort to control Casey's environment, Judy has built a prison for herself. Her every activity is dictated by Casey's limitations. She can do what he "permits" her to do. Her needs are not even considered as she puts all her effort into orchestrating Casey's days. She has dug a big hole and buried herself in it. But no one can accuse her of being an irresponsible mother!

Few parents can keep that kind of pace up indefinitely. As your child gets older and her interests expand, the number of things you could be responsible for, on her behalf, increases. Superresponsible parents are bound to become overextended or burnt out. Maybe it wasn't a strain to remind your daughter to take her lunch to school every day, but it becomes a different story when you must help her with piano practice, drive her to the library because she didn't finish her report for school, take her to her friend's house so she can get the book she left there, run home from the baseball game to get the glove she forgot, and walk her dog. If you have a second child, taking over all your daughter's responsibilities is not only exhausting, it is impossible, and you will have to leave her to face her consequences abruptly.

But parent burn-out is not the only problem. One of the most unfortunate results of your being a superconscientious parent is that you may begin to build co-dependence in your child. Remember that co-dependence is an unhealthy dependency that robs the child of the opportunity to grow. Two oft-repeated parental phrases that should warn you that you are developing an unhealthy degree of dependence in your child are: "Here, let me do that for you . . ." and "Oh, never mind! It's faster if I do it myself!"

A conscientious parent can become confused about what is healthy support and what is rescuing. Although child development books take a lot of the guesswork out of deciding what your child should be able to do for him- or herself, there are still personality differences, personal timetable differences, and the child's emotional background to consider. **Parents must keep asking themselves: Could my child do this for herself?**

SHARING POWER

Power is part of every relationship. It's like an atmospheric energy that surrounds two individuals or a family unit. The family power can reside in one dominant member or it can be shared equally by all. In some families the kids have all the power because the adults do not know how to defend their own rights. The parents watch TV shows that the kids pick and eat "kid food" at every meal. If the kids hate baby-sitters, the parents don't go out.

In other families the adults have all the power. They decide what the family will eat, what the family will do, and where the family will go, all without ever considering the childrens' preferences or needs. In these families, "Children are to be seen and not heard." The children are ordered around like dogs and beaten or punished unfairly if they don't comply. In other families, Dad alone wields the power and Mom must be as obedient as the kids.

When one sector of the family has considerably more power than the rest, the family is not healthy. There is sure to be an atmosphere of resentment and hostility. These "power trips" are so unnecessary. Children don't need to be ordered to do things. They will usually comply more quickly and more willingly if they are asked politely. It's OK to say "Please" and "Thank You" to your child. If your three-year-old drops his cup of milk on the kitchen floor, just mention, in a matter-of-fact manner, that he made a mess and state that it's time to clean it up. Hand him a rag, and when he is done, thank him even though he caused the mess to begin with. If you are cheerful and respectful about the spill, that's what his attitude will be about clean-up. If you are angry and pushy, he'll take his cue from you and stubbornly resist cleaning up. You can use your real power as a mature adult to set the mood of the day.

A good trick, when your child has misbehaved, is to let her set her own punishment or consequence. Kids generally know when they've done wrong and they will follow a rule they've made much more willingly and peacefully. A feeling of *shared* power should be your goal. Later we will be covering conflict resolution skills in detail (Chapter 13) but here, briefly, are some respectful skills we can use when negotiating with our children.

1. **Take turns:** Let your child decide what the family will eat for dinner or do on Saturday night every now and then.

2. **Make up:** If you have yelled or threatened, apologize later and explain that what you did was wrong and you will try not to do it again.

3. **Mediate:** You, your spouse, or even another child can mediate a conflict between you and your child. Listen respectfully to what your child says and how she feels. Try to reach some compromise that leaves her feeling as if she has had some power in the situation.

CHILDREN ARE UNPREDICTABLE

Children are one of the most uncontrollable elements in one's life. Conception itself may have been an accident (or difficult) and the precise time of birth is usually beyond our control. Suddenly schedules and habits must change. The crying of newborn babies cannot be controlled and toddlers are irrational. Indeed, the child initially exerts a great deal of control over the parents. Because children are always growing and changing, every time the parents master one of the child's stages, (for example, they learn to deal with his refusal to eat) they find the kid is done with that stage and ready to go on to something else. So parenting is very stressful. Kids' changes and natural growth are a constant source of frustration for parents. That's why rigid parents try to stop kids from growing. Once the parents have figured out how to deal with the child, they want everyone to "stand still" developmentally so that they can practice that new parenting skill. But healthy children are not so easy to manage. **Because children are ever-changing, they require flexible parents.**

Many ACODF may have actually managed to control most elements in their lives up until they have children. Then the ACODF may become very anxious. Children do not do what you ask just because you asked it. Children may forget to do what you asked, may be too preoccupied with something else to do what you asked, or may feel like asserting their independence. Even a very cooperative child may become too tired to do what you ask. Children are naturally self-centered. They do not come into the world knowing how to be considerate of others' feelings.

One of the traits that most characterizes dysfunctional adults is their lack of maturity and extreme self-centeredness. In fact, they act quite a bit like children. If you grew up in a dysfunctional home, you probably found that at least one of your parents (the other may have been superresponsible) would forget to do what you asked, was too preoccupied with their own interests to do what you needed, or sometimes just arbitrarily didn't "feel like doing" what you requested. Your own children are bound to restimulate the feelings of helplessness, hopelessness, hurt, and frustration that you felt when your parents did not respond to your needs. Only this time you are physically bigger and more powerful than your frustrator. Also, you might feel unable to control yourself or your environment and, as a result, see yourself as a helpless victim of life. Perhaps the only element in your life you feel you can control is your child. You have learned that if children won't cooperate willingly, you can intimidate them into cooperating by using threats and physical force.

With all of these bad feelings flooding your being, you are bound to feel the pent-up rage that you have carried since your disappointing childhood, and that anger may come out at your children. **In addition to all the normal challenges parents face with their children, difficult personality traits such as hyperactivity are often hereditary and tend to run in families with a history of alcoholism or mood disorder.** This compounds all the normal parenting problems and the parent's frustration-tolerance level can become dangerously low. Parents think, "I should be able to control my child! There's something wrong with me if I can't." ACODF are especially sensitive to perceived judgments of their parenting and feel humiliated by their child's misbehavior. Now their self-esteem is involved. There is a tremendous drive to become abusive: to insult, threaten, or hit your children to force their cooperation.

POWER STRUGGLES

Children, unlike mature adults, are irrational and driven by almost instinctive impulses toward independence or dominance. Parents can work with this instinct or struggle against it. Since independence is a healthy and essential skill, parents should try to "go with the flow" whenever possible. The child who wants to button his own shirt, even though it is going to make you late for work, is working on his autonomy, not spiting you. You are the one in the wrong if you have not allowed the child enough time to dress himself. You can often negotiate such a situation with respect by saying, "I see you are trying to learn how to button your shirt, and I wish I had allowed more time this morning for you to work on it. Would you let me do it today and I'll schedule an extra ten minutes tomorrow morning so you can learn to do it yourself?"

At the same time, parents need to differentiate between what is a "striving toward independence" and what is simple rebellion. The child who refuses to turn off the TV when she is supposed to be doing her homework is just testing the limits and needs a firm command. Parents should insist that rules about homework be followed, but they shouldn't expect the rules to always be followed "cheerfully." If your child wants to pout and stamp her feet on the way to the table, let it go. To make an issue of it is to ask for a power struggle.

Firmness without vengence should be your goal. **Give kids clear messages about what's debatable and what's not.** If you don't give your children something to push against, they'll fall flat on their faces. Don't come across as if everything is open to debate on a moment's notice. Kids often argue just to distract you and get out of their task. To avoid getting caught in a power struggle, make a clear statement like, "I will not argue with you about this." Then simply walk away, or tell the child that *after* the task is done, you will discuss it in terms of "fairness" or whatever the complaint was. Usually kids don't come back to talk about it.

You might want to "try your wings" at being firm yet flexible by tackling the age-old problem of eating.

◆ GINGER—FOOD!

"That's what the girls are having tonight for dessert," Ginger comments even before she says hello. I have agreed to meet her at a restaurant and I am eating a muffin when she arrives. "I use dessert as a bribe. It's a built-in reinforcement for whatever behaviors I'm working on right now," she continues.

Granted, we are in a restaurant, but I still find it striking that Ginger's first comment on her parenting has to do with food. Food is often the focus of power struggles in many homes. It is little wonder that children grow up with so many eating disorders.

As it turns out, dinnertime was a daily disaster in Ginger's childhood home. Her father was an alcoholic who became verbally abusive when drunk. Ginger tells me, "The evening ritual was that my father would come home from work and tell my mother what he wanted for dinner. Then she would take the car and go downtown to buy the ingredients. While she was gone my father would take a shower and go to the bar for a few drinks. My mother would come home and fix what he requested, but often he would not even come back to eat it.

"If we went ahead and ate without my father, when he came home he would say, 'Why didn't you wait for me? I told you I was coming home.' If we waited for him he would say, 'Why didn't you go ahead and feed the kids?' My mother was wrong no matter what she did. I coped with the stress at the dinner table by talking incessantly. I also spent a lot of time at the table after dinner because my mother believed you should eat everything on your plate.

"So dinner was always very stressful. Someone once said to me that children of alcoholics often have eating disorders and I said 'Oh, I didn't. I always hated food.' She said, 'That's a disorder.' "

Ginger, and her husband, Sam, both professionals, were able to adopt a child through the FOSDOPT program. Those available for adoption through this program generally come from dysfunctional families and have often been neglected if not abused. After months of preparation and training classes, Ginger and Sam received their daughter.

"When we got Kelly, I took her for a physical and the doctor told me that she had a weight problem. He recommended that I be careful about what I fed her." Kelly, six years old, is a compulsive eater and no amount is ever enough. At her previous foster home she was required to eat everything on her plate, and Ginger, who remembers being forced to eat as a child, has tried to correct this forced overeating. "I justs required her to *try* everything. I put reasonable portions on her plate and then I have to line everything up like dominoes: First you eat your salad, then you eat your vegetable, and so on. I have to hold off the starches to the end or she won't touch any of the vegetables."

With foster children food is often a big issue. Many have been deprived of food at some time. Or food represents being cared for and it is hard to get enough. Because of Ginger's background she was ripe to play right into this food game. While she uses an approach that is better than her mother's had been, she is blind to her own compulsiveness. Obviously, it is hard for any of them to be neutral about food.

I am not surprised when Ginger explains that all the conversation at the dinner table had been centering around Kelly and her food. "She would just go on and on about what she wanted to eat and what she didn't want to eat and how she felt about each piece of food."

Ginger had to make a temporary "no talking about food at the dinner table" rule before she could get Kelly to think about other things.

Modern nutritionists and pediatricians caution against making too big an issue of food. Left to their own devices, most children who are offered healthy food will ultimately choose a well-rounded diet. They might not eat a balanced meal each time, or their food throughout one day might not even be balanced, but a child's food choices across a week will often show the child eating a balanced diet. Also, while the child needs to eat some vegetables, it really is not important what vegetable the child eats. Let the child eat green beans for two years if that's the only vegetable she likes. She'll get tired of it eventually and try an alternative. Parents who are really nervous about their children's diets should give their children a multivitamin every day to fill in the possible gaps. This should give you the peace of mind you need to be able to let it go. Power struggles over food are the least effective method of getting children to eat. They invariably increase the child's resistance because **the child has a need to feel in charge of her own body.**

Unfortunately, this "laissez faire" attitude about eating may not work with compulsive eaters. Kelly overeats for emotional reasons and "sugary" things may make her feel more "loved" than vegetables. When eating is a long-term problem it is best to follow advice from a pediatrician who has examined your child and has tailored his or her recommendations to the needs of your particular child.

Ginger's technique of structuring how Kelly eats her food, although a bit too controlling, has also had its positive side. Due to Ginger's careful monitoring, Kelly's weight came down to normal within the first year with her new parents. "She used to say that no one liked her; no one wanted to play with her," comments Ginger. "And now she talks about how easily she makes new friends." Ginger no longer needs to monitor the amount Kelly eats. When Kelly overdoes it, she feels ill. "She is learning to set her own limit on what she eats. She now frequently acknowledges that she is full after eating reasonable portions." Ginger has stopped using dessert as a reward and they all eat sweets less often.

"I honestly don't believe that these changes would have taken place if I had followed the recommendation, in popular parenting magazines, that I allow Kelly to eat unlimited amounts of whatever she chose. She would not have eaten some of every food group throughout the week. She would not have lost weight, and she would have continued to suffer the social stigma and poor self-confidence associated with overweight children, as well as the long-term health risks noted by our pediatrician."

Ginger has also been able to see the positive side to Kelly's enthusiasm for food. Unlike many small children, Kelly is quite adventurous about trying new foods. Ginger delightedly points out, "Kelly especially likes to sample the strange things that Sam and I order at restaurants."

Ginger and Sam's method was effective on a short-term basis and fortunately Kelly was eventually able to become self-correcting. With some dependent and insecure children, parents have to be prepared to do a lot of gentle pushing. To help their child achieve independence, healthy parents gradually shift from being the rule setters to letting the child set rules for himself or herself. This happens in very small steps throughout the child's life. For example, the parents might let their six-month-old choose from foods set out on his tray and later allow him to select his clothes when he is a toddler. The school-age child can decide whether he would rather do his homework when he arrives home from school or after dinner, and the preteen can be allowed to take a bus to a friend's house across town. Hopefully, with all these successful experiments behind him, the teenage child can then be trusted to choose his own friends and avoid the kids "headed nowhere." We don't want to be so overprotective that our teenagers feel compelled to rebel against us.

HYPERVIGILANCE

Any parents who have struggled through recovery from alcoholism are bound to be "on guard" against drug or alcohol problems in their children. This is common sense and can be a healthy thing, but it can also be taken too far.

In the Ward family, Tom had been a "closet alcoholic" who rarely drank in his wife Janet's presence, but ultimately became a daily drunk. Tom drank while off with his son on errands or while working in the garage. Every evening he would be busy working on projects in the garage and then come in to fall asleep in front of the TV "exhausted." We might wonder how Janet could not have known her husband was sloshed each evening, but Tom was very careful and clever—so clever, in fact, that all their friends expressed their genuine astonishment when Tom's alcoholism was uncovered. Tom's tolerance had gradually increased with his increased intake of alcohol until one day he "crossed the line" and could no longer control his symptoms of drunkenness. Tom had a bad fall and Janet, mistaking his drunken weaving for signs of a serious concussion, wanted to call for an ambulance. In that moment Tom realized that his drinking had gotten out of control and he said, "Don't worry about it. I'm just drunk. I'm an alcoholic."

I interviewed Tom, Janet, and their oldest son, Greg, separately, to get a picture of the whole family from different perspectives.

◆ THE WARDS—HYPERVIGILANCE

TOM

When Tom was a child his father would come home from work, drink a pint of beer before dinner, and then sip wine all evening.

"My father has always been very sharp-tongued when he's been drinking," Tom told me. "He would reach a peak at dinnertime and dinner was always horrible. He would criticize us for every little thing. 'Hold your fork properly. That's not the way to pass a dish,' and so on. Most of the criticism was actually directed at my younger brother. I was the 'good son.' My father was a very frustrated and bitter man who hated his job but was afraid to let go of it. He is still drinking and my mother is still putting up with it."

Tom began drinking heavily in college but feels he "crossed the line" when he got married and had his first adult job. "I started coming home after work and pouring a tumbler of wine. I drank that out in the open and that would be it for the night. But Janet was very aware of my father's alcoholism. When I drank some of her cooking wine she had a big fit. I denied drinking it but then I realized that I would have to drink on the sly if I didn't want her to get mad at me. So I bought myself a gallon of wine to keep in the garage." It was not until ten years later that Tom's alcoholism was finally exposed.

JANET

For Janet, the most devastating effects were her loss of confidence in her own judgment and her broken trust in her husband. "I felt betrayed. I thought, 'What else don't I know about him?' It felt almost like he'd been having an affair I didn't know about. I thought, 'If I can't trust my husband, who can I trust?' It was very disillusioning.''

One reason that Janet might have missed seeing the signs of her husband's alcoholism was that she had been struggling with recurring depressions for years. Depression causes the victim to become so preoccupied with self that she can become unaware of much going on around her.

"The first time I got very depressed I was in high school. I felt just horrible, but no matter how depressed I am I can always function. So I remember sitting there working on my homework and tears were streaming down my face. My mother asked what was wrong and I said, 'I don't know,' because I really didn't know.''

"When I had Greg I became very anxious. Things in the paper would scare me. I would personally relate to all these disasters. The Manson trial was going on then and it got so I couldn't even read the paper anymore. I felt like it was my job to protect my child from all these horrors.'' Janet went for therapy but continued to have periodic recurring depression.

When Tom was three-years sober, the Wards' oldest son, Greg, entered adolescence. Because Greg had been an easy, compliant child, his parents were shocked at his teenage rebellious and destructive behavior.

"Greg's grades took a terrible drop. Third quarter of freshman year he got some F's. He'd always had excellent grades before. We got this parenting book out of the library and it described teenage behavior in levels from normal to very distrubed. Most of his behaviors fell in the normal column. But I don't know if I was just denying how he was really acting. A big part of the problem was that we just didn't know what was normal for a teenager. Of course, Greg would tell us that we were just too uptight about everything.

"Then there was this incident we blew all out of proportion. A neighbor had seen Greg smoking a cigarette and we got all upset about it, thinking one thing leads to another and all that. We were afraid for him because of the family history of alcoholism.

"We put him on restriction for a week but he kept provoking us and we'd add another day. Then Greg had this fit where he was ranting and raving. Tom took him to the doctor the next day and described what had happened. The doctor told us we better consider drug use. So we called around and found a therapist.''

Despite the therapy, a few months later Greg got picked up for possession of liquor and for curfew violation. He was taken to juvenile hall and had to serve one day cleaning up the park. "That was pretty minor. But then a few months after that Greg didn't come home one night. I went out looking for him and eventually found him passed out on our own lawn. He was drinking alcoholically and that was really frightening.''

GREG

Greg was nine years old when his father went into treatment.

"I can't remember if I actually saw my dad drinking much, but we used to have piles of beer cans in the backyard and one time when his friends were over playing pinochle he let me have a beer and that was really weird.

"When he was drinking he would do crazy things. We'd go to Taco Bell and then stop by the liquor store for a bottle for my father. I didn't think of it as him drinking. I just thought about myself. Like, 'Oh wow! I get to go to Taco Bell!' Then we'd go out on the highway and he'd go about ninety miles per hour in his Porsche. I thought it was a fun game. He never got caught. This was what we did for fun before. Then he turns around later and says that's wrong.

"I was pretty happy when I was little but our family never went anywhere. I'm not a home-boy type, and all they wanted to do was hang around home. I resented that. It was like we were shut off from society. I still just want to jump into my car and bail. Part of that is just that I was stuck here for so long. Like my parents were so superrestrictive. I wasn't even allowed to go downtown when I was in junior high. My mother had so much fear of the world and me being kidnapped and all. I think they thought I would eventually want to sit around reading books like they do. But I never will.

"If you ask me what the family was like before I was about seven or eight you'd get a totally different story than after that. When my father sobered up things were different. I was brought up in 'the alcoholic family.' But my brother has just lived in the normal family. I started to feel jealous when my brother was about five. He was the age where I first start remembering things. I was looking at him and seeing him being treated in a totally different manner. I know everyone is a different individual and all that crap, but he was getting a different type of attention than I had gotten. I knew that was because of my dad's sobriety but I felt like I was being cheated.

"Well, all the hate started coming out when I was a freshman. I came home from school one day and my mom asked me if I'd been smoking. I figured she must already know or she wouldn't be asking so I just said, 'Yes.' They grounded me for a week. I felt like they weren't listening to me or anything or willing to hear my side. I freaked out and I pushed my mom. So then they kept adding on to the punishment. They drove me to school. It was all such a big deal over nothing. They didn't realize that I was really so much better than a lot of other kids.

"Later on that year I tried alcohol and had some maybe three times out of that whole year—I was still pretty goody-goody. Then my sophomore year, I started drinking regularly. My drinking got serious fast. I was premeditating my weekends, thinking all week about how I was going to get ahold of some alcohol and what I was going to do. I was listening out for parties. I got totally obsessed with alcohol. But then a few weeks before my sixteenth birthday I got busted for alcohol. So I got into dope.

"At first it's fun getting stoned but then it doesn't work as well anymore. You just start getting anxious instead. You get stressed over it and you get concerned about where your dope is coming from. You can't think about anything else. I kept journals and I can see how it screwed up my head.

"After two years, I finally got off drugs because of a girl. We went to a party and I was smoking a joint and we were all going, 'Oh, my God! This is the best stuff I ever had.' I passed it to her and she made up this big lie about a friend of hers dying from a toke of dope laced with LSD. But I kept on smoking and I was saying all this stuff and then I'd look at her and realize she was totally sober, and I could imagine how I looked to her and I felt like such a jerk. This was the first time I ever took her out and she wouldn't talk to me until I was sober.

"I got that pride about how people look at you. I had to teach myself that—that it does make a difference what you wear or how you act—they're going to judge you by that. I didn't care before. Now I do care. I care that the car looks good. Like I dressed up for school last Monday and everyone was amazed and started treating me differently.

"My parents can't deal with the whole drug and alcohol thing at all. So I can't even tell them that I've worked through all this stuff and they don't have to worry anymore. I didn't get anything good out of it and I corrected myself. I wish my parents could see that. But I can't tell them how much I used to drink or do drugs because they couldn't handle it. They'd start restricting me *now!*"

(Continued in Chapter 12)

If you insist that your children never try a drink, you may be making it the most alluring temptation your child will ever have to face. The Wards understandably had trouble being objective about Greg's drinking. If alcoholism or addiciton runs in your family, you may need to seek the advice of a therapist or doctor to get a sense of perspective. If professionals think your child may be headed for trouble, seek help immediately. But if a reliable counselor who is familiar with alcoholism, drug abuse, or mood disorders feels your child's behavior is normal for his or her age, consider this opinion carefully before you launch into a moral speech for your children. When you do talk to your child about family illnesses, keep your eyes and ears open. If they begin to lose interest, stop. If they start to look alarmed, reassure. Let your values be known in a matter-of-fact (not preachy) way and then be ready to respond to your children's questions. Your talks should be conversations, not lectures.

Explanations should be tailored to the child's developmental level and interest, just as one would gradually reveal facts about reproduction. When they are young you can point out that alcohol is not nutritious, and just as you don't want them to have a heavy diet of candy, grown-ups should not make alcohol too large a part of their diet. Find parallels that are meaningful to your child at each age level. If you exaggerate the risk or act too self-righteous, you will damage your credibility in the eyes of your children. Explain the behavior of other family members in a neutral, compassionate way. If they sense you hate Uncle Harry for the way he acts, your children will not feel free to come to you when they find themselves acting like Uncle Harry.

Likewise, if you make acid remarks about all the drinkers at a party every time you return home from one, your children will not want you to know about their drinking experiments because they will fear your wrath. Family history might be enough to keep them from experimenting, but if it is not, you want to keep the door open. Show you can discuss the issue calmly and objectively, so that if they run into problems with alcohol (or fast living) they will still feel free to come to you and talk about it.

Remember, you are building a lifelong relationship. You may be your child's best resource when he or she is older and facing these hereditary problems.

Communication Skills

BARRIERS

BUILDERS

1) ASSUMING: If we assume our child will have the same reaction to a stimulus as they had last time, and act accordingly, we are ignoring the individual's ability to change.

1) CHECKING: By checking with the child each time we want them to attempt a behavior, we allow them to show how much they have grown since they last faced such a request.

2) RESCUING/EXPLAINING: If we step in and explain things or intervene so our child does not experience the consequences of his or her behavior, we deprive them of the opportunity to learn from their experiences.

2) EXPLORING: By exploring various solutions with our child by asking leading questions and allowing them to think about the answers, we help them develop problem-solving skills.

3) DIRECTING: If we direct our childrens' every move we are likely to be met with resistance and hostility and defeat our childrens' initiative.

3) ENCOURAGING/INVITING: By inviting participation and contribution instead of directing, we convey a feeling of respect for our child.

4) EXPECTING: If we expect perfection in the beginning, we will miss seeing the important little steps our children take toward mastery of a task and discourage them unnecessarily.

4) CELEBRATING: By praising small steps in the right direction, we affirm the child's progress and show our confidence in their potential for growth.

5) ADULTISMS: If we forget what it is like to be a child and expect, demand, or require the child to think like an adult, we produce feelings of impotence, frustration, hostility, and aggression.

5) RESPECT: By understanding that attitudes and behaviors come from perceptions and beliefs, we can recognize our child's different way of seeing the world and affirm his or her right to be a child.

COMMUNICATING WITH TEENS

Family psychologist Stephen Glenn (*Raising Self-Reliant Children in a Self-Indulgent World*) offers some good advice to parents who are trying to learn better communication skills so that they can "be there" at this critical time in an adolescent's life. His first admonition is: When in doubt, do nothing. Too many of us have been trained to give responses that actually block communication. Glenn defines the communication habits that discourage communication and describes the better alternatives. The chart above illustrates and contrasts these different approaches:[1]

The *builders* above all serve to build self-esteem in children, and your child's high self-esteem is his or her best armor against destructive temptations.

TRUSTING YOUR TEEN

Remember Gary from Chapter 3? He was a teenager during the sixties. One of five children in a family whose business had just gone bankrupt, Gary faced the "Will I or won't I?" drug decision.

◆ GARY AS TEEN

"When I was about nineteen—that awkward age where you're not quite an adult but you're still living at home," Gary began, "I had friends that started doing stuff that I didn't want to do. They were getting into drugs and so on—my best friend too—I just didn't feel comfortable around them. I found out that I wasn't being invited to parties because I wasn't any fun and I was crushed.

"I came home one night—I remember I had broken up with a girlfriend—and I'd basically 'broken up' with my best friend. I had the same kind of feelings," Gary explained. "I got home and my mom had turned my closet inside out because it was a mess. She was going to show me that it was time I started doing something around the house, but she really chose the wrong time to do it," he recalls. "I was so upset that I couldn't handle anything. I remember talking to her and telling her how mad I was and she said, 'Don't drive.' And I said to her, 'I'm OK, but I have to get out of here.'

"So I drove off and just parked somewhere until I cooled off. I was gone for a couple of hours. When I came back she had cleaned up my whole room."

Now a parent, thinking like a parent, Gary says, "I know she shouldn't have cleaned up my room, I should have cleaned up my room. But I remember coming back and thinking about what a nice lady she was and how thankful I was that my parents were so supportive and they knew how upset I was. She didn't say, 'I don't care about your friends. They're all dumb kids anyway. Now get in there and clean up your room.' But instead, by cleaning up my room she said, 'Your room is not that important but these other things are, and I think you made the right decision.' "

At this critical time that Gary recalls his parents being so supportive, his father had just gone bankrupt. Obviously this must have been a very stressful time for his parents, but Gary does not remember it as a crisis. He had put himself through the local college instead of going away to school like his older sister had done. But he felt no resentment about the work it meant for him. The family was still a warm, supportive nest. The parental relationship had not been torn apart by the bankruptcy. All that had been lost was money, and in that family money was a much lower priority than relationship.

The memory of that critical night has stayed in Gary's mind as an example of the tremendous trust his parents had in him and how much that trust always meant to him. He had given them very few details, but his mother had sensed what was going on with Gary. "I'm sure that the things that were bothering me about my friend were bothering them," Gary explains, "but they never said anything about it. They never told me to stop hanging around with him or said he was a jerk." As a parent, Gary now realizes how difficult that must have been—just to sit back and let him come to his own conclusion about his friend. But he also knows that he was very independent and that if they had criticized his friend he would have clung to the relationship all the longer, despite his own better judgment.

Each night at dinner Gary listens attentively to his daughters' daily trials, hoping that by the time they are teenagers he will be able to sense when they need his quiet *unspoken* support.

It is hard to strike a good balance between letting our children take the lead and letting them fall flat on their face. Every conscientious parent would like to spare his or her child from the pain of life, but this is not only impractical and impossible, it is also destructive. We all learn from our mistakes. If we protect our children from every mishap, they will enter adulthood with no defenses of their own. I remember complaining to my therapist once about having to be "on guard" with salesmen. I said I wished my parents had protected me more so that I was not so suspicious of people. "That's odd," he remarked. "Yesterday a client of mine was complaining about how 'on guard' she had to be all the time because her parents had overprotected her so much that she never learned for herself who or what to trust."

We cannot suffer our children's pain for them; they must suffer the pain of their own wounds. Such protection is not even an honorable or useful goal.

◆ ══════════════ **SUMMARY** ══════════════ ◆

Parents who have grown up in dysfunctional families often have a tremendous need to be in control. Not only do they exhaust themselves by running everything without help, they kill initiative in their spouses and children, thus fostering unhealthy dependence in those around them.

◆ ══════════════ **POINTS** ══════════════ ◆

1. When we have grown accustomed to taking on heavy responsibilities from an early age, we sometimes have difficulty getting out of "hyperdrive" and consequently overparent our children.

2. Many ACODF felt lonely and overwhelmed as children. When we remember our parents' neglect, we may overcorrect and do too much for our children, thus interfering with the child's development of self-reliance skills.

3. If the superresponsible parent becomes burnt-out, she may need to cut back abruptly on her care of her child. It is better if we can recognize our needs earlier, and gradually wean the child away from overdependence.

4. Healthy families share decision-making power with the children. If we give our children a say in setting rules and consequences, they will generally be more cooperative and less resistant.

5. We often want our children to "stand still" developmentally while we catch up or rest from the last parent/child adjustment. However, since healthy growing children are ever-changing, we need to be flexible parents.

6. By understanding our children's natural striving toward independence, we will interpret their motivations differently and be more tolerant of their oppositional stands.

7. It is very difficult for us to be objective when our children face a hereditary danger such as alcoholism. However, if we come on too strong, we will push our children to take up rebelliously the very behavior we dread.

NOTES

1. This chart uses concepts from Chapter 4 of Stephen Glenn's *Raising Self-Reliant Children in a Self-Indulgent World*, Fair Oaks, CA: Prima Publishing, 1987.

11

NURTURING RESPONSIBILITY

*12. ACODF either model irresponsible behavior
and create irresponsible children or are so
superresponsible that they become burned out
and dysfunctional.*

A strong sense of responsibility can be a curse or a blessing. More than any other characteristic ACODF struggle with, how responsibly we behave is often *reactionary*. It is very typical for marriage partners in a dysfunctional family to polarize around the issue of responsibility. If your father was an irresponsible drunk, your mother probably went overboard playing the responsible one. It is part of co-dependence not only to compensate for the other's weakness, but also to base our *comparative* self-esteem on how much better we are at that critical trait. If your parents polarized around the issue of responsibility, you have probably selected one parent either to emulate or react to.

If you favored your mother and she was the responsible one, then, like her, you will probably become superresponsible. On the other hand, if you felt oppressed by your mother's "controlling" behavior, you may instead go overboard proving that you can be a "fun" person like your dad. It is hard for ACODF to be balanced about responsibility because they have not seen balanced responsibility modeled. As a parent, you are likely to adopt either the superresponsible or superirresponsible attitude, and both are destructive to your child. If you are superresponsible you are probably holding your child back from learning to take responsibility for herself. If you are superirresponsible you are probably creating fearful feelings of neglect or abandonment in your child. Neither extreme builds confidence and self-esteem.

204

BEING REACTIONARY

Unfortunately, this dance between the superresponsible parent and the superirresponsible parent can become a vicious circle. The superresponsible parent who compulsively takes over all the responsibilities (because she can do a better job than anyone else) is fostering irresponsibility in the other parent. Not only does the superresponsible parent allow the other parent to be irresponsible, **she may actually push him into that corner of inactivity by doing everything "better and more efficiently."** Just as the discouraged child will give power over to the domineering parent, if pushed far enough, the discouraged spouse will give power over to the dominant spouse. The irresponsible parent might first give up territories of responsibility because he just doesn't want to fight about it, but eventually his limited position and power in the family will erode his self-esteem until he believes he really is not capable of being responsible. Hence, we have the superresponsible parent versus the superirresponsible parent. This phenomenon is called polarizing. It is most common for women to take over the superparent role because the custom has been the rigidly fixed male/female roles of provider versus caretaker. Other polarities are the disciplining parent versus the nice parent, or the dependency-encourager versus the shover-out-of-the-nest.

If you find yourself and your co-parent (whether you are still married to one another or not) polarizing so that you are now both exaggerated opposites of one another, take a close look at your dynamics. Does the children's father make a point of taking them on dangerous outings because he thinks you coddle them too much? Do you find yourself giving in to your children's demands more than you ordinarily would because their father is so harsh when he is around? **When you discipline or set rules for your children, are you acting in their best interests or are you** *reacting* **to your co-parent's excesses?**

To sort out whether or not you are being primarily reactionary, ask yourself: Who was I before I married? What role do I feel pushed into? If you feel as if one part of your personality is dominating much more than it used to (for example, were you always compulsively neat or are you just reacting to your husband's sloppiness?) decide if this is really a change that you have worked toward in a positive sense. Are you being more of something you always wanted to be more of? Or are you trying to make up for some negative trait in your spouse or co-parent? If you decide that you are primarily reacting to your co-parent, don't waste time waiting for him or her to change. "Who 'started' it?" is a moot point. Your children need balanced, reasonable parents, not the anxiety caused by two strongly opposing sets of values. Think of your children and ask yourself: What can *I* do to stop it? If you are being too lenient because you feel your co-parent is too harsh, stop and think through your actions and decisions. You needn't be harsh to reverse the trend. If you just start being reasonably strict, it will free your co-parent to give in a little. The more balanced you act, the more balanced your co-parent can act.

To nurture an independent, balanced sense of responsibility in your children, you will have to closely examine your actions in this critical area. The issue of responsibility is complex and ever-changing. As soon as your child masters one level of responsibility, he or she is ready to embark on the next challenge. Therefore, you need to examine—not once but over and over—what responsibilities you should take over for your child and what responsibilities you should leave in his or her hands. To remain flexible and keep current with your child's growing abilities in any and all areas, you need to save time every day for reflection and evaluation. Let's look at some common mistakes parents make in the area of responsibility.

THE OVERCOMMITTED CHILD

The responsible parent tries to provide opportunities for her children to discover and develop their talents; the superresponsible parent makes sure her kids have everything she didn't have, whether they want it or not. As mentioned earlier, it is a common mistake for each generation to project their needs onto their children so that no one is ever recognized for who they are, nor do they get their needs met. Grandma wanted to be a dancer but her mother kept giving her sewing lessons, so Grandma dragged Mother off to dancing lessons every week although Mother wanted to play baseball; now Mother is making Daughter play baseball when Daughter would rather be sitting in the grandstands wearing frilly dresses, and so on.

Baseball may have been the most important thing in the world for you as a child. Maybe you signed up for Little League and halfway through the season your mother got tired of driving you there. Perhaps you dreamed of becoming a professional ball player and had been told you had natural talent. If so, chances are you swore that your son would never go without organized sports, no matter what it took. So as soon as he learned to walk, off you went to sign him up for baseball. After your great generosity he ungratefully balks at going. What is wrong with this boy? Maybe he had no interest in sports and was destined to be a scientist; or maybe your son also had a natural talent for sports but he was so frustrated by trying to learn to run, catch, and throw before he had even mastered walking, that he was turned off to sports for the rest of his life. **Superresponsible ACODF parents often jump the gun. While trying to be the best Mom or Dad, they become a *spoiler*, not only spoiling their children but also spoiling everything for them.**

Not only are ACODF likely to project their desires onto their children, they may also lack perspective about just how much their children can or should do. If you dreamed about a lot of activities but were never allowed to try any of them, you may want to offer too much to your child. It is much easier to dream about participating in many activities than it is to participate in each and every one of them. In your effort to give your children what they ask for in addition to what you lacked, you may overwhelm them with extracurricular activities. Children tend to be impulsive as it is. They need you to model and suggest reasonable limits.

THE IRRESPONSIBLE PARENT

By contrast, some ACODF model irresponsible behavior and create irresponsible children. Of course, both extremes are damaging to children, but very irresponsible parents are a burden to the whole family. Not only do they fail to do their share of the work, they even create more work for the family to do. Either Mother becomes overburdened and cannot give the children the care and attention they need, or the children themselves are expected to do Daddy's work. Or perhaps Mom is chronically depressed and stays in bed like a sick invalid. Not only does she neglect her work, she requires others to wait on her. As the more responsible parent becomes preoccupied with controlling or fixing the irresponsible parent, the children often lose the attention and support of both parents. Life becomes chaos as promises are broken, schedules are ignored, and unaddressed problems pile up.

Raising children is hard work and two parents are needed. If you have been less responsible than you should be and have come to feel that your family may be better off without the meager help you could give them, think again. If you are not part of the solution then you are part of the problem. You may believe that by blending quietly into the background and letting your more eager partner take full responsibility for your children, you will at least do no harm. But the minute you become a parent you have tremendous power over another person (your child) and the only choice you have is how you will use that power. **Your child needs to feel that both her parents care for her.** When you withdraw and become a passive member of the family, your children take this as proof that you don't love them or care what happens to them. If you are feeling very depleted and poorly qualified to do much as a parent, start with a small task. Don't worry about being a "perfect parent." Perhaps you could offer to entertain the children while your spouse gets some work done. Then drive the children to the park. For the most part, they will be able to entertain themselves once you have placed them in the right environment. (At first they may constantly seek your attention, asking you to watch them swing or applaud their tricks on the jungle gym. This is a stage they have to get through.) By reasserting yourself, and making sure that you are an active parent, you provide a much healthier role model for your children. They will know what a true parenting partnership is and be able to create a more harmonious family for your grandchildren.

PARENTING ALONE

Sometimes there simply is no co-parent. Maybe you never married, your spouse died, the children's father moved away and does not write or call, or your new husband has let you know in no uncertain terms that he considers your children by your previous marriage to be *your* problem. Perhaps your spouse does not recognize that he or she has stopped co-parenting. Even though the children's other parent is still a member of the family, he or she may simply refuse or be incapable of acting the part of the parent. Maybe the child's mother is depressed, alcoholic, or "lost" in her career; or perhaps their very well-meaning, loving father travels on business two-thirds of the time. Whatever the cause, if you are parenting alone, remember that one consistent parent is better than two inconsistent parents. Take charge and set rules that you can live with. Don't plan so many activities and obligations that you need another adult to help carry them out. Keep your expectations within your capability as a solo parent. Be clear and objective with your children about why you can't do more. Cite the other parent's absence as a cause but don't do this in a blaming or accusatory way. Be as neutral as you can about the fact that Mom or Dad are simply not available.

The man or woman who has lost the support of his or her spouse in parenting tasks because the spouse is inaccessible due to an addiction—be it alcoholism, workaholism, golf or running addiction—is in an especially vulnerable position until he or she accepts the loss and moves on emotionally. For example, if the wife with an emotionally absent husband can function independently—make decisions, make friends, manage the money, and discipline the children—the whole family will be more stable because life will go on with less disruption when the spouse is not present, whether the absence was predictable or not. The children will be less disturbed about the missing parent if the one parent can function as two parents. This may be a bitter pill to swallow for the remaining parent, but once the loss is fully accepted, the abandoned spouse can begin to divide up family responsibilities more realistically, assigning tasks to the children to lighten her load. She can also reduce the stress of ambiguity for all. It is always more peaceful to feel in control of the situation.

Divorce is also an option; but if the spouse is still earning money and providing financial security for the family, staying intact as a family while acting as an independent parent may be less stressful than a divorce or separation. The newer research on divorce shows that, in most cases, children are better off if the parents stay married.[1] On the other hand, if you or the child are being seriously abused, you may both need to get out of the situation and divorce may be the only answer. However, in less extreme situations, you should try avenues such as counseling first.

One major frustration of parenting alone, in the case of divorce or the emotionally absent parent, is watching the children be hurt by an irresponsible parent who promises to take them places and repeatedly doesn't show up at the appointed time. Instead of having the children dressed and ready to go, the active parent can relieve some of the anxiety and unpleasantness by letting the children carry on with their activities or even visit friends nearby so that they can be assembled quickly when Mom or Dad finally arrives. Some abandoned parents may feel it is useful to let the children suffer the consequences of their parent's lateness, letting them sit down ready at the appointed hour waiting and listening for their parent's arrival, so that the irresponsible parent can see the pain he or she has caused the children by being so late. However, the active parent must realize that the "absent" parent is not likely to learn from this and change. The children are repeatedly suffering need-lessly. Instead, the active parent must overcome this temptation (and there is often a great temptation born of bitterness to have the children see how little that "rat" cares about them; but that will not help their self-esteem nor is it the best way to show them how much you care) and put what is best for the children first. Sitting and fuming is not best for the children even if it could teach the other parent a lesson.

Sadly, many careers demand that parents spend a great deal of time away from home. Doctors often have very demanding schedules and calls that take them away unexpectedly no matter what the family had planned. Military personnel are often sent off for ex-tended periods of time, leaving their families to fend for themselves. Anyone who wants to climb in a competitive company must be willing to travel. If the family benefits overall from the money that can be earned at these inconvenient jobs, it is best to have a positive attitude and make the best of the situation.

Losing a parent to a career is sometimes more difficult to cope with emotionally than losing a parent through death or divorce. The parent-at-home and children may feel lonely and abandoned even when the workaholic spouse is at home because he or she is often emotionally absent. Yet it is harder to recognize the loss and move on to a solution. The parent may feel foolish complaining about the spouse's absence to friends, and so he or she cannot even get the comfort that could come from talking to a sympathetic ear. Like-wise, the parent-at-home may feel like a single parent, but still be reluctant to make family plans and decisions on his or her own. The family will be "stuck" until they can intellectually declare the other parent peripheral. Naturally, this will all be easier if the parent-at-home has developed a network of friends and is comfortable with independence.

Taking command as if you are a single parent is not just a last-ditch effort in a bad situation. Even mothers and fathers in healthy families may have to be absent a great deal of the time because of business travel or other work demands that are an inescapable part of certain jobs. In the healthy family everyone, including the traveling parent, would consciously recognize that parent's inaccessibility and build a family system that can function fully without him or her. There are many things the traveling or absent parent can do to lower the stress even if he or she can't be there. For example, the less-accessible parent can let the family know ahead of time when he or she will be absent; stay in touch by phone when out of town; or schedule some family or spouse time into his or her new busy work schedule. The family might go along on a business trip, or the overly busy parent can meet his or her spouse for lunch. Also, the less-accessible parent's ability to quickly and smoothly change out of work-mode into his or her home-mode when with the family is also important. Obviously, that parent's ego must be strong enough to survive the family's making important decisions or having a good time without him or her, and it helps if the family can be flexible enough to include the other parent when he or she shows up unexpectedly at the last minute. Again, it is a matter of how the family perceives the problem.

If Dad is going to be gone for three weeks, it makes no sense to "wait until your father gets home" for discipline. Even more ludicrous would be waiting three weeks for some love or affection because Mom is out of town. Therefore, the solo parent must be a self-contained parenting unit. Of course, this can be very demanding and the solo parent should assemble his or her own support group to help them through hectic or troubled times. Churches often offer relief for parents by scheduling activities for adults with child care provided, and parents can meet other parents at church who might agree to some cooperative baby-sitting. It is also a good opportunity to get to know other parents so that you can call someone and talk if you need to. Often a solo parent wishes there were another knowledgeable adult around to help make a child-rearing decision, and neighbors or parents of your child's playmates can fill in as an "extra head." Unmarried parents can find comfort and family activities through organizations such as Parents Without

Partners. If you are parenting alone you may feel so overwhelmed by your parenting responsibilities and other demands, such as your career, that you can't imagine when you would have time to socialize. However, it is very important not to become isolated. The energy you put into making parenting friends will pay off one way or another—by emotional support, care-taking assistance, or simple breaks from the intensity of family togetherness.

Sometimes the nonparticipating co-parent is very much physically present. The spouse who is superirresponsible (due to alcoholism, drug use, or severe problems with maturity or intimacy) often seems like an "extra child" to take care of. You may feel that the family cannot get back on its feet unless the irresponsible spouse goes for therapy. This might be like waiting for hell to freeze over. In dysfunctional families, the poorest-functioning member is often the last to enter therapy. But family systems counselors are very optimistic about the family's chance of recovery even if this key member refuses to participate in family therapy. In fact, the whole family's way of relating and interracting can be changed for the better even if only one member goes into therapy.[2] Every unhealthy relationship is a dance and it takes at least two to tango. If your spouse is being very irresponsible or hostile, you are doing something to enable him or her to continue being irresponsible or abusive. As described earlier, you may have created an irresponsible spouse by aggressively taking on too much responsibility, or you may have become overburdened with responsibility in reaction to your spouse leaving so much undone. It doesn't matter how it began. You can change the pattern yourself. You need to calmly set limits on how much you will do, and firmly move forward doing things that make you feel stronger, healthier, and more capable. Sometimes it's easier to leave the spouse and sometimes it's absolutely necessary (when physical danger is present); but if you can hang in there and work it out, your children will get an education in conflict resolution and problem-solving worth more than a college degree. Remember, divorce is rarely the quick solution it appears to be in fantasy. Conflicts between parents can still go on for years after the divorce and there are fewer opportunities and less motivation to work on solutions.

WHO IS THE GROWN-UP HERE?

When an irresponsible parent is having a profound impact on the family, the children will sometimes "go with the flow" and become irresponsible themselves. But more often than not, the child's discomfort in the atmosphere of chaos forces him or her to mature quickly and become superresponsible. If both parents shy away from taking charge, this responsible kid (often the oldest sibling) becomes a parentified child, caring not only for himself or herself, but also for younger siblings. Although the child will gain much valuable experience in this role, this premature responsibility usually forces the child to "skip" many levels of development.

Parents coping with an irresponsible or missing spouse need to remember that every child, no matter how competent, needs to be guided and feel cared for. Competence is not the same as being emotionally ready. During wartime children can be startlingly resourceful, but no one should have to live as though they are in a war if they are not. Cut back on your demands and expectations until your child is free to be a child again. In other words, **if you need someone to lean on, don't lean on your child.** Lean on an adult, be it therapist, friend, or paid baby-sitter.

Obviously the best solution would be for the irresponsible parent to "grow up" and start taking some of the parenting burden back onto his or her shoulders. But excessive dependency (or codependency) is a habit that's very difficult to break. It is an addiction. The dysfunctional parent generally feels helpless and "stuck." He is afraid to care for himself, let alone be responsible for a child. This parent needs to realize that irresponsibility is a painful and limiting existence. There are great rewards in sharing the load and gaining the respect and companionship of his family.

CONSCIOUS PARENTING

Remember that if you are parenting from scratch you cannot rely on images and memories from childhood to instruct you in a pinch, but you can set aside time to teach yourself to be a better parent by honestly and objectively analyzing recurring problems. Why did your son throw a temper tantrum at two o'clock? If you stop and think about it you might discover that he throws a temper tantrum every Wednesday at two o'clock. Why is that? What happens on Wednesdays that sets him off? Is it the fact that Brian's mom baby-sits him in the morning while you go to your weekly meeting? Is he stirred up by Brian, angry that you are not there, high on junk food that Brian's mom had fed him, or just plain hungry? Or is it a combination of all of these? Once you take the time to think of all the possible causes, you can begin to narrow it down. Ask Brian's mom what your son eats there on Wednesday morning. If something is suspect, pack a healthy lunch for him next time. If it's a simple case of your son having trouble giving you up one morning a week, ask if there is something special he would like to do with you before you leave. Maybe you can both get up an hour earlier and snuggle with a book for thirty minutes or so. For one problem the best solution would be putting your son to bed earlier on Tuesday nights. If the sitter is the problem you might want to consider changing your day-care situation.

This detailed planning may seem overwhelming, but unfortunately you may have to go about many parenting tasks in this highly analytical manner because you cannot just rely on "what comes naturally." If your parents were abusive, neglectful, or unsupportive, these responses are what will "come naturally" to you. **We all revert to what we have seen modeled, when we don't think things through carefully or we are under pressure.** This is probably the greatest handicap for an ACODF. For those with good parenting models stored away in their memory, the task is so much easier. When their children hurl insulting curses at them, they promptly reply, "You just go to your room until you can be civil." When a child insults an ACODF, if the parent does not give in to impulse and smack the child across the face, there will be a "stop action" while the parent analyzes the situation. First he must ask himself if he should feel insulted, because his child has probably called him a name that is far less demeaning than the names his parents called him in the past. Once he determines that he has a right to object, the parent then has to ponder what is a reasonable thing to do in response. If he is lucky he has observed a neighbor or relative using some acceptable means of discipline. If not, he may sift through his mind looking for a relevant scrap from a parenting book he has read. If he is in a hurry and very worried about being abusive, he may do nothing, leaving a bigger problem to deal with next time. If this sounds like a tremendous effort, it is! No wonder your kids make you so tired. For an ACODF, parenting can be like a trip to a foreign land where one has had no formal training in the language spoken there. **With no good role models, each decision must be thought through from scratch.**

◆ GRACE—GAINING CONTROL

"I could have handled myself much better if I hadn't had Candy when I did." In Chapter 6 Grace described how difficult it was for her when she would be out working late at night and her daughter would try to wake her in the morning. "I would tell her to just let me sleep for an hour and I couldn't understand why she couldn't do that. But of course she couldn't tell time. I would snap and I would cuss her out and bang the door. I didn't lay a hand on her because I swore I would never hit her, but I would beat the door.

"Then when she was older I would yell at her for not doing what I told her or the way I wanted it done. Like if I asked her to set the table she would just go ahead and do it her way because she thought her way was better. But I would want it done my way. I had in my mind a certain way that I felt was correct and nothing else would do. I didn't see her as being 'creative' or anything like that. I thought she was defying me and it would make me so angry that I would end up blowing up at her.

"Every time that I yelled, like the minute after, I felt horrible and ashamed. I just couldn't stop myself. It would eat me up inside. One part of me would be saying, 'Stop it!' and the other part of me would go right on yelling. I would tell God, 'If this is the way I'm going to be for the rest of my life, I don't want to live.' It was myself that I hated even though it was others that I was yelling at. I didn't want Candy to grow up in the pain that I grew up in, so I would try to make things right with her."

Although Grace felt good that she was not hitting her daughter, she knew her yelling rages were almost as damaging. "At first the fear in her face would actually make me more angry because it made me feel so guilty. I knew how wrong I was treating her. That's when I would have to send her away. I would tell her to go in her room so that I could calm myself down and then I would start to pray. I knew it was the wrong way to handle things, so I would keep praying until I felt calm. Then I would go into her room and tell her that I was sorry and that it was wrong of me to yell at her like that. I would tell her that it was me, that it was nothing she had done. Then she would tell me how scared she was when I yelled, and I could see how much I hurt her."

(Continued in Chapter 16)

Sometimes parents are so ashamed of their weak moments that they want to sweep them right under the rug and pretend nothing happened. But the child knows what happened and if you don't talk about it, it just sits there. It's pain on top of injury. It's true that Grace's screaming fits were abusive, but it is very much to her credit that she could at least talk about it openly afterward and reassure her daughter that Grace herself was the one misbehaving. Still this should not be an end point for anyone. If Grace had not been able to correct her behavior, her daughter would be left with little faith.

If we never get beyond apologizing to *changing*, we have done little to restore our children's faith in us or their belief in a responsive world. Grace's aim was to change this behavior, and she focused all her energy on ridding herself of her pent-up rage so that she could be a responsible, responsive mother.

Here, ultimately, Grace is using responsibility appropriately. At first her expectations for her child were unrealistic. She didn't think about the fact that her toddler-daughter couldn't tell time and could not know when an hour was up. At a later stage, Grace's expectations were more reasonable (Candy was capable of setting the table), but she was being too rigid. Grace could have dodged personal responsibility for her yelling by blaming her daughter for "making her" yell by being disobedient. But Grace pushed herself to look at the circumstances more closely and be open to what fault she may have had that contributed to the situation. In other words, Grace was finally able to see that there really was no excuse for yelling at and terrorizing her daughter. Grace alone was responsible for her abusive actions, and Grace alone was the one who could change that behavior.

This kind of self-examination may sound like the hypervigilence I warned against in Chapter 10, but one big difference is that it is not eternal. With each successful experience you add to your knowledge of parenting. The next time the situation comes up, you can do the first thing that comes to mind because you have screened your responses to know what is useful and fair and what is not. No matter what age your child is when you begin conscious parenting, it will become easier as you establish well-thought-out methods and routines. Of course, your child is constantly changing, so what works now may not work later. That's the same fifty percent of the problem that any parent faces. Once you have developed a secure parenting base, it will all be less stressful. However, it only makes sense that you refrain from having any more children until you feel in command of your present situation. The next one can be a breeze if you wait until you are ready.

As a matter of fact, you should do as much as you can to keep all areas of your life as simple and uncluttered as possible while you are developing your parenting skills. It takes time to consider alternatives. You will need to lose your sense of panic about decisions, particularly those directly affecting your children. **If you act on impulse and realize later that you have been too harsh or too** lenient, don't be afraid to admit you were wrong and reopen the discussion. Solicit alternatives from your children. They may have seen neighbors (or a teacher) handle this type of situation well. Or postpone any decisions until you have had time to talk things over with a parenting friend, if you yourself cannot think of alternatives or imagine the consequences.

It is better to say, "I need some time to think about that," than to give the first answer that comes to mind. Anything that slows you down will actually increase your chances of making the right response. While you walk the dog, take a bath, or commute to work, don't let your mind fill up with details of your daily chores and tasks. Instead use this time to evaluate the past twenty-four hours. It is good to set aside a half hour or so each day to contemplate your choices and decisions. Some people find it easier to focus by writing. Begin to keep a parenting journal. List your goals. Tackle one behavior at a time only, and work on it until things are running more smoothly between you and your child.

Many situations can be thought through ahead of time. ACODF often have difficulty following through on discipline when chores are not completed or rules are broken. Some forethought can solve this problem. Very often rules have not been stated clearly enough. You might stop at the supermarket door and turn to your child with the warning, "Be good or you won't get any gum." What does "be good" mean? Children are not born knowing how to "be good." For one thing, social rules vary from one culture to the next. Much of what we consider good or bad are really value judgments that we have absorbed through acculturation. Children need specifics like: Don't run in the aisles, don't grab things off the shelves, and don't beg me for anything from the toy section. Some parenting advisers prefer that everything be stated in positive terms such as : Walk slowly and quietly, keep your hands to yourself, and the only prize we have money for today is a pack of gum for following our shopping rules. If your children have chores, write down what they are and put the list on the refrigerator. Decide ahead of time what the consequences will be if the chores are not done. The best policy is to plan something desirable that will happen after the chore is done. For example, "You may have an afternoon snack after the dog has been fed, and you can watch TV after you finish your homework." Or, "When the dinner dishes are loaded in the dishwater we will all have a nice dessert."

ANTICIPATION

Anticipation is the good side of control. If you are a "controlling type" you can learn to use this talent constructively. Many potential conflicts can be headed off by planning ahead. If you know your child disintegrates into a temper tantrum when he is hungry, bring a snack with you when you pick him up from school, ready to head off on two hours of errands. Agree on a pleasant key phrase to use in public when behavior is not up to par. "It's really too nice a day to worry about that! Isn't it, honey?" As part of that behavior contract have an agreed-upon consequence if it is violated.

How is this different from Natalie's overprotectiveness (Chapter 8), or Judy's superresponsible behavior (Chapter 10)? The difference is subtle but very important. By bringing a snack when you go on errands with your young child you are taking into consideration an unavoidable fact of his metabolism. Nearly all children are starving after school and are likely to be crabby and uncooperative if they do not eat. This is just the kind of sensible planning that healthy parents generally do without much thought. Natalie might see herself as "planning ahead" when she checks other schools for her child and "saves" him from poor teachers. If her child had had no problems with other teachers, and other parents verified that the first-grade teacher was incompetent, her pulling him out of the public school might have been reasonable. However, Jerry's problems follow him everywhere, and to keep him from "having problems" she resorts to removing him from society. This is an extreme solution. Likewise, Judy goes to extremes when she gives up all her personal activities and follows her child around the classroom.

Healthy parents do what is *reasonable* to make their children's days go smoother. It's the difference between being *supportive* and being *overbearing*. Thinking about and planning how many children to have, how much money to spend on a house, or what to do on vacation that is pleasant, not exhausting, is just common sense. ACODF should also consider their own personal limitations as a factor in their decisions. For example, if you still have a choice about it, keep your family small so that you will have enough time for each child. No matter how many children you now have, think about setting up a formal "private time" with each child so that you can give them individual attention *before* they are tempted to use negative means to get it. Don't forget to schedule in private time with your spouse too. It is much easier to be supportive of each other's efforts if you have time to discuss things (and some time together where you don't have to discuss things!).

Start by noticing your child's ups and downs and try to figure out what triggers misbehavior and what makes it easier for your child to behave well. By knowing what puts your child "on the fritz" you can head off many problems. Most children will have behavior problems when they are tired or hungry and many moms believe that too much sugar sets their children off. Is your child better with some friends than others? Does he play nicely with one other child but start crying and hitting when there are four children playing together? Does he seem more edgy when your spouse goes out of town on business?

You can plan special distractions for tough times. Help your child look forward to Mommy or Daddy going away by taking him to a restaurant or on a special activity that is reserved for only the two of you. My husband absolutely refuses to eat at Burger King, so that is where my son and I go when Dad is out of town.

Build a relationship with your child's teacher before she has reason to contact you for bad behavior. Ask about her classroom policies and be friendly and helpful. Even if you work during the day or are too busy to help out in the classroom, you can communicate your supportive attitude toward the teacher. Tell the teacher about your child's temperament and let her know what environments are best for the child.

Teach your child anticipation. Explain that Daddy likes quiet when he gets home from work. Tell her, "I'm in a bad mood today—watch out!" And help her anticipate and plan ahead for her own highs and lows. When an important day is coming up, explain to her, "You need some rest so you can have a good day tomorrow."

Be aware of your own potential stressors. Parenting experts agree that children under six or over thirteen are the hardest to handle. If your children are in these age brackets, slow down other activities in your life so that you have adequate energy to deal with your children. Be aware, too, of parental stress periods, such as mid-life crisis, that coincide with your child's stress periods (such as entering junior high.)

By educating yourself about normal child development, keep your expectations low enough so that you are often pleasantly surprised by your child's achievements, rather than disappointed.

Become informed about the unique pressures of children at various ages and stages. Be prepared for sleepless nights when your children are infants and then for the exhausting resistance of toddlers learning to say "no." Be ready to talk over school anxieties with your early school age child and burgeoning sexual development with your preadolescent. Then don't forget your children when they become teenagers. Late adolescents have many deep concerns and important decisions to work through. They will have to deal with heartbreaks, pressure to take drugs, and decisions about what they want to do with the rest of their lives all at the same time.

GIVING POSITIVE ATTENTION

If you frequently find yourself feeling overwhelmed by everyone's needs, you should try "getting ahead" on your children's needs. Neglected children will get to the point where they do irritating or destructive things to get attention. At this time, their needs have already come into the deficit column: They are already behind on getting their needs met. But if you can meet someone at the point where they have just begun to feel the need, what they want is generally reasonable and fairly easy to grant. For example, if you have to work overtime every Wednesday and as a result your children always act needy when you come home on Wednesday night, you can probably even things out and avert a crisis by spending extra time tucking them into bed. If you wait until Thursday the need debt may be higher. However, if you can get to them even *before* they feel the need—say by giving them a little extra attention on Tuesday when you know you will miss time with them on Wednesday, maybe they can accept your absence without a ripple. Sometimes two minutes of attention on Tuesday will satisfy the children as much as two hours of attention on Thursday.

By being alert to your children's mood changes, you can figure out when they need you more, even if they can't yet express that need directly. Children sometimes train us to anticipate their needy times by being exhausting and demanding when their needs aren't met. They have little "breakdowns" where they are incredibly irrational, prone to tantrums, and convinced that you don't love them. Then the child does self-destructive things, like running wild, screaming, or hitting another child. Naturally the parent has a hard time acting loving during such behavior. The child triumphantly concludes that the parent does not love him, just as he suspected.

It's a horrible, draining, vicious circle that should be avoided whenever possible. Sometimes you don't know ahead of time that you are going to have a maddeningly busy week where you can't pay adequate attention to your children. But often if you can acknowledge the busyness right away you can avert one of his "breakdowns." It's as simple as saying, "I know I've been very busy this week and this is going to go on until Saturday. I haven't been paying as much attention to you as I'd like. I see you need to spend more time with me and I miss you too. But there is nothing I can do about it until Saturday. Why don't we plan to go to the park for lunch Saturday and spend the whole afternoon together?" Then when you give him your undivided attention on Saturday as you promised, this tactic will work even better in the future. This builds trust while teaching children the important lesson of postponing gratification. Kids need to learn to live with frustration and disappointment in order to grow up happy, secure, and with reasonable expectations of life.

RULES, ROUTINES, AND RITUALS

Rules, routines, and rituals can lower the stress of day-to-day living; for decisions are stressful and they take time. Why begin each day as if it is the first day in the rest of your life? What's wrong with it being just like all the other days that came before? There is something to be said for not having to decide whether or not to get up, when to get up, when to brush our teeth, when to eat breakfast, and how to wear our hair each and every day, as if these were all new experiences. When you are all groping groggy-eyed through the house, it is very helpful to have an established rhythm that tells you when it's your turn in the bathroom. Routines allow much to be done without time-consuming discussion and debate. Rules with known consequences settle many arguments before they begin. When rules and routines are the "ruling authority" in your house, you will have fewer head-on power struggles with your children.

You can make rules to cover any recurring conflict. The notes hanging in my kitchen will no doubt tell you what the hot topics are at my house. They read:

1. Homework done by 5 P.M. to get ride home from Mom next day.

2. No Inspector Gadget until homework is finished (show may be recorded for later viewing).

3. Homework done and in backpack on washer before evening TV.

4. No TV viewing past 9 P.M.

5. Dressed, with jacket and homework on washer before breakfast or TV.

6. If you miss school bus and Mom must drive you to school, you lose TV privileges for 2 days.

I was not always this compulsive, but my son is a stickler for detail. Once we clearly established all these variables that affect homework and getting to school on time, we've never had an argument about it. When we see the school bus pulling away before he reaches the corner he says, "No TV for two days! It's my responsibility." And I peacefully drive him to school, knowing, by the way, that this will not happen again for months. And my son really doesn't think of me as the one who took the TV away.

Rules and routines also help us establish healthy habits. Our children need to know how to reduce their own stress before they become independent adults. We can help our children understand why it is important to eat regularly, get enough sleep, and exercise, by giving them the experience of feeling the benefit of a well-balanced life.

Rituals are really just routines. Any firmly established routine takes on the religious quality of ritual for a child. Children don't really like surprises. They want to be able to look forward to bath, cereal, and story before bed. Nighttime rituals are like meditations; they serve to calm the child gradually for sleep. And these same rituals can be used on baby-sitter night, thus leaving a little of Mother or Father behind for comfort.

ESTABLISHING RULES

Children need clear rules to live by. Many parents make the mistake of thinking children just naturally know how to behave properly. They drop the child off at the movie and say something totally vague like, "Be good." When the child misbehaves, the parent then assumes that the child is being defiant. But children really need to be *taught* how to act in different situations. A lot of their behavior habits will come from simply imitating you, but any new situation is an unknown for your child. Any time your child misbehaves, ask yourself, "Did I explain exactly what I wanted her to do and not do in this situation?"

The best way to increase the child's cooperation in following the rules is to have the child help set the rules. This can be done at a family meeting or by sitting down with the child to discuss the rules for her behavior one-on-one. All families have rules even if they haven't formally set them. In many homes, "Don't eat in the living room," is a rule that quickly becomes understood by all. According to parenting trainer Cynthia Walker, family rules generally cover a number of predictable areas such as personal habits, social conduct, respect for property, consumption, chores, school conduct and schoolwork. For example, parents should establish rules and routines to cover personal hygeine (when should the child take a bath, brush his teeth or wash his hands?); to teach social skills (say "please" and "thank you," and don't hit those you disagree with); to teach respect for property (treat yours and others' belongings carefully); to provide guidelines about what we put in our bodies (eat nutritious foods before dessert, and don't take drugs); to build responsibility through family chores (who does what and when must it be done?); and to help establish good learning habits (respect and pay attention to the teacher at school, and do your homework before after-school play.)[3]

Children really do need rules for all of life's situations. They must be taught to say "please" and "thank you." The more they know about behaving appropriately, the better accepted they will be. Like it or not, it's a simple fact that people will respond to your children more positively if they are clean and polite. They need to be told to say "excuse me" when they must interrupt others who are talking. They must be told which words are offensive to most people and what alternative words are socially acceptable. They are not born knowing any of these things. When you make a rule, tell why the rule is necessary. Rules should be simple, consistent, and clear. For example, if you use profanity in the privacy of your own home, your children will not automatically know they should not talk that way at school. You could make a rule that *you* may say swearwords but your child cannot. However, since children learn much by example, you are making it just that much harder for your child. Likewise, if you decide that your children may say "dirty words" at home but not at school, you are complicating the task. If "dirty words" become a habit at home, the child will have more trouble remembering not to say them in public. Part of any clearly stated rule is the consequence for not following it. For swearing, I would recommend that everyone, Mom and Dad included, be fined a nickel per swearword, payable to each person who heard it. Then be good natured about your child catching you.

Children also need to learn good table manners, how to share, and how to treat guests of any age. By teaching your children respectful behavior you will be heading off potential problems. **Rules also help parents to be consistent, because we cannot always remember where we drew the line on the child's behavior in the last situation.** We might have said whispering in church is OK (as the lesser of two evils) but giggling is not. If we reprimand them for whispering next time, we are being unfair and confusing our children. Discussing and writing down rules helps us remember what rules we have established. Our family rules can also give us a sense of dignity and pride. "We Smiths always serve our guests first."

◆ CHARACTER
Rachael Beck

What a drag it is
to build that kid's character!
I know it's better for him
if he learns
to clean the sink and tub,
wash dishes,
take out papers and cans for recycling,
and return those returnable beer bottles.
I know it's important for him
to Learn Responsibility at home;
but I'm exhausted
by the time I ask him,
persuade him,
coerce him,
listen to him tell me
he'll get to it—whatever the request—
as soon as he gets a break in his homework,
his music, or during the next TV commercial,
and then he doesn't move
till we go through it all again!
How long must I build his character?
When may I just do the chores
myself?[4]

Each family's rules will be different because each family's habits and life-style are unique. Some families would never let the dog in the house and others sleep with the dog. There is a lot of leeway for what is "right" in your home. You may have purchased dark durable carpeting just so you wouldn't have to worry about food in the living room since you value family snacks before the fire, or you may feel that the living room is sacrosanct and no one is ever to cross the threshold with food or a beverage.

If you find your children disobeying the rules or not doing what they've been asked, first consider whether or not the rule was fair. Would that task be considered adult's work in most homes? Are you really expecting too much from a child that age? Do his siblings have to follow similar rules? One must be realistic and consistent. Consistency not only means having the same rules from one day to the next, it also means being equally demanding of every child in the family (based on his or her developmental level).

Just as your rules reflect what you as a family consider important; rules in other families reflect their values. Your children need to learn that old adage, "When in Rome do as the Romans do." When they visit the homes of friends or relatives they should follow the rules of that home. You might help your child with this by asking the host or hostess what their house rules are. For example, your child needs to know if it's OK to run in and out of the house without knocking. You can also teach your child to be observant. I'm sure when you enter a house with no ash trays in sight, you don't light up a cigarette and tap your ashes onto the floor. Likewise, when your son or daughter enter someone's house and see toys lined up in neat rows on shelves in the playroom only, they can guess that this family may not want toys to be carried throughout the house. If you want your child to be welcome in the homes of others, you need to teach them how to learn about and respect the preferences of others.

FAMILY MEETINGS

More than half the parenting books on the market today suggest a technique called the "family meeting." This is central to more democratically based family decision-making than the old traditional authoritarian model. But this does not mean, as many fear, that the kids can make outrageous demands that parents have to obey. It simply means that you are committing to be genuinely open to your children's ideas. We make many rules for arbitrary reasons, usually patterned after our childhoods. My parents always insisted that the kids sit in the back of the car, assuming, I guess, that if they ever let a child sit in the front seat, they'd never get any of us into the back again. We are often far more rigid than we need to be.

If you have grown up in a dysfunctional family, you might even be rigid as a means of self-protection. So many things have gone wrong for you, or hurt you, that if something works once, you don't ever want to risk changing it. No matter how much effort it takes to get your kids to do the chores every week, you would rather go on with the old map of responsibilities than risk anyone trading chores as an experiment. But it is much easier to get cooperation from children when they have participated in the decision-making.

Holding a family meeting doesn't mean that your children can vote to abandon their chores and have you do them all. It means that the children gain a realistic sense of what must be done and why, because you have sat down together long enough to explain it to one another. If each person has some say in what they will have to do, they will feel less trapped and more respected. Everyone is different. One person might love to polish the chrome in the bathroom but hate to sweep the floor. Not everyone will think the chores you personally dislike are the bottom of the heap. If there are some chores that everyone hates doing, rotate them so each person only has to do each of these distasteful tasks once a month.

If you keep a loving spirit in your home, family meetings can be a wonderful tool to learn new parenting skills and attitudes. Your children are not yet contaminated by years of dysfunctional thinking. Stop and really listen to what they have to say. They may have a fresh way of looking at things that can turn a conflict into an interesting challenge. Maybe you are stuck back at square one thinking that five-year-olds must learn to tie their shoes, but your preschooler has noticed the velcro shoes everyone is wearing that go all the way up to adult sizes. Why learn to tie shoes ever?

Maybe you love to take walks at night and so does the dog, but you were brought up to believe that the kids wanted the dog and the kids should walk it. Don't get stuck repeating patterns that don't make sense. Take a turn at walking the dog yourself. You might discover a new pleasure. (And if you get excited enough about walking the dog, everyone else will probably start begging for the privilege at the next family meeting.)

Family meetings don't all have to be chore negotiations. Put a fun item on the agenda. Decide as a group what you will have for dessert on Sunday or where the family will go on vacation this year. Schedule time to discuss shared feelings and problems, such as the illness of a family pet. Remember that it is not always easy for a child to grab center stage when they have a problem. Even as adults we lose some of our assertiveness when we are being dragged down by adversity. Children are no different. When something is really bothering them they will often have an attack of shyness. Post an empty agenda in a prominent place where each member is free to write in an item for discussion at the next meeting. Then make sure each item gets touched upon. You will begin to know your children in deeper and richer ways.

Finally, the family meeting is probably the best vehicle for passing the torch of responsibility on to your children. By taking time to listen to their opinions and persuasive arguments you will be aware of their growing maturity. Children who feel free to express themselves will naturally ask for expanding privileges. The family meeting gives you a chance to discuss these issues thoroughly and determine if your child is ready for new privileges. Even when your child is not ready, you can take the time to explain to your child what signs of growing maturity are. ("When I see you feeding your frog regularly without being told, I'll consider your having a pet bird.") This helps your child learn how to correct himself or herself and also makes the decision less arbitrary by describing the behavior desired. This gives your child a much greater sense of controlling his or her own destiny. For ultimately, your child will have to do just that.

◆ ══════════════ **SUMMARY** ══════════════ ◆

The best parents allow time to evaluate their own performances as parents and make changes when needed. No one should rely solely on their parents as role models because today's world is so rapidly changing that what is appropriate today may be hopelessly ineffective tomorrow.

◆ ═══════════════ **P O I N T S** ═══════════════ ◆

1. Without reliable role models, the ACODF parent must use "conscious parenting." We must analyze every child-rearing situation, for to do "what comes natural" would be to imitate our own unhealthy upbringing.

2. Because *Conscious Parenting* takes a great deal of time and reflection, we must keep our lives simple and low-stress so that we have time to reflect on our parenting methods and goals each day.

3. We can use our "controlling" instincts constructively by anticipating problems and setting up clear solutions or consequences. We can also "get ahead" on our children's needs for attention.

4. Children need the involvement of both parents in order to feel fully loved and secure. If we have felt so inadequate that we have left all the parenting to our spouses in the past, we must push ourselves to become more active.

5. We must be careful not to become "polarized" against our partner's parenting methods. In the healthiest families each parent participates equally in both nurturing and disciplinary functions.

6. When we must parent alone, we need to keep our expectations within our capability as a solo parent. When we focus on "what is best for the children," we do not use them to express our resentment toward the uninvolved co-parent.

7. Every child needs his or her energy to work on age-appropriate developmental tasks. If we must carry the parenting burden alone due to divorce or dysfunction, we must not appoint one of our children as co-parent.

8. Rules, routines, and rituals make everyone's job easier and teach children how to organize well-balanced, low-stress lives for themselves.

───────────────

NOTES

1. Judith S. Wallerstein Ph.D. and Sandra Blakeslee, *Second Chances*. New York: Ticknor & Fields, 1989.

2. Eda LeShan, "Family Therapy Minus One," *Parents Magazine*. November, 1988.

3. Interview: Cynthia Walker, Licensed Clinical Social Worker who has conducted parenting classes at various counseling centers in Los Angeles area. She has specialized in Confident Parenting for black parents.

4. From *The Tie That Binds* (Sandra Martz, editor), Watsonville, CA: Paper-Mache Press, 1988.

12

CONSISTENCY AND SUPPORT

13. ACODF have difficulty following through on promises and agreements such as trips, outings, transportation, or allowances.

14. ACODF often seek approval from their children and consequently fail to be consistent with discipline or act responsive to the child's own need for approval.

Children need consistency and support in order to flourish, but people who have grown up in dysfunctional families have often been raised in the chaotic atmosphere of chronic tension. Their parents had difficulty following through on anything and everything from vacation plans to discipline. Your insecure parents may have had difficulty with commitments (even seemingly simple ones like planning a trip to the beach), and their guiding principle for discipline may have been to give in to you when they needed to feel "loved" and lash out at you when they had allowed you to overrun them too much. Like most troubled people, your parents were probably too self-centered to be able to think about your needs; and like most children, you probably didn't really know what you needed and couldn't give your caretakers clear messages. Therefore, one great handicap you will have in the area of consistency and support is the lack of a role model or a reasonable standard. The ACODF parent who was abused and confused as a child may treat her own child ten times better than she was treated and still be negligent or unsupportive by healthy standards. "How much is enough?" is a cloudy mystery to many ACODF.

If you have given your child nice clothing, food to eat, and an attractive bedroom, when you yourself never had these basics to rely on, you may be understandably baffled when you learn that your children actually need more. But they do. Each child comes into this world needing love and security to grow up undamaged. What you experienced as a child does not change what your child needs now. If your mother beat you and never told you that she loved you, that does not mean that your child will feel secure if you limit yourself to verbal abuse and tell her that you love her once a year. **The amount of time, attention, and consistency that kids really need can come as an astonishing surprise to someone who was neglected as a child.**

Cynthia Walker, a counselor and trainer in a special parenting program designed to meet the needs of concerned black parents in low socioeconomic areas of greater Los Angeles, commented, "They don't have the support themselves. They don't see their children as needing support. They say, 'My kids should be happy. They got food and roof over their heads.' But I tell them, 'Well, they can get that in jail.' "[1] There can be such a gap between what we had as children and what children really need to flourish.

CONSISTENCY

There are two areas of consistency that we need to look at. Do we act consistent or predictable in our own lives, and are we consistent in our dealings with our children? As we learned in Chapter 7, if we lead scattered lives where we often change jobs or move frequently, not only will our children be exposed to a poor role model, we will be so distracted by the confusion in our lives that we cannot possibly be consistent with our children. It takes some effort and quiet, thoughtful time to establish rules for our household, see that they are followed, and carry out consequences if they are not. **When we are preoccupied with our own changes, we cannot pay enough attention to what our children need.**

Further, we as children may never have had the opportunity to stick with something to the point of satisfaction. With everything we pursue in life, be it jobs, recreational skills, or relationships, there are going to be ups and downs. The greatest lesson we can learn is that there probably will be another up after the down. Did you have an opportunity to learn that as a child?

Were you forced to drop out of scouts before you even had time to become disenchanted, leaving you feeling that scouts is a relentlessly euphoric experience? If so, you probably won't be very sympathetic when your son complains about going on another long hike up the mountain. (*You* would have been grateful to have the opportunity!)

Did your parents stop taking you to scouts the first time you complained, so that your last memory of scouts is that it's fun at first but then it really gets to be a drag? If so, the first time your son complains about a hike you'll probably be relieved that he has found out the truth so soon and you can now stop pretending that scouts is the greatest.

Were you one of the lucky ones who complained about a scout hike only to have your parents say, "When you get to the top, you'll be glad you went?" If so, when your son complains you'll probably reassure him that everything isn't fun all the time, but if you stick it out, it will probably become fun again. **A down means an up is on its way.**

If you have no experience sticking things out, you will have little to draw on when you try to convince your child to do differently. You may even feel that you cannot expect anything from your child that you did not accomplish yourself, but this is not realistic or fair to your child. Your child probably has a better parent than you did. If you have helped your child keep up with homework, and your parent did nothing to help you, your child is probably getting a better education than you had. Remember, uneducated immigrants send their children to college every day, setting them up to achieve far more than their parents. Don't set your sights too low for your child. In other words, your children have an excellent chance of being happier and more successful than you were. The key lies in you knowing your child. You want to encourage your child in line with his or her natural abilities and needs.

Parenting is a demanding task for anyone. ACODF depleted by the stress caused by ill-thought-out decisions do not have enough energy to parent effectively. **As they model this impulsive behavior for their children, the children begin to emulate it and the chaos increases exponentially.** This can set off a terrible downward spiral that leads to self-loathing. Everyone has better hindsight than foresight, so we often realize what we could have done that would have brought us a better result. ACODF often experience so much remorse from their ill-thought-out decisions that they are blocked from learning from their mistakes. The healthy individual, who has been led and supported through failure to success as a child, can be more objective about her mistakes. She can say, "I won't do that next time!" and let it go at that. **But most ACODF do not have enough inner confidence to accept mistakes as a natural, normal part of life.**

One thing that confuses us and holds us back from being the best parent for our children is our preoccupation with our own issues and past hurts. If you find yourself confusing your wants and needs with your child's, that means it's time you fulfilled some of your own needs. It is better for you to take those piano lessons you missed (or were allowed to quit on) than to force your disinterested child to take the lessons. Let him go play soccer if that's his thing, and you stay home and play the piano. It's never too late for you and the sooner you start meeting some of your mourned needs, the sooner you will be able to see your child as a person separate from you with the wants and needs that grow out of his or her special personality.

BEING ASSERTIVE

As mentioned earlier, ACODF often seek approval from their children. Therefore, they may fail to discipline, set limits, or meet their children's own need for approval. This is related to self-esteem. **Parents have to feel good enough about themselves to be able to admit mistakes.** If the parent feels like a "bad parent," he may feel guilty setting limits. For example, the children's noise may drive him crazy, but he feels that if he were a better parent he would enjoy the children's noise. So, instead of setting limits on the children's noise, he might try to compensate for his "lack of patience" by gritting his teeth and letting the children do whatever they want. The insecure parent might think, "Who am I to tell him he can't? I don't know anything about parenting." As a consequence of the era of permissiveness, many parents have been reluctant to be the authority in the home. But healthy parents have the confidence to say, "Look, I'm the parent, and you're the child, and I'm in charge here."

◆ ROSALYN'S TOUGH LOVE

Rosalyn's son Richard presented so few problems as a child that Rosalyn did not need any more advice until her son turned thirteen. Then his whole personality seemed to change. He began to be belligerent and his grades started falling. One night she got up to let in the cat and saw that her son was not in his room. She knew these could be signs of drug involvement and she didn't want to take any chances. She needed to act and decided to begin with something visible that couldn't be denied—his drop in grades. She imposed a tough curfew and forbade him to hang out with a friend of his who had been picked up for shoplifting.

Richard raised no objections to the restrictions, perhaps a bit relieved that his mother had stepped in. Rosalyn felt that the book *Tough Love*[2] helped her a great deal at the time. When her son was caught cutting classes, she attended school with him for two days, following him from class to class, and sitting right beside him. She told him that if he cut class again she would return to school with him. He never cut again. As a counselor, she knew that she had been losing control of him and if she let it go on, she might lose him altogether.

"I told him: I'm the parent and you're the child. Until you are eighteen, you will have to live by my rules." One rule she made was that he must earn no lower than a C in any class. When he brought home some D's and an F, Rosalyn put him on partial restriction. "I wasn't going to ground him for ten weeks, because then I would have been grounding myself. Instead, I told him he had to be home at six o'clock on school nights and seven-thirty on the weekends. That gave him time to go out and complain to his friends about how unreasonable I was so he could get it out of his system. But it didn't make it very easy for him to get involved in parties where there might be drugs or alcohol." He had a little bit of freedom, but not too much.

She also used the "Tough Love" technique of emphasizing cooperation. She told him that he knew he was expected to get decent grades, and since he had not cooperated with his mother's wish, she would not do special favors for him until he cleaned up his act. She stopped making his lunches or giving him money for lunch but bought plenty of lunch items for him to make his own lunch. She stopped driving him to school and bought him a pass for the bus. "He knew that I meant business and I gradually reeled him back in." At the end of the ten weeks all his poor grades had improved.

Many ACODF have had trouble being assertive ever since childhood. As a child the ACODF may have worried that his parents would stop loving him if he demanded too much. After all, many ACODF did not even get their basic needs for security and nurturance met. Their dysfunctional parents acted as if being fed was an unreasonable demand. The ACODF are left feeling as if they have no rights.

FACING THE CHILD'S ANGER

When we fail to set limits or discipline our children, we are most often motivated by our desire to be liked. Add to that the discomfort of coming face to face with the child's anger and it is easy to see what a constant temptation it is to let children have their way. But when we do that, we are killing them with our kindness. Children must not only learn rules so that they can behave in socially appro- priate ways, they must learn to follow rules so that they eventually achieve a sense of self-control. Only through successful self-control can a child overcome that feeling of being at the mercy of chance. Once again we are being called upon to do something that we may never have experienced or seen modeled. It is in our hands to stop this sense of helplessness with our generation.

Children are quick to realize the power of shouting, "I hate you!" Those words are sure to bring back childhood memories of the hateful things your parents did. You will freeze at the sound of these words and ask yourself, "Am I treating my child like that?" If the answer is yes, stop the action and try a better approach to your child. But don't be too quick to jump to that conclusion. Normal children who love their parents also shout, "I hate you!" at their mom or dad. **What they are really saying is, "I'm angry," and no one can get through parenting without making his or her child angry many times.** It is children's nature to want to do what they want to do, when they want to do it. It is your job to see that they do what they need to do, when it needs to be done, not when they feel like it. That sets up an automatic conflict. What kid really *wants* to clean her room on Saturday morning just for the joy of seeing it clean? We could debate all day whether a child should really be expected to keep her room clean, since it's *her* room and you could just shut the door, but that would be missing the point. We all have to do things we don't want to do some of the time, and some of those things are exactly what will lead to success and happiness for us. There is value in learning to do what we don't want to do, just for the sake of discipline. Don't give up on your child by giving in in the face of her anger!

Exactly what you make your child do, whether it be cleaning her room or drying the dishes, is of little importance. She does benefit from being "made" to do things. There are two ways you could make this easier on yourself. Method #1 is to allow your child to have a say in *what* it is she will be "made" to do. She will have a wonderful sense of power over her own life if she gets to select the chore that bothers her least. The important thing is for her to learn to follow through on the task she has been assigned, ideally until she does not even need to be told. The lesson is not improved by her hating every minute of it with a passion. Method #2 is to select something that is not *your* pet peeve. If messy rooms drive you crazy, maybe you *should* shut the door and let her have it her way, because you are not likely to be neutral on this subject. If the child senses that this is very important to you it will only push on her need to rebel. When confronting your child's anger, try to be matter-of-fact. Step back, become objective, and you won't be crushed by her disapproval.

APPROVING OF YOURSELF

Starved of approval as children, ACODF constantly seek approval and affirmation from those around them, whether it be boss, friend, lover, or child. They are still eager and hungry to hear, "What a nice job you did!" However, seeking approval from your children is almost invariably inappropriate and frustrating. The need for approval is a self-esteem issue and, as such, gaining self-esteem should be the parent's first priority. The need for approval from others is also an insatiable addiction that leaves "the user" dependent on others for a sense of worth. In fact, the parent will never get enough at work, at home, at church, or on the golf course. The only approval that truly satisfies and doesn't leave one vulnerably dependent on others is self-approval.

Stop and take a positive inventory. What good skills have you inherited from your parents? (No one's parents were *all* bad. This activity can double as an exercise in forgiveness). What good skills have you acquired on the job or in relationships with friends? What positive parenting skills did you learn from childhood neighbors or your current neighbors? Picture yourself in all the various settings of your past and present life. List ten things that can be counted as strengths. Don't be modest. ACODF have a tendency to believe that they *earn* failure but gain their successes by *luck*. Give yourself credit where credit is due. You weren't lucky to get that A, that job, or that promotion. You were skilled and deserving.

Once you've made your list of strengths, examine them to see how they can help you to parent effectively. If you are superresponsible, look on the bright side and give yourself credit for being someone your kids can rely on to do what was promised. If you lean more toward being irresponsible, are you also more playful and lighthearted than your superresponsible spouse? The strengths that are most useful are the ones that you can keep in the midrange. Are you creative? Organized? Hardworking? Easygoing? Curious? Parenting is an occupation that uses everything you've got.

Although as parents we can learn from our failures, we can learn from our successes too. Don't just blame yourself for your child's bad days. Give yourself some credit for the days that run smoothly and give your child pleasure. Have faith that you have caused this good reaction in your child and then try to analyze what you did right as well as what you do wrong on the bad days. Make a list of the things you don't have to worry about.

REGRETS AND REMEDIES

ACODF often have difficulty following through on promises and agreements such as trips, outings, transportation, or allowances. Maybe you carry around a whole list of legitimate grievances your children could file against you right now. You have disappointed them so many times, you don't even want to promise them anything. "My kids have every right to hate me!" you may exclaim. But you can gain control over areas of your life where you have failed in the past.

Parents who have grown up in dysfunctional homes have often not learned the skills they needed to follow through and complete the projects and plans they have proposed. Their parental role models may have broken many promises and failed to come through on even the smallest commitments. Without guidance, these ACODF who are now parents may have no idea what goes into accomplishing a long-range goal. First they must have some idea what small tasks are needed to complete a large project. A simple family outing to the zoo in the nearest city can be paralyzingly complex for the inexperienced ACODF. Let's say Mom has promised to take the kids to the zoo on Saturday. Her first mistake may have been not allowing enough lead time. Does she know the zoo's hours? Does she know how to get to the park where the zoo is located? (Does she know where exactly in the park the zoo is and what park road to take?) Does she know how long it takes to drive to the zoo and how long it takes to see the zoo? Does she know if there is a tram or if they must walk the whole way and what sort of shoes and clothing they should wear to be comfortable? Does she know how much it costs to get into the zoo? Can they get back in time for Mom to get ready for the play for which she has tickets that night?

Mom has promised the zoo and the kids are excited. If someone informs Mom on Saturday morning, at 11 A.M. as they are preparing to leave for the zoo, that it takes two hours to drive there and at least four hours to see the zoo (even if you can keep the kids moving every minute), Mom may decide to cancel the plans. If the kids are vociferous enough about their disappointment, the family may go ahead to the zoo, but Mom will be nagging and rushing them the whole way. They might be cold, hungry, and irritable because they have worn the wrong clothes and Mom didn't bring enough money to cover the cost of the expensive concession food. Few alcoholic or other low-functioning parents knew how to plan successful family outings and once again the ACODF is parenting from scratch. Indeed, having no role model to follow, if the ACODF realizes all the complexities that must be considered, she may be too overwhelmed even to attempt family outings.

Perhaps you have already run up against this problem. You have been put off from making plans, or you have made promises that you could not pull off. Your children have little faith in you to follow through and you have little faith in yourself. Just as you would help your child learn to manage her own room or homework, you need to pick a task simple enough to assure success. Begin with a simple picnic in the park and work up to more involved activities. Give yourself lots of lead time for planning new experiences. Ask other people about the place you intend to visit and check your plans out with them before you announce them to your children. Probably someone from your workplace or neighborhood has been to the zoo before and can fill you in on the details. Allow enough time to find a map, talk the outing over with your children, and set rules for the trip. (We all stay together.) Your children will regain their trust in you, and you will develop more confidence in your ability to complete things with some practice and successful experiences.

TEACHING RESPECT

The most basic component of a good relationship is mutual respect. If you regret that you are not closer to your child, look at the level of respect you show toward each other. Teaching your child respectful behavior and showing respect for your child are the best remedies for a damaged relationship.

Children are the most receptive to change between age two and twelve. Most behavior is learned and therefore most behavior can be changed or unlearned. People learn either by watching and copying models or by experiencing the consequences of their behavior. Most children learn from how their parents behave and from how their parents respond to the child's behavior. If a parent changes himself during the child's formative years, he can (and probably will for better or worse) change his child just through modeling.

Take an organized approach to shaping your child's attitude by breaking it down into specific behaviors. If you want your child to act more respectful, decide what behaviors strike you as respectful or make you feel respected. Saying "please" when asking for permission, food, or service from the parent (a ride to school), and responding to parental requests immediately, might be two behaviors that strike you as respectful. Tackle one at a time. Explain to your child that you feel good about doing him a favor when he says "please" (and of course be sure you always say "please" to your child when making a request). Then watch for that behavior, and when he regresses correct the child with a neutral attitude. If he asks you to bring him a glass of milk and forgets to say please, just stand and wait until he remembers the "magic word."

This may all sound very elementary, but I often see mothers rushing about waiting on their children and not expecting any expression of appreciation. Parents get caught up in the doing and forget the importance of respect in smooth relationships. You may think that love means never having to say "please," but I believe parents not only deserve to be treated politely at all times, but benefit immeasurably from that treatment. Parenting is hard work and "please" and "thank you" at least symbolize the freedom you have to fulfill or not fulfill your child's request. **If you allow yourself to be taken for granted, your self-esteem will soon suffer.**

PRAISING EFFECTIVELY

Dislikable behaviors such as "baby talk" or overdependence will diminish if not rewarded or praised, but unfortunately good behaviors that are not praised will disappear too. Too often parents focus on the negative and forget to reward the positive. **A parent is responsible to teach the child what *to do* as well as what not to do.** Most parents do remember to praise for special favors their children do, but take children's everyday good behavior (getting dressed) for granted. If you don't let your child know that you really appreciate her picking up her towel when she is done showering, she just may stop doing it. She shows respect for you by saving you from this bit of "housework," and you show respect for her by showing gratitude. If you don't tell them the behaviors that please you, they really don't know what is important to you (or to most people in our culture.) Be generous with your praise, for praise not only builds self-esteem, it also builds a positive relationship between parent and child.

If you want to get the most out of praising your child follow these simple rules for praise recommended by parent-trainer Cynthia Walker:

1. Look at the child.
2. Move close physically.
3. Smile.
4. Praise the behavior, not the child.
5. Praise immediately after the desired behavior.
6. Be affectionate.
7. Respond to even the smallest improvement, not just perfection.

If you want to see for yourself what a difference praise can make, conduct this simple experiment. Select a behavior of your child's that you *like* and that can be counted. For example, you might like the way your child can entertain herself with her building blocks or toys. Over the next week count how many times your child does that behavior and write it down somewhere to have a record of it, (but do *not* comment on the behavior in any way.) The following week praise that behavior every time your child does it by saying something like, "I love to see you peacefully playing with your blocks." Reinforce this with a gentle pat on the head. The third week count how many times your child does that behavior (and continue praising her). Then at the end of that week compare the count from week 1 with the count from week 3. Is your child quietly entertaining herself more now? What feelings do you have while praising your child and how does your child seem to feel? Hopefully the outcome will justify the effort.

◆

Uses and Misuses of Healthy Parenting Skills

DO THIS	NOT THIS
1. Communicate • discuss, listen and respond	1. • chatter, lecture, react, ignore
2. Be supportive • affirm, support, encourage, • accept diversity, • nurture	2. • criticize, pressure, undermine, • overwhelm with expectations
3. Foster respect • respect individual differences, • foster self-respect and respect for others	3. • require conformity, • tolerate disrespect, • ridicule or disrespect others
4. Trust • Trust your children, • be trustworthy, • foster integrity	4. • withdraw, hold grudges, • break trust, deny problems
5. Set aside family time • Share time, play together, • maintain a sense of humor, • keep balanced interaction among members	5. • abandon family to work, sports, volunteerism, • excessive preoccupation with self, alcohol, drugs or other addictions; • form cliques or "triangles" within the family
6. Value responsibility • Foster responsibility, • share responsibility, • set reasonable expectations	6. • create dependent children by being super-responsible or rescuing • dump adult responsibilities on children, • expect too much or too little for the child's age or stage of development
7. Teach values • Talk values, • cherish traditions, • seek "value groups"	7. • laissez-faire, "law of the jungle" (or street smarts), • counter-culture cynicism
8. Get Help • Reach out to doctors, experts, advisers, counselors, friends.	8. • deny or hide family situation, • require children to keep "family secrets."

All this thinking, plotting, and planning may sound oppressively controlling (and we just finished learning about not being controlling). Influencing, nurturing, and supporting are words that better describe the attitude that should accompany your parenting efforts. And of course there should be some spontaneous playtimes when rules can be abandoned as long as no one gets hurt. But Conscious Parenting can be taken too far, until it becomes a crippling, damaging, very self-conscious parenting. Opposite is a list of do's and don'ts that should help you sort out how much is enough.

Striking the right balance between healthy parenting ("do this") and overparenting ("not this") can be difficult at first. Often our anxiety about our children pushes us to go overboard to destructively self-conscious parenting. We are most vulnerable to such excesses when our children are facing a potential danger. The Wards (Chapter 10) had difficulty deciding how much to say about drinking because of the hereditary weakness that would probably affect their son. It can be agonizing to let our children learn from their own experiences, but once we have made them aware of family problems there is sometimes little more we can do.

Fortunately, Greg Ward eventually grew through to recovery before he did irreparable damage to himself or his future. He is now in college majoring in creative writing, a talent he discovered after he "got sober." Greg's grandfather still drinks even though he's almost seventy, and Greg's father drank destructively for ten years; but Greg was able to process the whole thing in about two years. Because Greg was able to see his father go through this cycle, he didn't have to spend so much time doing it himself. Tom's early awareness of the problems drinking caused in his family of origin helped Tom realize that he had lost control, and this awareness made him willing to go into treatment at age thirty-seven. As we will see in an upcoming chapter, Greg's problems were not over when he thought they were. He too had to go into a treatment program before he was free of substance abuse, but Greg was only twenty when he faced his problem.

My own mother was alcoholic and I swore I would never be like that. Yet, halfway through college I started drinking destructively. I didn't become physically addicted and I never got in over my head with drugs. I think because I had observed my mother drunk, I was more aware, and I stopped drinking at age twenty-five. My mother didn't wake up about it until she was fifty. I feel that if I talk to my son about the alcohol problems in our family, I can condense the time it will take him to realize what a dead end drinking is.

Obesity often "runs in families," so if your mother weighed three hundred pounds you would be really aware of fat and you might have decided you never want to be fat like that. Everybody gets to a point in their lives where they've stopped growing and they just can't eat as much as they used to or they start growing "sideways." If you have watched somebody else get fat, you would probably notice right away when you start gaining weight. You might say to yourself, "I know where this is going." But another person who comes from a family where no one is particularly fat might not even notice the gradual weight gain until they've gained a lot and gotten into some pretty bad eating habits. The light didn't go on in their head soon enough. They are "naive." On the other hand, the children of the obese person would have a chance to stop themselves early because of their heightened awareness.

Before Greg went to college the Wards were able to face all this openly. Greg's first therapist, who never seemed to realize that Greg was attending the sessions stoned, not only failed to help this family, he directed the family toward what would have been a devastating blunder. After two years of therapy Greg had made no progress and Janet asked for a reevalutation by the staff.

◆ THE WARDS—RELAXING THEIR GRIP

"The therapist did a big workup," Janet explains, "and then told me we should send Greg away to a residential school for distrubed teenagers. Sometimes I had thought, 'I can't handle this kid! If he doesn't straighten out we're going to have to send him away.' But when it came right down to it, it just didn't seem to fit. I decided we needed a second opinion."

This second therapist looked at the whole family and he diagnosed Greg's difficulties as a family communications problem. "With the old therapist it was really more like we were ganging up on Greg with the therapist and that didn't help. The new therapist looks at everything in terms of family dynamics and helps us see what we all contribute to the situation instead of seeing Greg as the disturbed one. Since we've been working with this new therapist things have improved tremendously.

"For example, Greg's grades began dropping again. We had tried everything. We tried having a study hall time at home. We tried threatening him. We tried a laissez-faire approach. Nothing worked. Finally we realized that they were his grades and we told him that he was responsible for them and just let go of it.

"This has all happened since we started seeing the family systems therapist. He helped us understand that we need to let Greg make his own mistakes and live with the consequences. I now realize that Greg, to a large degree, was just rebelling. Once we put him in charge of his own grades, he started to improve. His attendance at school improved, his grades improved, and his attitude improved."

TOM

"Over the years I had talked to my kids about my alcoholism, but mostly just to let them know that it was a disease that could be passed on in families and that we were going to be strict about alcohol for that reason. But I didn't make amends to my kids because I felt that the only person I had hurt was Janet. I knew I had been less available to my kids, but I felt like the best amends I could make would be to live sober. Recently I've begun to make amends to Greg for things he's brought up that I don't even remember. When Greg has gotten very upset he'll blurt things out. For instance he complained that I hit him when he was little but I really don't remember doing that.

"For a long time I just felt dumped on, like I was getting blamed for everything wrong in our family even after I got sober, and I probably discounted what he said because of that. But just recently I've realized that maybe there is a lot of truth in what he says and he obviously needs me to try to make amends. These memories are bothering Greg. I think for a long time I just couldn't admit that I might have harmed Greg. Yet I know that because I had blackouts I could have done things that i don't remember. This anger just kept welling up in Greg and I felt like I wanted to do whatever it took to help him. So I've apologized.

"Yet, I still don't know how to be emotionally available. I grew up in a family where there wasn't much closeness and I have no role model. I really don't understand how to be intimate."

As Tom is telling me this I feel his warmth, his love for his child and his comfort with telling me these intimate details. I comment that he seems relaxed and open now.

He laughs. "I've been beaten down by a teenage son's problems! I've had to really face it. Besides, the new therapist has been educating us. One thing we've realized is that we had a lot of negativity in our family. We forget to praise, but by God, if you do anything wrong, you'll hear about it for the rest of your life.

"We gradually realized that we weren't getting anywhere with our old ways of doing things. We just had to try something new. I've stopped being pompous and lectury. I was a great lecturer. Now we're recognizing that that just leads to more problems. Instead I need to recognize the emotions Greg is having.

"I've caught myself leaning toward the old ways. Greg has a habit of exceeding the limit by one or two percent. So he'll exceed the limit and I'll come down like a ton of bricks. But then I'll get ahold of myself. I'll go to him and explain that when we're upset and he responds with some smart remark it makes us fly off the handle. I explain that I became irrational, and I take back the absurd punishment I made and come up with something more reasonable.

"We used to get frustrated. We would think, how many times do we have to tell him midnight means midnight? Even though it was only 12:05, two weeks without the car would seem appropriate when we were all worked up. Then because he would start screaming and yelling at us, we'd feel like we couldn't back down.

"The family counselor has pointed out to us that we've got a smart kid. Greg understands the limits but he is just unwilling to live by them. He's not exceeding the limits by a wide margin. It's not like he takes off and doesn't come home for days. He comes in fifteen or thirty minutes late after having called to say he'll be late. We resented him always calling to say he'd be late because we just plain wanted him home on time. But he isn't a bad kid; he just needs to push the limits.

"And I'm beginning to let go. In a few months he'll be going off to college and he'll have to make these decisions for himself. Why should I ruin our last few months together? As long as he meets my minimum standards, I can let it go.

"I talked to one fellow at work and realized that our problems with Greg are very small compared to the problems of some parents of teenagers. I'll go in and complain about Greg being forty-five minutes late and this guy will say to me, "Did he flunk junior year? Did he get pregnant? Did he smash your car up?" And I'll realize that I really don't have that much to complain about. I'm beginning to get educated about how most teenagers behave and what's worth getting upset about. My younger son, Lyle, will get more of the benefit from this than Greg did, but of course, the poor oldest child has to break the parents in. If we had a third child, he'd have it even better than Lyle. You get a perspective with each kid."

(Continued in Chapter 15)

My own son is a limit-pusher. He just has this tremendous need to be in control. If I ask him to be in the car in five minutes, he'll get there in six minutes just to prove that he's in charge of the decision. If I can let it go, it's just that small inconvenience of one minute. If I feel like I need to challenge him or show him he needs to obey me, we could spend half an hour arguing about it. It really makes more sense to let him have that extra minute or state things in a way that lets him feel as if he is in charge of himself. If I make a polite request instead of ordering him, or if I offer him a choice, I get a lot more cooperation. And it really costs me very little.

CONSISTENCY VS. RIGIDITY

When Tom Ward set a punishment and then backed down on it the next morning, wasn't he being inconsistent? Old parenting styles would demand that Tom stick to his guns whether he's wrong or right. But that is actually **rigidity,** not consistency. **Rigidity is a**

reactionary defense. If you actually feel as if you have little personal authority, you are more likely to resort to rigidity. It takes an open, flexible person to be able to admit he or she was wrong in the heat of the moment. This doesn't mean that Greg's parents shouldn't punish him at all when he is late. They could decide on a buffer zone in their minds. When Janet says she is going to be home to cook dinner at 6 P.M., is Tom ready to hit the roof at 6:15? We all seldom arrive on the dot of when we said we would. Adults might be early sometimes and late sometimes. Kids, by virtue of their station in life, are more likely to do the latter. How late is *late?* If you are genuinely worried if your children are not home before 12:15, then that's the real limit. A reasonable consequence might be requiring them to be home thirty minutes earlier next time they go out. Or if this will only cause repeated violations, they can be grounded for the next Saturday night. If you punish harshly for fifteen minutes of tardiness, what will you do if your adolescent is an hour late? Harsh, rigid, unreasonable punishments are rarely really effective because, contrary to what many think, they will lose you the child's respect. To look like thinking, conscientious adults, parents need to be flexible.

Rigid policies also stop parents from considering children's individual differences or better solutions to a problem. One child may live and breathe TV while another can take it or leave it. If they each lose an hour's TV as a punishment, you will not be treating them *fairly*, you will be punishing one more than the other. Do you buy your son a dress each time you buy your daughter one? Would it be effective to make your six-year-old spend as much time on his homework as your sixteen-year-old? Yes, your kids should each get dessert, but they should not all be required to eat the same size dinner before they get it. People, and kids are people, come in different sizes, have different preferences and different needs.

Tom used to find himself locked into a course of action. He was afraid to back down even when he later realized that his punishment had been irrational. He was not putting things into perspective. A teenager who calls home every time he is going to be late is a responsible teenager. Many would find this cause for celebration. In his heart of hearts Tom knew this. By sticking to his pronouncements, no matter what, he was bound to lose a little respect for himself. He has done what he knows is wrong. Given that he cannot gain control of himself quickly enough, it is more respectable to admit later that he was wrong. However, the best solution would be to postpone discussion of the matter to morning when everyone has had time to calm down.

Good parenting is very fluid. What works with one child may not work with another; what works one time may not work another time. Rigidity blocks out the responsiveness to each situation that would inform the parent of alternative courses of action. On the other hand, life would be too difficult if we had to make a new decision every time we are confronted with a situation. Some routines and rules need to be established. If consequences are also established beforehand, they are more likely to be reasonable. Most decisions can follow these patterns. Then the parent's mind is free to be aware of situations that merit a significantly different response.

There are also those parents who are rarely rigid, but neither are they consistent. Consistency in parenting can be particularly difficult for an ACODF. These parents often have weak boundaries and are too preoccupied with being liked. Children, by nature, will manipulate for what they want at the moment. It may also be hard for the ACODF to set limits because they are not used to thinking about their own needs. You may not feel consistently angry enough to stop a behavior each time. But you can establish firmer boundaries between you and your child. You can dare to discipline them, as your relationships with your peers improve and you begin to get approval from other sources.

BEING A ROLE MODEL

Last, but not least, try to establish and stick to some rules for yourself. Model consistency and perseverence. Keep regular hours; establish routines such as laundry on Monday (so everyone knows when they will have clean clothes); **keep plans simple so that you can complete what you set out to accomplish.** Even if your children battle with you on every point, they are watching to see how you do. You might lose the argument about a clean room, but you will have taught your child the value of keeping your house in order if you "have a place for everything and everything in its place." When you can find your shoes in fifteen seconds and it takes them fifteen minutes, you are having a long-term positive impact.

◆ ═══════════════ **SUMMARY** ═══════════════ ◆

Our children need to be able to count on not only our support and encouragement, but also our reliability. Through us they will form their opinions about whether our world is a benign place that can be trusted or a sinister place that must be feared.

◆ ═══════════════ **POINTS** ═══════════════ ◆

1. The amount of time, attention, love, and consistency that children really need to become competent confident adults can come as an astonishing surprise to someone who was neglected as a child.

2. We must be careful to separate our own talents and ambitions from those of our children. For example, if we were deprived of music lessons as a child, we should take lessons now instead of forcing our children to take them.

3. If our parents did not encourage us to complete projects despite frustrating setbacks, we may have inherited destructively low expectations for our children. With our gentle support our children may be able to accomplish more than we did.

4. Children need firm parents. We must learn to assert ourselves and set limits despite our feelings of insecurity and our children's angry protests.

5. To break out of destructive dependency patterns, we need to begin to appreciate our strengths and give ourselves the approval we failed to receive as children.

6. By learning to follow through on our own long-range goals and plans, we can model consistency while rebuilding our children's trust in us.

7. We have an obligation to teach children what to do as well as what *not* to do. When we demand respect from our children *and* act respectful of them in return, we teach them the most important social skill.

8. We can be consistent without being rigid. If there is a sound reason, it is better to change a rule or back down on a harsh punishment, instead of arbitrarily enforcing an unreasonable rule set in anger.

NOTES

1. Interview: Cynthia Walker, Licensed Clinical Social Worker who uses Confident Parenting techniques.
2. Phyllis York, David York, and Ted Wachtel, *Tough Love.* New York: Bantam Books, 1983.

13

RESOLVING CONFLICT

15. ACODF have few skills for dealing with conflict effectively.

Conflict resolution has long been neglected in our competitive society. To truly resolve conflicts one needs to act out of a spirit of cooperation and goodwill. This is the essence of maturity. Since the parents of ACODF are characteristically psychologically immature and self-centered, they rarely acted out of this spirit. Unresolved conflict is the pain and anguish of living. **Whatever still hurts is a conflict in you that has not been resolved.** You will go on acting out that conflict in every area of your life. If your parents criticized you constantly, you are still living with the anger of shame—that feeling that you will never be good enough. You may approach conflict with a "Get them before they get you" attitude. Or you may approach it with the old standby, "What's the use of trying?"

Sometimes ACODF imagine that most families are conflict-free and no one in their family should feel negative emotions if they are doing a good job as parents. But negative emotions and conflict exist in every family. The ACODF who doesn't realize this will undoubtedly discourage the expression of negative emotions, but the conflicts will still be there, undercover, doing as much or more damage than if they were expressed.

Psychologists have reduced our response to stress and conflict down to two polarities: Fight or Flight. Although these are the two most common human responses, and indeed may have been our only responses for hundreds of years, there is another alternative that humankind is ready to approach: Negotiation. We all know the

uselessness of the flight response. This leaves the conflict unresolved. And in our nuclear-age world the fight response has become
obsolete, as we realize that aggression begets counteraggression
and can lead to mutual destruction. In the smallest arena, the
nuclear family, to fight also means no winners, only losers. Negotiation, which has always been an effective tool, is now the one essential skill our children need for survival. But let's take a closer look at
these alternative responses to conflict and how they are acted out in
the family.

AVOIDING CONFLICT

Another term that describes the flight response is avoidance.
We can simply withdraw from the conflict and hope that it goes
away. Sometimes this is actually the wisest response. If some weirdo
approaches you on the street and says something insulting, it is
wiser to walk away than it is to stand there and defend your honor.
Similarly, if your child is overtired and beyond thinking rationally,
it is most sensible to ignore his or her provocations. Likewise, if the
matter is something that is not really important to you, such as
what cereal the child eats for breakfast, accommodating the child
by getting out a different brand of cereal may be the best course.
The old adage, "Pick your battles!" would make a good watchword
when approaching conflict.

But there are also destructive ways of avoiding conflict. These
are characterized by passive-aggressive tactics. This is often a favorite among children: Say "yes" to whatever Mom asks and then simply
forget to do it.

But parents also use passive-aggressive tactics. Kids often see
parents deal with conflict by walking away. Cynthia Walker, licensed
clinical social worker and parent trainer for Pasadena Guidance
Clinics, reports, "I once saw a four-year-old who walked around the
house saying he was going to kill himself. But that's how he saw his
mother deal with conflict. She would run out of the house, slam the
door, and say she was going to kill herself."[1] What is this parent
modeling? A variation on this theme is threatening to run away and
abandon the child. Many of us have probably felt like either running
away or taking the ultimate escape at one time or another. Usually
we are not standing there thinking, "What can I say to terrify this
child?" When we feel like that we are overwhelmed and we are

focused on escaping that terrible pressure that children can exert. Nonetheless, these tactics do create tremendous fear and insecurity in the child, and as the "grown-up," we need to button our lip and not let these words escape us. That's why it's so tough being a parent. You're being watched all the time. Parenting is a relentless responsibility. The bright side of realizing the influence you have as a parent, and how important it is for *you* to change, is that it's like an opportunity to "live your life over" and correct your mistakes. It's a good and valid excuse to improve yourself, to give to yourself.

Another way of avoiding conflict is the indefinite postponement. As stated earlier, postponing a conversation about a conflict or a decision about a punishment until we are out of the "heat of the moment" is a wise tactic—**as long as we do take it up later.** Unfortunately, postponement is too often abused. We postpone resolving the conflict while we are angry because it doesn't seem like a good time to settle things rationally, but then later, when things are calm, we are loathe to dig up the conflict again. We can convince ourselves that it really wasn't all that important.

However, unresolved conflict festers. If you outwardly exhibit patience or forbearance but inwardly you are seething with resentment, your child will pick up on your nonverbal messages. Children are usually still "in tune" with their intuition and often seem like mind-readers. My child is an excellent "face-reader." If we are riding along in the car and I am *thinking* about something disturbing, he will ask, "What's wrong, Mommy?" Likewise, if I am exhibiting a saintly amount of patience while I am thinking I would like to grab him and shake him, he will say, "Don't look at me like that!"

FIGHTING

For a long time expressing your anger loudly and aggressively was "in," but modern researchers such as Carol Tavris (*Anger: The Misunderstood Emotion*)[2] and Harriet Goldhor Lerner (*The Dance of Anger*)[3] have discovered that although expressing our anger might temporarily relieve some tension (and even that's debatable), if you want to go on having a relationship with the object of your angry outburst, you had better think about what you are saying. For the most part, uncensored expressions of anger just aggravate and enflame the bad feelings that are already there. Does this mean we should always smile and turn the other cheek? No. There is a difference between venting our rage and assertively stating what our needs are, and how we see them being violated. Even if our opponent is objectively despicable and one hundred percent at fault (unlikely), we are more likely to get the outcome we want when we control ourselves and treat him or her respectfully.

Let's take the touchiest of circumstances to illustrate this. Your ex-spouse always delivers your child an hour or two late when they return from a visitation. Not only do you worry each time, twice this has made you late for a support group meeting that is very important to you. What do most people do under these circumstances? First of all, depending on how outwardly aggressive one is, the offended parent is likely to scream and insult the visiting parent, threaten to get a court order to prevent visitations, be sarcastic and snide, or manipulatively lay a guilt trip on the ex-spouse. There may be a good chance that the ex-spouse is doing this to irritate you, but let's assume a spirit of goodwill. Before you blow up, think about why the child is repeatedly brought home late. Maybe your daughter is having a terrific time with her visiting parent and she delays the arrival home. Maybe your ex-spouse misses the child terribly and just can't let her go on time. Maybe they don't have enough time to spend together and visitation should be increased. Struggle to see the situation from the point of view of the other person.

No matter what the cause of your daughter's late return, an angry response on your part is not likely to inspire your ex-spouse to change. If he or she is doing it to get your goat, your anger will serve to cheer the ex-spouse on to greater displays of rebellion. If your daughter or your ex-spouse are suffering from a lack of time together, your threatening behavior will just raise their anxiety; even if you have scared them good, they will probably continue to be late because they are either too anxious to plan responsibly or they feel like each time might be their final visit and they had better make it last as long as possible. What outcome do you want?

First of all try to identify if what's really bugging you is that you don't have control over your child or the situation for that hour or so. If that is your primary motivation, you need to let go of your unhealthy need to control. Then, with a relaxed and respectful attitude, ask your ex-spouse and child to sit down and discuss the situation with you when the ex-spouse arrives for the *beginning* of the next visit. State at the outset of your discussion that your daughter can stay later this week since part of the visitation time is being used for negotiation. Be pleasant. Tell them both that the lateness has been a problem for you and you are wondering if there is anything you can do to make it easier for them to get home at the agreed-upon time. Be flexible. Be open to changing the allotted time to a more realistic and attainable one. Any offer on your part to be flexible will serve to lessen the tension of the issue. Believe me, this will work much better than hostility if what you really want is to *solve* the problem, not just have a good energizing fight about it.

ALTERNATIVE METHODS

A truly resolved conflict is one which has no residue of bad feelings. Below is a table created by psychiatrist and marriage counselor William Summers, M.D. (*The House of Marriage*), which shows four styles of conflict resolution and their resultant emotions:[4]

Methods of Resolution of Conflict

TYPE	ATTITUDE
Accommodation	+ I will change because *I* want to.
Acceptance (Forced accommodation)	− I will change because *they* will not change.
Compromise	+ We will both change.
Persistence (Forced concession)	− I will make you change to *my* point of view.

Summers explains that of the four methods of conflict resolution, only two leave positive emotions. Both Accommodation (especially when met by counteraccommodation) and Compromise resolve the conflict peacefully, with no hard feelings on either side. However, Acceptance and Persistence result in a negative emotional tone. What is your pattern of resolving conflict? Do you rely on positive or negative means of settling conflicts? Do you use the same methods with your spouse, kids, and friends? Love does *not* mean never having to treat your family respectfully.

Accommodation is one way to settle conflicts and it is sometimes the best way. But peacemaking is not always so peaceful. Sometimes we must insist that our rights and wants be respected. If we do not require our children to "give in" to us sometimes, we will begin to feel resentful. For example, say it is time to make dinner but your child wants to go to the store right now because he is afraid that someone else will buy the truck he has had his eye on. Although you have sixty other things to do, you play "nice parent" and drive him to the store. As a result, dinner is an hour late and you are too harried to remember your book discussion meeting that night. By the time they call to ask where you are, it is too late to bother going. Your whole evening is ruined and for three hours you have been snapping at your child because you feel harried and behind. Your son has no idea why you are being nasty to him. He asked you to take him to the store and you said, "Yes." He doesn't even know that his request was unreasonable but he is punished anyway by having to endure your bad mood. Really, that is worse for the child than just saying, "No."

What has gone wrong here? Let's take a look at this situation in terms of the four methods of conflict resolution. If you were truly feeling accommodating, you would have gone off to the store because you'd rather shop than cook anyway. The result would be that you and your child are two happy shoppers. You can eat out, bring Dad a burger, and still make it to the book meeting on time, relaxed and happy. But what if you didn't really want to go shopping just then but your protests had no impact on your child. You go to "shut him up." You will not end up feeling good about this outcome. You accommodated the request but not of your own "free will." You will probably feel resentful.

How could you have used compromise to solve the problem? You could have pointed out that you would like to accommodate your child but you simply can't do it now; you could offer to pick him up from school tomorrow and go straight to the store; you could suggest he ask Dad to take him after dinner while you are at your book meeting; or you could ask him what other solution he sees to the problem. This will give each of you a sense of having your needs respected and having power over your lives. What if you had taken a more aggressive stance in your refusal and shouted, "No! Can't you see I'm busy cooking? Get out of here and stop bothering me!" If forced to concede to your wishes without any consideration of his desires like this, your child would have been left feeling discounted and resentful.

You owe it to your children to model good conflict resolution. You need to show them how to take turns, postpone gratification, compromise, and "lose" gracefully. With these skills your children can attract and keep good friends. By contrast, if the accommodating parent always lets the child have his way, that child will have few friends. For the world is not accommodating (even though some parents knock themselves out trying to get the world to conform to their children's needs and desires).

CONFLICTS BETWEEN CHILDREN

The cry, "Pick your battles!" should be used often when approaching conflicts between children. Teachers and parents constantly struggle with how much one should get involved in children's battles. When should you stay out of it; that is, when should you let children resolve the problem on their own? I say, unless they are going at it with knives, let them work it out. You do need to intervene if one child is obviously larger and stronger than the other and he or she is taking advantage. The only other good excuse for getting involved is if you can really calmly and objectively use the situation to teach something about conflict resolution. This does not mean presiding as judge. That is usually a fruitless task. Very often all you will get is, "He started it!" from both sides.

If you think it can be constructive to get involved in the conflict, start by separating the two children and asking them each to think about the argument and some different ways it could be settled. Let them do this apart from one another (preferably not within sight of each other) for a period of five minutes (or until they cool off, however long that takes). Then bring them back together and have them tell you their proposed solutions. At first children may have no approach except "might makes right." They may need you to list alternatives. Here are a few that fit many situations:

1. Take Turns

This will probably solve 50 percent of children's problems. Who goes first? Flip a coin. If one complains that the other "won't" take turns, you have two alternatives. Help them decide what the consequences will be if one should refuse to give the other a turn; or cancel that activity for the day and politely tell them they can try again tomorrow.

2. Make Up

Have each apologize to the other for his or her part in the conflict, whether it was a response or a provocation. (It always takes two to tango.) If they are still too angry to do this, let them take more time out. This doesn't have to be done punitively. They can each go read a book in separate rooms until they cool off.

3. Mediate

Have them each tell what happened from his or her own point of view and how it made them feel. Make each one repeat what the other said, showing they each understood the feelings as well as the words. Next, summarize the situation for them using neutral language. Find some point of agreement, no matter how small. For example: They are both feeling hurt or angry and those are uncomfortable feelings it would be good to get rid of. Have them each suggest solutions and then help them evaluate the solutions by imagining the possible consequences. If it seems necessary, have them write down the solution they agree upon and sign it.

DO NOT try to find out who started it, decide who is to blame, ask *why* they did it, automatically defend the younger or less aggressive child, or solve the problem without the children's participation. These tactics are a total waste of time for everyone and only serve to blow the conflict out of proportion. The only exception to this would be if one of the children is markedly larger and more aggressive. He or she cannot be given free reign over the weaker child, but beware of the underdog's manipulation too.

CONFLICT WITH SPOUSE

Do you and your spouse peacefully share the power you have as parents? Your children will probably learn the most about how to resolve conflict by watching the two of you. Your home and family is an intimate glimpse into the private and real feelings of people in relationship. How you settle your differences is likely to be how they will settle theirs.

The best model for children is a **shared power** model. Both boys and girls need to see women being as strong as men, even if in quite different ways. They need to see Mom being as respectful of Dad as he is of her. Do you and your children's father have equal power in your relationship and in their management? If not, who is the more powerful? Where does his or her power come from? Right now, you are the only person you can change. Even if you are the more powerful one, you have no real power over whether or not your spouse changes. So you need to look at your role and change *yourself* if there is unequal power.

If you are the less powerful you will need to take back some of the power you have given up. Does your spouse have the power because he or she is the breadwinner? If money is a big playing card you may need to go earn some and exert power over it. Or you might think of ways your labor saves the family money and consider yourself to be earning that much. However, hurling the figure at your spouse and demanding more respect and power won't work. The change has to be *within* you. You have to *feel* and *acknowledge* your own contribution and give yourself the power you deserve. If you wish to have more power over decisions regarding the kids, take it. Speak up the next time you disagree with a discipline tactic or granted privilege. If the issue seems sensitive, ask your co-parent to go to another room to discuss the issue with you before making a decision. Let the child wait while you and your co-parent hash it out. If you just have a "bad feeling" about your spouse's decision but haven't had time to analyze the situation and present a rational argument, ask that the decision be postponed. Then stick to your guns. Be firm. If the decision seems to require an immediate response (like the neighbors have just asked if your son can go with them now to a PG-13 rated movie), explain that you need more warning and they cannot go this time but you will try to establish some rule that would apply to future situations. If you take yourself seriously, your spouse and child will too.

On the other hand, if you are the more powerful you must start giving back some of the power you're hogging. Being "the head" of the family all the time can be stressful and exhausting. If you have a pattern of being superresponsible you may have run your spouse out of the game long ago by always beating him or her to the punch. Give your spouse power over some "territory." For example, let your co-parent decide what the Saturday routine will be. Don't throw it out as a challenge. Say you are tired and would really appreciate some more help with the kids. Then don't criticize. If your spouse plans a disastrous Saturday, be sympathetic and try to remember that doing new tasks takes some trial and error. Don't jump in with your suggestions. Instead, ask your partner how he or she feels about the way the day went. Let your co-parent critique himself or herself. You should be working toward having some true "time off" from being in charge, so give your spouse and children space to solve their own problems. They might come up with creative new solutions that would never have occurred to you. If your spouse asks you directly for advice, don't take over. Be tactful and cautious. Keep in mind that if you have been hogging the power for a long time, it will take your spouse time to learn to be powerful again. Allow your co-parent the freedom to make mistakes and learn from them.

Think of your family power dynamics as an equation:

Powerful spouse ($+1$) plus powerless spouse (-1) equals zero.
Powerful spouse ($+1$) plus powerful spouse ($+1$) equals double power.

When one parent in the family has all the power, the children not only miss out on feeling like they have two parents they can depend on, they also miss out on the mitigating power of your influence. We all need feedback and fresh ideas now and then. If you are holding back your contribution to family decisions because you feel powerless, you are also letting your spouse be less than the great parent he or she could be. Divorce studies make it abundantly clear that children need *two parents*. **Whether you are married to or divorced from your co-parent, you must learn to share the power.**

Remember Susan who lost her children in Chapter 9? She had become a powerless person, letting her spouse trample over everything she believed in. She allowed the kids, who had rarely spent time in their father's care before the divorce, to be awarded to her ex-husband. By giving in without a fight, she abandoned the children she loved so dearly. Who lost the most in that divorce? When Susan came to her senses she took back her power.

◆ SUSAN'S STRENGTH RETURNS

Susan sought counseling and was assigned a wonderful woman counselor who said to her, "You're not crazy. I understand what you've done and you've done nothing wrong. You go back into those courts and demand your children back." She told Susan she had been driven by misplaced guilt and a misguided desire to do what was best for her children.

"Just her affirmation made me start to see myself realistically. I got a lawyer immediately but when I went back into court I was informed that I couldn't change the custody arrangement." Caught up in the blind machinery of social change, the divorce courts were bending over backward to be fair to the father. Bart was not expected to give Susan any child support, and Susan's teaching salary was much smaller than Bart's salary. "They did not question my fitness—the judge said he found me to be a very fit mother. But I could not support my children as well as my husband could."

Susan's ex-husband, Bart, was transferred to the East Coast and the children went with him. Bart finally became a parent to the children. "Bart would call me up and ask me how I had done things because he wanted them to have continuity. For the five years that I was separated from my children he actually was the father that they had never had. This was an invaluable experience for my children. Even though it was extremely painful for me, I am very glad that they were able to have that time. It was a very difficult five years for me. I called them every week and I sent for them twice a year. I never put him down in their eyes because I knew that wasn't good for them. Still, my kids would say they wanted to come live with me, so I pursued getting them back through the New York courts."

Nothing in Susan's circumstances had changed enough to make a difference until she remarried. "During the first year that I was remarried, my daughter, Jenny, then eleven, made it very clear to my ex-husband and his new wife that she wanted to come and live with me. She made it so uncomfortable that my ex-husband called us and said that if my new husband, Ed, was willing to adopt Jenny, we could have her. We sent for her immediately. My ex-husband sent the papers for us to adopt her. Her parting with her father had been very bitter. That next Christmas Jenny sent back presents to her father and stepmother with her brother, Brent, when he came out to visit, but my ex-husband told Brent to tell Jenny that she was no longer his daughter. He wanted nothing more to do with her. That was very hard for Jenny. She couldn't understand why it was all right when she lived with him, but it wasn't all right for her to live with her mother."

Brent continued to tell his mother that he wanted to live with her, and the brother and sister missed each other deeply. So Susan tried the courts again. Brent was taken into the judge's chambers. Susan's lawyer reported to her later that Brent marched up to the judge and said, "Is anybody going to listen to what I want this time? I've been saying for five years that I want to live with my mother. Now will you let me do it?" And the judge said, "Yes."

Susan, her husband Ed, her ex-husband Bart, and Bart's wife were in the courtroom when the lawyers and Brent came out of the chambers. "I thought I'd lost again but Brent and Jenny were shouting at me that we'd won. I didn't hear them, because I was too afraid to believe it. When I finally realized that we had won and the kids were mine again, I sat and cried. Then I looked over at my ex-husband and his wife and I began to cry for them. I said, 'Why did it have to be like this?'

"When my ex had the children he was very willing to raise them by my old rules so they could have some stability and I have to praise him for that. For that five years, he was an outstanding father. For him, the divorce was an awakening of fatherhood and he really rose to the occasion. It probably wouldn't have happened if it hadn't been for the divorce. The truth is that much good has come from all of that pain.

"We all suffered from the separation, but the kids have learned that sometimes life deals you something difficult but that doesn't mean that you fall apart, or turn to drugs, or become an alcoholic. It doesn't mean that you give up on yourself; you just go on. You have an obligation in this life to be the best that you can no matter what your circumstances are. I think that's been one of our sources of strength in this family."

(Continued in Chapter 16)

Susan and her husband had obviously polarized in their marriage. He assigned all the nurturing to her and became totally unnurturing. But then when she was out of the picture, he was able to let the nurturing part of himself emerge. He is a rigid person and it is easier for him to put things into little boxes. Unfortunately, when his daughter "rejected" him, he became totally unnurturing to her. It had to be black or white. His daughter had deserted him as his first wife had. Like Susan, Jenny would have to be out of his life forever.

The healthiest, happiest relationships are between two equals. When your child becomes an adult you will want him or her to have power equal to his or her mate. There are two ways you can prepare your children to share power in relationships. As we have mentioned, you can model a shared power relationship with your co-parent, but it is also important for you to share power with your child. You may be the older, wiser, and more responsible party, but there are many decisions that your children are capable of making. Be sensitive to these times and allow your children to exercise decision-making power whenever possible.

PARENTING TOGETHER

Studies on children of divorce show that when the two parents were both able to stay involved with the children and could cooperate enough to make the children's transition between them smooth, the children had fewer problems after the divorce and on into adulthood. **Children whose parents are in deep conflict feel pressured to take sides, but for them taking sides often means giving up a loving relationship with one parent.** This is clear-cut and obvious in divorced families, but Mom-against-Dad teams form in many intact families too. These alliances are just as damaging and may even be more destructive because the battle lines are unacknowledged. When parents cannot get along with each other there is a tremendous temptation to use the children in the war.

At different stages, and because certain personalities mix better than others, the children may show a preference for one parent over the other. When children are young they are often closer to the mother, but boys or girls may gravitate toward the father during preadolescence and adolescence. If you are angry at your spouse and you are the parent in favor now, the idea of gaining the child's sympathy to side with you can be very compelling. When parents do this consciously they often can recognize how wrong it is. But usually this "taking sides" is a subtle, subconscious movement. Mom may be feeling very angry at Dad, so when Daughter has a garden-variety conflict with Dad and complains about how unfair Dad is, Mom sympathizes a little too much, and the unhealthy alliance is born. The hardest task demanded of a parent is to set aside your own feelings and do what is best for the child. And it is best for the children not only to be free to love both parents, but also be encouraged to do so even when they are angry at a parent. If they are helped to turn away, they will grow up with tremendous guilt. In most cases, when the children realize what part one parent has played in alienating the children from the other parent, they become angry and turn against the parent they were "closer" to. If you help your children hate your spouse (even if he or she deserves it!) you might win the battle, but you won't win the war.

Whether married or divorced, you must learn how to work harmoniously with your co-parent for the sake of your children. Even Susan's ex-husband, Bart, filled with as much anger as he was, was able to consult with his ex-wife to provide consistency for the children. When Bart called Susan for advice she must have been tempted to refuse to give him guidance and let him fall flat on his face. Since he had had too little contact with his children, it would have been easy to make him look like an incompetent father. But Susan didn't want her children to suffer from their father's lack of parenting skill. **She kept focused on the children's needs rather than her personal conflict with Bart.**

The temptation to make the other parent look bad is present in intact marriages every day. Stay-at-home parents have tremendous power to discourage or encourage the children's relationship with the working parent. The traits you find most infuriating in your co-parent might be an element your child needs in his or her life. Polarizing, as Bart and Susan did, is common. When one parent is very strict, the other parent often compensates by being much looser than they would ordinarily be. If you're being the "fun" parent, your kids may need the sobering effect of the "serious" parent to keep balance in their lives. However, it is best if neither parent has to play such a fixed role. If you find yourself being pushed into exaggerating a quality of yours to compensate for your spouse, resist. Try to be as well-rounded as you can. That will free your serious co-parent to be fun sometimes.

Try to find respectful ways to support the efforts of the other parent. If you feel your co-parent is too harsh, don't make up for it by abandoning all the rules when your spouse is not around. Talk to your co-parent and try to get him or her to be more moderate. Unless the children are being abused (and then you *should* interfere and insist on family counseling), try to go along with your co-parent's discipline. If your co-parent is too irresponsible, be sure your kids feel safe and secure, and then try to loosen up at agreed-upon times. Let them eat candy for dinner on Friday nights if they've eaten nutritious food the rest of the week! For those readers who are mentally arguing with me, saying, "But you don't know how uncooperative my co-parent is!" I recommend reading the book *Getting to Yes*, by Roger Fisher and William Ury.[5]

Finally, I want to say what "parenting together" is *not*. Parenting together does not mean ganging up on the kids. If Mom says the kids cannot go out until they do the dishes, by all means support her and don't give them permission to go anywhere. But if Mom has been screaming and yelling at them, for whatever reason, and you are not in a conflict of your own with them, don't join her in screaming and yelling. You can do far more good staying out of the fray and being available as a sounding board, confidant, or mediator. This is not being disloyal to your wife. You can be supportive *and* not be angry at the kids.

Such a scene might go like this:

(Dad screaming in the garage at your eight-year-old son, Billy) "How many times do I have to tell you to leave my tools alone! Look at this saw. It's all rusted!"

(Billy runs to house crying.) "Dad's yelling at me. He almost hit me!" (Billy buries his face in your lap.)

(Mom, stroking Billy on the head.) "It sounds like Dad is really angry at you. What do you think he's mad about?"

"I left his saw outside and it got all rusty."

"Did you have permission to use his tools?"

"He lets me use them when I'm with him."

"Are you supposed to use them when you are not with him?"

"Probably not."

"What do you think you should do about this situation?"

"I should probably go tell him I'm sorry, but he's so mad I'm afraid he's going to hit me."

"He's probably calmed down by now, but if you want me to, I'll go with you."

"Thanks, Mom. Let's go."

Kids who have two parents who can cooperate are really fortunate. They can feel supported and lovable even when they are in trouble with the other parent.

CONFLICT WITH CHILD

Children are often irrational and they can do the most infuriating things. They can be very unfair, rude, and hurtful. Most of the conflicts we have with children grow out of the fact that they want to do what they want to do, when they want to do it. Childhood is a long process of finding that we can't always have things our way. Parents are the primary teachers of this terrible truth. Our roles are oppositional. The child strives to be independent and we strive to hold them back until they can handle what they are setting out to do. The old method for this was for the parent to simply say to the child, "No! Because I said so." Now children are saying, "No, because *I* said so!" And we do have to let them assert themselves. Authoritarian approaches are only useful as long as we will be *physically present* to protect them. When a fellow student offers them a joint, or an adult "offers" them sex, our children need to be trained to say, "No!" strongly and assertively out of their *own* free wills.

The 1990s call for a new approach. Children must be active participants in setting rules and consequences. At family meetings they can be made part of the process that protects them, so they can internalize this knowledge and become self-reliant. Parents must work *with* their children, not *against* them, as if it were a contest to see whose will will be done.

PHYSICAL PUNISHMENTS

Some believe that child abuse is on the rise now because life is much more stressful. Others think that our heightened awareness is just causing more cases to be reported. A generation ago beating your child was not considered abuse in many states. Parents could do what they wished until the child reached legal adult status. But whether or not parents abuse their children more now, children have lost some common protections. Before families moved around so much, nearby neighbors and relatives served as inhibitors. Children were able to form ties with neighbors so that the impact of the family situation wasn't so total. Now, not only are children more vulnerable to abuse by their parents, parents themselves are often stressed to the point of breaking because they have no friends or relatives nearby to relieve the pressure of children when the kids become unbearable.

Yet, I optimistically believe that we will live to see the end of physical punishment of children in this country. This is not really so farfetched. In Sweden it has long been a law that parents may not strike their children. If a mother slaps her child for grabbing things off the shelf in the supermarket, her child will be taken away from her. Of course, some hitting still goes on behind closed doors, but out there in public parents are being forced to learn other methods of controlling their children. I taught in the New Jersey public schools, where corporal punishment has been outlawed for more than a generation, and then later in New Mexico, where paddling was the solution to most discipline problems. In New Mexico, the other teachers were always amazed by my ability to control my students. (I taught delinquents.) I never once sent anyone to the office to be paddled. Growing up in New Jersey I had never seen a teacher solve any problems by striking a student. In a tense situation most of us will revert back to what we saw modeled. In my moments of greatest stress I went into "automatic pilot," and all I could visualize were teachers settling conflicts without physical violence.

On the other hand, my parents were strong believers in physical punishment. In my worst moments I have never struck my child (because of my strong convictions and access to alternatives) but I often pictured it. In fact, when my son said, "Don't look at me like that!" it seemed as if he could see the violent scene playing out in my head behind my eyes. I believe that anyone who was physically "disciplined" or abused as a child is at high risk for abusing his or her own children. I have seen some parents calmly and judiciously spank a young child as a means of discipline. For them, it may be a reasonable alternative, although physical punishment is *unnecessary* in any circumstances. But for the ACODF who was abused, even spanking is very risky business. It is just too easy to cross that line between spanking and beating.

If you were abused as a child, you have actually been *pro-*

grammed to abuse your child. That's a strong pull when you are under stress. By the same token, if you were hurt repeatedly as a child, you probably have a lot of pent-up rage inside of you which can come out when you are upset with your child.

Rage is not the same as anger. Although certain situations with your child may trigger rage, rage is not really situational. It is a feeling that lives in your body even when you are not conscious of it. The rage you feel is really toward your parents for abusing you, your relatives for not interfering, and society for allowing such things to happen. Nobody can change your past now. Releasing your rage on your child won't even serve to expel it from your body (as some anger advocates believe). Shouting will not leave you calm and peaceful. Instead, rage multiplies like a virus. Until your rage has been "worked through" in counseling or a group, it is likely to surface when you are angry at anyone and especially when you are angry at your child. (Because children are irrational by nature, until they are mature they can be very exasperating and generate the strongest emotions you will ever feel in your life.) Just as an alcoholic must decide never to take even one little drink again, I think that ACODFs who were beaten as children should never raise a hand to their own children.

To keep yourself from striking your child, start by preprogramming your mind. When you are alone and evaluating your parenting, give some thought to the situations which make you very angry. Picture the situation, feel the anger, then visualize yourself taking some action other than hitting. Some alternatives are offered below. Later, if you find yourself steaming with anger in a hot situation with your child, start counting to ten. Not only might this give your child time to come to his or her senses, it will give you a chance to cool down and consider alternatives. If you must, stamp your feet and shout, "I am really mad now!" to let your children know that you have reached your limit.

ALTERNATIVES TO PHYSICAL PUNISHMENT

There are many alternatives to physical punishment. First of all there is the whole area of rewards and praise. We talked about praise in the last chapter. Parents who participated in Cynthia Walker's parenting classes through the Center for Improvement of Child

Caring in Los Angeles, tried the praise method and saw good results within a few weeks. Walker comments,

> The kids also started to imitate the parents and praise them back. The parents were very surprised by that and it began a self-perpetuating positive cycle. It was good for these parents, who had never been praised before themselves. Praising also reduced some of the anger in the kids and they became less hostile so that they began to act more like kids. This helped the parents feel closer to them.[6]

Most of the kids showed a positive response to the praising within four to five weeks, but there is an old rule of thumb that says any change takes ninety days. So when you try this method, don't get discouraged for at least three months.

Rewards are also very effective and needn't involve spending a lot of money. A trip to the park, a visit with a favorite friend, the right to pick what dinner will be, or special time alone with you, are just a few suggestions for free rewards. However, in order for rewards not to be mere bribes, they require advance planning and may not work in unexpected situations. Knowing that she will get ice cream for dessert is often not enough to inhibit a child who would like to haul off and belt her little brother. Sometimes simpler more immediate responses are needed.

If your parents relied mainly on hitting, you may never have seen good verbal correction methods. Cynthia Walker points out that many parents are totally ineffective at correcting their children. They do it from other rooms; they yell and scream. You can't effectively teach or praise your child from another room either, but you can learn some good techniques that will help you correct, teach, praise, or discipline your child more effectively. First, you need to get very close to the child and talk to them quietly. Keep requests or statements brief and simple: Don't lecture, discuss, or argue. Standing up close to the child might also make you more aware of your voice volume. You don't need to shout at someone who is six inches away. When you see the expression on your child's face, you will also realize when you are frightening them or being ignored. If you are making a request, it's important to go back into the room later to see that your request is being followed.[7]

Ignoring is often the best technique to use against negative attention-getting behaviors. Remember, even negative attention will appeal to a child. Of course, part of the plan should be to pay lots of attention when the child is behaving appropriately, but you will also need to extinguish disruptive behaviors by removing your attention. If your childs sulks, pouts, cries, whines, or throws temper tantrums, the best policy is to turn away from the child and even leave the room if necessary. Keep your face neutral as if you hear nothing. Ignore any request that is made in a whiny voice, or is being coerced through tears. It's important to get others in the family to join you in ignoring these behaviors, because their attention can be rewarding enough to keep the child going. As soon as your child stops the negative behavior, make a point of going over and touching your child to show you still love him or her. In other words, catch them being "good" and reward this positive attitude immediately. Like the praising method, it may take a few weeks for the "ignoring method" to extinguish unwanted behaviors.

PUNISHMENTS VS. CONSEQUENCES

If you are trying to take a more positive approach it is also important to learn the difference between punishments and consequences. Punishment comes in many forms and any good ACODF is probably very familiar with them. As a matter of fact, an ACODF parent may be so well-versed in punishments that they fail to see the subtle distinction between punishments and **logical consequences.**

The best consequences for helping children learn the ways of the world are natural consequences. These are the things that will automatically happen to them if they do something they weren't supposed to do. If they touch a stove, they will get burned. If they hit their friends, the friends will go home. If they leave without their coats, they will be cold, and so on.

But sometimes the natural consequence is too delayed to be instructive or is simply too dangerous. For example, if your child does not brush his teeth or eat properly he may have poor health as an adult but then it will be too late to do anything about it. Also, while he is still a child you may not be able to convince him that this could really happen. Similarly, your child may well break his leg if he jumps off the roof but a responsible parent wouldn't take the child up to the roof to try it. So sometimes we need to set up consequences ourselves. The most effective consequences are logical consequences or those that are closely related to the behavior.

A logical consequence for someone who leaves her bike out on the lawn where it can be stolen is to lose the priviledge of riding that bike for a week (since she would not be riding it if it were, in fact, stolen). A logical consequence for someone who will not take his dirty plate into the kitchen after dinner is for him to find the dirty plate at his place at the next meal (since it didn't get to the sink to be washed.) However, it is not a logical consequence if the child is grounded for two weeks because she didn't put away the laundry. The consequence should have something to do with laundry. Perhaps she can be considered out of the family laundry arrangement for a week and she will have to wash her own clothes. (This is most effective if the time period exceeds the number of favorite outfits.) Neither is it a logical consequence to be slapped in the face for being rude. Instead, the child can be told that she will have no privileges until she apologizes. If she has been rude to you in front of her friends, then she should apologize in front of her friends.

Finally, there is usually a difference in the parent's attitude when he or she is setting up a logical consequence instead of a punishment. **Consequences should be unemotional. They should be stated neutrally and they should not give you sadistic pleasure.** If the phrase, "I told you so!" is about to escape your lips, your attitude is not neutral. Likewise, if you find yourself getting wickedly excited at the thought of the consequence you have devised, it is probably really a punishment.

Consequences allow you to keep a matter-of-fact attitude about disciplinary measures. "You broke the rule and this is the consequence." It is like a natural law. The agreed-upon consequence is enough. There is no need for a righteous or vengeful attitude. It is even fine to sympathize with your child. You can acknowledge what a shame it is that they have to miss the fabulous TV program coming up, but "Ah, me. Bedtime is bedtime!" And there's just nothing to be done about it (at least certainly not before the next family meeting).

In order for children to learn from their mistakes, they have to be permitted to make mistakes. They learn best from the natural consequences of their actions. If your child forgets her lunch, the natural consequence is that she will feel hunger. If your child leaves his truck in the street, it will get run over and he will no longer have a truck. If you run after her with the lunch or you make him march back out and get his truck out of the street (or feel sorry for him and take it out of the street for him), you interfere with the natural outcome of his or her irresponsibility. You can tell him that his truck will get run over if he leaves it in the street, but he won't believe you. He knows that what will really happen is either you will remind him to go pick it up or you will pick it up for him. For him, the natural consequence of not being responsible is that someone else will take responsibility for what he neglects to do. His life experience tells him this.

On the other hand, the "natural consequences" philosophy, taken to the extreme, can become an excuse for neglecting your child's needs. You might say that if your child forgets her coat on a snowy day, the natural consequence is that she will get pneumonia; if he doesn't set his alarm, he will be late for school; if she doesn't study, she won't get into college, and so on. So be it. Some will learn this way, but most need a little more guidance. When natural consequences are impractical or the lesson to be learned would be too harsh, parents must employ logical consequences. Each situation has to be judged separately. For example, I believe that no child will be seriously harmed by missing his or her lunch every now and then, so go ahead and let them miss it. (However, my son's school apparently disagrees with this judgment since they give him a free cafeteria lunch every time he forgets his lunch. Fortunately, my son hates the school lunch, so the natural consequence of having to eat that stuff is even more effective than going hungry.) However, if your child forgets her coat on a snowy day, pneumonia is too harsh a consequence. You have to create a logical consequence. You might logically keep her in after school that day because she has not demonstrated that she knows how to dress appropriately on a cold, stormy day.

Logical consequences, although slightly less effective than natural consequences, can be created for any situation. If it embarrasses your son very much to come to school late and have to "answer to" the school secretary, it may be appropriate to let him just suffer the consequence of not setting the alarm. But if confronting the secretary is not strong enough to be a deterrent, you will have to set a logical consequence. You could insist that he go to bed an hour earlier the next night so that he can wake up "naturally" in time to get ready for school. Then after he shows that he can remember to set the alarm, you can let him try staying up later again. **The idea is to stop the irresponsible behavior before it becomes a *habit*.**

Also, you need to ask yourself if the natural consequence has a long-term effect that makes it a costly lesson (like not brushing his teeth and having millions of cavities when he goes to the dentist), or if the consequence is just distasteful enough to make him not want to repeat the mistake. When Merissa made the rule that there was no TV watching until David was all ready for school, the logical consequence was just a loss of a valued privilege. She didn't require him to walk to school even though that would have been the most natural consequence of missing the bus, because his safety was at stake.

I must add one caution: Don't *set your child up* by helping the teacher "catch him," thereby engineering a "natural consequence." For example, if the teacher is not careful about checking homework, don't ask her to be sure to check your son's each day so that he will learn he better have it done if he doesn't want to be embarrassed. If this is not happening to all the other students, your son will feel manipulated. Sometimes it is a tremendous temptation to interfere like that so they'll see you are "right." But **what is "natural" is what happens if you *don't interfere.*** In real life, everyone gets away with breaking the rules every now and then. Who hasn't squeezed through a yellow light or driven over 55 mph on the open highway? If you make sure your child gets punished for every small transgression, this is just another way to get across the message that you expect your child to be perfect.

Similarly, allow your child some dignity when she is the victim of her own natural consequence. If she refused to bring a jacket even though you told her it was going to be cold when the sun went down, and now she is sitting there with her teeth chattering, there is no need to rub it in. It really is OK to sympathize with her. Forget who "won" the argument for a moment ("*See,* I was right, wasn't I?"). Clear your mind. Look at your child as you would if you had forgotten to bring a jacket for her, and you had none to lend her. Rub her arms and tell her you're sorry she's cold. You don't need to give her *your jacket* (and you shouldn't!), but you can give her your warmth and understanding.

PSYCHOLOGICAL ABUSE

Alice Miller probably captures the essence of a punishing attitude in the title of her well-known book, *For Your Own Good.*[8] Heinous crimes have been committed against children for the stated purpose of their enlightenment or character development. When Diane was in junior high school her family moved to a town ten miles away. She remembers how sad she felt leaving all her childhood friends. Diane had promised to stay in touch with her friends, but when her family got into their new house Diane's mother announced that they "couldn't afford" a phone. A few days later, when Diane produced the letters she had written to her friends, her mother told her that she wasn't going to give her money for postage or take her to the post office. Diane's mother explained that she felt it was best for Diane to give up her old friends because it would force her to make new friends and adjust to the new school faster. What might have been a gentle transition was changed to a traumatic event by Diane's mother's attitude (despite her "good" intentions). Such a need to teach by "the hard knocks of life" method belies a feeling of hostility, resentment, and probably jealousy of the child.

The most common means of psychological abuse is tearing away at the child's self-esteem through excessive criticism. Alice Miller dubs it "the systematic destruction of self-worth and identity." Parents who become too anxious about their children's appearance or performance often strip the child of confidence by never appreciating what the child *is* capable of doing. Name-calling and insults are even more directly damaging. A twelve-year-old who is told she looks ugly or horrible as she is leaving for school is liable to feel ashamed and self-conscious all day. **Never** and **always** can be the two cruelest words in the English language. "You *never* do anything to help me around here"; "You're *always* thinking of yourself"; "You *never* get these dishes clean"; "You *always* manage to make my day miserable"; are just a few ways to say, "You rotten kid."

Fear and intimidation are other means of psychological abuse. How many of your parents actually said to you, "So help me God, I'm going to kill you one of these days"? Or how about, "I'll make you sorry you were born"? Maybe your parents went in for more subtle messages like, "See what happens next time you ask me to do something for you," or "Maybe you'll get coal in your stocking this Christmas." "You'd better do what I tell you, or you'll be sorry," is another "tender" phrase. But my favorite is, "I'll give you something to really cry about!"

Verbally abusive statements like the above were common in the last generation, and most adult children have these choice phrases milling about in their heads waiting for a chance to pass through their lips. These little sayings are almost subconscious litanies that come out unexpectedly even when we don't mean them. With this kind of programming, we must be conscious and careful of what we say, especially when we are tired or irritable.

FORGIVING AND FORGETTING

A spirit of goodwill is most apparent when you can truly forgive and forget your child's transgressions. (We'll talk more about reading too much purposeful hostility into your child's actions in the next chapter.) Children bumble and forget a lot. They don't leave their coats in the middle of the living room just to bug you. Even when they scream, "I hate you!" because you said "no" to something they wanted, they do not really mean it. When you have a conflict with your child, try to dispense with it as quickly as possible. If your toddler throws a tantrum when you enter the supermarket because he has spotted some exotic junk toy and you have refused to give it to him, consider the matter settled once he stops screaming. When you turn up the next aisle and the toy is out of sight and therefore out of mind, the incident is probably over for your child. Don't hold a grudge and refuse him his pack of gum at the register because he wasn't an angel *the whole time.* If he was cooperative the majority of the time and especially for the last half of the trip, let it go. Way back in his distant past, twenty minutes ago, he misbehaved. Don't hold it against him forever.

Your love for your child really should be unconditional. The child shouldn't feel as if she has to do certain things to please you and thereby *earn* your love. Neither should she fear that she will lose your love when she misbehaves. Her transgressions should be regarded as *mistakes,* and we all make mistakes sometimes. A child who has been emotionally supported really will learn from her "mistakes of behavior." As she grows older, she may go on making as many mistakes, but they will not be the same ones. Children need to be secure in the knowledge that even though you don't love what they *do* sometimes, you always love *them.* Your love and loyalty should not be commodities for bartering.

One of the things I am most proud of in my parenting is my ability to forgive, to wipe the slate clean each evening with my child (and often even ten minutes or two minutes after an infuriating incident.)

Each night when he goes to bed, if we have had a fight that day, I remind him that I always love him even when I'm mad at him. He responds with obvious gratitude and relief. He wants to hear this before he goes to bed at night. We might even have an impending punishment; perhaps he has already lost a privilege for the following day. I won't rescind it. It's just a fact, an objective reality to be lived through the next day, like having already spent your allowance when you see the toy you'd rather have. But we do put the emotional fire behind us. It is in the past.

Many who would find it impossible to forgive or be nice at the time of the incident (or even hours after!) can let go of it at the end of the day when they've had time to cool off. It is sure to make your child's sleep more peaceful, and you'll get a better rest too.

◆ ════════════ **SUMMARY** ════════════ ◆

Settling conflict by force damages the "loser's" self-esteem and is bound to leave behind a residue of hostility and resentment. Therefore, to truly end a conflict, it is more effective to use cooperative methods that focus on making everyone a "winner."

◆ ════════════ **POINTS** ════════════ ◆

1. Because our children will need to know peaceful conflict resolution strategies to survive in tomorrow's world, we must learn to move beyond the "fight or flight" reflex and acquire the skills of negotiation.

2. Although it is wise to avoid dangerous or pointless confrontations, "running away" from conflict with our children not only provides a poor role model, it can leave them feeling emotionally abandoned.

3. Accommodation and compromise are two peaceful means of conflict resolution, but *forced* accommodation and *forced* concession foster anger and resentment that really prolong the conflict while pushing it underground.

4. After we teach our children effective conflict resolution skills, we need to step out and let them work things out between them.

5. In our dealings with our co-parents we should model respectful, peaceful conflict resolution, and strive to share power equitably.

6. We should avoid "ganging up" tactics where parents side together against a child, or parent and child side against the co-parent. Instead, we need to allow each family member to have a "sacredly separate" relationship with every other family member.

7. If we were physically abused as children we have been programmed to physically abuse our children. Therefore, we should make a commitment not to use physical means of discipline.

8. Rewards and praise are far more effective means of altering children's behavior in a long-lasting way than threats or violence. These means also leave self-esteem intact.

9. Children will learn from their mistakes and achieve self-discipline if they must deal with the consequences of their own poor decisions.

10. The greatest gift we can give our children is true forgiveness for their transgressions and a fresh start. We should settle the day's conflicts at bedtime and let the child awaken to a clean slate.

NOTES

1. Interview: Cynthia Walker, Licensed Clinical Social Worker who has specialized in Confident Parenting.
2. Carol Tavris. *Anger.* New York: Simon & Schuster, 1982.
3. Harriet Goldhor, Lerner, Ph.D. *The Dance of Anger.* New York: Harper & Row, 1985.
4. William Summers, M.D., *Building the House of Marriage.* Rolling Hills Estates, CA: Robert Erdmann Publishing, 1990.
5. Roger Fisher and William Ury, *Getting to Yes.* New York: Penguin Books, 1981.
6. Cynthia Walker, interview.
7. Cynthia Walker, interview.
8. Alice Miller, *For Your Own Good.* New York: Farrar, Straus & Giroux, 1983.

PART III

PARENTING STRENGTHS

Parenting Strengths of Adult Children from Dysfunctional Families

1. ACODF have a warm, positive vision of family life that inspires them to strive for a more harmonious home.

2. ACODF are able to question their judgment as parents and this motivates them to seek out parenting advice and strive for better parenting skills.

3. An ACODF who is overwhelmed by the needs of her young children can turn this into a positive by teaching the children to help in many small ways appropriate to their age and developmental level.

4. When ACODF learn to keep better boundries, their children will experience the warmth and joy of a parent who is not afraid to be close.

5. By recognizing their lack of experience anticipating problems, ACODF will be motivated to become less impulsive, and take the time they need to make careful, considered judgments.

6. The ACODF's vulnerability to stress ultimately forces them to lead a simpler life and make child-rearing a higher priority.

7. ACODF can tolerate a child's difficulties or other family problems until the best approach or solution can be determined.

8. A soul-searching ACODF will realize the loneliness and isolation their critical nature has caused them. When a new, more relaxed, attitude brings them support and friendship, the example will teach their children to be more accepting.

9. The ACODF's childlike fear of harsh judgment can help them empathize with their self-critical children, and together they can learn to be more accepting of self and supportive of one another.

10. If tempered and softened, the ACODF's rigidity can be transformed into reliable consistency and scrupulously equal treatment of all children in the family.

11. When ACODF can attain some healthy distance from a situation, their strong will can be channeled into setting clear, firm limits for their children.

12. When "tamed," the superresponsible ACODF provides a strong sense of security, and the irresponsible ACODF can teach more serious family members the meaning of play.

13. As ACODF struggle to become more organized and reliable, their efforts to bring order out of chaos, and the greater peace this brings to the family, will serve as an inspiring example for their children.

14. The ACODF's hunger for approval helps them understand how important it is for children to be recognized and appreciated. When they begin to set good boundaries through discipline, they will feel nurtured and valued by their children's respect.

15. In the absence of learned skills for dealing with conflict, ACODF can be more open to the new focus on cooperation and democracy in the family.

Remember the big fifteen parenting pitfalls listed in Part II? These were distorted feelings and perceptions and dysfunctional behaviors that grew out of our outmoded childhood adaptations. Now that we understand our old motivations and have a new perspective of what makes a good parent, we can rewrite that list in our life. **Every adaptation has a negative and positive side.** We need to focus on the good strengths and skills we can draw out of our tough beginnings.

· 14 ·

TEMPERAMENT AND STYLE

THE SERENITY PRAYER
God grant me the serenity to accept the things I cannot change;
The courage to change the things I can;
And the wisdom to know the difference.

—Anonymous

We have parental role models whether we acknowledge them or not. Stored in our brains are parental behavior tapes that influence each word we say to our children. Your obvious role models are your parents. Like it or not, you will do as they did if youdo not consciously decide to do otherwise. As we discussed earlier, if you disapprove of the way your parents raised you, just doing the opposite of what they did is not an adequate solution. Like the overly permissive parent "compensating" for his or her own parents' harsh authoritarian discipline, we can sometimes do as much harm (or more!) in the opposite direction.

How, then, do we program ourselves to be better parents? My parents were not my only models. I spent a lot of time in other kids' houses during my childhood. I knew there was something wrong in my house, but I wasn't sure what. I watched my neighbors closely to see how they did things. My next-door neighbors were big on budget. One day when my neighbor's parents were not at home my friend let me come in and view the sacred budget book. There her family had accounted for nearly every penny. They never told tales of the electricity being turned off, and they took a two-week family vacation every year. My friend showed me how they kept track of how much money they would need for each bill and the startling entry where they saved money toward vacation. I vowed I would live by a budget when I grew up.

Another girl's mother was the only mother in the neighborhood to laugh and play with us sometimes. She would help us put on shows and sell cold drinks. I wanted to be like her when I was a mother. There was the neighbor down the street who had yard parties that brought the neighborhood together annually, children dancing the polka in the yard with the adults. But most important to me were the parents of my best friend, who lived directly behind me.

Mr. Zetwick was a calm, fair, firm, assertive, warm, understanding man. I never saw him enraged, I rarely saw him angry; at most he got a little mad sometimes. Fortunately for me, when Anna Marie and I did something wrong he didn't send me home. He would sit us *both* down and talk with us about it. Since I went everywhere with Anna Marie, when she was grounded, I was grounded. My own father was emotionally absent. He drank, he slept, he worked compulsively in the yard. I had my first two-way conversation with him when I was twenty-one years old. What a terrible impact that would have had on me if I had not had Mr. Zetwick as a surrogate father!

There was one lesson I learned through this family that stands out the most clearly for me. I was beaten at home, but Anna Marie's parents had vowed never to strike their children. Mrs. Zetwick was not American-born. She had come from Iceland, a cold Scandinavian country with long nights, where people, crowded together in close quarters for the winter months, had come to understand the need to find gentle means of disciplining their children. She brought this revolutionary idea with her to America. In the 1950s they were the only parents I knew who did not hit their children. Often terrorized by my father, this idea struck me as a great enlightenment. To top it off Anna Marie was probably the best-behaved child in the neighborhood. She had not been the least bit spoiled by the sparing of the rod.

When I was angry at my child, the first images that came to mind were violent. After all, I witnessed far more discipline at home than I had at Anna Marie's. But if I resisted the urge to strike and held my mind still long enough, the other images would enter in. I am still raising my child, but I rarely see violent images anymore when he makes me angry. I have resolved much of my inner rage through therapy, but perhaps equally or even more important—I have stretched my memory to fill it with the better examples of parenting styles I saw as a child. There are good role models around us everywhere. We don't have to settle for the legacy of our natural parents. Search your memory. Was there a teacher, a neighbor, or older sibling that treated you the way you needed to be treated? Even characters in novels can offer us alternative patterning.

When the past fails me, I round out my knowledge by paying careful attention to the parents around me now whom I admire. Because of the dramatic changes in family structure, we are a generation that must model for each other. Few of us had working mothers to observe, involved fathers to model ourselves after, or single parents to show us how to parent alone effectively. Do you see some teenagers who look secure and healthy? Ask their parents how they disciplined their children when they were five or six years old. Seek and ye shall find.

PARENTING STYLES

For nearly thirty years psychologists and family specialists have been looking at parenting styles to see what kind of offspring they produce. In 1963, W. Hugh Missildine, M.D., (author of *Your Inner Child of the Past*—the first book to talk about the now-popular concept of the "child-within") published his theories on excessive parental attitudes and how they affect children. This research focuses on the negatives and will be discussed in the section entitled *Negative Parenting*. About the same time, Diana Baumrind, Ph.D., (director of the University of California Family Socialization and Developmental Competence Project) was carrying on a study of parenting styles at the University of California, Berkeley campus. To this day she has been following a group of families for more than one generation to see how children parented different ways turn out as adults. This is the first carefully controlled scientific study of parenting methods. Following is a thumbnail sketch of her results as they were summarized in a chart in pediatrician Glenn Austin's book *Love and Power: Parent and Child.*[1]

Results of Parenting Types

PARENT TYPE	COMPETENCE OF CHILDREN							
	fully competent		partially competent		incompetent		numbers	
	boys	girls	boys	girls	boys	girls	boys	girls
Rational-Authoritative	83%	86%	17%	14%	00%	00%	6	7
Traditional	43%	50%	57%	33%	00%	17%	14	6
Authoritarian	18%	42%	55%	58%	27%	00%	11	12
Permissive	20%	00%	60%	71%	20%	29%	5	7
Rejecting-Neglecting	00%	00%	33%	63%	67%	27%	9	8
Total							45	40

As we can see, according to Baumrind's thirty-year study, about 85% of all children raised by rational-authoritative parents grew up to be fully competent, confident adults, while less than 50% of all children raised by traditional parents did. Only about 30% (boys and girls combined) of those raised by authoritarian parents and about 10% (boys and girls combined) of those raised by permissive parents became fully competent, while none of the children raised by rejecting-neglecting parents grew up to be fully competent adults. A brief description of each of the parenting styles is presented below:

◆ BAUMRIND'S PARENTING STYLES DEFINED:

Rational-Authoritative parenting: They demand good behavior but rely on praise more than punishment. They are firm but not strict or harsh. They provide opportunities for their children to learn responsibility by caring for a pet or by earning money for a desired item. If they must threaten, they always follow through. They respect the child and the child respects them. They raise responsible, confident, caring adults.

Traditional Parenting: This is characterized by the father who is both provider and disciplinarian and a mother who is nurturing and subservient to her spouse and children. This role has worked well in the past but in our changing society girls and boys need role models who are more well-rounded. To be secure a girl should have a career and a boy needs to know how to cook and clean for himself.

Authoritarian Parenting: Characterized by little respect for the child and harsh discipline. They allow their children little power to make choices about their own lives. Because these parents are overcontrolling, the children may become depressed, hostile, or passive-aggressive.

Permissive Parenting: Some permissive parents seem to have given up disciplining their children in frustration, and others are basically disorganized. Divorced parents who feel guilty for breaking up the child's home or who try to compete with the ex-spouse are also often permissive. Permissive parents generally give children too much power and consequently these children grow up selfish, self-centered, dependent, and spoiled. As adults, they will often seek someone else to take care of them.

Rejecting-Neglecting Parenting: Emotionally absent and often physically absent, these parents fail to care for their children. Alcoholic or mentally disturbed parents often neglect their children. Raised by themselves or an older sibling, the children grow up with few parenting tools and will become rejecting or neglecting if they do not have opportunities to observe more active parents.

Rational-Authoritative parents are balanced, calm, confident parents who make clear requests and are respectful of the child but still set limits and teach self-control. They produce healthy children who feel needed, in control, confident, competent, and secure. They have high self-respect and high self-esteem. Traditional parents have been effective in the past but may not prepare children for the challenges of today's world. With so many two-career families and the percentage of working mothers constantly on the rise, the majority of parents cannot make use of the Traditional Parent model. If you grew up in a dysfunctional family, your parents were probably one of the other three types: Authoritarian, Permissive, or Rejecting-Neglecting.

Although Authoritarian parenting does produce some competent children, its success is determined by the reasonableness of the authority in charge. Unfortunately, the authoritarian style is often destructively exaggerated in dysfunctional homes. When the person-in-charge is a parent with the negative qualities described by Missildine (see chart p. 285), his or her authority is often harsh.

There are as many different systems of categorizing parenting styles as there are parenting books. I couldn't present them all here, and I wouldn't want to. Therefore I will run the risk of adding to the confusion by creating my own system that uses the concepts developed by others and reorganizes everything in behavioral terms under three broad categories: Aggressive Parenting, Passive Parenting, and Assertive Parenting. Both Aggressive Parenting and Passive Parenting do not provide the support children need to flourish, and so they will be explored more fully when we discuss Negative Parenting.

POSITIVE PARENTING

Fortunately, there is much agreement in the literature about what kind of parenting produces the most confident, competent children. The characteristics do not differ from system to system, only the labels change. My Assertive Parenting is the same as Rational-Authoritative Parenting (presented above), the PRICE system's Balanced Parenting,[2] Popkins' Active Parenting,[3] and the Effective Parenting method taught by the STEP program,[4] just to name a few. (See footnotes for fuller citations of the above parenting systems.) The traits and methods described in these programs are also consistent with the characteristics of parents in healthy families.

To review, **Assertive Parents** demand good behavior but rely on praise more than punishment. They are firm but not strict or harsh. They provide opportunities for their children to learn responsibility by caring for a pet or by earning money for a desired item. If they must threaten, they always follow through. They respect the child and the child respects them. They raise responsible, confident, caring adults. The suggestions for becoming a more sensitive, caring, and open parent provided throughout this book are consistent with the traits and responses of Assertive Parents.

NEGATIVE PARENTING

What we think strongly influences what we do. We each bring to our decisions a set of beliefs that govern our lives. In its most simple form, we generally have one of two basic attitudes: People are good and will remain so if they do not have to struggle against harsh circumstances and negative influences; or people are basically evil and must be kept in line through threats and punishments. The latter attitude is the underlying philosophy that has supported negative parenting styles for centuries. In the 1960s Missildine was defining negative parenting styles. Since many of today's parents were raised by these parents, it is useful to look at some of Missildine's descriptions of negatively focused parental traits and see what kind of children they produced.

<hr>

Missildine's Negative Parenting Traits[5]

1. OVERCOERCION (most prevalent according to Missildine)
   Parental Traits: Controlling. Constantly directs and nags the child.
   Child's Traits: Passive resistance, procrastination. Adult child often feels chronically fatigued and has trouble meeting his or her own daily goals.

2. OVERSUBMISSIVENESS (second most prevalent)
   Parental Traits: Overly permissive. Fails to set limits.
   Child's Traits: Demanding, self-centered, impulsive. Incapable of sustained effort. Adult child feels unloved whenever he or she can't have his or her way. If they must work hard for something they are angry and resentful.

3. OVERINDULGENCE
   Parental Traits: Gives the child everything *before* he or she asks for it. Anticipates child's every desire.
   Child's Traits: Bored, tired, listless.

4. PERFECTIONISM
   Parental Traits: Pushes children to behave and achieve beyond their developmental level. Hypercritical.
   Child's Traits: Very accomplished. Nearly perfect people with high standards. Unable to recognize or gain satisfaction from accomplishments. Adult child is hypercritical of own child.

5. PUNITIVENESS
   Parental Traits: Excessively harsh and strict. Assumes child will do wrong at first opportunity. Vents feelings of hostility and aggression on child. Younger parents who feel strapped by parenting responsibilities are prone to becoming punitive. Punishments are often more the result of the parent's mood than they are of the child's behavior.
   Child's Traits: Feels he or she is bad. Feels guilty, vengeful, and fearful.

6. NEGLECT
   Parental Traits: Fails to attend to the child's physical or emotional needs for whatever reason—be it death, mental illness, volunteerism, or a career. Takes no real interest in the child and his or her activities. May try to buy way out of parental responsibilities by purchasing expensive gifts, clothes, etc., but is never actually around to attend to child.
   Child's Traits: Anxious, lonely, fear of intimacy, no sense of belonging.

I break this down into two basic types of negative, ineffective parents: Aggressive Parents and Passive Parents.

Aggressive Parenting, or harsh authoritarian styles of parenting, pits us against our children almost as if they are our enemies. The parent feels he or she must win every conflict and any means justifies this end. They withhold love to punish their children. They feel morally bound to teach the child that they "are not the center of the universe." They generally demand excessive gratitude for every gift or concession. This parent loathes "weakness" and is prone to cruelty. He or she would typically make the child tough it out in the dark without a night-light, force her to eat foods she loathes, wash the child's mouth out with soap, and take away her "blanky."

To make matters worse, if Aggressive Parents are not aware of the qualities they dislike most in themselves, they are likely to "project" those faults onto their children. This means that they see their children as having their worst faults, magnified and multiplied. For example, if your child is messy (and you are messy but don't really admit to yourself just how messy you are), the child's mess added to your mess will look like an overwhelming, maddening mess. The child's mess alone, or your mess alone, might each be manageable, but as your eyes scan the room you see your child's clothes and toys at the top of the heap on the dining room table and imagine that the whole pile belongs to her. Although half of your disapproval should be directed at yourself, the child gets the full measure of your wrath.

Passive Parenting is the lackadaisical parenting most often labeled "permissive." There are probably three basic motivations behind this style. Some parents are too passive in providing guidance, direction, or rules because they have a misguided notion of what makes a carefree childhood. Often reacting against their own overcontrolled childhoods, these parents want to allow their children to "express themselves." Unfortunately, these children are often disliked and rejected by others because not everyone is delighted with their self-centered expressions. These parents are committed to their passive parenting style and will meet criticism with a shrug of the shoulder, dismissing the critic as unenlightened.

A second type of passive parenting is represented by the disorganized, unenergetic parents who can't even care for themselves properly. Often chronically depressed, they never have enough energy to do housework, enough confidence to pursue activities for their children, or enough emotional stability to stop thinking of themselves and their problems long enough to consider the needs of their children. They may be drug abusers, alcoholics, suffering from mood disorders, or simply so lacking in self-esteem that they cannot assert themselves against their environment in any way.

The more energetic passive parents might be real go-getters at their jobs, housework, or volunteer activities, but put their children as a very low priority. Children's needs are attended to after scores of other things have been accomplished. Often these parents never get far enough down the list to address the children's needs. If the kids want breakfast, they had better make it. If they want clean clothes, they had better wash some. If they want to be in scouts, they should find themselves a ride. These parents just don't see themselves as being "responsible" for the children's problems or even maintenance.

Whatever style of negative parenting your parents used, the result is the same. You will grow up with low self-esteem and little confidence. Your basic life-view will be negative and this negativity will distort the way you interpret events and social interactions. You will bring this life-view to bear on your relationship with your children, often interpreting their actions in an unrealistically negative light.

NEGATIVE THINKING

If we grow to adulthood with the negative feelings caused by our poor rearing, we can wrongly misinterpret our children's actions and intentions by distorting what we see as it is filtered through our poor self-esteem. In *Feeling Good: The New Mood Therapy*, David Burns, M.D., explains the concept of cognitive therapy by showing how our distorted thinking traps us into negative assumptions.[6] The cure is to stop feeling sorry for ourselves, guilty, angry (and a host of other negative debilitating feelings) and replace our distorted thinking with rational responses.

Although some of us vacillate, we can generally relate to one of the three basic styles described above. Aggressive Parenting would encompass overcoercion, perfectionism, punitiveness, and rejection; Passive Parenting would encompass oversubmissiveness, overindulgence, and neglect; and Assertive Parenting is my all-encompassing term to describe modern healthy parenting methods suggested in most of the recent parenting literature.

Below is a chart that shows how these three types of parents would be likely to react to a stimulus problem from their child.

Parental Attitude Chart

Event: Monday Evening Dinner
Issue: Clean-up and dishes.

Scene: After an exhausting Monday-morning-catch-up workday, you come home tired and hungry. Your spouse has gone out of town on business and you are left caring for your two children, Tommy, age five and Lena, age eleven. Not wanting a hassle at dinner, you have spent an hour preparing the kids' favorite foods. At dinner Tommy eats enthusiastically but Lena just stares at her plate and says she isn't hungry. You remind the children that it's Tommy's turn to clear and Lena's turn to do the dishes. Tommy jumps up to clear the plates but Lena says she shouldn't have to do the dishes because she didn't eat anything.

NEGATIVE THOUGHT	TYPE OF NEGATIVE-THINKING RESPONSE	RATIONAL-THINKING RESPONSE (ASSERTIVE)
1a. No matter what I do these kids never want to eat my cooking.	1a. All-or-nothing-at-all thinking. (Passive)	1. Tommy loved my cooking and Lena usually eats these foods.
1b. I cooked even though I was tired. Lena will do the dishes even if I have to stand over her with a whip!	1b. All-or-nothing-at-all thinking. (Aggressive)	1b. Lena doesn't seem to be herself tonight. I wonder if she's sick. I'd better take a new approach.
2. What's the use? I can never get these kids to do anything.	2. Overgeneralization. (Passive)	2. Tommy is ready to help. Maybe Lena will pitch in once we get moving.
3. My evening is ruined. I won't be able to concentrate on my work later.	3. Mental filter. (Passive)	3. If the dishes don't get done, close the door and let them wait until tomorrow.
4. Lena must be hungry. She's just doing this just to irritate me.	4. Mind-reading. (Aggressive)	4. Nonsense. Lena is ruled by her stomach. If she were hungry she would eat.
5. I should have known with these kids. The whole week is going to be like this.	5. Fortune-telling. (Aggressive)	5. Snap out of it. Everyone will feel better after a good night's sleep.
6. I'm such a bad parent. I can't get these kids to cooperate.	6. Magnification. (Passive)	6. Nonsense. They were cooperative all day yesterday.

7. What difference does it make if they don't do the dishes this one time.	7. Minimizing. (Passive)	7. This is giving in too easily. Make some agreement that shows this is not going to be acceptable every night.
8. Tommy will clear the table. Big deal. What about the rest of this work?	8. Discounting the positive. (Aggressive)	8. Tell Tommy how much you appreciate his help. He deserves positive feedback.
9. I can't stand it anymore. I hate being a parent.	9. Emotional reasoning. (Aggressive)	9. Calm down. Weren't they fun at the park yesterday?
10. Lena should know I had a terrible workday. If only she could be more considerate.	10. If/Should statements. (Passive)	10. She's just a child. You need to tell her when you are edgy and why.
11. Lena is such a spoiled brat.	11. Labeling others. (Aggressive)	11. You raised her. Don't you feel very proud of her assertiveness sometimes?
12. I'm such an insensitive lout. It's her birthday!	12. Labeling self. (Passive)	12. Give yourself a break. Now that you remember, do something about it.
13. It's ALL her fault for not reminding me.	13. Blaming others. (Aggressive)	13. Let go of your guilt so you can be responsive instead of defensive.
14. It's ALL my fault. I should have remembered.	14. Blaming self. (Passive)	14. Blaming yourself won't make her feel better. Wish her happy birthday instead.
15. Lena is not usually like this. Something must be bothering her. I need to check this out with her.	15. None. (Assertive)	15. Feeling good as a rational assertive parent.

The basic message of Burns's book is that we can change our life-view. We can stop the "negative tapes" running in our heads and supplant them with more positive interpretations of events. It just takes some practice. When you find yourself assuming the worst about your child or co-parent, take a moment to imagine a more positive interpretation of their actions. Give them the benefit of the doubt.

TEMPERAMENT

Having grown up in a world where things were often inexplicably unfair, the ACODF sometimes goes to extremes to be fair to his or her children. Treating everyone the same seems like a simple, straightforward way to go about being absolutely fair. But such dedication to fairness without considering variables can lead to rigid parenting. Although some parents make all their children go to bed at the same time regardless of their age differences, many parents make allowances for older children to stay up later than their younger siblings. But this may be where their flexibility ends.

Children have many other differences besides age that require special consideration. Every child in a family may have a different temperament. Some may need less sleep than others; some may be early risers regardless of what time they go to bed; and others may be afternoon nappers who get a second burst of energy after dinner. What makes sense for one child, is not necessarily the best approach for another. Some children should do homework the minute they come home from school because their concentration declines throughout the evening; some children may work best after having an after-school recess; and other children might be most alert for homework in the morning before school. Having a family rule that everyone must do their homework when they get home from school would not meet the needs of all of these children. Parents must be aware of temperamental differences in their children.

Exploring and responding to differences in temperament is still a new science and there are many new theories and systems for looking at temperament. Keith Golay, a popular temperament theorist, divides people into four basic types that are represented by four animal figures: the ape (about 40%) is outgoing and experiential; the bear (about 40%) is stable and traditional; the owl (about 10%) is intellectual; and the dolphin (about 10%) is motivated by relationship and cooperation.[7]

Janet Hackleman, a parenting specialist at The Family Connection in Colton, California, who runs groups for parent trainers as well as parents, is an advocate of Golay's system and feels that there are certain kinds of temperaments that tend toward each different kind of dysfunction. Hackleman finds that awareness of temperament types can help people to understand their tendencies toward certain dysfunctional parenting behaviors. Golay's types are described in terms of learning styles and motivations. These factors are the two most important components for communication. Hackleman states:

> I need to know what motivates you and how you learn best if I want to affect your behavior. There are certain pathologies that go with each temperament types. The Apes are addicts, the Bears are depressed or hypochondriacs, the Owls are obsessive-compulsive and phobic—the handwashers—and the Dolphins are eating disorders and schizophrenics. They really don't cross. Each of these types have a strong motivation at the center of their being. They have a strong drive to have that motivating thing. You could call that an addiction but I prefer to call it the central motivator. These people need this thing to feel right with the world and sometimes if they don't have it, they try to get it in dysfunctional ways. They should be able to get those things. It's just that they don't know how to do it, so they are screwing themselves up and everyone around them because they are trying to get it in wrong ways. But I would say that what they need is OK to have and if they learn how to get it appropriately, then they are healthy.[8]

Hackleman analyzes the various types in terms of their likely parenting behavior. She explains that an Ape parent might come across as very rejecting because children interfere with one's freedom. Bear parents, if they are not very healthy, are going to foster dependence. They may make neurotic little hypochondriacs out of their children. They want to be needed. Says Hackleman, "They are the servants of the world and if you don't act grateful, they are the martyrs. They are the classic unappreciated Jewish mother. They get depressed and feel terrible because they are always being abused."

Owls are distant, cool, detached—they are often not even aware that their kids have emotional needs. An Owl father may love the child dearly but the child will not feel it. The Owl does not use feeling words and they are not demonstrative, so the kids might grow up in an emotional vacuum. On the other hand, Dolphin mothers tend to be so concerned about their children's psyches that they want to prevent them from experiencing any emotional pain, so they will talk their kids out of their feelings. Hackleman explains their thinking: "They reason, 'If I am a good mother, my child will not have any kind of psychic pain.' So if the kid says, 'Mom, I feel

very sad today,' the Dolphin thinks, 'Oh, I'm a terrible parent!' "
Dolphins put a lot of effort into making sure nothing happens to
upset their child.

Hackleman uses a lot of temperament theory in family counseling. She helps parents learn to tailor their parenting skills to the
individual child. For example, when dealing with most children, one
should go over and place a hand on the child's shoulder, look him
or her in the eye, and use a direct command, such as, "Pick up your
toys." But that doesn't work very well for Apes. For starters, you may
not even get eye contact with the Ape child. Explains Hackleman,
"The Ape is a freedom lover and if you get too close to his personal
space, his fight/flight reflex kicks in, and he will fight you. It's better
if you touch him, give him the command, and get out of there. As
you're walking away you can say, 'Thanks for taking care of that,'
even though he is ignoring you. He just has to feel like he's the one
in power."

Unfortunately, Golay's character descriptions are sometimes so
general that they begin to sound as nebulous as daily horoscopes.
Regardless, these temperament resources are useful for making the
point that we each may see things differently and may need to be
treated and interracted with accordingly.

How can we analyze our children's temperaments so that we will
know the best way to approach each child? The most useful approach I have found is the one described in Stanley Turecki's book
The Difficult Child.[9] Turecki defines eight variables that are most
helpful for analyzing a child's temperament:

---◆---

Temperamental Traits

1. Activity Level: How active is the child?

2. Distractibility: Can the child pay attention or is he or she easily distracted?

3. Adaptability: How well does the child adapt to changes?

4. Approach/Withdrawal: Does the child draw back in fear in new situations or is he or she generally outgoing?

5. Intensity: How loud or demanding is the child?

6. Regularity: How predictable are the child's appetite, sleep habits, bowel habits?

7. Sensory Threshold: How sensitive is the child to noise, light, tastes, or smells?

8. Mood: Is the child generally cheerful or negative?

Some children are born easier to manage than others. The child who is only mildly active and adapts readily to changes and new people is going to be easier to be with than the child who is hyperactive and has a tantrum every time he or she must change activities. By the same token, parents have unique personalities that are made up of the various temperamental traits, and some parents will "fit" better with a certain child than another parent would. If you are a boisterous, outgoing extrovert you may not like a quiet child any more than a shy, quiet parent would like a noisy, active child.

What is your natural temperament? How does that mesh with the temperaments of your children? It is a two-way street. If both you and your child are very distractible, you may find that you are always late for appointments, as the two of you exponentially become distracted by everything in your environment. If you are negative, a negative child will drive you further down and make your climb up from a low mood even more difficult.

Another factor that dramatically affects your success with a particular child is your natural or learned level of nurturing behavior. An easy child and a nuturing mother will have few problems. A nonnurturing mother with an easy child or a nurturing mother with a difficult child will balance each other out pretty well. But woe unto the nonnurturing mother who inherits a difficult child. There will be too little positive attention to go around.

You may want to use the following chart to compare your temperament traits with those of each child by placing your and the children's initials in each category under the appropriate description.

♦

Turecki's Temperamental Variables (Checklist)

TRAIT	Column 1 (difficult)		Column 2 (easy)
ACTIVITY LEVEL	very active	–to–	sedentary
DISTRACTABILITY	easily distracted	–to–	attends easily
ADAPTABILITY	resists change*	–to–	very adaptable
APPROACH/WITHDRAWAL	introverted or shy*	–to–	extroverted
INTENSITY	very intense*	–to–	quiet and easygoing
REGULARITY	unpredictable	–to–	creature of habit
SENSORY THRESHOLD	very sensitive	–to–	mellow
MOOD	pessimistic*	–to–	optimistic

(*These are the most critical in determining if the child will be easy or difficult to raise. Negative, highly reactive, emotional, or withdrawn children with poor adaptability are very difficult to raise. They are also very vulnerable to stress, especially high parental expectations.)

THE DIFFICULT CHILD

How well do your temperamental traits match up with each of your children's temperaments? Turecki finds that the more traits the child has in Column 1 above, the more difficult the child is to raise. Likewise, parents who have many traits in Column 1 are difficult to be with. In this case, opposites may balance each other. Common folk-wisdom tells us that we have the most difficulty with the child who is "just like us." Temperamental traits do show up consistently from generation to generation and are considered hereditary. (Geneticists have even located which gene causes shyness!) The traits that Turecki defines as difficult are also the traits that are used to classify children as *hyperactive* or having *attention deficit disorder*. As we mentioned earlier, "hyperactivity" does seem to run in families, especially families with a history of alcoholism.

Turecki has studied a number of families with difficult children in them. In many cases the parents have other children who are not difficult, so one can see that the child's poor temperament is not the result of "poor mothering." But what effect do these children have on their mothers? Turecki has found that mothers of difficult children are often bewildered, exhausted, angry, guilty, embarrassed, depressed, and isolated. They feel inadequate and trapped and find that mothering such children gives very little satisfaction. Some children are so difficult to parent that the mother naturally becomes overinvolved or overcontrolling. In short, the mothers begin to exhibit all the anxious, unhealthy behaviors of adult children of dysfunctional families.

If the mother had a very easygoing disposition before she began parenting the difficult child, she will be able to stand up to the stress of this child better. If, however, the parent is also a supersensitive distractible type, she is bound to fall apart under the stress of parenting her difficult child. Turecki has seen even the healthiest of families seriously damaged by the pressure of caring for a difficult child. The marital relationship is generally disturbed, the other children are neglected, the mother becomes too worn out to cope, and divorce is often an outcome. This lays the groundwork for generations of dysfunctional families to follow.

This is much like the question, "Which came first: the chicken or the egg?" If you are raising a difficult child, the answer doesn't matter much. What is important is a commitment to stop the spiraling dysfunctionality with this generation. Turecki has found that with proper training and attention to temperament, parents can learn how to raise the difficult child to be a happy, competent adult.

◆ THE BRADFORDS' DIFFICULT CHILD

Brenda Bradford was a blessed difficult child who shows how successful these children can be if nurtured and supported. Although her temperament differed strongly from her mother's calm, orderly manner, this was offset by her healthy family atmosphere. Her parents, Carol and Henry Bradford, had both come from supportive families and had grown up to be "all they could be." Carol had graduated from a prestigious university and taught in the public schools before she married Henry, a practicing lawyer.

The Bradford children, Brenda and her younger brother, Mark (who have now both completed college), never had problems with drug or alcohol involvement. The parents had purposely kept in very close contact with their kids by being involved in their activities. Carol and Henry were scout leaders, soccer coaches, youth group leaders, or whatever the situation demanded. In this way, they had many opportunities to know their children's friends and keep in touch with what their kids thought. As Henry says, "We had them so involved in constructive activities that they didn't have time to get into trouble."

The kids did have Saturday nights free and could have gotten involved in drugs or alcohol if they were motivated to, but it just didn't come up as a problem. Sometimes Brenda or Mark would come home from parties appalled and disappointed in friends who were using drugs and alcohol. Henry sagely remarks, "The kids they associate with in high school have tremendous impact on their behavior. We influenced who their friends were by encouraging their healthy relationships. We hosted overnights and other activities and tried to make our house a gathering place. We provided lots of entertainment and constructive activities so that they didn't have to depend on other kids to provide things to do."

This may all sound very simple and easy, but nothing with Brenda was ever really simple and easy. Brenda, Carol Bradford's first child, was a very difficult child by anyone's standards. She scored high on the difficult side of six out of Turecki's eight traits. She was very active, easily distracted, shy with peers, very intense, unpredictable, and very sensitive. Her great saving grace was that she was an optimistic, cheerful child with contagious enthusiasm. She could also adapt to new situations fairly well and has always been at ease with adults.

Carol muses, "Brenda's extreme UP personality is one of the joys she has brought to our family."

As an infant Brenda was just too restless to nurse past six weeks. Her mother's milk didn't come down fast enough for her, and Brenda switched to a bottle enthusiastically, probably because it allowed her to be "in charge" of the situation. Brenda was not able to cuddle and didn't like to be held long. She seemed to be in perpetual motion. When Brenda began to walk, Carol realized that this child was going to require a lot of energy. Carol remembers that one night she had to put her daughter to bed twenty-five times. She has this accurate count because they had company who counted for them! Carol comments, "She was always into something and has the scars to prove it. There was one from the time she fell off the sewing machine. If she couldn't see something, she would climb up or in to get a better view."

When Carol began to feel bewildered by her daughter's wild behavior, she went to her mother for counsel. "Because she was a grandmother now and saw Brenda from a greater distance than I did, she had lots of good advice for me. She also understood me very well. I couldn't take advice from Henry because he was so like Brenda and I didn't want my daughter to be disorganized like him! But I trusted my mother." Carol's mother, who had been a difficult child herself, always counseled Carol to be patient.

As Carol thinks of Brenda's early years she recalls, "Brenda was a go-getter from the start. She walked early, she talked early. She had her own way of doing things. You couldn't show her anything. You had to wait for her to ask. She hated to be told what to do. She'd rather find her own way to do it. She was very very strong-willed."

How did Carol discipline this rambunctious child? She occasionally used spanking as a form of discipline but more often she used isolation. Because Brenda was very sociable this was quite effective. Carol also read Dr. Spock and various articles on parenting in magazines to learn what to expect from her children at certain ages.

When Brenda was an adolescent, Carol and Henry developed ways to deal with Brenda's stubbornness constructively. Since Brenda strongly resisted any direct advice or instruction, the Bradfords would often find articles or tell stories about other people who had solved a problem similar to the one Brenda was having. "We also have a tradition of writing notes to each other and sending them through the mail when we have a very important issue to discuss.

Brenda's brother, Mark, was born when Brenda was two years old. Mark was as easy as Brenda had been difficult. He scored high on the easy side of six of Turecki's traits. Mark was only somewhat active, could easily stay on task, was at ease socially, popular with his peers, extremely consistent and predictable, and was calm and responsive to discipline. On the negative side he was rather intense, liked routine, and did not respond well to change. He was also reserved and worried needlessly. But overall, Mark had millions of positive ways to gain his parents' attention, while Brenda always seemed to be doing something that would win her a reprimand.

Concerned that Brenda would grow up feeling "less loved" than Mark, Carol consciously thought through how to treat the children equally. Both parents were involved and supportive in both children's activities. In fact, the whole family did almost everything together. Brenda went to Mark's Cub Scout meetings and Mark went on Brenda's Girl Scout camp-outs. Brenda's father even joined Brenda's dance company with her, although he had never danced before. Carol and her husband often discussed how to make both children feel appreciated and included. It was a family value. Everyone would attend Brenda's recitals and everyone would attend Mark's games. The children were taught that their attentions were valuable and wanted by their sibling. To this day, the children have little sibling rivalry and not only like each other, but are proud of one another.

Carol thinks back and recalls what made her finally appreciate Brenda for who she is. "We had an exchange student who was very orderly like me and that was hard for Brenda. She felt like I cared more about that girl. But actually I learned that this very orderly girl was boring as I would be very boring if left to my own devices."

Brenda does have a lot of spunk! Just one year out of college she has already purchased her own house. Dad expresses his admiration for her teaching ability. "She has so much enthusiasm for what she does. Brenda has always loved life and gone after it with both hands. Those students are sure lucky to have her for a teacher!"

The parenting techniques recommended throughout this book will be useful for dealing with the difficult child, but I will highlight a few of Turecki's most important points here. First of all, it is important to keep a positive and open attitude. Assume that the child is not being difficult just to get your goat. Probably the child balks at the entrance to the supermarket, not to make shopping harder for you, or to show you that you can't make him behave; he is balking because he is overwhelmed by the sights and sounds of the store. Your threats or entreaties will not lessen that fear. So what should you do instead?

Two alternatives are avoidance or preparation. If you find your child is repeatedly uncomfortable and uncooperative in a certain situation, stop and determine if it's really necessary to put him in that position. Perhaps you should consider leaving him with a sitter or shopping when your husband is home to care for the child. Or if the situation is unavoidable (like attending public school) prepare your child by talking through the newness before you arrive. If he will be starting in a new school, take him to the school beforehand, perhaps when the children have gone home for the day and he can quietly meet his teacher-to-be. Then make a second visit with children in the classroom and explain that the same children may not be there when he starts in the fall.

In other words, try to sort out the feeling that is causing the difficulty and then be supportive and reassuring rather than more forceful and demanding. Stop and think about the child's behavior from her point of view. Don't say, "You are driving me crazy. Why do you always do this to me?" Instead say, "You are getting overexcited. Calm down so you don't create more problems for yourself." Teach your child about her own temperament so she can learn to control the stresses in her life as she grows older, and so she can tell her teachers and caretakers what approach will work better with her. Help her learn "cooling off" activities that give her an opportunity to get calm when overexcited. Help the child ease into new situations by building "bridges." For example, bring along the curtains from his old room when you move to a new house, or let him carry the same old lunchbox to the new school. Develop routines that make everything as predictable as possible. Feed the child what she likes to eat instead of turning every meal into a power struggle.

A difficult child takes more time and attention, and even when you are managing him or her well, you will have to remind yourself to save some time to relax after interacting with the child. Likewise, you must set aside time for your spouse and other children. If possible, you should slow down on career plans during the difficult child's early years. If not, then invest all you can in stable, supportive, understanding child care.

Then do yourself one last favor. Avoid people who are critical of your parenting and instead seek out those who understand temperamental differences in children.

BEING CHILD-CENTERED

Your children may have to learn that they are not the center of the universe, but there is no harm in their being the center of your home. Being child-centered, as opposed to work-centered or self-centered, is the central component in a positive parenting attitude. Healthy families give their children first priority. This doesn't mean that the children become little dictators in the home. Rather, well-balanced parents always put what is best for the child first (even though children don't necessarily always want what is best for them). Neither does it mean that Mom and Dad have to sacrifice all their hopes, plans, dreams, ambitions, or nights out alone together. Part of what is best for the child is a happy parent. You need to save some attention for your "child within."

◆ GAIL'S CHILD-CENTERED HOME

Gail's parents were very impulsive, but Gail and Steve (whom we met in Chapter 4) like to think things through before they act. "We are child-centered and we really try to understand our child. When Ariel is tired and cranky we stop and think about it, and maybe we realize that we have pushed her too hard by expecting her to sit in her stroller for two hours. It's not fair to punish a child for not being able to do what she isn't capable of doing. I don't think my parents had any understanding of that. I think they just expected us to be perfect and didn't understand why we weren't."

Gail fears she has a tendency to be controlling, but she consciously tries to build independence into her child. "My daughter tends to be rather clingy. I don't know if she's that way because I had to leave her as a baby and go to work or if that's her natural temperament. But I do encourage her to try things on her own. I coax her to climb up the stairs and tell her all the while that she can do it. I insist that she put her toys away. I let her choose what she wants to wear, what she wants to eat, or what books she wants to hear. But then I make her stick to her choice. We praise her and build her up a lot and try to give her opportunities to be competent. This didn't come naturally. I read these things."

Gail's husband is very good with the baby and has a strong bond with her. A calm, easygoing guy, he has a natural talent with children. "I remember watching my husband with Ariel during our last Christmas vacation. We were all home together, and my husband was in on the bed with Ariel bouncing her up and down. They were totally absorbed with each other. It seemed so strange to me. I could never relax like that with her."

"Now I realize that there are a lot of acceptable ways to be a good mom and some of them include working. My daughter was only three weeks old when I first took her along to Jazzercise. Some of my friends would say, 'I can't believe you are taking a three-week-old baby out like that.' But I knew that I needed to keep up with my exercise and interests. It had been such a long road to get myself feeling good emotionally and I didn't want to risk losing it all by getting cut off from myself. I felt like a happy mom is a good mom."

Whenever possible, parents should try to "go with the flow" of the child. Why should an infant go hungry if his parent can be available to feed him on demand? Parents should honor the natural rhythms of the child (eating, sleeping, playing) whenever feasible. You want to build a positive supportive relationship with the child. In the beginning, these nonverbal communications are all you have.

Another way to build a positive relationship is by keeping the home consistent with the child's developmental stage. If your child is at a curious exploring-with-the-hands-and-mouth stage, keep everything that you don't want her to touch or savor out of her reach. Child-proofing your home allows you to say, "Yes!" more than "No!" By accommodating the house to the child instead of the child to the home, you will have more time to sit back, relax, and enjoy the sight of your child playing.

Children benefit immensely from time with their parents. It raises a child's self-esteem (and probably his IQ!) when a parent is around to answer those endless questions. If you must work, be assertive about how many hours you will put in and make sure you have allowed time for relaxed conversations and outings with your *children's interest levels* in mind. Time for volunteer work should be allotted *after* you have designated time to be with the children. Everyone really does have a limit on how many hours they can put in on various projects. Some scream, "Enough!" *after* they have given the children's time away, while others draw the line sooner.

A good way to avoid overload while feeling like you are carrying your weight in society is to volunteer for only those projects that allow you to be with your child. Nothing tells your child how much you value her more than your active participation in her activities. And as the Bradfords show, you can get a lot of mileage out of participating in scouts, Campfire, church groups, team sports, or school activities with your child. Not only can you screen the activities to see that they represent values you want to teach your children, you have an opportunity to meet your children's peers and encourage healthy friendships. Perhaps an even greater benefit you get from working with your children's activities is the support of other child-centered parents.

In the chaos and pressure of rearing children it is sometimes easy to forget what makes them so wonderful. Children are our chance to see the world through new eyes. Most children are optimistic, even in the face of very difficult circumstances. They are quick to forgive and want to think the best of us. Be sure to take the time to watch your child playing or sleeping so that you can be reminded of the positives. This will refuel your commitment to be an assertive, accepting, "positive parent."

◆ ════════════ **SUMMARY** ════════════ ◆

We must remember that, like us, each of our children is unique in all the world. We need to "tune in" to what works best for getting cooperation from each of our children, given our own temperamental characteristics.

◆ ════════════ **POINTS** ════════════ ◆

1. We needn't accept our parents as our only role models. Parents of friends, childhood teachers, and present-day neighbors can offer more constructive images.

2. Children turn out best if their parents are balanced and calm, make clear requests, treat the children with respect, set firm limits, and teach self-control.

3. Being fair does not necessarily mean treating all our children the same. We need to reward each child by offering what is a "treat" for someone with his or her unique personality.

4. Our relationship with each child is strongly affected by our temperament, the child's temperament, and how compatibly these two variables match up.

5. Some children are so temperamentally difficult that they create unbearable stress in the family. Blaming or despairing is unproductive. The parents of such children need to accept the child's limitations and bring their expectations in line with the child's capabilities.

6. Being child-centered, as opposed to work-centered or self-centered, is the central component in a positive parenting attitude.

NOTES

1. Glenn Austin, M.D., *Love and Power/Parent and Child*. Rolling Hills Estates, CA: Robert Erdmann Publishing, 1988.

2. Lou Denti and Kevin Feldman, *P.R.I.C.E. (Positive Responsibility Influence Consequences Encouragement).* unpublished.

3. Dr. Michael H. Popkins, *The Active Parent* (Video Series—1989). 4669 Roswell Rd. NE, Atlanta, Georgia 30342, 800-235-7755 ext. 200).

4. Don Dinkmeyer & Gary D. McKay, *The Parent's Handbook.* Circle Pines, MN: American Guidance Services, 1982.

5. W. Hugh Missildine, M.D., *Your Inner Child of the Past.* New York: Simon & Schuster, 1963.

6. David D. Burns, M.D., *Feeling Good.* New York: Signet Books, 1980.

7. Keith Golay, *Learning Patterns and Temperament Styles.* Fullerton, CA: Manas-Systems, 1982.

8. Interview: Janet Hackleman RN/MFCC of Family Connection, Colton, California, has developed a series of in-depth parenting courses and has trained parent trainers in her methods.

9. Stanley Turecki, M.D., and Leslie Tonner, *The Difficult Child,* New York: Bantam Books, 1985.

15

THE BUCK STOPS HERE

*As you build a secure and nurturing home for
your children, the child in you will rage at the
recognition of the deprivation he or she
suffered. . . . You will have to parent the child in
you and your children with the same understanding and love.*
        —O'Gorman and Oliver-Diaz, *Breaking the Cycle of
        Addiction*[1]

As I pointed out earlier, there is ever-mounting evidence that alcoholism, mood disorders, "hyperactivity" (or attention
deficit disorder) in children, and many other psychological problems
are hereditary and chemical in nature. Although some still argue
that these are habits passed down by example from parent to child,
adoption studies and studies with twins show there is surely a
relevant biological connection. Experts can go on debating about
whether heredity or environment is the root cause for these disorders being passed on to the next generation, but it is widely accepted
that these disorders do "run in families" for whatever reason.

As a base point, it would be wise to see what family handicaps
your children may be up against so that you can educate them in
prevention long before the need is critical. Try to draw a **genogram**
of your family. A genogram is a family tree that includes known
psychological disorders. (An example is given below.) What "runs"
in your family? Search your memory or interview your relatives
about habits and peculiarities of both your mother's and father's
parents and siblings.

MAURA SHULTZ FAMILY HISTORY

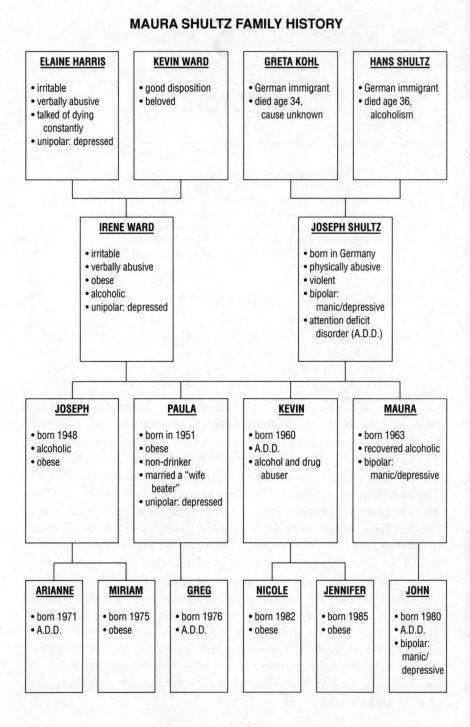

Remember, many are not comfortable with the term "alcoholic," and in earlier generations mood disorders were usually not diagnosed unless they were so totally debilitating that the person had to be hospitalized. Here are some less-threatening questions you might try asking:

---◆---

Family Genealogical Survey

1. What family stories did they tell about Grandma? Grandpa? Uncle Jim? Aunt Susie? etc.

2. What did your (or my) grandparents die of and how old were they?

3. Did anyone have reading problems in our family? (attention deficit disorder)

4. What were your brothers and sisters like when they were little? (hyperactivity often means attention deficit disorder)

5. Was anyone in our family very overweight or exceptionally thin? (eating disorder)

6. Were any of our relatives known for their bad disposition or wild shopping sprees? (mood disorder)

7. Did anyone in our family talk about dying a lot? (mood disorder/depression)

8. Was anyone in our family known for their *extreme* outgoing nature or boundless energy? (mood disorder/manic)

9. Was anyone in our family known for being very critical of others? (mood disorder/depression)

10. Was anyone known for being very nervous or jumpy? (mood disorder)

11. Was anyone in our family known for being overly pessimistic? (mood disorder/depression)

12. Was anyone in our family known for being very hot-tempered or violent? (mood disorder)

13. Were there things that you knew were kept secret in the family such as illegitimate births? Hospitalizations? Criminal records?

14. Has anyone in our family been in trouble with the law?

15. Has anyone in our family had a lot of trouble sleeping at night? (mood disorder)

16. Did anyone in our family take any prescribed pain killers, sleep aids, or tranquilizers? (mood disorder/addiction)

17. Did anyone in our family ever attempt suicide or talk about killing themselves? (mood disorder)

18. Did anyone in our family get too heavily involved in drugs? (addictive tendency)

19. Do you remember anyone in our family who drank a little too much? (alcoholism)

20. Did anyone in our family abstain totally from alcohol? (alcoholism)

Try to elicit remarks about behavior and then use these remarks to pinpoint suspected psychological problems. Mood disorders generally fall into two basic categories: bipolar, or manic/depressive, where the person is alternately depressed or wildly active and optimistic; and unipolar, where the person's mood varies from depressed to normal but never swings to a manic high mood. More subtle is a condition called "cyclothymia," where the person experiences high and low moods in rapid cycles. For example, they could be severely depressed for five days and then go into a manic period for just a week before returning to normal.

Pay attention also to relatives who are teetotalers. In our society, people rarely abstain totally from alcohol unless there is good reason. Do they abstain because they were hurt by parents with alcohol problems as children? Or do they abstain because they learned long ago that they couldn't "handle" alcohol? **Whether or not your parents drank, they can still pass on the genes that will make social drinking difficult for you.** Likewise, if one of your parents was actually wise enough to realize that poor diet and too little sleep always triggered a depression, and lived a health-conscious life as a result, you will not "inherit" the good health unless you follow the healthy habits. Neither will your diet keep your children from inheriting these disorders. **You must teach your children how to care for their own bodies given their genetic weaknesses.**

◆ LILLIAN'S MOODY FAMILY

Lillian's parents were in their early to mid-twenties when she was born. Her father was in the military and was often gone for long periods. In fact, her father was gone so much of the time that when her mother became pregnant with Lillian's younger brother, her father asserted that it was not his child. Fortunately, Lillian's brother looked so much like her father that the paternity was no longer questioned after the baby was born.

"I'm sure it was very hurtful for my mother. Even when my father got out of the Army he wasn't around much. When he was, he smelled of whiskey."

Lillian's parents separated when she was five. "We just packed up and moved to my grandmother's house. My mother didn't tell me anything about the divorce. My father was simply gone as usual. A year or so after that, I remember crying for my daddy and my mother told me he wouldn't be coming back."

Lillian's mother, Joan, worked six days a week, ten hours a day, and Lillian was left with her grandmother. Joan would come home after dinner, eat by herself, and then go read a paperback. Lillian recalls, "She was tired all the time—always struggling to keep things together."

Joan never treated Lillian badly but she was around very little to give Lillian any positive attention. The grandmother was cruel. She complained of headaches and was always taking phenobarbitol. When she wasn't "sick" in bed, the grandmother would beat Lillian with a switch or belt. Lillian doesn't remember any particular thing she did to deserve these beatings, and she feels the punishment was always too severe.

Lillian suspects her grandmother may have been unipolar (depressed only). Always a very negative person, the grandmother is now taking antidepressants. "I've heard horrible stories about my grandmother's mother. I think depression runs in our family. My mother hated her grandmother, probably for much the same reasons that I hated mine. However, I really wouldn't describe my mother as depressed. She was even-tempered like her father.

"My son was a very easy baby. If you didn't want him to do something, you just told him not to. I didn't realize I would need any help with parenting skills until I had my daughter. She wants to do what she wants to do no matter what anybody says. She has to test every rule. If you say, 'We don't draw on walls,' as soon as I'm out of the room she would go get her crayons and draw on the wall. Her attitude is, 'You can't stop me.' She was a totally different personality and I didn't know how to deal with it."

Lillian went back to college to take child development classes and read every parenting book she could get her hands on. "I already had a good sense of what to expect from Karen in terms of developmental level because I had read books on that, but what the class did make me realize was that a difference in temperament can matter a lot. My son and my daughter were just very different from one another. And I think I had expected my daughter to be just like my son, who is actually exceptionally well-behaved. He's totally left-brained and could respond to rational arguments at a very early age. Then I had this right-brained impulsive daughter who talked late.

"I really needed some 'how to's' to deal with my daughter, because I knew I didn't want to just go out and cut a switch to beat her with. If my blood sugar's low and I'm feeling irritable, hitting is still the first thing that comes to mind, but I don't let myself hit her. After all these years and all I've learned, under stress what still comes into my mind is, 'I ought to take a belt to you.' "

Lillian later worked in Karen's parent-participation preschool for a year. "I saw other kids who were as impulsive as she was but they were always hyperactive boys. Still, it made me realize that Karen is impulsive more than she is rebellious. Sometimes she'll do something I told her not to do, but then she'll immediately look guilty and scared and try to undo it. She does a lot of things without thinking. She'll say, 'My brain got twisted, Mommy.' My object in life right now is to teach her to slow down and think."

(Continued in Chapter 16)

BREAKING THE CYCLE

As you reorganize your life in reaction to your parents' hereditary tendencies, beware of overcorrecting. If we try to become the
opposite of our parents, we may become so evangelistic that our
children will rebel and become the opposite of us (or *like* our
parents). Rigidity in any direction does not work. We just create a
flip-flop cycle with each generation having the illusion of progress.

Your children should be aware of the hereditary risks they face.
Even four- and five-year-olds can be told this in a casual manner. If
diabetes or cancer ran in your family, you would want to emphasize
the need for regular check-ups. This doesn't have to be frightening.
You can emphasize that most illnesses are easier to cure, the earlier
you and your doctor know about it. It is *helpful* to know what runs
in your family because your knowledge can possibly help the doctor
narrow down exactly what illness your symptoms indicate. If many
family members have "caved in" from manic-depression in their late
thirties, **your child should know that when he is older, if he feels
very very sad or has trouble sleeping, he should be sure to let the
doctor know that this illness runs in the family.** These things
should be mentioned casually, in context, when your children are
young. It should just be something they have always known about
themselves, like their ethnic background.

If your children have seen you as an active alcohol or drug
abuser, living a life of recovery will be the strongest message you
can give. Remember Greg Ward in Chapters 10 and 12? The genetic
pull toward substance abuse turned out to be more than he could
overcome alone. Janet Ward contacted me a year after my interview
with Greg to give me a disturbing update.

> "What Greg told you was a pretty whitewashed version of the truth as we are
> beginning to find out," she wrote. "Addiction made him an accomplished liar and
> manipulator. Greg checked into a drug treatment program two weeks ago because he
> realized his life was totally out of control. He is just now starting to seem his old
> self—twelve or thirteen years old. I think he is beginning to face the fact that his
> emotional development slowed way down as soon as he started using (and he tried
> everything, I think, but heroin) and that he is now faced with the tough task of
> growing up as well as staying sober and straight.
>
> "We go to a family session with other patients' families, private family sessions,
> and visit him once a week for a few hours. Yesterday's visit was as draining as a
> therapy session but it was wonderful to hear him really talking to us again without
> his nasty, tough-guy persona."

The Wards were naturally quite disillusioned at that point. Seeing his father sober up and knowing about the alcohol problems that plagued earlier generations in his family were apparently not enough to keep Greg from falling prey to drug dependency, but this knowledge did finally help him enter a drug-rehab program willingly. Although he has "lost time" developmentally since he was thirteen, Greg has still sobered up nearly twenty years earlier than his father had been able to at age thirty-eight.

If you have never used any drugs or alcohol in front of your children, or since you have had your children, it is even more important to make sure you explain these family handicaps. Without direct experience, your children will not realize the potential danger of alcohol abuse any more readily than they will believe car accidents are terrible things to be avoided if they have never seen or been in one. Don't be so overprotective that you never let them see the dark side of your family. You may have avoided your family of origin in the past because you didn't want your child to be exposed to their "irresponsible" behavior, but you may be passing up one of the best opportunities to educate your child. Be frank and open about the problems alcohol or drugs have caused for you, your siblings, or parents.

Education about substance abuse should begin in a casual manner while the children are young. Because of your own childhood experiences you may have *very strong* feelings about drinking or the use of drugs. You will have to censor and "tame down" these feelings as you discuss these issues with your children. For example, it would be better to admit that some people can drink just a little alcohol and have no craving for more, than to imply all drinkers become alcoholic.

At the same time, remember that even though certain psychological disorders run in your family, it does not mean that all of your children are at risk. Geneticists have been developing tests that can determine a child's susceptibility to certain diseases, alcoholism among them. Consider having your children tested if your genogram shows they are at high risk. Let your children know that it is a strong possibility and something they need to be aware of, but don't try to make decisions for them by indoctrinating them through heavy preaching.

Without forbidding your teenager to drink, you can let him know that his body may react differently to alcohol than his friends' bodies do. This is like an allergy that runs in your family. Caution him that all addicts are prone to cross-addiction, so no drugs are really "safe" for him either. Tell him you hope he will wait until he is twenty-one to try alcohol, but you want him to talk to you about how it affects him whenever he does decide to try it. Keep in mind that not all your children will automatically inherit these weaknesses. There is no reason for your son or daughter to give up having a drink or two on special occasions when they become adults if it causes no problems for him or her. It is reasonable to ask them to wait until the legal drinking age before they try alcohol, emphasizing that they will have "stopped growing" and have better judgment by then, so that they can determine more objectively how the alcohol is affecting them. By giving your children a sense of choice, or freedom to decide for themselves, they will not have to use your cautions as something to rebel against. Let them horrify you with their hairstyles instead!

SHARING CHILDHOOD MEMORIES

A general family history is only part of what you should share. Your children may need to know about your particular childhood hardships and fears. Remember, family secrets can be as poisonous as lies. We cannot deal with unnamed terrors. Your childhood has inevitably left you feeling anxious about many things. If you went hungry, you are probably anxious about having enough food. It is better for your child if you can explain, "I'm sorry I seem worried about us having enough money for groceries. Our family has never run out of food or money for food. There is no reason for you to worry. I worry needlessly because when I was a child, we didn't have enough to eat, and it's hard for me to realize that I'm safe now." The alternative is for the children to sense your anxiety, and even though they have never gone hungry, they may begin to worry about going hungry.

Also, you want your family to have open communication. This cannot be one-sided. You must be willing to share your childhood with them, and openly acknowledge your lingering fears. You cannot really protect them from this knowledge. You can keep the facts and details from them, but you cannot stop them from sensing that something is wrong and that you are keeping it from them.

If you have had a very unhappy childhood, your children will sense this when you talk about childhood memories, no matter how well you "censor" what you tell them. They will notice omissions or sugar-coated explanations. Not talking about your childhood traumas only makes it a taboo subject. Dr. Druno Bettleheim, the renowned child psychologist and author of *A Good Enough Parent,*[4] noticed that Jewish children who were told about the family's Holocaust tragedies were less fearful about the subject. Of course, at the same time you need to try not to make your stories terrifying or overwhelming for the child. You can say that your father hit you as a child and it was very frightening, without giving a blow-by-blow description that makes your children feel the fear as you did. Then, assure them that you are OK now and you do not need *them* to make up for it. By the same token, you can calmly let your children know that you sometimes feel jealous of the good childhood they have by comparison. Limit your comments so that these revelations do not turn into "bitching sessions" that will make your child anxious. Casually bringing these feelings out in the open gives the feelings less power.

Your children won't hate Grandma if you can say you forgive her, that she couldn't help it, or that you are trying to forgive her. **Be compassionate toward your parent and someday your child will be compassionate toward you.** You are writing your future with your child by modeling forgiveness (or malice) now.

MEDICATION AS SOLUTION

If you grew up in the "drug generation" of the sixties and seventies and were either hurt indirectly by drugs or have felt their devastating effects in your own life, you may very likely be strongly "anti-drug." Sixties "pro-drug" propaganda was quick to point out that parents had been "getting high" on Valium, barbiturates, or tranquilizers, and there was really no difference between that and smoking pot. While it is true that even prescription drugs were often abused, it is not drugs *per se* that are our enemy. Drugs can be used constructively or abused. One advantage of getting drugs through a physician is that he or she can be more *objective* about the drugs and their effect on you than you can. A pusher is not about to tell you that you are taking too much and should try to lower your dosage, but a physician gains nothing by having you continue a drug if you don't really need it.

Naturally our concern about the possible negative effects of drugs coupled with the wisdom of the health-food movement will make us hesitant to give even prescribed mood-altering medications to our children. Drugs have been overprescribed in the past and we should move with caution. Many of the most effective drugs for "hyperactivity" in children are very new (with the exception of Ritalin) and there has been no long-term research on possible side effects down the road. There may be some truth to allegations that schools are using drug therapy for kids to solve what are really problems caused by overcrowded classrooms.

If you have fought hard for your "sobriety," you probably see a lot of merit in solving problems without the use of chemicals. You may worry that your child will never build enough "character" to live without the crutch of drugs once they have been offered, or you may feel like you are "copping out" if you permit your own problems coping with your child to be solved "the easy way." Medication is not the best solution for all emotional problems. Each situation must be evaluated separately.

When it comes to medication and children, all other alternatives should be tried first, if only for the parent's peace of mind. Some children respond to regimens such as sugar-free diets, additive-free diets, or the Feingold diet.[3] Others respond to a more carefully structured life where eating habits, sleeping habits, and exercise are used to help the child achieve a more balanced existence. Still others may be helped most by the parent taking corrective drugs and/or engaging in therapy.

But if all these alternatives have been tried and the child is still having problems, medication should be given serious consideration. Just as we would condemn a parent who would withhold insulin from a diabetic child, we should question ourselves if we are not willing to permit drug therapy to be tried on our child when all else has failed. If a child is suffering from low self-esteem because he can rarely act appropriately, it is cruel to deny him an opportunity for a "normal childhood." We have all met children who are just too difficult to be around. We avoid inviting them to our houses, we hear them discussed by neighbors, we see that snap of irritation flash on the teacher's or group leader's face. Everyone rejoices when he is absent. At best, they kindly tolerate his presence, but they never look forward to seeing him. How do you think it feels to be that kid? No matter how hard adults try to hide these feelings, kids sense them. And other children rarely try to hide these negative feelings at all.

The proper drug given in the proper dose really can transform these children into calm, likable children who are a pleasure to be around. We have had it hammered into us for decades that "you can't just take a pill and expect all your problems to be solved." However, for some children, this seems to be an empty proverb. For those who really have an imbalance in their brain chemistry, drug therapy can be an instant "miracle cure." For others, medication is only part of the solution but it is a necessary component for helping the child break the downward spiral. Changes in life-style should accompany most drug therapy, and in many cases, the life-style changes and behavior training possible while the mind is calmed by medication, can later maintain the child's positive transformation while the drug is phased out.

Anyone who has suffered from manic-depression and had that mental suffering cured by new antidepressents or lithium treatment, regards these new medical advances with awe and gratitude. Affected children don't have to grow up "losers" anymore. When mood disorders and distractibility run in families, medication can help everyone in the family live a happy, productive life.

◆ JUDY'S SELF-DISCOVERY

Judy eventually had to admit that Casey had not adjusted at all. Instead, Judy had adjusted the world to him and it was one exhausting task. Despite all her efforts, there were just too many things she couldn't control, and after six months of preschool he was still being sent to the time-out chair every day. Casey was beginning to hate himself. He would ask her every ten minutes if she still loved him. He would make her promise that she would never leave him. He would require her to write love notes. Not only would these demands for reassurance have annoyed anyone, Judy was finding it harder and harder to sound genuine because she could not quell the tremendous resentment building up in her toward him and his excessive needs.

It had been months since she had done anything for herself. She wanted to be able just to sit and read a book uninterrupted for more than five minutes. She wanted to be able to go out with a friend and stay out until she felt satiated with conversation. She was sick and tired of preparing all their food from scratch and she was tired of eating the boring concoctions she could make without using any ingredients that contained artificial color, artificial flavor, or preservatives, or even perfectly healthy food like apples and oranges that were forbidden on Casey's diet.

To top it off, her self-esteem was still dangerously low and suffering daily blows. She had begun to accumulate "mother clothes." There was no point in buying anything expensive or dressy because she had no place to wear it, and even if she decided to get a little dressed up for the fun of it, Casey was sure to smear it with peanut butter the first time she wore it anyway. She also didn't bother wearing makeup because she wasn't going anywhere. She had been used to eating a light lunch or skipping it, and now she didn't dare keep many of her usual foods in the house because if Casey couldn't eat them it just made sticking to his diet all the more difficult. Besides, it broke up the day to have a sandwich at the park and a snack in the afternoon. In short, she had gained about fifteen unattractive pounds.

When she caught glimpses of herself in the mirror she had to admit she was starting to look like the typical depressed, dowdy housewife. And she was being treated that way. People she met talked down to her. Salesladies sneered at her as if they wondered if she really had enough money (or taste) to shop in their store. Clerks waited on the more prosperous-looking people around her, and even her husband seemed to have forgotten her master's degree, increasingly addressing her in condescending tones. She had no props, no proof of her competence or worth. She began to believe she was the person she looked like—ignorant, self-abasing, and narrow. Even little Casey had begun swearing at her and criticizing her ministrations as never good enough—she cooked the egg wrong, she had packed what he wanted for lunch every day for the last two weeks but hadn't divined that he hated muffin and cream cheese *today.* And she had slowly, unconsciously stopped noticing his abuse (which was much less severe than the abuse she had suffered as a child.)

Her therapist would try to remind her of her education and skills and her simple right as a human being to be treated respectfully, but for a long time it seemed as if he were talking about another world, another lifetime, another dimension. Yet, she was slowly beginning to feel the rightness of it, even though she couldn't act on it. Then she realized she was going to have to start to "fake it" at least—pretend to be angry at what should make anyone angry whether she felt it or not, pretend she has something important to do that day that requires dressing up, pretend that she could expect respectful treatment from her son even if she didn't quite believe he was capable of it. She had to start setting limits for his sake as well as hers. She had to give up her belief that people should treat her like a professional whether she looked like one or not, and that people should love her son because he was healthy, handsome, loving, brilliant, talented, and affectionate, even though he had been nothing but rude and belligerent in their presence. And in order to have any chance at success she had to start accepting the help that was being offered.

Judy decided to take Casey to the staff psychiatrist, and after taking an elaborate family medical history the psychiatrist prescribed an antidepressant. Judy was ready to cooperate and Carl had no objection. As a matter of fact, he had long been ready for something that could help him treat Casey better and relieve some of his guilt. Within two weeks, Casey was chosen to take the "good behavior bear" home from school, signifying that he had not been sent to "the chair" once during that week. He began to play alone for longer stretches; he began to absorb rules (such as don't rock in the chair) after ten repetitions instead of one hundred; he was slower-moving, less agitated, and more patient. It was like a miracle and the miracles built on the miracles.

Time and space and stillness opened up for Judy. Carl was slower to escape Casey's presence at night and Casey began warming up to him. Judy began to indulge herself, taking up where she had left off when Casey was born. There had been a whole childhood of wanting and being denied that she had to "rewrite." She started with simple extravagances filtered through a new awareness. When she and Casey were in the toy store trying to decide what to spend his birthday money on, she simply could not spark his interest in *Sea Monkeys*. Instead of trying to outwit him for his own good and convince him to buy them, instead of surprising him with them later because she just knew he would love them, she decided to face the issue head-on and buy a package for herself. And when Casey was reluctant to move from rhythm class on to piano lessons, she looked that old demon in the eye and signed up for her own lessons. Freed from the tyranny of Casey's diet they could both eat store-bought, low-fat yogurt again. He no longer needed Judy to go to preschool with him every day, so she signed up for an exercise class. The better she treated herself, the better she liked being with Casey, and the better he seemed to like being with her.

Judy was experiencing islands of euphoria, but they were still punctuated by mysterious bouts of depression all out of proportion with her improved circumstances. It was true that Carl was still failing to be supportive and had not acknowledged Judy's positive changes, but on her good days she was strong enough to believe in and support herself. Carl's lack of recognition was not enough to explain the depth of her intermittent depressions. Even her therapist was disturbed and surprized that she was still periodically sinking so low. He referred her to Casey's psychiatrist. To Judy's surprise, the psychiatrist nodded and listened as if he had anticipated her descriptions of the low periods of extreme withdrawal that overtook her in the midst of an outgoing, confident period. He diagnosed her as having a milder form of the affective disorders that had plagued her family of origin and prescribed the same medication for her that he had prescribed for Casey. She was stunned, then relieved. He had given years of suffering a name. She was no longer weak, self-pitying, and morally lazy. She was cyclothymic.

The medication made it possible for her to think clearly, to hold onto thoughts, and follow through with action before she was distracted. Casey's excessive demands struck her as simply unreasonable, and she slowly, calmly, methodically began to refuse to gratify his every wish, pushing him toward greater independence. Within a few months both Judy and Casey were ready for him to extend his time at the day-care center adjoining the preschool.

Casey was still more intense than the average child and Judy was still more fragile than the average adult. She realized she might never be able to manage a full-time job while she mothered this particular child, but it was possible to consider another part-time job. Attainable, reasonable, manageable—these were new words that described her dreams and existence. Boring to many, they were full of exciting new possibility for her.

In the case of Judy's family, medication was like a miracle cure. It turned neither Casey nor Judy into a "zombie." There were no noticeable signs that they were taking medication, because the psychiatrist had carefully adjusted the dosage so that the drug was not at all debilitating. With this medication Judy now felt "normal" for the first time in her life. Experiencing this change herself made her even more aware of what a blessing it was that Casey could be cured so young. She realized he would never have to go through the years of painful depression that she had suffered. Life was now indisputably "worth living" for both of them.

NONGENETIC DYSFUNCTION PATTERNS

Traumatic events or long-term illnesses can also set off patterns of dysfunction that can go on for generations. Divorces can sometimes be so bitter that the parents fight a "no holds barred" battle that goes on for years, with no consideration for the children caught (and sometimes even used as weapons or convoys of hatred) in the fray. Mothers and fathers who were supportive, nurturing parents before divorce, will sometimes abandon the children entirely or simply become so distracted by their own internal pain that they cannot even consider the welfare of the child.

A father returning from a war such as Vietnam, a mother who has been raped, or a child born with a birth defect can all traumatize a family so deeply that they cannot function normally. Unless there is therapeutic intervention these problems can affect generations to come. **If a parent is distant and unreachable, for any reason, it will surely affect parenting in the next generation as the child grows to adulthood and tries to sort out, from scratch, just how parents should behave.**

Any long-term or terminal illness of any family member is also a damaging trauma that even the strongest families cannot absorb without repercussions. Sometimes a conflict appears to have been worked through for the moment, but the damage of these psychological scars crop up later, triggered by some similar event. Miriam Wiseman's exceptionally bright daughter, Lisa, suddenly and inexplicably withdrew and became suicidal when she was sixteen. Lisa's early childhood years had gone smoothly. Anyone would have described her as a vivacious girl, active, capable, loving, and well-loved. Miriam had been content to stay at home with her children and was active in PTA, civic organizations, and all the children's activities. They were a happy, healthy family. Then the walls caved in. It took nearly two years of family therapy to unravel the threads of what led to Lisa's breakdown. In the end, more of the answer to the riddle was found in Miriam's life than it was in Lisa's. Lisa just seemed to be a vessel that carried a lot of grief and pain Miriam had never let herself experience.

◆ MIRIAM'S TURMOIL REVISITED

Age sixteen had been the hardest year of Miriam's life. Her warm, supportive mother had just died of Hodgkin's disease, and Miriam subsequently "lost" her father to his all-consuming grief for his wife. The disease itself was not hereditary but the emotional *dis*-ease felt during this painful year went on affecting Miriam and in turn, her daughter.

After a week-long shiva, Miriam remembers coming home to the family meal following the burial. "I remember feeling like I had had such a great mother for however long. And for a long time after that, whenever I came home I would see my mother's car there and I would think, 'Mom's home from work!' and then I would remember that she was dead."

During her childhood all Miriam's affection had come from her mother. Her father, like many 1950s fathers, had always been physically distant, and now he was totally engulfed in grief, wanting to die and follow his wife to the grave. To make matters worse, the father's mother had died just three months before his wife. He was incapable of coping with a teenager.

"I was involved with a loser of a guy who was going nowhere. My father forbid me to see him. But I would sneak out to meet this boy. My father, usually a very mild-mannered man, actually had a fistfight with this boy in the street. I was wild and out of control. I wasn't doing drugs or drinking or anything, but I couldn't concentrate on my schoolwork and I was just being a rebel. My father didn't know what to do with me."

He finally decided to send Miriam to live with her aunt and uncle on the East Coast. Miriam was isolated and lonely without familiar high school friends and resented being sent away. Still, she managed to finish the school year and was allowed to return to California.

While Miriam was gone, her father had started his "new life," and shortly after she returned, he leapt into marriage with a woman he scarcely knew. This new wife immediately got rid of every reminder of Miriam's mother and alienated every member of the family. When she suggested the father push Miriam out of the house, he came to his senses and divorced the woman. They had only been married six months, but the damage done to Miriam was long-lasting. Despite her father's final rally to her defense, she felt unloved and emotionally abandoned.

Then Miriam started college and discovered she could lose her grief in sex. She majored in "romance" and began missing a lot of classes as well as many nights of sleep. Sophomore year she dropped out mid-semester and went to work. "It was really good for me," recalls Miriam. "It was the first time I had to be responsible." Shortly after that Miriam met her husband, Jerome, and ended her intense adolescent rebellion with a traditional temple wedding. Within two years she gave birth to Lisa.

"When my daughter, Lisa, was born she was incredibly responsive, active, and hard to discipline. She could never calm herself down after a tantrum. She needed someone to sit and explain things to her." Overjoyed to have a family, Miriam had all the patience she needed for the task. She talked with Lisa patiently, read to her, took her to the park. When Lisa started nursery school, everyone began telling Miriam and Jerome how bright Lisa was. Lisa could read long before she went to kindergarten. "I was trying to be the perfect mother," Miriam explained. Two years later she gave birth to a son and they all lived the idyllic middle-class life. "We were all very busy doing all the right things. I chauffeured my kids to dance lessons, soccer, and so on."

Then Lisa entered adolescence and their problems began. "At first I didn't realize that there was any problem. She had been early at everything, so when she became sexually active at fourteen I thought that was normal. My parents had been very repressed sexually and I didn't want to be that way with my daughter, so we discussed methods of birth control. It was all very reasonable. I thought I should be permissive and open with Lisa, but I went overboard. I remember she brought home a black teddy that she was going to wear prom night and I said, 'Isn't that pretty! I bet your boyfriend will like that.' What a stupid thing for a mother to say!"

But Miriam had had no role model after age fifteen. Her only guideline was a conviction that she would not be as strict and rigid as her father had been. "Lisa's therapist later told me that up until the age of ten (the same age Miriam was when her mother became fatally ill and began her five-year decline toward death) my daughter had had a good solid normal life and then something went wrong. He said if she hadn't had that good foundation, she would have killed herself."

Lisa's first real boyfriend caused trouble between Lisa and her best friend. Lisa wanted to be with the boy all the time and her friend was very jealous and vindictive. She started doing things to "get even" with Lisa. She would call her up and call her a slut. About the same time some kids from school scrawled a swastika on Lisa's windshield.

"She would come home from school, go straight to her bedroom, close the door, and cry. I would go down, open her door and say, 'Honey, is there anything you need help with? Can I do anything?' And Lisa would say, 'No. I'm just upset.' She kept it in. When I talked to my other friends with teenagers they would say, 'Oh, it's normal adolescent problems!' "

Then Lisa began to have trouble sleeping at night. Miriam could sometimes hear Lisa talking on her bedroom phone in the wee hours of the morning. Finally, Miriam realized that her daughter hadn't slept for a week. Lisa came to Miriam and said, "I'm breaking down." She had realized she needed help. Miriam took Lisa to a therapist immediately.

"It was so frightening. The therapist called us in and said, 'I can guarantee her safety when she is with us. And I can guarantee her safety while she is in school because she has things she has to do that keep her occupied and going. But I cannot guarantee her safety—her life—when she gets out of school.' "

They had to commit Lisa to a psychiatric hospital for her own safety. "Lisa went willingly with me but when I left she was crying and crying about being left there." Within two weeks she had let go of all the feelings she had been holding back and regressed emotionally to the level of a two-year-old. "We had promised her that she could come home in two weeks. But at the end of that two weeks she was a hundred times sicker. In fact, she had been put on a suicide watch and it was against the law for us to take her home. Still we felt terrible about breaking our promise."

Lisa had to be transferred to a hospital that worked exclusively with adolescents. She was all bandaged up because she had tried to cut up her arms. The new therapist looked at Lisa's arms with concern and told Miriam and Jerome, "We've got to put a stop to this right away. When she gets out, she won't want to have these scars."

"They talked about when she would get out as though, of course, she was going to get over this," Miriam relates, as if she is describing a miracle. "I had reached the point where I thought Lisa was just going to be rocking back and forth like a maniac for the rest of her life." Then Lisa went through a stage where she blamed Miriam for everything. "This was very hard for me," Miriam recalls. "I had stayed at home and not worked so that I could raise the perfect child and this was the fruit of my labor. I felt like I wanted 'out.' I had another child to raise." At the therapist's advice, Miriam stayed away, but after a few weeks Lisa began asking for her.

"We did a whole lot of family therapy. It wasn't easy. There were times we would come out of a session ready to tear each other apart. But the therapist was so good. I felt like we were honored and blessed to have this man in our life. He pulled Lisa from the depths of despair. He got her out of that hospital in four months."

They thought a regular college prep program at her old high school wouldn't be too much pressure, but Lisa was back in the hospital three months later.

"That second commitment was so hard," Miriam recalls. "It was December and everyone was rushing around getting ready for the holidays. Our family had planned to go on a cruise—which is a reward we had promised Lisa for getting out of the hospital. The doctor told us we had to go ahead without her because my son had been looking forward to it and we shouldn't disappoint him. Lisa couldn't go. The doctor said it was just too risky. She was regressing and no one would be able to deal with a nervous breakdown out in the middle of the ocean. So I signed her into the hospital when she knew we were all going on *her* cruise. I saw her little face in the door as I drove away. It was so hard. Her birthday is in December. We put her in two days before her birthday."

(Continued in Chapter 16)

On the surface it looked as though Miriam had done all the "right things." She was indeed a highly functioning parent until her daughter reached the age of Miriam's own mother's death. In many ways Miriam had never matured beyond fifteen. She never learned what type of sexual behavior is healthy for an adolescent. As teenagers we all might have complained about the restrictions our parents put on us, but as we mature we come to understand our parents' viewpoint and motivation better. Miriam never had the opportunity to work through adolescence to maturity with her mother. Once her mother had died and was not available to comment on Miriam's behavior, Miriam was free to imagine that Mother would have approved of what Father condemned. When Miriam's daughter, Lisa, became a teenager, Miriam began to function more like a "pal" (an uncritical teenage confidant of Lisa's) than like a mother. Miriam had no idea how the mother of an adolescent should behave.

Many of us lack role models for parenting our children effectively through critical periods in their lives. We need to take an honest look at ourselves and make the best use of our past hardships. We can do nothing about the past. It's time to let go of our grievances and get on with the business of growing up. It doesn't matter how many mistakes you have made or how many disappointments you have endured if you have learned from them. Examining our past experiences and future plans to see what we can learn from each of them will change our basic perceptions about our life. What was a handicap becomes a challenge and an opportunity for enlightenment.

SURVIVAL SKILLS PUT TO GOOD USE

After hundreds of pages describing all the many ways ACODF may be dysfunctional parents, we need to pause and look at the picture in context. If you are reading this book you obviously have a desire to change and be a better parent than your parents were to you. For you to have come out of a troubled home and now be seeking better ways, you must have strength and many good coping skills. The trick is to learn to put your skills to good use. What is the positive side of each of your adaptive behaviors and what is the negative side? Don't throw out the baby with the bathwater. If you played a fixed role in your family, such as the hero, you need to determine which characteristics have been beneficial to *you* and which served only your parents' needs. For example, it may be time for you to give up "parenting" your younger siblings so that you can devote more attention to the children growing up in your own family right now. However, you can still *gain* from the caretaking experiences forced on you at a young age, by recognizing the parenting skills you learned. When processed carefully, these early "parenting" experiences can give you more confidence in handling your own children.

On the other hand, if your role does not seem to benefit you anymore, you should probably try to give it up or outgrow it. For example, if you played the "lost child," you have probably developed a habitual lack of assertiveness. The only positive use I can see for that role is to help you be aware of how sensitive, unsure, and helpless children are. But now, you must be the grown-up for them and show them how to get what they want and need.

USEFUL DEFENSES

The adaptive behaviors that ACODF have learned while growing up in a dysfunctional family are what psychologists call defenses. No one can live without defenses. Whether intentional or accidental we will all experience "hurts" in our lifetimes again and again. If ten people apply for a job, nine will be rejected. If we let ourselves be as vulnerable as children, we might spend every day "crying in our soup." To be *defenseless* is not our goal. Rather we need to learn what defenses, taken to what degree, are healthy and enabling, and what defenses are crippling and limiting. We need to determine what are *reasonable defenses.*

It is reasonable and healthy to protect yourself from the excessive demands of others. That includes both pleas from volunteer organizations and demands from your children. What is excessive is determined by your current stress tolerance. If you are burned out, volunteer for nothing until you feel yourself filling up with excess energy. If your children are drawing too much out of you so that you feel depleted, you must set limits. You may feel your child is seeking so much attention because he truly needs it (and it's all your fault he feels so neglected!). Regardless, you cannot give what you don't have. Everyone may have to live with less than they would like for awhile. You are the goose and they will just have to wait patiently for your next golden egg.

On the other hand, if you find yourself refusing to give of yourself because you fear criticism, rejection, or failure, it may be time for you to drag yourself out there and line up with the rest of us. You will only develop courage and confidence by trying and (eventually) succeeding. If you draw back from closeness with your child because you fear being hurt, you are also missing out on the joys and warmth of shared confidences and growing trust. You may be successfully avoiding life's pain, but you will also avoid all of life's joy. This is being *too safe* for comfort.

Remember the rules of dysfunctional families?

1. Rule of ridigity
2. Rule of silence
3. Rule of denial
4. Rule of isolation

These all represent crippling defenses. Our rigid expectations and behaviors keep us and those dependent on us from growing. It's safe, it's predictable, but it is deadly boring. In fact, ridigity creates a "living death" that eventually becomes chronic depression.

The rule of silence also contributes to depression. When we are not allowed to talk about our intense feelings and fears, they stay inside our bodies and poison us. By not talking, we also fail to take the first step toward change and resolution. We cannot begin to change our lives until we can define what is wrong.

Denial is not a solution either. Our problems will not go away if we avoid thinking about them. Those who are in strong denial have the mistaken belief that if they don't advertise or admit to their problems, no one else will know about them. I have known women separated from their husbands who went on giving an "intact family" story to the neighbors, as if the neighbors would never have noticed that the spouse's car had been missing for two months. Denial doesn't keep the secret from others. It keeps the secret from yourself and blocks you from receiving comfort from others.

So it is with isolation. If you fear the criticism of others, there are many safe places to go with your first efforts to reach out. The safest place is one-on-one counseling with a competent therapist. Churches and synagogues are often safe places to experiment. If Sunday morning coffee hour seems too threatening, go have a private talk with the minister first and get a sense of the openness of the church. Parents of your children's friends are also good risks. End your own imprisonment by taking a chance.

It is fine to be cautious at first. You don't have to run out and tell your neighbor your whole life story. That might prove foolishly risky. Feel people out gradually. Reveal your least sensitive fears first. Try sharing that you worry you don't expect enough of your daughter and ask the other mother what her daughter does in the way of chores. If your son's teacher has seemed cold and aloof, risk asking his classmate's mother if the teacher strikes her that way too. If you are looking for friends, be willing to admit that you feel lonely sometimes. If your companion doesn't suggest a social outing with you, ask her where she has been able to make friends. Try not to be too "heavy" until you know people well. Once you have done some sorting and gathered a small nucleus of friends around yourself, you will find yourself feeling comfortable and able to give up your most isolating defenses.

KNOWING WHAT BAD PARENTING IS

Ironically, one of the greatest advantages you may have going for you is your childhood experience with misguided parents. When you know what foods you *don't* like, it makes ordering from the menu much less complicated! There are good parents, poor parents, and mediocre parents. If you had good parents you will probably just do as they did and do a fine job (as long as nothing unusual happens—such as the birth of a handicapped child). If you had mediocre parents you may feel like you are developing pictures in the dark. You just can't tell how they'll come out yet. You may have very unclear ideas about what your parents did well, and what you should not imitate. If you had very poor parents you will be way ahead of the game if you can objectively put your knowledge to good use.

First, you will be more motivated to learn better parenting skills. You will not have a false sense of complacency. Better ways of doing things may have been made very clear to you by suffering through your parents' mistakes. Not only have you learned first-hand how it feels to be belittled and criticized, you have also seen the effects of your parent's behavior on your siblings. If one of your brothers or sisters seems to be less affected by the negative parenting, you can analyze that and try to determine what mitigating factors helped this child through.

Not only will poor parents give you some concrete ideas about what should be done differently, your personal suffering will give you a motivating hunger for change. Misery creates a preoccupation with self that can be channeled into a positive direction. Many who have grown up in dysfunctional families are very introspective. Through self-examination they have made themselves grow a great deal, long before they became parents. Parenting calls for new skills and new insights, so it can initially be very overwhelming and discouraging. But if you have worked through other passages and important transitions in the past, rest assured that once you lose your sense of panic, you will triumph in this situation too. **Remember, people who question are more likely to learn.** As we said earlier, this intense self-awareness allows you to become a *conscious parent* who takes the time to think through things to the best solution instead of just *reacting*.

Last but not least, if you grew up in a dysfunctional home you probably come to the job of parenting with some first-hand experience. If you weren't expected to care for younger siblings, you probably found yourself taking care of yourself pretty often. Your parents may have put you in many tight or embarrassing spots that improved your ability to "think on your feet." You can think of the chaos in your childhood home as *crisis training*. The same cognitive skills you used during childhood to determine which closet it was best to hide in, given ten seconds to make a selection, can help you get your entire family out of the house in the event of a fire!

Earlier we talked about how childhood crises can go on making you feel unsafe even when there is no rational need. The example we used was a fear of running out of food even though your family income is more than adequate to keep you all eating in style. There is another side to this coin. Your childhood hardships may give you a sense of perspective that other parents lack. If you can both remember your hardships, and assess your present situation realistically, you may find much cause for joy that the average person overlooks. You can feel a warm sense of overwhelming gratitude toward the forces of good, just because your husband comes straight home from work every night instead of stopping at the bar. Or you can feel blessed that your wife has a calm steady rhythm of moods that never shoots too high or dips too low. You can look at the love in your child's face when you tuck her in at night, and thank God for the miracle of her birth and this opportunity to live a happier childhood this time around.

◆ ═══════════════ **SUMMARY** ═══════════════ ◆

In the past twenty years researchers have learned so much about psychological disorders that many people who were once considered hopeless are now virtually curable. We need to end the

cycle of suffering in our families by taking advantage of the medications, therapy, and support available today.

◆ ══════════════════ **POINTS** ══════════════════ ◆

1. Research shows that alcoholism, mood disorders, hyper-activity, and other psychological problems are hereditary. Our children need to be informed about what disorders run in our families and what living habits help keep these disorders under control.

2. From a very early age, children should be told about hered-itary problems in a casual manner. We keep the doors of commu-nication open by modeling a mature, compassionate attitude to-ward our relatives' transgressions.

3. Medications exist which can end the suffering of mood-disordered, hyperactive, or alcoholic adults and children. If other approaches have not been effective, we should be open to trying medication as a solution.

4. Traumatic events or long-term illnesses can set off pat-terns of dysfunction that go on for generations. If a parent is distant and unreachable, for any reason, this will surely affect his or her child's later parenting abilities.

5. We need to sort out what defenses, taken to what degree, are healthy and enabling, and what defenses are crippling and limiting.

6. Our children often provide the impetus for us to outgrow our own limiting, unproductive behaviors. To grow and change we need to be open to help from friends, neighbors, support groups, or therapists.

7. Although our parenting difficulties often seem like unjus-tified punishment, by working through our pain and confusion we will gain new insights that enrich our own lives as much as our children's.

NOTES

1. Patricia A. O'Gorman and Philip Oliver-Diaz, *Breaking the Cycle of Addiction.* Pompano Beach, FL: Health Communications, Inc., 1987

2. Bruno Bettleheim, Ph.D., *A Good Enough Parent.* New York: Alfred A. Knopf, Inc., 1989.

3. Ben F. Feingold, M.D., *Why Your Child Is Hyperactive.* New York: Random House, 1974.

16

THE SUPERSURVIVORS

The pupil dilates in the night, and at last finds day in it, even as the soul dilates in misfortune, and at last finds God in it.
— Victor Hugo, *Les Miserables*

Those who have studied survivors, whether survivors of war, concentration camps, or cancer, have noticed the survivor's remarkable flexibility of character. Their personalities are generally made up of polar opposites. This is how Bernie Siegel, M.D., describes survivors in his popular book *Love, Medicine, and Miracles:* "They are both serious *and* playful, tough *and* gentle, logical *and* intuitive, hard-working *and* lazy, shy *and* aggressive, introspective *and* outgoing, and so forth." They are complex people with many strong needs such as survival, acceptance of others, self-esteem, self-actualization, and a deep inner drive to have things work well for others as well as themselves. Despite the obvious internal conflict it must create, survivors pursue all of these aspects and interests simultaneously. They are compelled to leave the world a better place than it was.[1]

Interestingly enough, psychologists I interviewed kept pointing out that adult children from dysfunctional families often focus on the black and white of things, rarely seeing the gray. The faults that ACODF parents commit generally have to do with excesses. They take a trait that would be neutral in moderation, such as responsibility, and turn it into a monster by being superresponsible or superirresponsible. They struggle with these strong drives and if they win the battle against their excesses, it means that they have finally been able to integrate the opposing parts of their personalities in a way that allows them to be strengths.

This often involves a dramatic shift in thinking that many identify as a spiritual experience. It is as though they have had two weak-muscled eyes that have each focused outward for years, splitting the world into two contradictory images. A psychologist, mentor, or god lends them a pair of corrective lenses and the world is transformed into a whole that is more than either of the parts. This new perspective transforms their understanding of motivations and relationships. What was once an insurmountable problem is reinterpreted as a blessing.

◆ SUSAN—FROM DYSFUNCTION TO SUCCESS

Susan (Chapters 9 and 13) thinks back on her beginnings trying to trace her will to survive. "I survived my childhood just because I had an inkling and a faith that things could be different. I did a lot of observing in other families. I had a lot of friends. They didn't know about my family because they never came to my house, but I was welcome in theirs. I was involved in a very powerful youth fellowship where the leader taught us to find our own faith and think for ourselves." Susan had a close supportive relationship with a high-school boyfriend who was also the child of an alcoholic. They broke up when they each went off to different colleges—two survivors setting out on different paths.

Susan has suffered some very low periods in her life, but she has always believed that things can be better. She works toward a positive future and tries to look at the past as a learning experience. Although the greatest pain she ever felt came out of her first marriage, she now views that marriage as a growing time that gave her two beautiful children. She comments, "It was a difficult time, but it was not a waste of time."

As she looks back at her great depression at the end of her marriage, she realizes that during her childhood she had been emotionally used up by the needs of her parents and siblings. When she needed strength, her strength account had been overdrawn and her family was not there to lend her new strength. "At the bottom I realized that I was the only person I could count on. I was the only one there and I could see myself and my strength for the first time."

Susan's younger sister, the "lost child" of her family of origin, has submerged herself in her husband's career. Married to a physician, she is his receptionist and has no friends or interests outside of her marriage and her husband's career. In contrast to her sister, Susan feels she overcame a similar "loss of self" when she escaped her marriage. She took responsibility for her own life. She said to herself, "This is it. There is only me."

Others may realize this in gentler terms as a part of maturing, but the adult child of a dysfunctional family has grown up hoping and praying that, somewhere out there, there are people who can be depended on—Prince (or Princess) Charming. Usually when ACODF are young children, no one is dependable, but they keep looking for that dependable "parent" that they believe in. It is the ACODF's dream that he or she will finally be able to let it all go and be taken care of. They each typically think, "I know while I'm in this crazy family, I'm the only one I can count on. I'll just have to hang on tight until I get out of this family, and I can give all this responsibility for myself to someone else." There are stages that the ACODF goes through when this dream crashes into reality.

The Four Stages of Caretaking

Stage 1: "I take care of myself because nobody else will."

Stage 2: "I'm going to let this person take care of me."

Stage 3: The terrible realization: "He is not going to take care of me."

Stage 4: "Nobody is going to take care of me ever, so I'm going to have to learn to take care of myself. That also means no one else should expect me to take care of them. I'm the only one I can depend on, but I'm also the only one I have to take care of."

Some ACODF become bitter at this point. They feel they are missing out on something everyone else got. In some ways this is true. Children who had responsible, mature parents have already had their need for care satisfied by the time they reach adulthood. Once you've missed this opportunity in childhood, you can't really go back and get it. The time for it has passed. The ACODF can make mutual-nurturing contracts with others, but they can never hope to be totally cared for as children are. They can only get this kind of care in an extremely dependent relationship or a mental hospital. Most feel, and rightly so, it is not worth the sacrifice.

Once we all reach adulthood, we are on equal ground. Many children from good homes wish they could continue to cling to Mom and Dad. College, or a post-high-school career or marriage, is often that transition time when the child has one foot in his or her family of origin, and the other foot in the world of the independent adult. The less-fortunate ones never really do get both feet out of the hearth. But for those who want to mature to full adulthood, the need and ability to be self-reliant is an ultimate truth that even they must face.

Who and what can any of us trust? We can trust that others will do whatever is in their best interest. If we use this as our guideline we will rarely be disappointed. This may sound rather cold-blooded. What ever happened to brotherly love? People do, at moments, reach out and even sacrifice themselves for others. But most of the time anyone with a healthy survival instinct will only give what he *has* to give. He may need the good feeling that comes from giving you his last sandwich more than he needs that sandwich. But whether he chooses to keep the sandwich or give it away will depend on his own needs, not yours.

When you are down and out, the person you turn to might love you and want to help you, but she might be having her own nervous breakdown just at that critical moment. Learning to be self-reliant is at the core of breaking out of co-dependency. It is different from having a self-sufficient chip on your shoulder. Rather than being a depressing realization, it is a relief to understand this. Once you know deep down inside that you are the only one you can really count on, you can move ahead under your own steam. (Of course it helps if you have let go of the burden of taking care of the whole rest of the world before you try to come to your own aid!)

◆ SUSAN

"When I was a small child I was always off finding myself. I would go off to think. I had a relationship with nature and God. I've always been very creative. I used to escape into books and had read my way through the children's library by the time I was ten. I was always considered older. I had a goal since I was a young child. I was going to be a teacher. I had ambition and direction. I was a very determined person.

"My actions as a teenager would have made you believe that I already knew that I had to make my own way in life," Susan tells me. "I was holding down two jobs trying to earn enough money for college. A part of me knew I had to count on myself, but I was too young to recognize the truth. I believed that everyone else had someone he could rely on. But it is an enormous relief to know that even in the most loving circumstances, ultimately you are the only person who will act in your best interest. Then you can get control of yourself and your life and say, 'OK, what do I like and not like about this? What am I willing to do without?' And you have to recognize it's your choice. Everything is your choice. If you decide to stay in a horrible situation, then that was your choice to do it. Nobody is making you do it. But when you recognize that, you also recognize that you have the right to say no. Before that, I didn't feel as if I had the right. In the way I was raised, I had responsibilities and obligations but I had no rights. Once I took responsibility for my life I also had the right to decide what would happen from then on out. It gave me a whole different perspective. It said, 'You're fine just the way you are. There's nothing wrong with you.' "

It is important for ACODF to be able to learn to trust. But this also ties in with the idea of "reasonable defenses" we discussed in the last chapter. ACODF often grow up cynical, believing that no one can be counted on. It isn't any wonder. In an alcoholic family, or any other dysfunctional family, there is nothing you can really depend on because you never know what's going to happen. And there isn't honesty. So you can't rely on what your eyes tell you or what your ears hear. Your parents say one thing and do another. When there are real problems they don't face them; they simply pretend the problems are not there. You begin to doubt even your own perceptions. If you stop counting on your parents that is probably a reasonable and healthy defense. If you then decide *everyone outside your family* can be trusted, you are setting yourself up for disappointment. The truth lies somewhere in between. Many people can be trusted much of the time. But *no one* can guarantee you that they will be there whenever you need them. This is a romantic notion that many of us cling to. Just as you can't *promise* your child that you will never die, your friend or spouse can't promise you that he or she will always be there.

> Susan recalls how she coped with the uncertainty in her daily life as a child. "Everything is like a movie going on around you. You become a superb actress so that you can handle any role at the last minute. I could be whatever anyone thought I was.
>
> "And I continued to do that into my marriage. I was supposed to be the military wife, but in my heart I was a peace activist! I had to create dialogue for dinner parties. My husband would remind me that his promotions could be made or broken by what I said. I had to dress and wear my hair and makeup a certain way. And in many ways this fit with the ideas from my small hometown about how a woman was supposed to be. Certainly my mother taught me to be an uncomplaining wife and bear up under any burdens my husband put on me."
>
> Susan's early training made her think of herself as almost a god. Regardless of who she was, she seemed able to fill any gap, solve any problem. All she had to do was give up her authentic self. But in her first marriage she finally learned to say, "NO!"
>
> "I still am a "yes" person and I have to watch it. I sometimes still say "yes" when I really don't have the time. I still respond as if I am Ms. Superwoman and can do anything, and I have to back off and take a realistic look at myself. I have to face that I have a limited amount of energy. Now when I'm tired, it's a healthy tired—not the exhaustion that comes from having nothing left. I have learned to cry. It's much easier for me to cry now. It feels good. It's a release. I don't have to pretend to be tough anymore. I don't have to feel guilty."

Susan feels her recovery grew out of her early self-reliance, her drive, her therapist's intervention at a crucial moment, and her relationship with her very supportive second husband. She also speaks of a "faith" that things would get better, that she would have the strength to make it through.

SPIRITUAL RECOVERY

While interviewing people for this book, I found that nearly every parent who had overcome his or her dysfunctional training talked about feeling a spiritual intervention. They asked God for guidance or they felt blessed and watched over. The strongest example of this is Grace.

◆ GRACE—A SPIRITUAL RECOVERY

"This marriage (I've been married over three years) has been a real struggle for me because I had become too independent. And just now, everything is starting to smooth out. It's because of God. I've been to a lot of psychiatrists—since I was thirteen years old. And I've put myself in the hospital twice and I was very self-destructive. I was one of the angriest people you've ever seen. I've been in more fights than most men have. I've even gotten in fights with men. I was extremely violent and extremely angry at the world. And now it's all gone. It's completely gone out of me. All these years I've been waiting to be this way. This is what's kept me going. I had faith that some day I would come to this point—where Grace didn't hate herself anymore—and I didn't blame myself for everything. I used to take the guilt of the world on me.

"About three years ago I began the process of being healed by God. And I don't mean religion. Religion and God are two different things. But God has really changed me.

"Ever since I met my husband I have felt myself moving toward God. I had always prayed to God when I was going through all this stuff. And when I was so lonely and alone with Candy I had prayed to God, 'God, I'll serve you for the rest of my life if you'll just give me a good husband and a safe home.' And then I met my husband and he was a minister. I started turning myself over to God. I would pray and ask him to heal me and I would feel God giving me the strength to overcome things. I would think of the way I would do things before and it never worked and then I decided to try doing things God's way and things would turn out better. I started becoming this new person. I wasn't hurt anymore; I didn't have so much anger in me. God would speak to me in different ways and he would use people to minister to me. Now I have so much faith inside me, even though I haven't grown up in churches. I now feel like my whole life is something God allowed to happen so that when I finally came to God, I would be a really good witness to God for people that really need it. Because to come out of what I've come out of and be healed and be as 'normal' as I am now is like a miracle.

"God has taken the bad feelings out of me. I have to accept something in myself and then it just happens. He speaks to me in dreams or when I go for walks. I ask God to help me with my children and he answers all my prayers."

Grace is acutely aware of how this spiritual transformation has affected her ability to parent. She had her first child, Candace, when she was nineteen, deeply insecure, and self-destructive. After she had been married to her second husband about two years, and felt whole and healed, she decided to have a second child. Parenting each of these children has made it crystal clear to her how much one's degree of inner peace and life-attitude influence the way we treat our children.

In *12 Steps to Self-Parenting*,[2] based on the respected 12 steps of AA, the authors talk about discovering your "Higher Parent." The spiritual aspect of AA has always referred to a "Higher Power" or "God as we understood Him." O'Gorman and Oliver-Diaz also describe God as "Good Orderly Direction."[3] There are many ways to think about the source of our spiritual guidance. Psychologists might call it a "will to live." In our unconscious mind, the place where our dreams and intuitions come from, we have the knowledge and understanding we need to live a happy, fulfilled life. Carl Jung called it the collective unconscious; metaphysical spiritualists may think of it as the spirit we were all born from and to which we will return. Scientists and atheists might prefer to call it the "survival instinct." Whatever practical or ethereal name you give it, you do have the knowledge you need to parent in a nurturing, affirming way.

"The difference between how I am now with this baby and how I was with Candy is enormous. I have an abundance of patience with this boy, but I had no patience with Candy. I was just so distressed all the time that I always wanted somebody to take her off my hands. It was a relief to leave her with my aunt while I worked, but now I don't even want to leave my baby. I don't yell at him. When Candy was just three months old and she had been crying and crying I remember yelling at her. But now, even though this baby has kept me up a lot, I have a lot of patience. Candy was a burden, and this baby is a joy. He brings me so much happiness. Candy was a real easy baby to take care of. This baby is a lot more trouble than she was. He's into everything. You would have never even known when Candy was teething, but he drools and gets sick.

"All along the way I've had so much more patience with him. When he cried I would just think about how he was feeling and try to comfort him. With Candy it was always such a traumatic thing, but now I'm more matter-of-fact about it. I really love taking care of my boy. I would rather be home with him than out working. He really makes me feel happy inside. I'm amazed that a child can make me so happy."

"Candace has heard me talk about the difference between how I was with her and the baby to other people. I do tell her that it was very hard for me, that I was very emotional back then. I told her that I had to go into the hospital. I've told her that I prayed for God to help me to not yell at her anymore.

"First I became sick about how I was acting. I would actually feel sick to my stomach when I would yell like that, so that I knew that I had to stop it. I had to change because I just couldn't live with that feeling anymore. Then I began to have faith that God would help me change, and I would trust and wait for a sign from God. I would try to be open to God's message whoever it came from. Like maybe the day I yelled and then prayed for guidance, I'd be with somebody who would tell me how they used to yell at their kids and how they overcame it. There were a lot of little coincidences like that. Or God would give me the strength to just say I was sorry to the person I had hurt and just let my part of the argument go—I didn't used to be able to let it go. Sometimes I would just see things differently—like where I had felt attacked I would realize someone was just trying to help me. Or sometimes in the middle of yelling I would see her young face and how vulnerable she was. I could see the damage I was doing when I saw the fear in her face. She once said to me, 'I know you would never hurt me, Mama, but when you yell at me like that it scares me so.' I had to be able to accept the correction I needed. I felt like I just never had the strength on my own, but the strength finally came from God.

"I don't yell at her hardly ever anymore. I don't feel as angry anymore. I don't feel the need anymore. It's wonderful to feel that it's gone. I get mad at her sometimes now, but I can correct her before it bothers me so much. I can stay calm and focus on the fact that she is actually a very good girl. It's just in the last few years, or actually the last few months, that I have felt like I have become the kind of mother I had wanted to be for her.

"People have told me, 'Grace, you've done a fantastic job with your daughter.' And I believe that. She's not all screwed up. She's very bright and she'll sit and talk to you like an adult. I think that after I came to God I began to feel a lot of peace in myself and now I can give my daughter all that love that I've been wanting to give her.

"Right now her teachers tell me that she's a very well-adjusted child. They say she's very secure in herself. I try to give her lots of praise to make up for the way I used to be. She's very mature for her age. She's gifted and I think that helps her to understand me. I used to feel a lot of guilt for the way I was with her. But I think, in spite of everything else, I must have shown her a lot of love back then."

Grace's story is perhaps the most moving and uplifting. As we hear about her severe childhood beatings and the sexual abuse by her father, we marvel that anyone can survive such a childhood. As one would expect, Grace grew up hostile and hard. She worked as a barmaid when her daughter was small, and Grace even told me tales of fistfights she had with drunken men. Yet today her face is full of light. She has not denied her past nor is she hiding from it in any way. When she recounted painful childhood memories to me, she would break down and cry. I think a large part of Grace's ability to be so responsive to her children is that she lets herself be open to her feelings, no matter how painful. She has not forgotten what it is like to be a small helpless child at the mercy of adults.

Grace believes she has received personal guidance from God in a number of forms. She speaks of other people as being messengers and she also talked of taking solitary walks and listening for answers to the questions she was struggling with. Like Grace, try to spend quiet time with yourself listening to that inner voice. Then, whatever it tells to do for your child, do for yourself as well.

EMERGING AWARENESS

As I listened to my interviewees, who had faced and surmounted parenting crises, describe their journeys from onset of the problem to recovery, they seemed to follow a predictable pattern.

Stages of Parenting Crisis

1. Birth of first child or other stressful event such as divorce or move to a new town
2. Childhood depletion catches up
3. Child shows signs of stress but parent denies it
4. Child's distress can't be ignored (authorities step in, fear of battering, or problems with school, church, neighbors, etc.)
5. The crash and shame
6. The rebuilding process (therapy, church, support groups)
7. Pain of remembered childhood
8. Parent grows up
9. Child becomes more manageable
10. Joy of more fulfilling life than ever thought possible!

The above sequence shows the natural resistance we all have to admitting that the family we grew up in was troubled, and in turn, the denial that anything is wrong with the current family in which we are parenting. It is amazing how people will cling to the belief that they came from a "happy" family, despite beatings, mental cruelty, and the chronic stress of never being quite sure what was going to happen next. We all have an instinctive social need to "fit in." We want to be part of a group. **Ironically, it is our drive toward health that creates one of our most debilitating characteristics: denial.** It is healthy to want to be accepted by people who grew up in healthy families. This is movement toward light. But that desire also causes us to lie to others (and ourselves) about our families. We don't want others to know anything is "wrong" because we fear they will reject us. At the same time, we are subconsciously attracted to people who grew up in dysfunctional families, though they deny it too. First, we share outrageous fictions about our families. As we get to know each other better and negative details about our families of origin emerge, we feel all the more "normal," and think we have made it. But we are all involved in an incredible masquerade.

When something happens to crack the facade, we feel very unfortunate. We wish our children did not "act out" and call attention to the family. We are terrified when we lose our ability to blend in. We feel singled out and cursed, asking, *"Why me?"* Some get by without exposure and we see them as the lucky ones. But in reality, our turmoil is our sign of blessing. *We have been singled out, not because we didn't try hard enough, but as one who has been chosen to break the cycle.* This challenge is really our vehicle to a happier, more fulfilling life.

◆ LISA'S RECOVERY

After a few more months, Lisa (whom we met in Chapter 15) stablized, was released from the hospital, and began taking simple electives at the local junior college. She was in therapy with an excellent therapist on an out-patient basis. She had a couple of brief hospitalizations—two separate weeks a few months apart.

Miriam and Jerome talked to Lisa about going away to school at a big university, but Lisa was afraid to try. Miriam hated to see Lisa waste her talents. "I sent her on a vacation to visit my relatives in San Francisco. Lisa was always interested in medicine and Lisa's aunt, who works in a hospital, got permission for Lisa to watch an operation. But Lisa's greatest thrill came from holding a one-pound baby in her hand. She began to get ahold of the possibilities for her. When she came back I said to her, 'Do you see what I am telling you? There's a big beautiful world out there for you to see and for you to experience. You're free. Your parents can afford to send you to college. Take it. Enjoy it!' And she is finally realizing that it's true. Now she's thinking about being a doctor.''

Lisa decided to go away to a college where no one would know her past and she could just start fresh. She continued occasional out-patient therapy visits while she was away, and she still takes Desaryl (an antidepressant medication) at night, but she came home from a successful freshman year excited and glad to be alive. ''For her to go away to college and live in a dormitory!'' Miriam relates. ''She went from being agoraphobic to going off on her own in just two years. This is like a miracle. But she's worked very hard to get there and we've worked very hard too. I feel so proud of myself now for coming through this. I really felt like we did our best. She's not only making it in college, she's not even calling home anymore! She's doing her own laundry, buying healthful foods for her dorm snacks—she's taking care of herself!''

''Right now we're just so grateful that we've gotten through all this,'' Miriam says. ''When Lisa brought her friends home from college recently she introduced Jerome and me and said, 'I have the best parents in the world!' We've come full circle. I asked her recently, 'Do you feel afraid you'll get sick again?' And she said, 'I will never get that sick again, ever.' I asked, 'Do you feel strong?' And she said, 'Very strong.' We know that she could have another episode of depression. Who knows what stressful situations will come up in her life? But now she knows when she needs help. She has learned what to look for and how and where to get help.''

Research on gifted children shows that they have a very high suicide rate and often feel isolated and painfully different. It's highly likely that if Lisa had been a late-bloomer her crisis could have come her first year of college, when she was far from her supportive family. Miriam may not have known how to be an appropriate mother for an adolescent, but she was always there for her daughter. As soon as Lisa confessed the depth of her depression to her, Miriam took immediate action. Miriam realizes how fortunate they were that Lisa's breakdown came when she was in high school. Although it was hell for them all to live through, Lisa did ultimately come away with an understanding about taking better care of herself and watching for signs of depression. No depression in the future will ever be as bad as this one was. For in her crisis, Lisa went all the way down to the bottom of despair and then saw herself recover. Therapy and proper medication restored her promising life the first time. Not only will she know where to turn next time, she will also know that she can find the strength and support she needs to recover.

ACODF parents have found many different ways to heal and gain the knowledge they needed to be better parents. For Susan, the support of a wise therapist was pivotal, but Grace never ''clicked'' with any therapist. She needed a more spiritual approach to give her the patience to "sit out" her parenting trials until self-examination and advice from others could cure her. She believed these moments of enlightenment were the result of divine intervention. Maryanne (Chapters 3, 4, and 9) also spoke of praying when she was at the end of her resources, but her first realization about her lack of parenting skills came when she saw a segment on child abuse on "The Phil Donahue Show." Many interviewees have described this sense of feeling "blessed" at some point, as a neighbor, teacher, or friend took a special interest in them that made a world of difference.

SELF-HELP BOOKS

Lillian (whom we met in Chapter 15) has also felt blessed, but her "messengers" have been the authors of books. Through education and self-help books Lillian *read* her way to health.

◆ LILLIAN—THE SELF-HELPED WOMAN

Lillian's mother, Joan, was not "left." Instead, Joan chose to leave her alcoholic husband. This is actually a very positive sign that speaks well of Joan's ability to refuse abuse and take charge of her own life. Even today many women find it impossible to leave an alcoholic husband, and back then (1950s) there weren't as many jobs available to women. It must have taken a lot of courage for Joan to strike out on her own. Lillian was fortunate to have this role model.

"Finally, when I was thirteen, my grandmother was treating me so badly that we moved out. I would have welts all over my body from my grandmother's beatings. I remember my mother came home and I was crying and crying from a very bad beating my grandmother had given me for something I hadn't done. I told my mother it wasn't fair. We moved out that same week."

One year later, Lillian's mother remarried, quit her job, and decided to stay home with her son and daughter. "We became very, very close but my stepfather was very jealous of me. Then the marriage broke up. I felt like my mother gave up the marriage for me and my brother. I felt guilty about it for many years, but now I realize the marriage wouldn't have lasted anyway and I just feel good that my mother chose to stand by her children. We were more like buddies and she and I became the two parents of my brother. It was like we were equals. She didn't set limits; she didn't give me curfew; she never punished me or made any rules. I was just on my own. I behaved and there weren't any problems."

Lillian was sixteen by then and she went on living with her mother until she got her AA degree. As soon as Lillian had a good job, and a serious boyfriend, she moved out of the house to have more privacy. Joan accepted this well. "I felt like she loved me," Lillian reports. "She seemed to admire my independence. I didn't make any demands on her. She's always been very proud that I'm a self-made person and got myself an education." Although Lillian has had lifelong recurring problems with depression and low self-esteem, she benefited greatly from this belated two-year boost of attention from her mother.

Lillian married shortly after that and she and her husband, Michael, spent five years together as a couple before they tried to have children. "It took three grueling years of temperature-taking and fertility tests. When we had given up and I went back to work full-time, I became pregnant. We had our son, and then two years later, we had our daughter. They were very wanted. My husband and I had been together over ten years and we had a house. We were in our early thirties. We stopped at two because I think we both realized that we couldn't do as a good job with three. We knew we'd reached our limit, so my husband had a vasectomy."

When Karen was born Lillian suffered serious postpartum depression. "I felt exhausted all the time. I thought about suicide from time to time, but I knew I wouldn't carry through with it because of my children. When I'm not going through some big hormonal change I don't get all that depressed. So I never really thought about going to counseling for the depression.

"Most of my emotional recovery, learning to keep my depression at a safe level and raising my self-esteem, has come through reading self-help books. I've learned to take better care of my body and to accept myself instead of being so critical. Also, I had a wonderful friend who was getting a masters in counseling and we had a lot of good conversations.

"When I went back to work I decided I would only work part-time instead of wearing myself out. I've made a conscious effort to understand what I really want instead of just doing what I think I *should* be doing. I've put my foot down on a lot of things with my husband. I've insisted on only working part-time so I could be with my children more, and so that I could do more things for myself. I used to feel bad all the time because my house was messy. Now I wish it wasn't messy but I realize I just don't have that much time to clean." Lillian explains that she gradually realized that guilt doesn't accomplish anything. She advises, "If you feel guilty about something that you really should do, get up and do it. But if it's a situation that you can't do anything about, just forget about it and accept things the way they are.

"I don't have an aversion to housework, I just have higher priorities—like my kids. So I don't feel bad about myself for that anymore. I took guilt and threw it out the window."

Lillian works in sales as an independent contractor. She got this job by answering a blind ad for someone who was a "self-starter." If I had to select one label to describe Lillian it would be that: self-starter. Fortunately for Lillian, the person who meant most to her (her mother) modeled, valued, and encouraged independence. Lillian epitomizes the independent spirit that runs through the stories of the most successful and fully recovered ACODF. Most ACODF I interviewed had put themselves through college or taken bold steps to get better jobs. They rose above incredibly debilitating circumstances with the stamina and drive of the survivor.

STARTING WITH THE SELF

Independence and self-direction are important not only for taking care of ourselves but also for developing healthy relationships with others. We need to attract and be accepted by healthy, whole people, and to do that we need to become whole ourselves. As we discussed earlier, dysfunctional people are only half-realized people. They cannot function or be happy unless they have someone to complete them. This need makes them demand too much of others and repel healthy people. Being in a relationship with a dysfunctional person can feel like being pulled down into quicksand. If we want others to look forward to being with us, we must develop ourselves as fully functioning people.

I only recently identified that the predominant feeling I have had toward my own mother was guilt. She left me no room to miss her or want to see her or talk to her. She always seemed to be hovering over me like a heavy mist, expecting more from me than I could give, so she was perpetually dissatisfied with me. She didn't take care of her own needs. As a result, my siblings and I were all expected to fill the tremendous vacuum in her life. Having a relationship with my mother felt like falling into a bottomless pit.

The flip-side of guilt is expectation. People with excessive expectations cannot simply "accept the things they cannot change." My mother often goes on and on about how my brothers have let her down. However, her expectations are so unreasonable in the first place that they can't help but let her down. No one could deliver what she expects. I heard a speaker recently who said, "The most you should expect from anybody is disappointment and then all the rest will be gravy."

If we hope to have a warm, reciprocal relationship with our children as adults, we must begin now to lower our expectations of what they will do for us. If we feel empty, we need to seek friends our age and support groups to relieve our loneliness. We must build a life that is self-sufficient and engineer our futures so that we will not have to depend on our children for our sense of worth, our future well-being, or even companionship. This is not to say that we should not look forward to spending time with our children as adults. But if we want them to look forward to spending time with us, we must have the attitude that it's all "gravy." Not "I have a rich fulfilling life *because* I have children," but **"I'll have a rich fulfilling life whether I see my children or not."**

Ultimately, it really doesn't matter if your child is difficult to manage because of temperament or due to your poor parenting skills. You are the adult and it is your responsibility to solve the problem. If you have a very difficult child, your parenting skills may even be superior. Regardless, if you do not have control of your child, or he is behaving in ways that make him a social outcast, he may be fortunate to have been born to you, *but* you will have to learn different parenting skills just the same. If what you have been doing has not worked, you must try something new.

First, you have to have the stillness of mind needed to analyze the situation and sort through your alternatives. If you are still feeling weakened from your childhood, you will have to start by taking better care of yourself. Sometimes it is necessary to delve back into childhood memories to discover the source of your hurts. You may have many tears bottled up in you that should have been cried out long ago. Crying can bring a tremendous sense of release. Thinking back on your childhood losses may also give you clues about what needs were never met so that you can begin to meet these needs for yourself. If you were physically neglected as a child, feed yourself healthy food and bathe and pamper your body. If you always wanted to be a scout, take den leader training and find yourself a group of children to grow and play with. In other cases, you may simply have to mourn your lost childhood.

There is a tremendous temptation to view our relationship with our own child in contrast to the tear-streaked vision of our past. If our parents never signed us up for lessons or made our lunch, we expect our children to be deeply grateful that we are performing these routine parental duties for them. We think they are spoiled or insensitive if they don't show their undying appreciation. Ironically, the better you take care of your children, the less they will know deprivation; they will have no measuring stick to judge their idyllic life against. Should you let them starve three days a week so they can learn to appreciate food? That would be as foolish as having them walk through a burning fire to learn what "hot" means. We can learn to appreciate what we have without being deprived of it. You can model this behavior just by joyously appreciating what you have. You can feel grateful for your warm home just because you have it, regardless of whether or not you had one as a child. Warm homes are objectively wonderful. You just need to stop and "smell the flowers" in front of your children so they can learn to do likewise.

What undermines this feeling of gratitude most is an attitude of resentment on the part of the giver. This is what you must guard against most carefully. If you find yourself resenting your children because they are "ungrateful," you are probably comparing their childhood to your own. Stop and compare their childhood to that of the other children on your street. This puts the issue out where you can be more objective.

WHERE TO GET HELP

As you can see, while taking these difficult steps you will need support and objective feedback. As my interviewees have done, you can find that support in books, classes, self-help groups, parenting organizations, group therapy, family counseling, or private counseling sessions. All major bookstores have self-help book sections and a wide selection of books for Adult Children of Alcoholics (and other dysfunctional families) or co-dependents. Many community colleges now offer adult education courses on various psychological problems, and Adult Children classes are becoming increasingly available and popular. Call your local community college for a schedule of classes. There are many good parenting education programs being offered now that are often free through the public schools or local churches.

Self-help groups come in all forms from light to intense. For some, organizations such as Parents Without Partners (PWP) offer enough information and support to bring these suffering parents out of the doldrums of isolation. Others may want the more intense involvement of Parents Anonymous (for parents who have hurt, or fear hurting, their children physically or psychologically) or Parents United (for families with a sexual abuse problem). All of these organizations have groups throughout the United States and can usually be found in the white pages of your phone book. Through Alcoholics Anonymous (AA) (also in most phone books) you can locate Al-Anon or Adult Children of Alcoholics (ACOA or ACA) groups, and these groups welcome adult children from other types of dysfunctional homes who find the meetings helpful. Most of these groups offer free support and advice or charge a nominal fee. If you have no insurance and cannot afford counseling, these groups can be a godsend.

Family counseling centers are springing up everywhere and usually take a family systems approach to problems with children and parents. You may not feel comfortable sharing your feelings in a group and may prefer private sessions with a therapist. Most insurance companies cover services offered by any licensed counselor. If you have no insurance and cannot afford counseling, you can sometimes get free counseling through Child Protective Services or can pay on a sliding scale at county or state funded agencies. A good place to start looking is in the yellow pages of your phone book under *Counselors.* In some communities these organizations and those mentioned above can be difficult to track down, so if you get discouraged in your search, drop in on a local minister or rabbi and ask them to help you. Most make it their business to know what resources are available in their communities.

It may take some determination and persistence, but if you want help it is available at a price you can afford. Just keep looking and be frank about your need.

THE RIGHT THERAPIST

If you can afford it, private therapy is often the best way to go. The role of the therapist or counselor is actually quite similar to that of a healthy parent. They will be supportive, gently correcting of your negative attitudes, and can help you safely work through your past. Under the guidance of a good therapist, the journey will be like traveling back in time with a supportive adult by your side.

However, since individual therapy is usually the most intense and expensive alternative, how do you determine if you need private counseling sessions? **You can try a self-help group first, but if you find you usually feel worse after the meeting, or you think about the problems of others more than your own between meetings, or other group members are impatient with the amount of time you need in the group, you probably need a one-on-one relationship.** If at all possible, try not to use your friends for this. Many can be a friend-in-need for occasional crises, but if you are always the one in need you will wear out your welcome. It is better to keep your friendships available for celebration and less intense sharing. Unfortunately, friends, being what they are, will seldom tell you directly when you are taking too much. If close friends have hinted that you may need therapy, they are probably telling you that they cannot give you what you seem to need. If you continue to try to pull this nurturance out of friends, they will have to make polite excuses to avoid you. The exception to this is an equally needy friend, but these bitching sessions of the blind leading the blind are seldom fruitful. You will just run in circles together.

If you decide to go into individual therapy or a group led by a licensed professional, what should you look for? You should feel comfortable with the person. Even the most competent therapist may have a personality that clashes with your own. It's OK to "shop" for a therapist. If you have never been to a counselor, try at least two and ask for an initial interview. Many counselors will allow you one "look/see" session for free. Any good counselor knows you need to be comfortable with him or her, and some may turn you down because *they* can sense a personality conflict! (They will often suggest someone else as an alternative.) If the counselor balks at the idea of your checking her out, steer clear. If she is good, she'll have plenty of clients and won't need to intimidate you into accepting her whether you like her or not. Even if you are receiving free counseling through social services, you have a right to ask to switch therapists if you are not comfortable with the one assigned to you.

Be sure the therapist has knowledge and training in areas that are important to your background. If your problems are related to alcohol in any way, the therapist should be familiar with the Adult Children of Alcoholics movement and should have read literature or attended a seminar on this subject. If manic-depression runs in your family, make sure your therapist is aware of new drug treatments and can refer you to a psychiatrist (who is an M.D.) in case you need medication to correct your mood swings. If drug addiction has been a problem for you or anyone in your family, you should find a therapist who is knowledgeable and experienced in this area.

I strongly favor counselors who are familiar with family systems theory and methods. These counselors may meet with one, two, or all of you, as the situation demands, but they will explore how the members of your family interract and affect each other. They can be especially helpful and supportive when one family member resists the healthy changes you are trying to make in yourself and your family. Communication problems are best solved with a family systems approach, and negative patterns of relating can be corrected much more easily with full family involvement.

Finally the therapist should be someone you can like and trust. If you don't feel comfortable or supported after four or five sessions, you would be better off "losing" that time and starting fresh with someone else, rather than letting a sluggish counseling situation drag on.

MAKING AMENDS

If you have been parenting for years before you realize you have taken some wrong approaches, chances are you have made some mistakes and have unwittingly hurt your children. Whether or not your children can identify this pain, it will be with them until you two clear it up.

Before you can ask your child to forgive, you must forgive yourself. And it may be that before you can forgive yourself, you must forgive your own parents. Both of these things must happen before healing can take place, in whatever order is most comfortable for you. We are the product of our experiences. If your parents were especially cruel to you, and actually seemed to hurt you on purpose (physically or psychologically), see if you can discover how that parent was treated as a child. If goodness has been encouraged in us to any degree, we will all strive to be better parents. No matter how cruel your parents were, chances are they were kinder than their own parents. Think about what it must have felt like to be them and try to be grateful for whatever they *could* give you despite their upbringing. My father was an orphan, pretty much incapable of showing love as a parent. He touted himself as turning out fine although he had had no father, and didn't see why we needed him to be a father. However, he felt very strongly that he could have turned out better if he had not lived in a city slum. His goal was to house his family in the suburbs and he achieved that goal. He would wave that flag of accomplishment at us whenever we complained about his absence and disinterest in our lives, and we would sneer at it, believing that it made no difference whether you lived in the slums or the country.

Now that I am older and able to see how much I learned from the families around me, families who expected their kids to go to college and required that they be in after dark, I realize what a great gift he did give me by being able to do that one thing. My father didn't know how to be loving, but he could work and earn money to buy us a "nice house." And my life has been better for it.

Stop dwelling on what your parents didn't do and try to understand what they *did* do. No matter how incompetent they were as parents, rest assured they did the best they knew how. And that is what you have done for your children. If you look at your parenting now and judge it inadequate, don't waste time berating yourself. Change.

If you can pinpoint certain things you did to your children that you regret or feel were wrong, it is valuable to let the children know that you are sorry and will try not to do it again. If you can handle it without having a need to retaliate, let them express their anger and tell them you accept and forgive their anger. There is a good chance they will not believe you truly intend to change or that they simply will not take a chance on loving you for awhile. Slates are not easily wiped clean. Waste no more breath. **In time, your changed *actions* will convince them.**

At the same time, no one changes overnight. You might vow not to yell anymore, as Grace did, but it is a habit and old habits die hard. The important thing is that with earnest effort you will begin yelling less and less often, until you have changed the pattern and become someone who yells "once in a while," instead of someone who yells "all the time."

SELF-PARENTING

At the end of this book I must send you back to begin at the beginning. Now that you have come to better understand how you have been hurt and how you can avoid leaving your child with such a legacy of pain, you are probably anxious to go forth and give, give, give to your child. But that is not the beginning. There is a child who needs you more—your **child within.** You cannot be a healer until you have been healed. You can spend the rest of your life feeling bitter or damaged because of all the love and support your parents could not give you. Or you can begin life anew today by promising your inner child that he or she will now get some proper parenting. You cannot rewrite the past. You will probably never get the nurturing you need from your parents, and you may still need so much nurturing that you cannot expect your spouse to provide all of it. All you can change is the future. You can move into the future as a loved, well-cared-for child by giving yourself that nurturing that you need. Instead of running yourself ragged trying to wear too many hats, or meet too many people's needs, step back and look at the worn-out needy child within you. Say, "You're overtired; you need some rest. Come lie down and listen to some music. I'll read you a story until you fall asleep."

NOTES

1. Bernie S. Siegel, M.D., *Love, Medicine, and Miracles*. New York: Harper & Row, 1986, p. 161–162.

2. Philip Oliver-Diaz, and Patricia A. O'Gorman. *12 Steps to Self-Parenting*, Deerfield Beach, FL: Health Communications, Inc., 1988.

3. Patricia O'Gorman and Philip Oliver-Diaz. *Breaking the Cycle of Addiction*. Pompano Beach, FL: Health Communications, Inc., 1987.

EPILOGUE

Throughout this book the case presented as Judy's story has been my story. Sharing what I learned through my own parenting crisis has been my central motivation for writing this book.

When the director of my son's preschool hinted that he was hyperactive (at best) or emotionally disturbed, I was confused, angry, and embarrassed. Most of all, it seemed so unjust! I had spent years in therapy working hard on myself in an effort to become "normal." I had waited until I felt I could handle a child. I had done everything "right," and it was not fair that my child was disturbed. I was still exhausted from the psychological effort it took to overcome my childhood trauma. I was no longer hostile, disorganized, drunk, or self-righteous. I deserved to have a happy, normal child for all my efforts.

The preschool director, the pediatrician, the child psychologist, my therapist, and all the parents I complained to would tell me how *lucky* I was to discover my son's problem so early. But I felt like the unluckiest person on earth—unfairly punished by fate.

As I saw it, I had had my life "all together" and my son had torn it all apart.

Today I feel more than lucky. I feel graced. It has been almost five years since my little son, barely out of diapers, was pronounced "incorrigible."

He no longer takes medication. His activity level is normal and he is assertive (perhaps pushy) but rarely aggressive. He has many friends and there always seems to be one here for dinner. He is in a special class, but his distinguishing label is "gifted." When his first-grade teacher told me that she could always count on my son to be doing the right thing when she wanted a positive example to bring the class under control ("Look at how nicely Casey is behaving . . ."), I wept.

I am so very very lucky that my son's problem was discovered when it was. My son seemed destined to be a juvenile delinquent, and now it looks as if he is headed for . . . the Presidency? The Nobel Peace Prize? Who knows? Albert Einstein was hyperactive.

But my son's bright future is just one small part of my blessing. There is the daily joy of being with him (I love being with him—he's delightful) and there is my own brighter future.

Medications for mood disorders were still in the experimental stage when I had had my last debilitating depression almost ten years before my son was born. When I was getting ready to marry, my therapist, in a fatherly fashion, asked to meet my then husband-to-be. He told us I would always have periodic, terrible depressions and asked my fiancé if he was prepared to accept these low moods. It was simply a fact of my life I had to live with. For years I spent low times hiding in my house until I got over it. Overall, I wasn't a "happy" person. The shadow of depression seemed to follow me everywhere, waiting for a weak moment to jump in and take me over. But I had come to believe that that was as good as life was going to get for me. I had given up therapy with a "what's the use?" attitude.

Now I *am* happy. And like all people I am sad sometimes, even depressed. Because of my son, I was forced to go back into therapy and discover that there are new treatments for depression, and, yes, a pill *can* make me better. I credit my son's problem behavior for freeing me from a horrible bondage.

But I am not the only one in this family who has been helped by my son's problems. My husband's characteristic reaction to personal problems had always been to retreat further and further into work. He lost out on a lot of closeness with his sons by his first marriage. My son's problems forced us all into therapy, and my husband has learned to relax and let work take a lower priority in his life. Now my husband not only has a rewarding intimacy with our shared son, he is also finding time to become closer to his three oldest sons.

We have grown with our son. This is the best you can ask for as a parent, as a family, and together we have earned it!

BIBLIOGRAPHY

ACOA AND GENERAL PSYCHOLOGY

Ackerman, Robert J., Ph.D., *Let Go and Grow: Recovery for Adult Children of Alcoholics.* Pompano Beach, FL: Health Communications, Inc., 1987.

Bach, George R., Ph.D. and Wyden, Peter, *The Intimate Enemy: How to Fight Fair in Love and Marriage.* New York: Avon Books, 1968.

Beattie, Melody, *Co-Dependent No More: How to Stop Controlling Others and Start Caring for Yourself.* New York: Harper/Hazelden, 1987.

Beattie, Melody, *Beyond Co-Dependency: And Getting Better All the Time.* New York: Harper/Hazelden, 1989.

Black, Claudia, Ph.D., *It Will Never Happen to Me!* New York: Ballantine Books, 1981.

Bowen, Murray, M.D., *Family Therapy and Clinical Practice.* New York: Jason Aronson, Inc., 1978.

Bradshaw, John, *Bradshaw On: The Family.* Pompano Beach, FL: Health Communications, Inc., 1988.

Burns, David D., M.D., *Feeling Good: The New Mood Therapy.* New York: Signet Books, 1980.

Curran, Dolores, *Stress and the Healthy Family: How Healthy Families Control the Ten Most Common Stresses.* Minneapolis: Winston Press, Inc., 1985.

———, *Traits of a Healthy Family: Fifteen Traits Commonly Found in Healthy Families by Those Who Work with Them.* San Francisco: Harper & Row, 1983.

Feingold, Ben F., M.D., *Why Your Child Is Hyperactive.* New York: Random House, 1974.

Figley, Charles R., and McCubbin, Hamilton I., eds., *Stress and the Family, Volume I: Coping with Normative Transitions.* New York: Brunner/Mazel, 1983.

———, *Stress and the Family, Volume II: Coping with Catastrophe.* New York: Brunner/Mazel, 1983.

Fisher, Roger and Ury, William, with Patton, Bruce, ed., *Getting to Yes: Negotiating Agreement Without Giving In.* New York: Penguin Books, 1981.

Forward, Susan M.D. with Buck, Craig, *Toxic Parents: Overcoming Their Hurtful Legacy and Reclaiming Your Life.* New York: Bantam Books, 1989.

Friel, John C., Ph.D. and Friel, Linda, *Adult Children: The Secrets of Dysfunctional Families.* Pompano Beach, FL: Health Communications, Inc., 1988.

349

Glasser, William, M.D., *Reality Therapy: A New Approach to Psychiatry.* New York: Harper & Row, 1965.

Gil, Eliana, Ph.D., *Outgrowing the Pain: A Book for and About Adults Abused as Children.* New York: Dell, 1983.

Gold, Mark S., M.D., with Morris, Lois B., *The Good News About Depression: Cures and Treatments in the New Age of Psychiatry.* New York: Bantam Books, 1987.

Golay, Keith, *Learning Patterns and Temperament Styles: A Systematic Guide to Maximizing Student Achievement.* Fullerton, CA: Manas-Systems, 1982.

Goodwin, Donald W., M.D., *Is Alcoholism Hereditary?* New York: Ballantine, 1988.

Gravitz, Herbert L., Ph.D., and Bowden, Julie D., *Recovery: A Guide for Adult Children of Alcoholics.* New York: Simon & Schuster, Inc., 1985.

Gurman, Alan S., Ph.D., and Knisken, David P., Psy.D., eds., *Handbook of Family Therapy.* New York: Brunner/Mazel, 1981.

Hochschild, Arlie, Ph.D. with Machung, Anne, *The Second Shift: Inside the Two-Job Marriage.* New York: Penguin USA, 1989.

Kritsberg, Wayne, *The Adult Children of Alcoholics Syndrome: From Discovery to Recovery.* Pompano Beach, FL: Health Communications, Inc., 1985.

Lerner, Harriet Goldhor, Ph.D., *The Dance of Anger: A Woman's Guide to Changing the Patterns of Intimate Relationships.* New York: Harper & Row, 1985.

Lewis, David C., M.D., and Williams, Carol N., Ph.D., eds., *Providing Care for Children of Alcoholics: Clinical and Research Perspectives.* Pompano Beach, FL: Health Communications, Inc., 1986.

May, Rollo, *The Courage to Create.* New York: Bantam Books, 1975.

Mellody, Pia with Miller, Andrea Wells and Miller, J. Keith, *Facing Co-dependence: What It Is, Where It Comes from, How It Sabotages Our Lives.* San Francisco: Harper & Row, 1989.

Miller, Alice, translated by Ruth Ward, *The Drama of the Gifted Child.* New York: Basic Books, Inc., 1981.

———, translated by Hildegarde Hannum and Hunter Hannum. *For Your Own Good: Hidden Cruelty in Child-Rearing and the Roots of Violence.* New York: Farrar, Straus & Giroux, 1983.

Minuchin, Salvador, *Families and Family Therapy.* Cambridge, MA: Harvard University Press, 1974.

Oliver-Diaz, Philip and O'Gorman, Patricia A., Ph.D., *12 Steps to Self-Parenting: For Adult Children of Alcoholics.* Deerfield Beach, FL: Health Communications, Inc., 1988.

Peck, M. Scott, M.D., *People of the Lie: The Hope for Healing Human Evil.* New York: Simon & Schuster, 1983.

Satir, Virginia, *Conjoint Family Therapy: A Guide to Theory and Technique, Revised Edition.* Palo Alto, CA: Science and Behavior Books, 1967.

Scarf, Maggie, *Intimate Partners: Patterns in Love and Marriage.* New York: Random House, 1987.

Seixas, Judith S. and Youcha, Geraldine, *Children of Alcoholism: A Survivor's Manual.* New York: Harper & Row, 1985.

Smith, Ann W., *Grandchildren of Alcoholics: Another Generation of Co-Dependency.* Pompano Beach, FL: Health Communications, Inc., 1988.

Tavris, Carol, *Anger: The Misunderstood Emotion*. New York: Simon & Schuster, Inc., 1982.

Whitfield, Charles L., M.D., *Healing the Child Within: Discovery and Recovery for Adult Children of Dysfunctional Families*. Pompano Beach, FL: Health Communications, Inc., 1987.

Woititz, Janet G., Ed.D., *Adult Children of Alcoholics*, Pompano Beach, FL: Health Communications, Inc., 1983.

The World Book Medical Encyclopedia: Your Guide to Good Health, Chicago: World Book, Inc., 1980.

LECTURES, JOURNALS AND MAGAZINES

Brandt, Anthony, "The Sins of the Children," *Parenting*, May 1988, pp. 84–90.

Fassel, Diane and Schaef, Anne Wilson, "Hooked on Work," *New Age Magazine*, Jan/Feb 1988.

Greenleaf, Jael, "Co-Alcoholic, Para-Alcoholic: Who's Who and What's the Difference?" Presented at the National Council on Alcoholism 1981 Annual Alcoholism Forum, New Orleans, Louisiana, April 12, 1981.

Wright, Rosalind, and Jacobbi, Marianne, "In Families Like Ours," *Ladies' Home Journal*, April 1988, pp. 111–113, 157–163.

Zigler, Edward, Rubin, Nancy, and Kaufman, Joan, "Do Abused Children Become Abusive Parents?" *Parents*, May 1988, pp. 100–106.

PARENTING PROBLEMS

Aitchison, Robert, and Eimers, Robert, *Effective Parents/ Responsible Children*. New York: McGraw Hill, 1977.

Ames, Louise Bates, and Ilg, Frances L., *Your Six Year Old*. New York: Dell Publishing, Inc., 1979.

Austin, Glenn, *Love & Power/Parent & Child*. Rolling Hills Estates, CA: Robert Erdmann, Publishing, 1988.

Bettleheim, Bruno, Ph.D., *A Good Enough Parent: A Book on Child Rearing*. New York: Alfred A. Knopf, Inc., 1989.

Bodenhamer, Gregory, *Back in Control*. New York: Prentice Hall Press, 1983.

Brenner, Avis, *Helping Children Cope with Stress*, Lexington, MA: Lexington Books, 1984.

Briggs, Dorothy Corkville, *Your Child's Self-Esteem*. New York: Doubleday and Company, 1970.

Brondini, Jeanne, et. al., *Raising Each Other: A Book for Teens and Parents*. Claremont, CA: Hunter House, Inc., 1988.

Dinkmeyer, Don, and McKay, Gary D., *The Parent's Handbook: STEP*. Circle Pines, MN: American Guidance Services, Inc., 1982.

Dobson, James C., Ph.D., *Dare to Discipline*. Wheaton, IL: Tyndale House Publishers, Inc., 1970.

Dodson, Fitzhugh, *How to Parent*. New York: Signet, 1970.

Dreikurs, Rudolf, *Children the Challenge*. New York: Hawthorne Books, 1964.

Elkind, David, *The Hurried Child*, Revised Edition. New York: Addison-Wesley Publishing Co., 1981.

Faber, Adele and Mazlish, Elaine, *How to Talk So Kids Will Listen and Listen So Kids Will Talk*, New York: Avon, 1980.

Glenn, H. Stephen and Nelsen, Jane, *Raising Self Reliant Children in a Self-Indulgent World*. Fair Oaks, CA: Sunrise Press, 1987.

Lickona, Thomas, *Raising Good Children*. New York: Bantam Books, 1983.

O'Gorman, Patricia A., Ph.D., and Oliver-Diaz, Philip, *Breaking the Cycle of Addiction: A Parent's Guide to Raising Healthy Kids*. Pompano Beach, FL: Health Communications, Inc., 1987.

Newman, Susan, *You Can Say No to a Drink or a Drug: What Every Kid Should Know*. New York: Perigree/Putnam, 1986.

Osborne, Philip, *Parenting for the '90s*. Intercourse, PA: Good Books, 1989.

Sanderson, Jim, *How to Raise Your Kids to Stand on Their Own Two Feet*. New York: Cogdon & Weed, Inc., 1983.

Silberman, Mel, *Confident Parenting*. New York: Warner Books, 1988.

Wallerstein, Judith S., Ph.D. and Blakeslee, Sandra, *Second Chances: Men, Women and Children a Decade After Divorce*. New York: Ticknor & Fields, 1989.

Wilmes, David J., *Parenting for Prevention: How to Raise a Child to Say No to Alcohol/Drugs*. Minneapolis: Johnson Institute Books, 1988.

York, Phyllis, York, David, and Wachtel, Ted, *Tough Love*. New York: Bantam Books, 1983.